Promoting Flourishing, Authentic Relationships, and Growth in Learners in the Digital Age

Raymond Aaron Younis
University of Sydney, Australia

IGI Global
Scientific Publishing
Publishing Tomorrow's Research Today

Vice President of Editorial	Melissa Wagner
Director of Acquisitions	Mikaela Felty
Director of Book Development	Jocelynn Hessler
Production Manager	Mike Brehm
Cover Design	Jose Rosado

Published in the United States of America by
IGI Global Scientific Publishing
701 East Chocolate Avenue
Hershey, PA, 17033, USA
Tel: 717-533-8845 | Fax: 717-533-7115
Website: https://www.igi-global.com E-mail: cust@igi-global.com

Library of Congress Cataloging-in-Publication Data

Names: Younis, Raymond Aaron, editor.
Title: Promoting flourishing, authentic relationships, and growth in learners in the digital age / edited by Raymond Younis.
Description: Hershey, PA : Information Science Reference, [2026] | Includes bibliographical references and index. | Summary: "This book will examine these significant developments, risks, threats and challenges, and explore timely solutions which promote the flourishing of young learners, among others, and which will be of benefit to all whose lives have been affected by the epochal and accelerating convergence of education, information, communication, technology and the "digital age""-- Provided by publisher.
Identifiers: LCCN 2024040520 (print) | LCCN 2024040521 (ebook) | ISBN 9798369309971 (hbk.) | ISBN 9798369350386 (pbk.) | ISBN 9798369309988 (ebook)
Subjects: LCSH: Internet in education--Psychological aspects. | Social media in education--Psychological aspects. | Education--Aims and objectives. | Critical pedagogy. | Well-being.
Classification: LCC LB1044.87 P756 2024 (print) | LCC LB1044.87 (ebook) | DDC 370.15--dc23/eng/20241019
LC record available at https://lccn.loc.gov/2024040520
LC ebook record available at https://lccn.loc.gov/2024040521

British Cataloguing in Publication Data
A Cataloguing in Publication record for this book is available from the British Library.

Table of Contents

Detailed Table of Contents

In this chapter, the concept of flourishing is defined in terms of individual values and interconnections. The authors propose that aligning the ideal of flourishing with society's current approach to learning requires a grounding in systems thinking, particularly living systems principles. Addressing not only intellectual, but also affective needs of learners is considered in the application of living systems principles to the creation of learning sanctuaries and other opportunities to promote belonging. These concepts are considered against the backdrop of the challenges and opportunities inherent in a digital age.

The digital era has changed learning, communication, and success. This chapter examines the complex link between thriving, lifelong learning, and success in the digital era, emphasizing flourishing's significance. Wellness is the cornerstone of digital life in many ways. In an age of continual technological change and unpredictable job markets, lifelong learning empowers people to adapt, flourish, and find fulfilment. Educational institutions and organizations pursuing digital well-being projects are given a set of digital success tips. Personal development requires a growth attitude and lifelong learning with digital technologies. Responsible digital citizenship and honest online connections foster a pleasant online environment. Mindfulness, digital detox, and digital or non-digital activity limits are crucial to well-being. This holistic approach helps individuals, educational institutions, and businesses thrive digitally while retaining their well-being and values by recognizing the complicated relationship between technology and personal growth.

This chapter introduces the reader to emancipatory education within the institute of higher education. Emancipatory education is an approach that empowers learners by promoting critical thinking, autonomy, and social justice. Its principles energize students by having them actively engage in their learning process and question norms and structures. It liberates minds by having students practice prioritization of historically marginalized perspectives and drives social justice efforts involving collaboration with communities to transform educational systems. Emancipatory education goes beyond traditional teaching methods. It encourages students to critically examine their experiences, societal structures, and power dynamics. By fostering awareness, it emboldens them to challenge injustice. Emancipatory education aims for liberation—both personal and collective. It seeks to transform oppressive systems and create a more just society. Teaching methods that emancipatory education supports include dialogic teaching, problem-posing, and participatory action research. These approaches prioritize dialogue, collaboration, and student voice.

Human flourishing is the end of education, mandating institutions to put an emphasis on the psychological and psychosocial health of the students. In a way, Neocalvinism forms a nexus with schools, demanding humanity to perform at its best to contribute to the flourishing of children. This study revolves around the self-reflection of the teacher-researcher who professes this system as a presupposed ideology in his professional practice, believing that it advances the well-being of children. Through thematic analysis, key patterns are identified and analyzed towards a distinct teaching framework. This study contributes to the present discourses on the influence of religion and spirituality in education, particularly from the perspective of professional development and classroom performance toward human flourishing.

This chapter analyzes opportunities students, in digital environments, have to grow in and apply virtue. The authors of the chapter, who work at a faith-based institution, share their observations and insights as they have actively sought to assist with the promotion of flourishing and growth in learners at their university within the Digital Age. The beginning of the chapter will provide readers with an overview of terms used within the chapter (e.g., virtue, flourishing, personal vocation) as connected to postsecondary outcomes or goals. Next, we will highlight information about technology and the impact it can have on virtue building followed by a section on personal vocation. We will then provide a reflection on encouraging students to be critical consumers as they engage in prudence with regards to use of technology in the learning environment and will conclude the chapter with a call to action.

Higher education needs social and digital media in the digital age. This chapter examines how these tools help students develop logic, self-awareness, and self-understanding. Strategic integration allows educators to build a dynamic learning environment that gives pupils modern-day abilities. Students develop rationality through critical thinking, different perspectives, and digital debates. The wealth of knowledge helps them make decisions and solve challenges. Students can document their experiences and growth on social media. It increases self-awareness and personal growth. A well-planned approach is needed to integrate social and digital media into higher education. It requires integrating technology with educational goals, choosing appropriate platforms, stressing digital literacy, and encouraging reflection and cooperation. Methods are evaluated and updated to stay current, accessible, and sustainable. Social and digital media in higher education are helpful and essential in an age of digitalization.

This study investigates the impact of Facebook usage on the academic performance of university students, particularly during the COVID-19 pandemic. The study surveyed 220 students from public and private universities in Bangladesh using a mixed methodology, removing invalid responses. Results show that students use Facebook for communication, entertainment, and educational activities like collaborations, live classes, and teacher interactions. However, challenges like distraction, harassment, unverified content, and spam hinder its effective use for educational purposes. Most students still have a positive opinion of Facebook despite these problems, even though 73% think that excessive socializing and distractions are harmful for their academic performance. Facebook is a helpful teaching tool, but excessive use might negatively affect students' academic performance. According to the study, students can use Facebook more effectively for academic success if they receive additional support in the form of financial aid, emotional counseling, and clear guidance.

India's cooperatives, including Gujarat Cooperative Milk Marketing Federation (GCMMF), Indian Farmers Fertilizer Cooperative Limited (IFFCO), and Krishak Bharati Cooperative Limited (KRIBHO), have a global reputation for their success and excellence. India's cooperative enterprises, accounting for one-fourth of the world's enterprises, contribute to the economy and promote ethical business practices. A review chapter reveals initial challenges faced by these enterprises, based on secondary data and research. The chapter delves into the fundamental aspects of achieving inclusive growth and sustainable development through various cooperative types. The chapter examines the impact of cooperatives, such as consumer, dairy, fisheries, women's welfare, and sugar cooperatives, on market prices in India, focusing on high-quality products and affordable prices. The chapter discusses recent efforts to support cooperatives and suggests further steps to strengthen them for inclusive growth and sustainable development through their successes.

As digital technology rapidly evolves, education has shifted from face-to-face interactions to more virtual experiences, especially following the COVID-19 pandemic. This shift has emphasized the need to examine the impact of technology on students' mental well-being, personal growth, and authentic relationships. The integration of artificial intelligence (AI) and virtual reality (AR) in education offers new possibilities for personalized learning and fostering stronger connections between students and teachers. However, as technology transforms the educational landscape, there is a growing concern that it may impair meaningful human interactions, which are crucial for academic performance and emotional health. This chapter explores how AI and other emerging technologies can be thoughtfully integrated to support both learning outcomes and student well-being, ensuring that technology enhances, rather than diminishes, the importance of human connections in education.

Preface

INTRODUCTION

Many have written on flourishing, and *eudaimonia*, and not surprisingly, many have subsequently sought to explore the significant relationship between these and modern education. First of all however two questions must be answered: what is flourishing and what is its relationship with education in the 21st century, dominated as it is by the accelerating technologies of the digital age, increasingly technologized, and dehumanised, modes of learning, and emerging dynamic systems of artificial intelligence which can generate AI personas, fake content and deepfakes to a hitherto unprecedented degree in order to reach a hitherto unprecedented number of students and learners?

This introduction will seek to clarify the key terms, examine some recent attempts to provide applied frameworks in education or to formulate formal criteria for flourishing as an educational aim, and set out some preliminary reflections which will hopefully open up new paths of investigation and exploration into our ways of understanding flourishing, its significance and relevance, and ways of applying it to education and higher forms of learning now (that is forms of education which recognise and emphasise flourishing as a key concept, and ethic, in the learning, growth and development of students, and which highlight the critical relationship between ethical deliberation, knowledge, habituation, choice, action and personal and interpersonal ends).

Julia Annas, among many others, recognises the importance of reason, practical reason, human capacities, virtue and human flourishing, and offers a notable, clear and cogent defence of it in many works (see for example, 2017, 2016, 2015a and 2015b, 2011, 2009, 2006, 2004, 1999 and 1993; see also Audi 2015, 2009a and 2009b, 2008, 2006, 2004, 2002, 1997 and 1993; Hursthouse 2011, 2007, 1999, 990-1991;

Foot 2001, 1995, 1994, 1978; Kristjansson, Carr and Arthur 2016; Kristjansson 2016, 2015, 2013, 2007; among many others). She argues that

Eudaimonism is the structure of all ancient ethical theories, with only one notable outlier. It wobbles into view in the pre-Socratic Democritus in the fifth century BC, and the neo-Platonist Plotinus is in the third century AD still working out his own version of it via criticisms of his predecessors. The only outliers are the minor school of Cyrenaic philosophers. In the ancient way of thinking about ethics, the entry point for ethical reflection is one which an adult will most likely take up at some point in his or her life: thinking about her life as a whole. It will start from questions such as: How is my life going? Clearly such a question can only be posed by someone who already has a life– who has been brought up by particular parents and educators in a particular culture, functioning in a particular language and so on. Eudaimonist theories do not set out to convince some philosophical skeptic that it is worthwhile to think ethically, but rather to enable us all to improve in doing something we are already and unavoidably doing, namely living our lives. Few if any of us are satisfied with our lives the way they are. Dissatisfaction may come from factors such as lack of talent, a society hostile to our ideals, or shaky health. This leads to reflection as to how we might deal better than we are with those or other challenges (2017, p.264).

Clearly then, flourishing, especially in its ancient Aristotelian sense, concerns our life conceived of as a whole, how we live it, how we choose to live it, how we might decide to deal with challenges in the course of our lives, especially moral ones. But she notes significantly:

Eudaimonist theories present themselves as systematic ways to think about your life and your sources of satisfaction and dissatisfaction, and then rethink your ways of living towards doing better, living a better life. Underpinning this ordinary way of thinking is the implicit idea of a final end. This is emphatically not the idea of an already fixed end or life plan, towards attaining which your life should be organized. The thought is rather that you can think of your life, as it proceeds, in two ways. There is the every day way, made salient to us by the demands of daily life: You do first this and then that, till the time (hour, day, lifetime) is used up. There is also the way that becomes apparent as a way to think about your life when you first ask yourself why you are doing what you are doing. Thinking about the action you are performing now, you ask yourself why you are doing it. The answer here is given by the goal you have in doing it. Many of your goals reveal themselves to be important only in the light of other, larger goals of yours. You shop to get food, to eat, to keep going, for example. You study to understand the subject, to get a job (let us say), to earn money, to maintain a higher standard of living than mere survival. Thought about the ways your goals hang together makes it clear that you have several large-scale goals:

to have a satisfying job, to make money, to have a family life, perhaps to travel and soon. You have several goals you are set to achieve in your life. But – you have only one life. All these goals have to be achieved in one temporal stretch (2017, p.265).

So, in this context, we consider sources of satisfaction and dissatisfaction, happiness and unhappiness, perhaps, even fulfilment or unfulfillment, success or disappointment, well-being or otherwise, and then we rethink our ways of living, and one might add, our decision-making processes, our choices, in order to pursue what Annas calls a "better life", that is to say, a more ethical, a more fulfilling, successful, healthy or prosperous life. It does seem obviously true that we have, or can have, small scale and large-scale goals, short term and long term aims, and that we, speaking generally, can reflect on and act on such goals and aims, all of which we might aim to achieve in one human life.

We also have conceptions, one might add, of such goals and aims, as well as conceptions of what a human life can look like, so to speak, of the shape we can choose to give it, so to speak, in the long term, through the habits and dispositions we develop, our choices and acts and the virtues we choose to instantiate as well as the vices we choose to avoid with some final goal or goals in mind - all of this makes sense within such a framework; certainly it is a meaningful, coherent and significant conception of human life, as far as it goes.

But Annas adds:

You might try to achieve only one, hoping that after that you can take care of the others (in some kind of "bucket list," for example). You might give some up when you think about the difficulty, or perhaps impossibility, of achieving them in a way compatible with your achieving other, more important, goals. Whatever you do, you have to organize your goals somehow into the living of a single life. If you give up on this, life will just do it for you, and you will be left with regrets that you didn't order things better while you still had options. In thinking of your life as the single life in living which you have to organize and integrate your various goals, you have implicitly recognized your final end – the goal which is overarching in that you achieve it in achieving your goals, whatever they are, in a coherent way which enables you to live a better life than you would have done had you given the issue no thought. An implicit such end whose pressure is unconsciously felt is a hupotelis, but ancient thinkers are, disappointingly for us, not much concerned with the pre-conscious roots of ethical thinking, and the final end is nearly always discussed as your telos, your explicitly recognized final end (2017, p.266).

The relation between flourishing and our goals, personal and interpersonal, the organisation of these goals through deliberation, choice and action, the quest for a better life, the avoidance of an unreflective, thoughtless or, in a Socratic sense, an unexamined life, and so on, seems quite clear, even if some of the details could be unpacked and elucidated a little more. It is not entirely clear what *pre-conscious roots* might mean here, admittedly, but the *conscious roots* of ethical thinking, reflection, choice and decision making and action, anchored, for example, in habits or dispositions which can be chosen and cultivated, as well as habits and dispositions which can be avoided, are not counter-intuitive, and quite defensible.

Annas argues, with some justification, that the end which one seeks is neither fixed nor static; it is "simply the goal you are trying to achieve in your life as a whole, the goal that all your other goals are means to or help constitute (2017, p.266). That end is flourishing, and perhaps as she puts it, happiness (2017, p.266). But it is important to maintain a distinction between flourishing and happiness for the sake of greater clarity here. Although happiness might conceivably be part of a flourishing life, the two are not the same, and should not be conflated. One might be happy and amoral, for example, or excessively selfish, even vicious; perhaps one finds happiness even in causing pain to others. A flourishing life in this sense cannot be constituted simply by a feeling or a state of being which turns on pleasure or joy or satisfaction, or other such things. It must include objective goods as many thinkers realise, also.

It is questionable also to assert as Annas does that in ancient Greece, "happiness is what you aim for in everything you do, while you do not aim for anything further in aiming at happiness" (2017, p.266). If the distinction made above is a meaningful one, then flourishing is a higher goal than happiness since it includes happiness conceivably but also objective goods like knowledge, learning, well-being, success, friendship, and so on. In this context, the Aristotelian argument broadly is that "everyone agrees that their final end" is eudaimonia (flourishing) though "they disagree as to what" it is, exactly (2017, p.266). It is logically questionable to say that *everyone* agrees on this, of course, since there is no way in which an Aristotelian could possibly ascertain or demonstrate this or even the presumption that eudaimonia is everyone's *final end,* for the same reasons – there is much scope here for complexity, nuance, disputation and differentiation, to be sure. But the general thrust, namely that eudaimonia is a desirable final end for human beings, in general, perhaps the most desirable for many, or most, or something worth pursuing in a human life, is certainly defensible.

She does argue, correctly, that there are distinctive aspects of eudaimonism such as the view that eudaimonia is a final end, although "it is what I aim at in my life, you in yours, and so on… not a merely prudential end" (2017, p.266). In other words, one's practical thinking, or deliberation, is not only about one's own interests over and against the interests of others - it is about how best to live one's life among others such as children, parents, relatives, friends, employees, and so on. She notes persuasively that concern for others is an integral part of one's concern for, and one might add, active and deliberative pursuit of, eudaimonia (2017, pp.266-267). Not having any concern for others, as she points out, is "never an assumption in ancient thinking" (2017, p.267); eudaimonia in this context cannot be achieved by choosing and cultivating, or habitually practising, excessive selfishness, or by disregarding the rights, or entitlements, of others. It is important to remember here, for example, the significance of virtues such as hospitality among the ancient Greeks, among others. Eudaimonia, then, "cannot be achieved without virtue" (2017, p.267). It cannot by extension be achieved by living a life of habituated viciousness (in the sense of a disposition towards choosing vices like callousness, intemperance, injustice, and so on, over virtues in one's relations with others).

There are some, of course, who argue against this connection between virtue and flourishing, as she notes. Some find it "implausible or even absurd", though it is difficult to see how eudaimonia could possibly be achieved in the absence of virtues, or in the presence, so to speak, of vices (such as callousness, injustice and intemperate behaviour), and others note the fact that there are "divergent theories about this", but Annas notes also that "most people thought that virtue must have some part in a life well lived" even if they did not have a clear understanding of the importance of that part or of the relation between it and "other things also regarded as requisite parts of a eudaimon life, such as money or status" (2017, p.267).

It does need to be noted here that the mere fact that there are divergent theories about the link between eudaimonia and virtue, does not necessarily mean that there is no significant and meaningful relation between the two. Theories can be partial, misguided or just plain wrong. This much is obvious (for example, from the available history of theories in philosophy as well as the sciences). Annas notes correctly also that "nearly all philosophers agreed that virtue could not merely be one part or aspect of a eudaemon life along with others; it must in some way be the dominating aspect" or, one might add, a crucial aspect (2017, p.267). The question is not a straightforward one to be sure, but its answer must await a future investigation.

So Annas is correct in claiming that virtue is "necessary (but not sufficient) for Aristotle, and necessary and sufficient for the Stoics" (2017, p.267). It is possible also, and quite coherent, to argue that virtue is an essential part of a eudaimon life, in general, since, for example, it is difficult to see, in logical and empirical terms, how the absence of a disposition towards virtue, or the presence, so to speak, of a disposition to act viciously (in the sense outlined above), can actually result in a fully realised eudaimon life. There is no getting around the troubling implication here: the negation, or neglect, of virtue or its integral importance in such a life entails, logically, the negation, or neglect, of justice, or compassion, or moral courage, and so on, as well as the negation, or neglect, of their integral importance in such a life.

So, what "does it mean to say that virtue is crucial for this?" Annas asks (not a moment too soon) (2017, p.268). The central claim is that one will not "succeed in living a eudaimon life if the virtues do not have priority in the way you live your life" (2017, p.268). True; but it goes well beyond priority, it must be said. To give virtues priority is to give them a proper place, but it is necessary to go further. They must be known, considered, chosen, instantiated, as habitual things which are good for us are known, considered, chosen, instantiated, in the pursuit of eudaimonia. So, she uses the example of "money-grubbing": this is a vice and clearly so, since it is based on an excessive desire for, and choice of, more and more money, without limits; it is clearly intemperate, that is to say, lacking in self-control. She argues persuasively that it" will not lead to eudaimonia, but neither will a lofty indifference to money" (2017, p.268).

Of course, we all have to deal with money in our everyday lives, as she notes, and "some of us are brought up to be honest with money, others not; and some of each kind endorse their upbringing while others reject it" (2017, p.268). But there are clearly virtuous and vicious ways of dealing with money, for example, by giving money to charity freely and deliberatively, or by taking it by force from others who have no wish to give it away. In any case, Annas is right to note that we cannot avoid dealing with it though it is our responsibility to decide whether or not to use it honestly or dishonestly, for example, virtuously or viciously. And one might add, this is something that has important implications for education, and more broadly, learning. It is no surprise for example to find many books, podcasts and classes now on responsible and ethical, sustainable, financial management.

The nexus here between virtues (such as honesty) and finance, on the one hand, and vices and finance, on the other hand, and education, or more broadly, learning, could hardly be more important at a time when some powerful nations, and indeed, organisations, some of them affiliated, are actively disposed towards, choosing and funding terrorism, terrible violence, chaos and/or disorder in numerous parts of the world. The role of education, especially in the context of the global village, as an instrument of enlightenment and emancipation, in some senses, has never been more important; the challenges have rarely been more acute, especially and perhaps most meaningfully, in relation to the pursuit of viciousness in all of its forms and structures, and in all of its nefarious, threatening, lethal, intemperate, de-stabilising global manifestations.

The claim, she argues,

most ancient philosophers make is that only dealing with money (and status and so on) virtuously, rather than viciously or indifferently, will form part of a eudaimon life. We cannot avoid this kind of choice in the way we deal with money, status, and other aspects of life –in our relationships with others, for example. We have to deal with these things in some or other way, as that is just what it is to live a life in the society and culture in which we find ourselves; so we cannot escape choosing to deal with them virtuously or not, where this will require endorsing or rejecting parts of our upbringing. This, incidentally, shows the mistake in the claim that thinking in terms of virtue will tend to endorse the standards one has learnt and so be conservative. This does not appear to be true on the level of ordinary ethical living, and it is wildly false of ancient philosophers, whose claim that you need to live virtuously to achieve eudaimonia was, over a wide range of time and different societies, standardly quite at odds with the culture of the day (2017, p.268).

On this basis, Annas argues convincingly for the meaning, structure and significance of the relation between eudaimonia, virtue and coherent, forceful, timely and engaged ethical thinking.

In other recent works, she argues that intelligent virtue is sometimes conceived of as a "simple perceptual response", but in fact it is an "educated and intelligent response, even where the content of the education is not explicitly rehearsed before the action. this is what distinguishes it from mere routine", or skill (2015a, p.286). One might add that it is also distinguishable from mere routine or skill by the fact that it has an incontrovertible ethical dimension, a deliberative or reflective dimension and a critical dimension, that is, it involves an ongoing evaluation of dispositions or habits which direct a life, so to speak, or the way in which one lives, through virtues and self-control, and away from vices, excess and deficiency, towards flourishing, and in that sense, goodness.

This kind of approach does go, as she realises, "beyond the skill analogy, since it is essential to a trait's being a virtue that it involve a commitment to goodness, which is not required of a skill" (2015a, p.287). It also, one might add, involves a commitment to deliberation, and good thinking, for example on the logic of choices and actions, moderation, excess and deficiency, and viciousness (in the sense mentioned above) and indeed on choices and actions which promote flourishing, broadly conceived (that is, an ethical but also, for example, as a humanitarian, egalitarian, political, socio-economic and psychological category, amongst other things). So, it in this context that flourishing may be called "activity (*energeia*) in accordance with virtue" (1993, p.13), but it is also possible to call it, coherently, thoughtful or deliberative activity in accordance with virtues which direct one's life, one's way of living, or human lives, more broadly, consciously, freely and habitually towards flourishing.

The question of which virtues ought to be chosen or valorised is an important one, given obvious differences in various communities and cultures but that is a question for another time and place; it is sufficient for our purposes that some virtues such as justice are recognised and actualised by different communities and cultures in the same, or analogous, kinds of ways, or that some virtues, such as kindness or mercy, are recognised and actualised across communal or cultural or national boundaries, and even across communities, cultures and nations which are otherwise marked by deep enmities, contradictions or radically divergent values or value systems.

*

For these reasons, among others, it is, then, not at all surprising that eudaimonian ethics (and what one might call in a broadened key, outlined above, humanistic eudaimonism) has attracted a great deal of attention recently from philosophers, scientists and educators, among many others. Some, also not surprisingly, have attempted to provide applied frameworks in education (for example, Kristjánsson; Norrish, Williams, O'Connor and Robinson; and Wolberta, de Ruytera and Schinkela, among many others).

Norrish, Williams, O'Connor and Robinson argue that

> *Eudaimonia as a philosophical tradition posits that happiness results from the actualisation of individual potential and from fulfilling one's daimon or true nature (Deci & Ryan, 2008). Where hedonic approaches focus on how people feel, eudaimonic approaches focus on what people do, how they act, and the choices they make… involves more than feelings of happiness and entails personal growth, giving to others, and living in accordance with values (2013, p.148).*

A number of points need to be made here. First of all, as noted earlier, it is important to observe the logical distinction between happiness and flourishing; the two are related conceivably but they are not the same, and they are certainly not necessarily the same ends for the reasons noted above. One could conceivably pursue happiness without any thought for the wellbeing of others, or without any concern for the wellbeing of others, or even in a cave. There is no necessary logical identity between the two. So, the philosophical tradition also posits a possible difference between happiness and eudaimonia. The tradition, broadly conceived, also posits more than the claim that "happiness results from the actualisation of individual potential and from fulfilling one's daimon or true nature" (2013, p.148); it is not in any obvious sense individualistic, inasmuch as the Aristotelian aspects of the tradition posit the social nature of human beings, and inasmuch as this tradition also posits agreement among men and women on eudaimonia as an end in human lives, in general (rightly or wrongly). It does posit as Norrish et al. state, "more than feelings of happiness" and does indeed entail "personal growth, giving to others" and one might add, importantly, interpersonal growth; it is not enough to argue that it involves "living in accordance with values", for it involves knowledge, deliberation, habituation and choosing a life or lives which are in accordance not with any values (such as hedonistic or egoistic values) but with specific virtues such as justice, temperance and so on.

They are correct to argue that flourishing in schools "exists on multiple levels. Individual students may be considered to be flourishing when they are happy, thriving in their social relationships, achieving their goals with competence and confidence, and making valued contributions to others" (2013, p.149). It is important to think beyond common conceptions of happiness, such as merely hedonistic or ego-centred conceptions; students (and teachers) may be considered to be flourishing when they are happy, thriving in their own lives and in their social relationships, achieving their virtue driven, one might say, ends, with knowledge, thoughtfulness, deliberation as well as competence, habituation and confidence as persons *and* citizens, and making valued contributions to their own orientation, success, wellbeing and so on, and to the orientation, success, wellbeing and so on, of others. This much is coherent, cogent and defensible.

On a practical level, Norrish et al. posit and discuss six domains which they claim are "central to wellbeing", namely positive emotions, positive engagement, positive accomplishment, positive purpose, positive relationships, and positive health, all underpinned by a sustained focus on "character strengths" (2013, p.150). This is valuable work indeed, although it is possible to go further, as this volume demonstrates.

A school or an institution might affirm and implement this framework, and students systematically might learn the value of positive emotions, positive engagement, positive accomplishment, positive purpose, positive relationships, and positive health, and become aware clearly and coherently of the meaning and importance of character and "strengths", and even know, say, how to make decisions or choices which would help them to achieve these six things. However, positive emotions, engagement, accomplishment, purpose, relationships and health may be necessary but they are not sufficient.

Eudaimonism also requires knowledge, even discernment, good critical deliberation, or what one might call more broadly the development and cultivation of reason, some understanding of logic (for example, which would allow the subject to distinguish clearly and coherently between deficiency and excess, and vices from virtues); it also posits an element of good fortune, or a good guide, according to the Socratic, Platonic and Aristotelian philosophical traditions, which cannot be concealed, ignored or dismissed, and systematic ethical reflection, as well as habituation which follows from the kind of deliberative process outlined above, amongst other things. It is imperative that educational institutions capture, in any attempt to put eudaimonism into practise, its reasonableness, thoughtfulness, richness, complexity and multifariousness. This task is by no means out of the question either (based on the personal experience of the author, for example, in the implementation and delivery of core curriculums at a number of educational institutions in the last two decades).

*

Others, like Wolberta, de Ruytera and Schinkela attempt, again not surprisingly, to formulate formal criteria which would begin to allow us to defend flourishing as an "ideal aim of education" (2015, pp.118-129). This work is very valuable as far as it goes; it does need to be said however that flourishing need not necessarily be restricted to an *ideal* or an *ideal aim* of education; an understanding of it and a carefully cultivated pursuit of it, can be emphasised in much if not all of its reasonableness, thoughtfulness, richness, complexity and multifariousness in educational curriculums and more broadly, in the fabric of pedagogy. It certainly has practical applications amongst other things; it should not be considered only as an ideal educational aim or structure.

They propose two criteria, "of which the second criterion has three sub-criteria" and argue that every actual conception of flourishing should be in accordance with the five criteria and sub-criteria (2015, p.7). They note that it is possible to use the term in ways that do not meet the criteria, but these "fail to capture what is distinctive about flourishing as opposed to for instance happiness" (2015, p.7).

The first criterion is *flourishing is intrinsically worthwhile* (that is, it is pursued for itself and not for any other end); the second is *the actualisation of the human potential;* the second criterion produces three subcriteria, namely *life* [conceived of or understood] *as a whole; a dynamic state; and objective goods* (2015, pp.7-8). All of this is largely consistent with some of the key aspects of classical Greek eudaimonism. They point out that within this framework "there are things that are good for everybody" (objective goods) and that these are "constitutive of a flourishing life, for example social relationships" and "other objective goods are good capacities, the development of which will contribute to the flourishing of human beings, for example phronesis, practical wisdom, which Aristotle deems necessary to exercise all other virtues" (2015, p.11).

They note also, importantly, that flourishing "inevitably" centralises "an ethical question" in educational theory by "asking what those 'good' capacities could be, and who can judge whether they are really 'good'" (2015, p.18). Eudaimonism certainly puts such a question at the centre, amongst other things, such as ethical answers, theories and explanations. The question of who can judge is also an important one, with *phronesis*, or practical wisdom, amongst other things, at the forefront of the discussion.

But they ask, "is this not asking too much of children, risking to turn them into stressful, unhappy overachievers? Should we not just try to equip children to have a nice life, and focus on being satisfied with whatever it is that happens to them in life (be happy with it)?" (2015, p.18). They agree that the answer is "no"; there is no necessary or self-evident connection between the pursuit of flourishing and "stressful, unhappy overachievers" (2015, p.18). Indeed, the latter would seem to need a few lessons on the distinction between flourishing and happiness, and on the virtue of moderation!

But the authors are right about optimal educational conditions: it is important "for both educators and children to have high aims, so that educators will strive to create the optimal conditions for children and for children to get the best chance to develop themselves towards the ideal of an optimal life" (2015, p.18). However, an optimal life is not the end of eudaimonism; a flourishing life is the end, and this end, as argued above, is not necessarily an ideal. It is one which can- one might argue that it ought to - be pursued and achieved in the here and now, especially since all of the key constituents discussed above – knowledge, deliberation, habituation, choice, the practise of virtue, the use of practical reason, the orientation of one's life between the poles, so to speak, of excess and deficiency, the pursuit of success, wellbeing, friendship and love, and so on and so forth, are all achievable, at least in principle, in our lives. They are not necessarily or self-evidently impossible.

In seeking flourishing lives for students, one is not seeking or demanding perfection, as the authors realise. One cannot seek, or demand, the unattainable. Seeking or demanding this from anyone, let alone children, might serve as an example of how the logic of deficiency and excess, so crucial to the choice of virtue and the avoidance of vice, for example, is misunderstood, or violated. The demand for perfection, in the sense of demanding a life of perfect virtue always, is clearly excessive, therefore it is not a virtue, and by extension, then, should be rejected as such in any eudaimonian framework.

The following chapters explore the nexus between flourishing and education in the broadest sense. Flourishing can have multiple meanings, forms and structures, to be sure, especially in the digital age in which human relationships and interconnections are being redefined and reconfigured globally. But flourishing requires authentic relationships. These go well beyond I-You relationships in Martin Buber's sense of that term, though these are no doubt crucial; for example, they require not only positive inter-personal or intersubjective dimensions, but many other things, for example, positive environmental, mental and physical, metaphysical, political, ethical, educational, emotional, health-related, rights-related, work-related, means-related dimensions as well as a recognition of and/or commitment to human goods, at the very least, personal dignity, respect, liberties, compassion, practical wisdom, courage, justice, and so on and so forth.

They require qualitatively different virtual relationships also, in the digital age, especially relationships which are based on well-being, honesty, tolerance, respect, compassion, critical thinking and reflection, practical reason, prudential patterns of relation and consumption – in short, professional, responsible, informed and ethical netizenship, one might say - and ideally, a systematic response to, and repudiation of, numerous forms of dehumanising virality, addiction, irresponsibility, exploitation, bullying, predation, excess, greed, fraud, fakeness and, indeed, viciousness in all of its physical and metaphysical, digital and virtual forms, more broadly.

Such relationships are vital preconditions of positive growth and development in many different settings and contexts, virtual or otherwise. This much is clear from the essays in this volume.

In "Living Systems and Learning Flourishing in the Digital Age", Belinda Rudinger and Kim Wahl focus on flourishing in terms of personal values and interconnections. They propose that an alignment of the ideal of flourishing with approaches to learning now requires a foundation in systems thinking, especially living systems principles, so that learning sanctuaries may emerge as well as other opportunities which emphasise belonging, especially in the context of challenges and opportunities which have emerged in the digital age.

In "Promoting Flourishing in the Digital Age The Interplay of Well-being, Life-long Learning, and Success", Ranjit Singha and Surjit Singha argue that the digital era has altered our understanding of learning, communication, and success. They focus on the relationship between flourishing, lifelong learning, and success in the digital era. They argue that wellness and fulfilment are crucial aspects of digital life. They provide tips for digital success in the context of development, lifelong learning, responsible digital citizenship and honest online relationships, and remind us of the important connection between technology and personal growth.

In " Cultivating Flourishing and Resilience in the Digital Age: Addressing Digital Addiction with Multidimensional Addiction Behavior Scale", Ranjit Singha and Surjit Singha focus on the crucial question of digital addiction. They explore various strategies which can mitigate digital addiction and promote flourishing and resilience. They understand digital addiction in terms of compulsive behaviour in relation to digital devices and platforms; they recognise the harm it causes, and the profound threat to flourishing that it poses, especially in the context of personal health and mental and physical well-being. They produce practical educational, policy and community-based approaches which can help us to develop healthier forms of digital relationships, in an age in which digital technologies are pervasive.

In "Creativity and Critical Thinking in Students Through Non-Traditional Teaching Methods", Mohit Yadav, Pankaj Jain, Rajeev Goyal, Ajay Chandel and Ta Huy Hung focus on the impact of non-traditional teaching methods and their effects on the creativity and critical thinking skills of students. They take a case study approach and look closely at qualitative and quantitative data to investigate the connection between teaching methods and student outcomes and argue that non-traditional approaches, for example, problem-based learning, can significantly improve the creative and critical thinking skills of students, with appropriate teacher training and institutional support.

In " Emancipatory Education in Higher Education: A Transformative Approach", Pam Epler focusses on emancipatory (higher) education, which she argues, promotes critical thinking autonomy and social justice and therefor empowers, and emboldens, learners. It is based on the critical investigation of the experiences of learners, social and power structures and encourages them to confront injustice, to seek a more just social order. Epler explores various approaches including dialogic teaching, problem-posing, and participatory action research to promote that end.

In "Pedagogy of the Impressed: Classroom Reflections Toward a Neocalvinistic Teaching Framework", Jeremiah Paul Giron Manuel argues that human flourishing is the proper end of education with primacy given to the psychological and psychosocial health of learners. Neocalvinism, he argues, requires human beings to do their utmost to promote and actualise the flourishing, and especially the wellbeing, of learners in childhood, and is therefore worthy of consideration, especially in the context of possible teaching frameworks.

In "Virtue as Applied to Digital Learning: Observations from a Faith-based Institution", Megan Reister and Liz Allgood focus on opportunities which online students have to grow, and to learn to apply virtue and develop authentic relationships in digital learning environments. They clarify virtue and flourishing, and link these to postsecondary outcomes and goals. They then look at the impact digital technologies can have on the development of virtue and reflect on ways of encouraging students to be critically and prudently engaged consumers in the digital age.

In " Social and Digital Media: Promoting Rationality, Self-Knowledge, and Self-Understanding in Higher Education", Surjit Singha argues that higher education requires social and digital media now, since these offer tools which can be used to develop logic, deeper self-awareness and self-understanding in students; which can be used to increase self-awareness and growth. So, it is important to integrate social and digital media into our higher education institutions and practises. In this way, we, as educators, can promote digital literacy and encourage critical reflection, sustainability and interpersonal cooperation.

In "Digitalization and the Impact of Facebook Usage on University Students' Academic Performance", Md. Ashrafuzzaman and Sabbir Ahmed explore the impact of Facebook usage on the academic performance of university students in the COVID-19 pandemic. They survey 220 students and find that they use Facebook for many reasons for example, communication, entertainment, and education. A number of challenges are discussed, for example, harassment, the problem of verification and spam but they point out that most students take a positive view of Facebook, even though a large percentage believe that excessive socializing and related distractions have negative effects on their academic performance. The authors recommend additional forms of student support especially in terms of counselling and clear guidance.

In " The Role of Cooperatives in Driving Inclusive Growth and Sustainable Development", V. Venkatakrishnan, Srilata Patnaik, Debasish Mohapatra and Surendra Kumar Jena point out that India's cooperatives, including Gujarat Cooperative Milk Marketing Federation (GCMMF), Indian Farmers Fertilizer Cooperative Limited

(IFFCO), and Krishak Bharati Cooperative Limited (KRIBHO) are known globally for their success. They point out also that these cooperative enterprises contribute significantly and positively to economies and promote ethical business behaviour. They outline initial challenges which these enterprises face and look at ways of achieving inclusive and sustainable growth and development and explore efforts recently to support such cooperatives. They conclude by outlining some steps which will further strengthen these cooperatives in order to promote inclusive success, growth and sustainable development now and in the future.

In " Pioneering Pathways: Future Directions and Innovations in Fostering Well-being and Genuine Connections in the Digital Era", Gregory Harrison and Emily Duplantis argue that as digital technology grows, education shifts from face-to-face interactions to virtual relationships especially after the COVID-19 pandemic. This change means that we need to examine the impact of technology on the well-being and growth of students and indeed on authentic relationships. The convergence of artificial intelligence (AI), virtual reality (AR) and education opens up new possibilities for learning and relationships, for example, between students and educators. They note an emerging concern: this convergence could make meaningful human interactions, which are important in terms of academic performance, health and wellbeing, more difficult to realise. So, it becomes important to explore how AI and emergent technologies can be effectively integrated, and harnessed, to promote positive learning outcomes and well-being; to make sure that digital technologies enhance, rather than diminish, the fundamental significance of human relationships and connections in the lives and experiences of students in the digital age.

It is hoped that these essays will stimulate further thought and debate on the meaning, place and function of critical thinking, moral deliberation, the promotion and development of healthy and positive, authentic relationships, wellbeing, virtue (and viciousness), the ethos of sustainability, human goods, safety online (and offline), and responsible, informed, reflective, ethical, one might say more prudential, citizenship and netizenship (in a world in which fragmentation, division and hostility seem to be on the increase), and so on, in relation to education, and the pursuit of higher forms of learning, and understanding, now; that they will open up further questions for investigation and critical inquiry, and increased engagement, at the vital, dynamic, but in some respects, troubling, intersection between artificial intelligence (and radical forms of simulation, and indeed, dissimulation), technology, communication, human inter-relations, education (and learning), flourishing and the digital age.

Raymond Aaron Younis

University of Sydney, Australia

REFERENCES

Annas, J. (1993). *The morality of happiness*. Oxford University Press.

Annas, J. (2016). Learning virtue rules. Developing the virtues: integrating perspectives, 225-233.

Audi, R. (1993). *Action, intention, and reason*. Cornell University Press.

Foot, P. (1978). *Virtues and Vices*. Blackwell.

Foot, P. (1994). Rationality and Virtue. In Pauer-Studer, H. (Ed.), *Norms, Values and Society* (pp. 205–216). Kluwer.

Foot, P. (1995). Does Moral Subjectivism Rest on a Mistake? *Oxford Journal of Legal Studies*, *15*, 1–14.

Hursthouse, R. (1990-1991). After Hume's Justice. *Proceedings of the Aristotelian Society*, *91*, 229–245.

Hursthouse, R. (2011). Virtue Ethics and the Treatment of Animals. In Beauchamp, T. L., & Frey, R. G. (Eds.), *The Oxford Handbook of Animal Ethics* (pp. 119–143). Oxford University Press.

Hursthouse, R., & Ethics, O. V. (Oxford University Press. Oxford, 1999).

Jenkins, W. (2016). The Turn to Virtue in Climate Ethics. *Environmental Ethics*, *38*, 77–96.

Kristjánsson, K. (2007). *Aristotle, Emotions, and Education*. Ashgate Publishing.

Kristjánsson, K., Carr, D., & Arthur, J. (Eds.). (2016). *Varieties of Virtue Ethics*. Palgrave-Macmillan.

Kristjánsson, K.Virtues and Vices in Positive Psychology. (2013). *A Philosophical Critique*. Cambridge University Press.

MacIntyre, A., & Virtue, A. (Duckworth, London, 1985).

Norrish, J. M., Williams, P., O'Connor, M., & Robinson, J. (2013). An applied framework for positive education. *International Journal of Wellbeing*, *3*(2), 147–161.

Wolberta, L. S., de Ruytera, D. J., & Schinkela, A. (2015). Formal criteria for the concept of human flourishing: The first step in defending flourishing as an ideal aim of education. *Ethics and Education*, *10*(1), 118–129.

Chapter 1
Living Systems and Learning:
Flourishing in the Digital Age

Belinda Rudinger
https://orcid.org/0000-0002-5253-0391
East Texas A&M University, USA

Kim Wahl
University of Wisconsin-Madison, USA

ABSTRACT

In this chapter, the concept of flourishing is defined in terms of individual values and interconnections. The authors propose that aligning the ideal of flourishing with society's current approach to learning requires a grounding in systems thinking, particularly living systems principles. Addressing not only intellectual, but also affective needs of learners is considered in the application of living systems principles to the creation of learning sanctuaries and other opportunities to promote belonging. These concepts are considered against the backdrop of the challenges and opportunities inherent in a digital age.

INTRODUCTION

In this chapter, we highlight the term flourishing and define its value to us as individuals and collectives within society. In other words, we define what it means to flourish and why it is worth seeking. After establishing a definition of flourishing, we consider what needs to change to arrive at such a point. Namely, we encourage balancing out our current mechanistic approach to include an appreciation of the

DOI: 10.4018/979-8-3693-0997-1.ch001

holistic approach to teaching and learning and making room for ourselves and others as whole creatures on this planet. In order to apply a more holistic approach to the pursuit of flourishing, we turn to systems thinking as a means of navigating the messy complexity of a holistic approach to flourishing. Systems thinkers across disciplines invite us to consider "hidden connections" and a new way of seeing that recognizes the ways in which we are inextricably linked with one another and our given contexts.

Using a systems lens allows us to identify these networks and connections and better ground and understand our actions within a given system. Within these connections, we also note the power of authentic relationships to our sense of well-being and our universal drive for belonging. Finally, with a common understanding of what we seek, why our approach needs to change, and how we can maneuver these pathways using systems thinking, we turn our attention to a final task of examining both the opportunities inherent in our current state of being in the digital age. Given these affordances and constraints, how do we take action toward flourishing using a holistic approach informed with an understanding of systems? These considerations can be applied at an individual and organizational level and to different fields such as business and personal development. For the scope of this paper, we choose to explore the following question: how do we align the concept of flourishing with our systems approach to learning, particularly in this digital age?

WHAT IT MEANS TO FLOURISH

Philosophers, writers, and scholars have long considered what makes a life worth living. Various terms have been used to capture this ideal, whose components include learning, growth, well-being, happiness, and authentic relationships. Various fields such as positive psychology, sustainability, and contextual behavior science have offered definitions of flourishing with their own metrics and descriptions. Father of Positive Psychology, Martin Seligman (2011), in his book *Flourish,* identified this concept as the new ideal for psychology. Seligman (2011) defined the term through a new model called Positive Emotions, Engagements, Relationships, Meaning, & Achievement (PERMA). His framework inspired a multitude of follow-up studies within Positive Psychology (Huppert & So, 2013; Rusk & Waters, 2015). Inspired by Seligman's PERMA model, Butler & Kern (2016) defined flourishing as "a dynamic optimal state of psychosocial functioning that arises from functioning well across multiple psychosocial domains" and created a measurement tool for its specific assessment (p. 2).

Definitions of Flourishing

Inspired by the work of Seligman (2011) and other positive psychologists, O'Brien (2010) applied the work of studying happiness to the field of sustainability. Emerging from the combination of positive psychology and sustainability, O'Brien's (2010) approach underscores the importance of inspiring people with something to strive for and that also moves beyond happiness or flourishing of a given individual in isolation. O'Brien (2010) has defined sustainable happiness as "happiness that contributes to individual, community and/or global well-being without exploiting other people, the environment or future generations" (p. 2). Grounding the pursuit of happiness within the context of sustainability ensures attention to the fact that one person's happiness should not come at the expense of another person's happiness. Furthermore, this definition recognizes that each individual stands within a network connected to others. O'Brien's (2013) definition intentionally "underscores the interrelationships between happiness, well-being, and sustainability" (p. 232). O'Brien (2012; 2013) shares real-world examples of infusing her ideas of sustainable happiness into various educational programs to promote education for sustainability. Perhaps the most significant contribution of sustainable happiness involves its recognition of interconnection and interdependence (O'Brien, 2013). As O'Brien (2012) noted, "Our natural desire for happiness can become the entry point for discovering that our well-being is inextricably linked to the well-being of others and the natural environment" (p. 45).

Sustainability scholar and MIT engineer John Ehrenfeld's ideas about flourishing bloomed from the original seeds of sustainability as applied to science (Ehrenfeld & Hoffman, 2013). Considering growth and limits to growth from a scientific approach, they determined flourishing, or *flourishing-as-sustainability,* to be a more authentic term to capture what humankind seeks (Ehrenfeld & Hoffman, 2013). "Flourishing is the result of acting out of caring for oneself, other human beings, the rest of the 'real, material' world, and also for the out-of-the-world, that is, the spiritual or transcendental world" (Ehrenfeld & Hoffman, 2013, p. 17).

According to Ehrenfield and Hoffman (2013), "Sustainability... is about the way we live. It is about living authentically; it is about our relationships with nature, with each other, and with ourselves" (Preface). Flourishing within the context of these relationships means not only to grow, but "to grow well" (Ehrenfeld & Hoffman, 2013, p. 6). This idea captures "what it truly means to be a human being living in an interconnected and complex world. It is a desirable future; one built not just on technological and material development but also on cultural, personal, and spiritual growth" (Ehrenfeld & Hoffman, 2013, p. 6). Ehrenfeld (2020) states that,

"Flourishing lies in the choice to lead an authentic life...on the path set by your commitments" (p. 22). He notes that flourishing is not measured by successful

performance, but by identification and commitment to "the design of one's life" (Ehrenfeld, 2020, p. 22).

This description of flourishing as an authentic alignment between identification and follow-through of one's commitments is reminiscent of the contextual behavior science approach to well-being. Grounded in hundreds of scientific studies, Hayes' (2019) work promotes a concept he has named psychological flexibility. Rather than considering only optimal functioning and avoidance of negative feelings and experiences, Hayes' (2019) contextual behavior science recognizes the inevitable suffering that occurs within human life. Rather than turning away from difficult or sub-optimal experiences, Hayes' (2019) science of acceptance and commitment provides impactful and actionable tools to deploy toward one's identified core values. Hayes defines psychological flexibility as "the ability to feel and think with openness, to attend voluntarily to your experience of the present moment, and to move your life in directions that are important to you" (Hayes, 2019, p. 5). Hayes' notion of developing psychological flexibility through acceptance and commitment is grounded in multiple techniques for use in both training and therapy settings (defusion, present-moment awareness, self-as-context, values, committed action, and flexible perspective-taking), with a strong research base (2019). While research has demonstrated the quantitative utility of these techniques, they are primarily utilized at the individual level, rather than within a systemic approach. They provide part of the approach to flourishing, but we assert that flourishing for a given individual must be rooted in an awareness of the given system.

Moving Toward Flourishing

To move toward flourishing, Ehrenfeld & Hoffman (2013) suggest two shifts in thinking. The first involves recognizing the systemic context of this pursuit, and the second is the importance of recognizing the value of subjective and qualitative ways of knowing in this arena. The objective metrics that serve science so well cannot alone capture the fullness of this endeavor. Rating scales and similar quantitative assessments will fall short; as Ehrenfeld (2020) noted, "Flourishing is a special quality of living and is not reducible to a numerical or other metrical value" (p. 15). While we can gather quantitative data on well-being assessments and questionnairesand determine the efficacy of specific behavioral interventions through single subject design studies, there is an element of flourishing that requires a qualitative perspective that considers the significance of relationships and connections. As Capra and Luisi (2016) noted, "relationships cannot be measured and weighed; relationships need to be mapped...when we map relationships, we find certain configurations that occur repeatedly" (p. 83). Capra and Luisi state that these repeated patterns of organization are typically found in living systems and can include boundaries and cycles (2016, p. 83).

Like sustainable happiness, sustainability-as-flourishing involves the recognition of connections to the rest of the world. According to Ehrenfeld and Hoffman (2013), "Care reflects a consciousness of our interconnectedness with the world (the web of life) and the historic recognition that well-being depends on acting to keep these relationships in a healthy state" (p. 84). Robinson and Moraes-Robinson (2017) concur on the significance of these connections within a system, defining sustainability as "the quality of our relationships" (p.6). Furthermore, their definition of authenticity is "the maximum coherence between what a person says, what they mean, and what they do" (Robinson & Moraes-Robinson, 2017, p.6). Each of these definitions of flourishing include alignment between value, intention, and action (Robinson & Moraes-Robinson, 2017; Hayes, 2019; Ehrenfeld & Hoffman, 2013).

Relationships are nested within systems, placing individual action in a connected network of the potential impact upon others. While positive psychological definitions of flourishing recognize the importance of relationships to well-being, the sustainability field extends this by recognizing the connections inherent between people and nature. As noted by Capra and Luisi (2016), strengthening connections between individuals also strengthens the success of a given system or network.

The use of the term flourishing captures a vision and a hope for the future, a powerful ideal to strive toward. This approach moves beyond a solitary, isolated conceptualization of "happiness" at the individual level and roots the ideal of flourishing firmly among connections to other people and life on this planet. While a positive psychological approach to flourishing may identify part of the same priorities, contextual behavior science looks at individual psychological flexibility to promote individual well-being, Concepts such as sustainable happiness and sustainability-as-flourishing recognize the significance of interconnectivity and living in systems.

Recognizing this, our working definition of flourishing for the scope of this chapter includes authentic alignment between values and commitments at both the individual *and* systemic/relational level. At any scale, Ehrenfeld (2020) notes that "any change that rebuilds connections should work to create the context for flourishing" (p. 130). Flourishing, in this chapter, refers to individuals within a system. There must be connectedness within oneself and between individuals in a given system. Strong, healthy connections from a systems view, both individually and socially, lead to flourishing systemically.

In the next section, we explore how systems thinking, primarily using principles of living systems, can promote the qualities needed for flourishing within a context of learning. This could include both youth and adults, formal educational settings, and also informal opportunities for growth and development. Applying living systems principles to learning (such as autopoiesis, dynamic balance, and individual development) can promote flourishing in space, person, and place. Relevant applications include creation of safe learning sanctuaries, building a sense of belonging, and creating inclusive communities.

WHY WE NEED A SYSTEMS APPROACH

We may long for flourishing at both the individual and system level, but our organizations, businesses, and societal norms do not yet reflect the optimal conditions. Hayes (2019) describes this need to make a change, noting that despite improvements brought on by modern science, "life should be getting easier, but it's not…too many of us struggle to live meaningful, peaceful lives full of love and contribution" (p. 3). Nowhere is this clearer than in our educational systems– where learning and subjects are separated into isolated parts without an understanding of the whole. We need to consider the relationships between the parts as we work to understand the whole. This requires a systems approach, however, our society's approach to learning has been largely mechanistic. An approach that promotes linear thinking to the exclusion of other types of thinking. We 'transmit' information in traditional lecture formats and have viewed education through a reductionist lens (Freire, 1970). The mainstream narrative of education continues to focus on products, competition, and individualism, and the westernized model of splitting up subjects and transferring information from the teacher, who is considered the 'expert,' to the student. In this case, education becomes transactional, with teachers making "deposits" that students receive and store. This transactional approach excludes space for meaningful engagement and exchange of ideas. (Freire, 1970).

When education operates in this manner, it denies the importance of the whole and reduces humans to simply their parts. As Immordino-Yang and Damasio (2016) noted,

> *Modern biology reveals humans to be fundamentally emotional and social creatures. And yet, those in the field of education often fail to consider that the high-level cognitive skills taught in schools, including reasoning, decision making, and processes related to language, reading, and mathematics, do not function as rational, disembodied systems, somehow influenced by but detached from emotion and the body. (p. 28)*

In treating learners with this approach, we are losing the most valuable aspect that makes us human – our connections and interrelationships that make us whole learners within our social systems.

We need holistic education that reunites the parts with the whole, using a systems lens for teaching and learning. To promote flourishing in the area of learning, we need to move from a mechanistic approach to a systems approach. To do so would allow us to create the conditions for learners to feel comfortable and have learning readiness. Under these conditions, learners would have the opportunity to grow, and "grow well" as described before. Ehrenfeld (2020) stated that, "flourishing is a name for a real condition; it is emergent and can be observed. It depends on how the parts of the world and their interrelationships are working as an integrated system" (p. 16). We see here that flourishing could become an emergent property of a given system. To promote flourishing in the context of learning and education requires systems thinking, including an understanding of interrelationships within an integrated system.

Systems thinking offers a view of the world that offers the following perspective: one can view the whole system while also recognizing the parts and relationships. In other words, a systems view allows us to see the forest *and* the trees. Meadows defined systems as "as a set of things-people, cells, molecules or whatever- interconnected in such ways that they produce their own pattern of behavior over time" (Meadows, 2008, p. 2). Alexander (1974) described a system as a network of organized components that are framed into a structure or pattern that has a given function or purpose. The purpose of a system is essentially to maintain a dynamic balance or equilibrium among the network of interrelationships to successfully sustain itself, thrive, and persist indefinitely over a long period of time. The goal is to have flourishing members within the system to maintain an overall healthy dynamic within the system and its interrelated parts. According to Meadows (2008), the components of a system include elements, interconnections, and a purpose. These components can adapt and self-organize themselves, maintaining themselves even in the face of disruption (Meadows, 2008).

A system has a purpose, including a boundary through which matter and/or energy may pass through for the exchange of information. The interrelated component parts share this common purpose as a whole system, so boundary is established according to the achievement of that purpose. Yet, the system reacts to the environment outside of the system. The system can either be open or closed, which determines what can pass through the boundary. This factor also influences how the system can perform its tasks collectively. Information flows move in and out of the system through this boundary. The system regulates itself through feedback loops that serve to maintain a dynamic balance or equilibrium. Places to make change within a system (leverage points) include examining feedback loops, monitoring flows, identifying the rules of the system, the goals of the system, its power distribution, and its governing paradigm (Meadows, 2008).

Applying this perspective to social and educational systems, including learning communities, opens the door to a new approach to learning with the potential to promote flourishing. A learning community is defined as "any facilitated group of students or professionals in higher education who come together for a defined period of time for a predetermined overall purpose having to do with intentional learning" (Widhalm, 2011, p. 2). It is a system of learners with the purpose of learning. Viewing learning communities from a systems perspective allows us to understand them better, while also identifying potential opportunities for change. Learning communities reflect systems in that humans consistently take in and process information (flows) to develop an understanding of the world. It is this feature that perfectly poises them to promote flourishing. Learners in these systems receive constant feedback from their social environment, while connecting this feedback to their previous knowledge and mindsets. As humans, we depend on information flows, connections, and feedback in systems to maintain stability. This dynamic equilibrium keeps us grounded in our own well-being, constantly re-balancing itself as new information is taken in from our surroundings.

This sense of connectedness and dynamic equilibrium relative to how we navigate the world reflects a systems thinking approach. This holistic approach balances out our current reductionist tendencies to better capture how humans learn. This approach is crucial in promoting equitable and welcoming educational environments that foster authentic relationships (the interconnections of the system) and learning experiences. Authentic relationships are inspired by authentic actions (Ehrenfeld, 2019). Authentic relationships and actions promote transparency, intentional vulnerability, and cultivate spaces where individuals feel comfortable to contribute to learning while being their true best selves. As the result of authentic interpersonal relationships, including behaviors and attitudes of selves and others, the space for meaningful learning is created (Bandura, 1971).

One particular type of system is a living system (Capra, 2002). A living system consists of a single living organism or several living organisms that work together for a common purpose and that respond to their environment. There are living system principles which support the function of a living system. Considering learning communities as living systems and applying living system principles to learning communities can help us understand more about the nature of complexity and the learners themselves. In doing so, we can begin to build more inclusive, flourishing learning communities (Widhalm, 2013; Capra & Luisi, 2016). This living systems approach more accurately mirrors our natural and social systems as we navigate more sustainable teaching practices (Widhalm, 2013). Table 1 lists the principles of a living system and describes them. Living system principles can help us shape learning experiences that foster a culture of care and authentic relationships where learners can flourish.

Table 1. Living Learning Principles

Living System Principles	Descriptions
Nested Systems	Individual systems layered one within another, encompassing a greater whole
Network	A group of interconnected members
Diversity	Variety and difference within a system promote resilience
Interdependence	Organisms do not live alone–they receive support from other living and nonliving structures in a given environment
Autopoiesis	A given system can self-organize and self-generate
Dynamic Equilibrium	A system maintains its continual and dynamic balance by self-regulation
Cycles and Flows	Systems have energy flows that move in and out of the system. Systems have a circulation of resources in the form of cycles or feedback loops. Systems have energy flows that move in and out of the system.
Development	System development, including learning and adapting, occurs at the individual level

(Capra, 2007)

Considering Learners & Learning Communities as Living Systems

An individual human is a living system and "is capable of adapting itself to the sorts of new and diverse circumstances that an active agent is likely to encounter in a dynamic world" (Davis & Sumara, 2006, p. 14). Because learning communities are composed of multiple humans (other learners and people playing the role of 'teacher'), we can consider them to have the same properties as living systems. From this perspective, the living system of a learner is nested within a learning system, such as a learning community. "Approaching learning communities as living systems represents a shift away from viewing education as something that can be compartmentalized, planned and pre-designed, measured, and quantitatively assessed with learning outcomes and grades" (Widhalm, 2011, p. 5). Here, we contend that learning systems may include both systematic processes, where you can plan and pre-design, but also the systemic processes necessary to promote flourishing. The key here is to dynamically balance both approaches to ensure holistic practices. We can develop a design or metapattern that is a living, flexible design that is adaptable and resilient based on feedback from partners within the learning community.

The Systemic Structure of the Learning Community

A system has a purpose and boundaries. For a learning community, the purpose includes meaningful learning experiences related to the healthy growth and development of the learners. This purpose may also be more specific to the content area and objectives of each particular learning community. The boundary is set by the students, instructor, and any individuals that strengthen the learning experiences (for example, guest speakers or community members working collaboratively on a project with learners). Information flows into and out of the system through the boundary of the system. As we set our purpose and boundaries of our learning community, we need to consider larger systems (for instance, a school, school district, or institution), and be sure the purpose and boundaries align well within the larger system. This can be challenging as larger systems may be more traditional in their approach to education.

As we consider the boundary of the learning community system, we should not only consider the elements or individuals. We need to consider the procedures and expectations that strengthen the overall system, so that individuals are aware of how to navigate the system to achieve its purpose. The learner should have a voice in how we structure the learning environment as well. The expectations put forth by the instructor and students include student input and feedback, and should set a flexible, adaptable, and dynamic boundary of learning. Learners will be more comfortable being familiar with the set boundaries while knowing there is room for flexibility and adaptability based on ongoing feedback from learners and instructor. The key to the success of the system is continuous work to dynamically balance the system. This happens by asking for feedback during class while also having more formal structures to garner feedback, such as holistic rubrics. These rubrics could also help students self-reflect on their own learning and contributions to an inclusive learning environment.

In setting boundaries to establish the learning community, there are two structures of procedures that we will address here: formal procedures and informal procedures. Formal procedures include such things as goals, learning objectives, written expectations, budgets, distribution of power, and so forth, whereas informal procedures are protocols that are more focused on communication and building relationships. There should be a dynamic balance of both structures of procedures, and they both need to be grounded in equitable practices in order to design a learning community in which learners may flourish (Figure 1).

Figure 1. Boundary Procedures

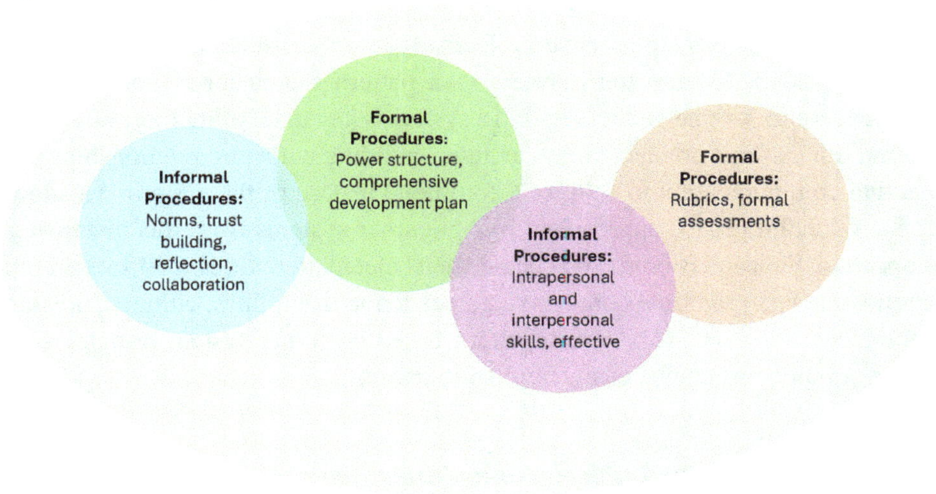

In formal procedures, the issue of power should be addressed, as it is a part of any community. Distribution of power that empowers its members is critical to success. The more people that feel empowered, the stronger the relationships and the learning community. As you go over formal procedures, a class discussion or ways to initiate student input is crucial to student engagement and successful learning outcomes. In addition, the instructor should recognize that a difference in structures that is far different from other courses within the larger educational system may lead learners to feel uncomfortable, so connecting to the larger system and other classes may lead to greater comfort for learners. For informal procedures, process and experimentation are just as important as outcomes. This includes freedom in learning, the opportunity to make mistakes, and a safe space to cultivate this growth mindset (Capra & Luisi, 2016). By increasing collaboration and improving informal procedures, a healthier community will result. Establishing trust is a component of creating a safe, confidential space for sharing. When educators establish clear transparent expectations, trust is built. Creating procedures agreed upon by students and teachers can be important in moving forward in a learning community to achieve the purpose of the system. A living systems approach to establishing all procedures is important as we consider individuals as living learner systems and the learning community as a living system itself. We can look to living system principles in helping us shape learning experiences which help us promote flourishing learning communities.

Living System Principles as a Metapattern for Learning

Living system principles have collectively been considered as metapatterns (Widhalm, 2013). Metapatterns refers to a pattern that inspires connectedness (Bateson, 2002). Connectedness within a system is key to learning more about oneself and others. This connectedness includes building authentic relationships with effective communication to achieve a common purpose of the system (Meadows, 2008). Widhalm (2013) approached living learner systems from this metapattern perspective. Volk and Bloom (2007) stated that "metapatterns are broad, overarching patterns that span multiple contexts (e.g., academic disciplines, cultures, personal experiences, etc.)" (p. 46). A metapattern based on living system principles and system components can be easily applied to learning.

Table 2. Living Learning Principles as a Metapattern

Living System Principles	Learning Connections
Nested Systems	Learners are within learning systems (classes/learning communities) that are nested within larger systems. Connections between systems impact processes and outcomes.
Network	We need to understand our relationships and how we communicate with one another within our learning systems.
Diversity	Diverse perspectives lead to stability of a system and the potential to come up with innovative solutions to problems.
Interdependence	Interpersonal relationships with peers, instructors, and the environment is crucial to effective communication and success of processes and outcomes of the overall learning system.
Autopoiesis	Occurs as new material and information is presented to students. Students integrate the new information into their previous mindset and knowledge base – their way of being in the world. Students self-organize to accept this new information into a potential new mindset.
Dynamic Equilibrium	Instructors and students work together to increase the success of the system through dynamically balancing processes and products. Based on ongoing feedback.
Cycles & Flows	Behavior and decision-making is ongoing and impacted by members within the learning system through feedback loops. Students and instructors are impacted by environmental conditions and the flow of energy in the system. In this case, flow can be considered learning and engagement in the course.
Development	Development occurs when members of a system adapt and evolve with new learning experiences.

Core to these metapatterns are the principles that contribute to structure of the system. The system structure includes the purpose of the system, the boundary, the component parts or elements, and the interrelationships between the elements. The interrelationships between the elements are impacted by living system principles as well as the whole system itself and all of its parts. Principles of living systems include such things as the nested system structure, the network, diversity of the system, dynamic balance, flows, cycles, autopoiesis, development, and the interdependence among the system components and living and nonliving components in its surrounding environment. The system structure and principles must be kept in mind when designing meaningful learning experiences and while building learning communities where learners can flourish. For instance, consistency and emphasis on the purpose and transparency of the boundaries of the system should be laid out in the beginning of the learning process, while also circling back to clear expectations of learning goals and objectives. The diversity of perspectives and styles of learners needs to be integrated throughout the learning-teaching process to promote inclusivity and a culture of care. Systems can be nested within one another, while still affecting the learning community. For example, a particular class is a system nested within the broader system of a school, which is then situated within another system, such as a district. Class goals and learning should connect to the larger system's vision. Networks and interdependence and the corresponding relationships are the bridge to living principles that build processes to promote learning and development, such as autopoiesis and dynamic equilibrium. These two principles, autopoiesis and dynamic equilibrium, consider all other principles and are the keystones that promote flourishing learning and development for learners.

Living System Principles: Autopoiesis & Dynamic Balance

A living system relates to its environment structurally through autopoiesis. Autopoiesis refers to how a system sustains itself through a network of reactions. "According to the theory of autopoiesis, a living system relates to its environment structurally—that is, through recurrent interactions, each of which triggers structural changes in a system" (Capra & Luisi, 2016, p. 135). Autopoietic organisms self-generate and self-organize as part of their growth and development process. Maturana and Varela (1980) refer to autopoiesis as a fundamental process of living things. Autopoiesis has also been referred to as homeostasis in which Damasio (2018) states that it "ensures that life is regulated within a range that is not just compatible with survival but also conducive to flourishing, to a projection of life into the future of an organism or species" (p. 25). Autopoiesis is a living system principle that continually needs to happen to promote emergent flourishing. Autopoiesis does not happen in isolation but occurs as flows of information and changes in connections happen between the learner and with others and the environment.

This process is supported by dynamically balancing feedback as the learning takes place to contribute to the overall purpose of the learning system.

Connectedness and dynamic equilibrium, including feedback loops, play an integral role in designing meaningful learning experiences. Teaching-learning systems need to have a dynamic balance and the flexibility to provide students with a comfortable learning space. This space can be referred to as a learning sanctuary (Lange, 2009). Learning sanctuaries are safe and comfortable spaces that support sharing and growth to create meaningful learning experiences. They promote a sense of belonging or a feeling of connectedness to the learning where learners feel valued and accepted for themselves. To promote learning sanctuaries and belongingness, educators and learners must consider ongoing feedback from each other and their surroundings since a learning community is a complex adaptive system (CAS).

A CAS evolves and adapts to ongoing feedback and change based on relationships and interactions with components and the environment. Learning communities may be considered a CAS in which we design a living system metapattern while knowing that it will need to change and adapt according to who is in the room, the context or learning environment, and feedback from the learners, instructor, and any additional learning community members. "Learners respond to their environment in the form of people-place-things through feedback loops that impact their overall dynamic balance or equilibrium and structure as a living system" (Wahl, 2020, p. 151). Autopoiesis manages dynamic equilibrium (Capra & Luisi, 2016) which reflects "adaptability, open systems, learning, feedback, communication and emergence" (Mason, 2008, p. 17). Emotions, in response to feedback, drive behaviors in living learning communities. Living learning systems strive to maintain an equilibrium or sense of stability and comfort while learning. From a systems perspective, learning happens away from equilibrium, and there is ongoing self-organization of new information. We can consider learning happening in liminal spaces where we are away from our usual 'equilibrium' and comfortable, older ways of knowing.

Figure 2. Learning & Lack of Learning Feedback Loops

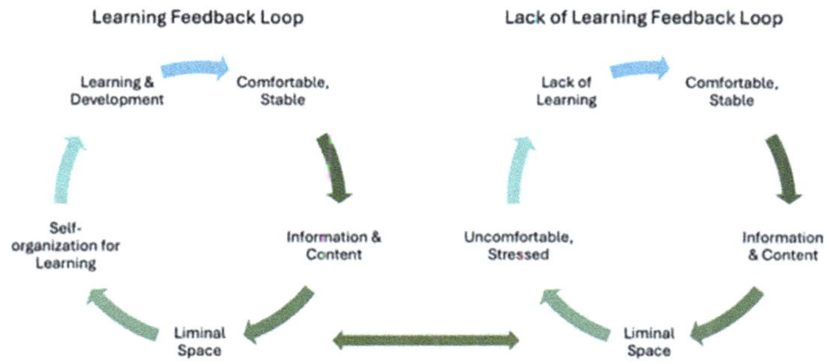

Note. Adapted from "Defying gravity: An affective photovoice lens on transformative sustainability learning" by Wahl, K., 2020, ProQuest Publishers. Copyright 2020 by ProQuest Publishers. Adapted with permission.

Learning happens at the liminal edges of the living learner system. Inspiring and promoting authentic real-world experiences for learners, along with a learning sanctuary, will promote growth and development where learners can flourish. This occurs as new material and information is presented to students. Autopoiesis, along with structural coupling and self-organization, is at the heart of this learning. In systems language, structural coupling involves connecting to and making sense of information from our environment (Capra, 1996). As we continue to adapt our behavior to our environment, we self-organize ourselves and our identities within a larger network – the learning community. By facilitating a learning sanctuary and by fostering a sense of belonging for learners within the learning community, learners will have a greater chance of flourishing within the learning system.

Learning Sanctuaries & Belonging for Flourishing Development

Flourishing is not an isolated state, such as a state of happiness, but an emergent property of the learner living system. Conditions to promote flourishing can be achievable when considering the development of the learner. Development includes growth through learning and occurs when learners are comfortable in their learning environment. Learning happens away from equilibrium and may cause discomfort, so a learning environment where learners are comfortable with a learning readiness is crucial to promote a flourishing learner and learning community. The living system metapattern approach focused on autopoiesis and dynamic balance is necessary to promote such an environment - an environment that reflects a learning sanctuary.

Originally, learning sanctuaries were associated with transformative learning and adult learners (Lange, 2009). Mezirow (1991) theorized transformative learning as a shift in perception as to how a learner views the world, sometimes referred to as a change in their frame of reference. "Frames of reference are structures of assumptions and expectations that frame an individual's tacit points of view and influence their thinking, beliefs, and actions" (Taylor, 2007, p. 5). A learning sanctuary is a place that provides support and comfort for learners in adult education (Lange (2009). Providing learners with a safe and comfortable space for learning facilitates an inclusive learning community that fosters a sense of belonging. A learning sanctuary and a sense of belonging are needed to promote learning readiness, which leads to 'learning as flourishing.'

Designing a learning sanctuary is conducive to learning readiness, where students are open to learning new concepts and can integrate new learning into prior mindsets and meaning-making schemes, as shown in Figure 3. Setting up a learning sanctuary may be based on Lange's (2009) elemental design in which learners explore not only new ways of thinking, but new ways of being within this safe space.

Figure 3. Belonging & Learning Feedback Loop

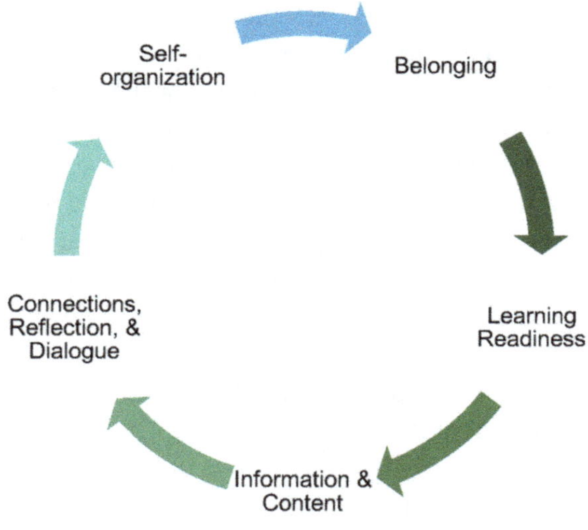

Note. Adapted from "Defying gravity: An affective photovoice lens on transformative sustainability learning" by Wahl, K., 2020, ProQuest Publishers. Copyright 2020 by ProQuest Publishers. Adapted with permission.

Based on the living learning metapattern framework, a learning sanctuary may be established by a pedagogy that is open to emergent learning where learners flourish. We can design and create opportunities for connections to social and environmental systems (including built, natural, and technological systems), and develop safe and trusting connections within the learning community. This includes peers, as mentioned by Lange (2009), but also with the instructor as a trusted facilitator of learning processes. Designing spaces that reflect learning sanctuaries need to be intentional, thoughtful, and authentic – in this case, without intent to transform as students must be honored for what they bring to the learning as learners. It is the role of the educator to provide information and cultivate spaces for learning. This begins with a learning sanctuary which leads to cultivating spaces for building a sense of belonging.

From a systems perspective, there are different levels or types of belonging. The first system level is a sense of belongingness with oneself which includes connections to our affective and cognitive dimensions and having an awareness of navigating and making connections for our overall health and well-being. The next system level is a sense of belonging to a social system or social belonging and connectedness within social systems. Lastly, is our connection to our environment – our sense of belonging to natural, built, and technological environments. These are nested systems of belongingness and should all be addressed when cultivating a learning sanctuary where learners thrive.

Cultivating a sense of belonging is key to ongoing meaningful learning experiences. Defining a sense of belonging or belongingness varies, but one that encompasses our work here is "the subjective feeling of deep connection with social groups, physical places, and individual and collective experiences – is a fundamental human need that predicts numerous mental, physical, social, economic, and behavioral outcomes" (Allen et al., 2021, p. 1). We can look to living system principles and equate belonging to the positive, healthy connections we have in the system in which we feel valued and accepted for our way of being in the world. These connections are dependent on dynamic equilibrium and feedback loops where we continually self-organize information to learn, grow, and develop within the learning community.

In a sense, belongingness is about connectedness, building community, and having support. Learners have a sense of belonging when they have autonomy – voice and choice – and interest in their learning (Du Toit-Brits, 2022). Learners with a sense of belonging are motivated and engaged with strong self-determination and self-direction (Allen et al., 2021). "Nurturing a sense of belonging can generate a learning community where (a) learning can flourish, (b) learning is directed, (c) learners can share their thinking, and (d) learners will be interested in their learning" (Du Toit-Brits, 2022, p. 63). When learning connects to purpose, has boundaries as well as transparency of processes and products, this further develops clear communication and aids learners and instructors to self-manage their learning while supporting one another in the learning community.

Building a sense of belonging, a feeling of connectedness, creates learning sanctuaries where learners are more open to reflect, discuss, and share their learning experiences (Wahl, 2020). Promoting a culture of care and sense of belonging should be prioritized as essential values in transitioning to more inclusive learning communities (Bizerril et al., 2022). In order to foster a sense of belonging to create a learning sanctuary, we need to consider affective learning. Affective learning may be defined here as a dimension. Ekkekakis (2012) stated that different emotional states are interconnected in a systemic fashion. We refer to the affective dimension as the "significant dimension of the educational process which is concerned with the feelings, beliefs, attitude and emotions of students" (Lang, 1998, p. 4). We will specifically center on emotions related to affect and learning.

For years, society's focus and energy has been on the cognitive dimension, but emotions are core to our way of being. Schutz et al. (2006) stated that emotions contain behavioral, biological, and psychological attributes. We need to support cognitive and affective processes as part of providing comfort where students feel open to learning, because emotions tend to drive our behaviors as we navigate our learning communities– they are a part of our embodied learning experience. " 'emotion' is a name we give to the multidimensional processes…we 'feel' our way through life in an embodied engagement" (Kövecses, 2000, p. 53). Embodied learning includes cognitive, affective, and somatic (body) dimensions of learning, and the role of emotions in learning and as part of this process is key to understanding how we navigate systems.

Essentially, emotions can be referred to as drivers of our learning and development. Strong research in neuroscience has supported this concept, most notably work in which individuals that have had prefrontal brain damage and how that relates to social functioning. Immordino-Yang and Damasio (2011) found that "emotion-related processes are required for skills and knowledge to be transferred from the structured school environment to real-world decision making because they provide an *emotional rudder* to guide judgment and action" (p. 115). Emotions guide our decisions. By addressing emotions in learning, we can focus on key aspects of the affective dimension, such as emotional intelligence.

Emotional intelligence is having the ability to name and manage your emotions while also being able to recognize the emotions of others and being able to respond well to their emotional behavior (Ott, 2017, n.p.). According to Goleman (1995), there are four domains of emotional intelligence: self- awareness, self-management, social awareness, and relationship management. Self-awareness is being aware of our emotions and our thinking about such emotions. The ability to know and understand your own emotions is the first step in being able to manage them. Self-management (or self-regulation) is the ability to manage your emotions in ways that are effective and helpful in how one relates to others and the environment (Ott, 2017). Successful self-management leads one to feel a sense of well-being and confidence in navigating social and environmental systems. Social awareness is the ability to recognize how others are feeling and to appropriately interpret social situations. Empathy is an important aspect of social awareness.

Empathy, or viewing things from another person's perspective, is crucial in understanding social situations and how to effectively react to diverse perspectives. Empathy includes self-reflection along with having the ability to enter into other perspectives with care and openness for other individuals (Boyatzis, 2012). Knowing ourselves along with effective communication and active listening is crucial to understanding another person's perspective. Perspective learning, including developing empathy, in systems thinking helps learners and the instructor view things from different angles while honoring diverse viewpoints."Perspective learning is learning about and analyzing diverse perspectives, integrating that learning, and can involve shifting perspectives" (Wahl, 2020, p.129). Giving opportunities to learn from diverse perspectives is important to perspective learning and circles back to the diversity as a living system principle. Being open to learning from others can help deepen empathy and strengthen relationships as you work to understand how each of you view the world. In essence, empathy is the bridge between social awareness and relationship management. Relationship management is about considering your own and other's emotions to manage healthy relationships.

All of these domains should be addressed as we learn to cultivate belongingness – a reminder that emotions are the driver behind our behavior. Naude et al. (2014) noted that emotion is connected to an individual's identity and relationships. As the authors stated, "Emotion can permeate the educational experience in a variety of ways and, therefore, play a complex and dynamic role in shaping the learning experience" (Naude et al., 2014, p. 214).

Emotions influence how we navigate our learning systems and our perspectives and how we view the world, and this view is shaped by our selves, social systems, and our environment. Our environment not only includes our built and natural environment, but also our technological environments. These environments are becoming increasingly important as we tackle the digital age while also trying to develop rich, meaningful learning experiences where learners flourish.

HOW TO PROMOTE FLOURISHING FOR LEARNERS IN THE DIGITAL AGE

In many ways, humans view technology as a tool, and a means to an end. And yet, as Arthur (2009) noted, "We place our hopes in technology…to make our lives better, to solve our problems, to get us out of predicaments, to provide the future we want for ourselves and our children" (p. 17). We have been increasingly dependent on technology as a way to navigate and obtain information, process information, and communicate with one another. With this globalization of information, we have been faced with opportunities and challenges in education. As we teach and learn, we need to keep in mind that "globalization requires that organizations increase their ability to learn and collaborate and to manage diversity, complexity, and ambiguity" (Ulrich, 1998, p. 126). We also need to keep in mind how we learn – through autopoiesis and dynamic balance – and that we are members of a learning community that takes into account our technological environment. The dynamic balance of information from our environment, including natural, built, and technological, should be considered as we build learning communities as living systems. We need to find comfort in the support that technology may provide us value as learners versus the additional stress of technology – the overuse or misuse of technology or navigating misinformation – all of which causes learners discomfort in connecting to their technological environment.

Arthur (2009) describes a tension felt between what technology can offer, and some of the ways that it also takes direction and control. He asserts that "the story of this century will be about the clash between what technology offers and what we feel comfortable with" (p.18). This tension can be felt as technology is applied toward learning. The effusive nature of technology today can lead to both intentional and accidental use in educational contexts. The field of positive technology provides initial guidance in navigating healthy relationships with technology which enhance learning to help us flourish.

Positive Technology

The field of positive technology offers an approach to provide grounding in the digital age. Positive technology is an emergent field that combines positive psychology with the use of technology. This field offers options for intentionally harnessing the power of technology toward the aim of flourishing and can be applied toward learning in technological environments. Drawing from the field of positive psychology and the importance of affect, engagement, and connectedness, Riva et al. (2012) classified technology in three corresponding ways: hedonic, eudaimonic, and social/interpersonal. Hedonic technologies promote experiences of pleasure while eudaimonic technologies promote engagement and self-actualization that are related to well-being. Finally, social and interpersonal technologies promote "connectedness between individuals, groups, and organizations" (Riva et al., 2012, p. 75). These conditions or processes – pleasure, engagement, self-actualization, and connectedness – are also important concepts of learning based on autopoiesis and dynamic balance in learning as flourishing. We want to be engaged in our learning to provide us with joy and pleasure as we reach a healthy self-actualization. These processes happen as we work through living system principles such as autopoiesis and dynamic balance, which considers all living systems principles to promote flourishing.

In another application of positive technology, Villamil and Heshmati (2023) note that while more research has focused on negative effects of technology for well-being, three themes have arisen for positive effects of technology use in the current digital age: seeing good, feeling good, and doing good. "Seeing good" refers to the specific visual experiences from pictures, graphics, and video. "Feeling good" relates to the sensation experienced while using the technology. Doing good refers to the actions taken while using the technology, such as contributing money to a good cause. Villamil and Heshmati (2023) use these three themes to create a conceptual framework for using technology to support well-being, called the Engagement in the Good with Technology. The interaction of these three variables creates a network of potential engagement that can be used to promote technology use that aligns with flourishing within a given system. As Villamil & Heshmati (2023) advise, "how we choose to use technology is ultimately the main predictor of how it impacts us" (p. 8). These three themes can be integrated into both research and practice. Both of these approaches in positive technology reflect living system principles and systems thinking – a necessary approach to promote flourishing.

A Systems Approach to Technology

Intentionally aligning technology use in learning with an overarching idea of flourishing requires thinking in systems. Considering technology as an environmental system that mimics many features of living systems, including system structure, supports a holistic approach to learning. In a holistic, living system approach, working with a systems structure involves defining the purpose and establishing boundaries of the system. Rather than subconsciously allowing available technology to exert direction and control, when we define the purpose of technology use, we also choose when and how we will use it. Establishing these boundaries by intentionally adjusting settings allows us to use these tools with intention. As Robinson and Moraes Robinson (2017) noted, "while technology has given us untold abilities to interact across traditional boundaries, the networks we develop are not going to be authentic and therefore sustainable without people who have an expanded level of consciousness. (p.5).

At the same time, recognizing that technology exists as a system reminds us that it does not exist in a vacuum. It is connected to learners as learners take in information to process. As we take in information, we should have a way to reflect, share, and dialogue how we construct meaning in learning communities to build successful learning experiences.

In addition to learners and learning communities, we need to consider structurally coupling relative to the technological system. What information is provided, along with how it supports affective and cognitive learning is crucial as we become engaged in our learning. A holistic, systems approach to education includes technology as part of the network of interactions within a learning community. Referring back to the living system principle of interdependence, learners are supported by other living and/or nonliving factors in their environment. Living learner systems are taking in information from our technological environment through flows and cycles in a dynamic balance to promote autopoiesis as a part of our learning, growth, and development. In addition to this living systems approach to the whole learner and their environmental systems, we can also consider technology as a system that mimics biological systems in order to fully understand how technological behaviors can align with our notion of flourishing for learners.

Technology in its advancing and evolving state can be conceptualized as a metaphorical living system that experiences autopoiesis through the combination and recombination of its possibilities within evolving contexts (Arthur, 2009). Complexity theorist Arthur (2009) notes that technology "is a system, a network of functionalities—a metabolism of things-executing-things—that can sense its environment and reconfigure its actions to execute appropriately" (p. 247). In appreciating its increasingly biological and organic qualities, Arthur (2009) described technology by: "its connectedness, its adaptiveness, its tendency to evolve, its organic quality. Its messy vitality" (p. 235). Although the authors recognize technology as a nonliving system, the behavior of technological systems can be compared to living system behaviors as we relate to our digital environment. Arthur (2009) states, "Technologies are acquiring properties we associate with living organisms. As they sense and react to their environment, as they become self-assembling, self-configuring, self-healing, and 'cognitive' (p. 229). In other words, the more advanced and evolved technology grows, the more it mimics attributes of living systems. This approach moves from a mechanization perspective of technology to a biomimicry perspective in which systems mimic biological systems. Understanding it from this perspective may help us draw parallels to living system principles to enhance learning processes with technology as our contextual environment.

Technology can enhance learning that leads to flourishing if we consider the how, what, where, and when the technology is being used in the process of autopoiesis. We initially need reliable information as we set the purpose and boundaries of any technological learning experience. We then need to continue to design experiences that promote conditions for a learning sanctuary and sense of belonging. This begins by honoring the learners and balancing autonomy, student-centered learning, and intrapersonal growth. This learning can be somewhat self-directed and should allow for some flexibility in which learners participate and progress in their learning

(Summerville & Johnson, 2006; Vanides, 2007). We also need to balance intrapersonal growth and development with interpersonal growth while building authentic relationships.

We can dynamically balance learning processes, both intrapersonal and interpersonal learning experiences, to promote flourishing and learning sanctuaries to promote belongingness. Having diverse ways to learn, share, and dialogue information is important to process and self-organize information in autopoiesis. While connecting, reflecting, and sharing information, we also need to balance affective learning with cognitive learning. Affective learning ties back to emotional intelligence and considering emotions and caring for each other as we bring our authentic selves into our learning environments. Dynamic equilibrium involves ways of learning holistically. As we consider affective learning and cognitive learning, we need to consider teaching approaches and ways of using technology to engage both ways of learning. Critical thinking should be balanced with creativity to engage learners within the learning community.

Creative ways of using technology to connect are necessary to balance diverse learning styles and to engage learners. Creative ways to approach learning experiences may include arts-based assignments in which poetry, photography, systems diagrams, movies, and so forth may extend beyond commonly used written formats. Students should also be encouraged to work through their understanding with peers and the instructor. Authentic relationships are key to feeling valued, cared about, and to develop a sense of belonging to the learning community. As we creatively develop learning experiences, we need to circle back to connect to living system principles and the structure of systems to monitor and improve learning process and design conditions where learners flourish.

The technological system structure must have a purpose and have boundaries that provide time to process learning. Technology should reflect the overall learning goals and be consistent and transparent to learners. Knowing the boundaries includes the learners and self-directed learning while also finding time to critically reflect and dialogue with learners and the instructor. Connections between all members of the learning community are important to develop trust. Trust may be established early on through technology etiquette or norms collaboratively discussed with the class and built upon and strengthened as learning and growth occurs together in the learning community. As efforts are collaboratively worked on to build trust and honor diverse perspectives, dynamically balancing learning types (affective and cognitive learning), types of assignments (written versus other ways of knowing), and checking on student feedback for improvement will help in maintaining a learning sanctuary to allow for autopoiesis or integration of learning where learning community members may flourish.

Life in this digital age requires an intentional awareness that keeps the ideal of flourishing in perspective and illuminates the need to act in accordance with values with respect to relationships and well-being within the context of our digital system. Technology (when recognized and used as a tool) doesn't change the ideal of flourishing, or the reality of nested positions within systems, or the importance of authentic relationships. Technology can be leveraged to build connections and enhance relationships while promoting sustainable happiness, growth, and well-being. Yet, it cannot do so without an intentional approach. The ubiquitous nature of technology underscores the necessity that now, more than ever, an understanding of values, systems, and relationships must be seen within this systemic context. When a holistic, living systems approach is used to move toward the goal of flourishing, within the context of living systems principles, and by harnessing the power of authentic relationships, technology can be seen as providing opportunities for growth and development where learners can flourish.

CONCLUSION

Flourishing can be seen as a dynamic striving at both the individual and system levels of life. It includes the ability to grow, and to "grow well." Flourishing is not an isolated period of time, a momentary moment of joy or period of happiness. Rather, it is a continual process whereby flows and cycles of information are self-organized for learners to navigate life successfully. It can be considered developing a 'climate of flourishing' – a long-term way of navigating life where one embraces learning to promote development and growth to live well presently and in the future. Flourishing with respect to learning is the continual outcome of ongoing learning processes within the learner and within a learning community. The process of how we learn is crucial. The abstractness of learning versus the physical space of living organisms leads to different complexities within our learning communities, and we often negate time to processes in lieu of mechanized approaches to develop products. We cannot flourish as learners without a systems approach to learning.

Understanding the structure of a system – its meaning or purpose and the boundaries – are the initial first steps of developing comfort in navigating learning as it leads to feelings of belongingness. Fostering a learning sanctuary where autopoiesis and dynamic balance are consistently facilitating belonging will strengthen the purpose and meaning of the system itself. In particular, a living systems approach is key in developing a climate of flourishing in learning communities, especially related to our connections to self, peers, instructor, and the environment. Living system principles developed into a metapattern should be considered and implemented thoughtfully and intentionally in ongoing learning processes as we foster authentic relationships.

How students absorb information and integrate it through autopoiesis is important and considers emotions as drivers of behaviors. Again, holistic learning from a systems view will be crucial to learning success. The concept of autopoiesis can be applied to living learning communities as well. As we view autopoiesis related to learning communities, we look to symbolism, ideas, and communication as learners take in information and how learners self-organize together as a group. In addition to autopoiesis, there needs to be ongoing efforts to implement dynamic equilibrium through considering cycles and flows of information. Crafting ways to balance affective and cognitive learning, process and products, and diverse learning experiences will help to support a learning sanctuary where learners flourish and feel a sense of belonging. Core to this work are authentic relationships and allowing connections that promote dialogue about learning and the time for these processes to take place. Creating space for these processes along with building positive connections to the environment are components of a living learning system.

This work is all the more important when considering the influence of technology in our current day and age. As a tool, the power of technology can be harnessed in service of the ideals of learning and flourishing. With our society's rampant use of technology in this digital age, an intentional and mindful approach is essential. As the field of positive technology shows, these tools offer opportunities to promote well-being when used thoughtfully, with the end in mind. This approach, combined with an application of systems thinking, can identify ways to meet learners' needs even in contexts that are infused with technology. Taking action while utilizing principles of systems thinking offers ways to promote authentic relationships and belonging. In many ways, technology offers broader boundaries, overcoming barriers of distance and time to allow for increased interconnections within a networked system. Ultimately, an intentional approach to the powerful tools of technology will allow for an alignment between flourishing and living systems of learning, within the backdrop of our digital age.

REFERENCES

Alexander, R. D. (1974). The evolution of social behavior. *Annual Review of Ecology, Evolution, and Systematics*, *5*, 325–383.

Allen, K., Kern, M. L., Rozek, C. R., McInerney, D. M., & Slavich, G. M. (2021). Belonging: A review of conceptual issues, an integrative framework, and directions for future research. *Australian Journal of Psychology*, *73*(1), 87–102. DOI: 10.1080/00049530.2021.1883409

Arthur, W. B. (2009). *The nature of technology: What it is and how it evolves*. Free Press.

Bandura, A. (1971). *Social learning theory*. General Learning Press.

Bateson, G. (2002). *Mind and nature: A necessary unity*. Hampton Press.

Bizerril, M. X. A., Arrais, A. A. M., & Silva, N. P. M. (2022). The culture of care and sense of belonging as drivers of sustainability in higher education. *Revista Tempos e Espaços em Educação*, *15*(34), 1–13. DOI: 10.20952/revtee.v15i34.18037

Boyatzis, R. (2012). Neuroscience and the link between inspirational leadership and resonant relationships. *Ivey Business Journal*, *76*(1), 26–28.

Butler, J., & Kern, M. (2016). The PERMA-Profiler: A brief multidimensional measure of flourishing. *International Journal of Wellbeing*, *6*, 1–48. DOI: 10.5502/IJW.V6I3.526

Capra, F. (1996). *The web of life: A new scientific understanding of living systems*. Anchor Books.

Capra, F. (2007). Sustainable living, ecological literacy, and breath of life. *Canadian Journal of Environmental Education*, *12*, 9–18.

Capra, F., & Luisi, P. L. (2016). *The systems view of life: A unifying vision*. Cambridge University Press.

Damasio, A. (2018). *The strange order of things: Life, feeling, and the making of culture*. Pantheon Books.

Davis, B. & Sumara, D. (2006). *Complexity and education*. Routledge: Taylor & Francis Group.

Du Toit-Brits, C. (2022). Exploring the importance of a sense of belonging for a sense of ownership in learning. *South African Journal of Higher Education*, *36*(5). DOI: 10.20853/36-5-4345

Ehrenfeld, J. R. (2019). Flourishing: Designing a brave new world. *The Journal of Design, Economics, and Innovation*, *5*(2), 105–116.

Ehrenfeld, J. R. (2020). *The right way to flourish: Reconnecting to the real world.* Routledge Press.

Ehrenfeld, J. R., & Hoffman, A. J. (2013). *Flourishing: A frank conversation about sustainability.* Stanford University Press.

Ekkekakis, P. (2012). Affect, mood, and emotion. In Tenenbaum, G., Eklund, R. C., & Kamata, A. (Eds.), *Measurement in sport and exercise psychology* (pp. 321–332). Human Kinetics., DOI: 10.5040/9781492596332.ch-028

Freire, P. (1970). *Pedagogy of the oppressed.* Seabury Press.

Goleman, D. (1995). *Emotional intelligence.* Bantam Books.

Hayes, S. (2019). *A liberated mind: How to pivot toward what matters.* Avery.

Huppert, F. A., & So, T. T. C. (2013). Flourishing across Europe: Application of a new conceptual framework for defining well-being. *Social Indicators Research, 110*(3), 837–861. DOI: 10.1007/s11205-011-9966-7

Immordino-Yang, M. H., & Damasio, A. (2011). We feel, therefore we learn: The relevance of affective and social neuroscience of education. *LEARNing Landscapes*, *5*(1), 115–131. DOI: 10.1111/j.1751-228X.2007.00004

Immordino-Yang, M. H., & Damasio, A. (2016). We feel, therefore we learn: The relevance of affective and social neuroscience to education. In Immordino-Yang, M. H. (Ed.), *Emotions, Learning, & the Brain: Exploring the Educational Implications of Affective Neuroscience* (pp. 26–42). W.W. Norton & Company.

Lang, P. (1998). Towards an understanding of affective education in a European context. In P.

Lange, E. (2009). Fostering a learning sanctuary for transformation in sustainability education. In Mezirow, J., & Taylor, E. W. (Eds.), *Transformative learning in practice: Insights from community, workplace, and higher education* (pp. 193–204). Jossey-Bass, John Wiley & Sons, Inc.

Mason, M. (2008). Complexity theory and the philosophy of education. In Mason, M. (Ed.), *Complexity Theory and the Philosophy of Education* (pp. 1–15). Wiley-Blackwell. DOI: 10.1002/9781444307351.ch1

Maturana, H. R., & Varela, F. J. (1980). *Autopoiesis and cognition: The realization of the living*. D. Reidel Publishing Company. DOI: 10.1007/978-94-009-8947-4

Meadows, D. (2008). *Thinking in systems: A primer*. Chelsea Green Publishing.

Mezirow, J. (1991). *Transformative dimensions of adult learning*. Jossey-Bass.

Naude, L., van den Bergh, T. J., & Kruger, I. S. (2014). "Learning to like learning": An appreciative inquiry into emotions in education. *Social Psychology of Education*, (17), 211–228. DOI: 10.1007/s11218-014-9247-9

O'Brien, C. (2010). Sustainability, happiness and education. *Journal of Sustainability Education*, *1*(1), 1–18.

O'Brien, C. (2012). Sustainable happiness and education: Educating teachers and students in the 21st Century. In Bartels, K. A., & Parker, K. A. (Eds.), *Teaching Sustainability / Teaching Sustainably* (pp. 41–52). Routledge. DOI: 10.4324/9781003447429-5

O'Brien, C. (2013). Happiness and sustainability together at last! Sustainable happiness. *Canadian Journal of Education*, *36*(4), 228–256.

Ott, C. R. (2017). *Assessing awareness, perception of importance, and intention to practice new skills in team emotional intelligence with Ohio State University Extension teams* [Master's thesis, Ohio State University]. OhioLINK Electronic Theses and Dissertations Center. https://rave.ohiolink.edu/etdc/view?acc_num=osu15119902457882

Riva, G., Baños, R. M., Botella, C., Wiederhold, B. K., & Gaggioli, A. (2012). Positive technology: Using interactive technologies to promote positive functioning. *Cyberpsychology, Behavior, and Social Networking*, *15*(2), 69–77. DOI: 10.1089/cyber.2011.0139

Robinson, S., & Moraes-Robinson, M. (2017). *Customer experiences with soul: A new era in design*. Holonomics Publishing.

Rusk, R. D., & Waters, L. (2015). A psycho-social system approach to well-being: Empirically deriving the five domains of positive functioning. *The Journal of Positive Psychology*, *10*(2), 141–152. DOI: 10.1080/17439760.2014.920409

Schutz, P. A., Hong, J., Cross, D. I., & Osbon, J. N. (2006). Reflections on investigating emotion in educational activity settings. *Educational Psychology Review*, *18*, 343–360. DOI: 10.1007/s10648-006-9030-3

Seligman, M. E. P. (2011). *Flourish: A visionary new understanding of happiness and well-being*. Atria Books.

Summerville, J., & Johnson, C. S. (2006). Rural creativity: A Study of District Mandated Online Professional Development. *Journal of Technology and Teacher Education, 14*(2), 347–361.

Taylor, S. E. (2007). Social support. In Friedman, H. S., & Silver, R. C. (Eds.), *Foundations of health psychology* (pp. 145–171). Oxford University Press.

Ulrich, D. (1998) *A New Mandate for Human Resources*. Harvard Business Review. https://hbr.org/1998/01/a-new-mandate-for-human-resources

Vanides, J. (2007). Online professional development that works. *Learning and Leading with Technology, 34*(8), 10–14.

Villamil, A., & Heshmati, S. (2023). Engaging in the good with technology: A framework for examining positive technology use. *Frontiers in Psychology, 14*, 1175740–1175740. DOI: 10.3389/fpsyg.2023.1175740

Volk, T., & Bloom, J. W. (2007). The use of metapatterns for research into complex systems of teaching, learning, and schooling, Part II: Applications. *Complicity: An International Journal of Complexity and Education, 4*(1), 45–68. http://ejournals.library.ualberta.ca/index.php/complicity/issue/archive

Wahl, K. (2020). Defying gravity: An affective photovoice lens on transformative sustainability learning. (Publication No. 28156446). [Doctoral Dissertation, UW-Stevens Point, WI]. ProQuest Dissertations & Theses Global.

Widhalm, B. (2011). Nature as guide for vibrant learning – a living systems framework for academic learning experience design toward a thriving sustainable world. (Publication No. 3489705) [Doctoral Dissertation, California Institute of Integral Studies, CA]. ProQuest Dissertations & Theses Global.

Widhalm, B. (2013). Teaching living systems awareness as a change agent skill for a vibrant sustainable world. In *Proceedings of the 56th Annual Meeting of the ISSS-2012, San Jose, CA, USA*. https://journals.isss.org/index.php/proceedings56th/article/view/1852

KEY TERMS AND DEFINITIONS

Autopoiesis: The process when self-bounded living systems self-generate and self-organize as they structurally relate to their environment.

Belongingness: Feeling healthy connections while being valued and accepted within a social system for our way of being in the world.

Development: A process in which learning occurs for an individual and includes emergence and growth and occurs away from equilibrium in a living system.

Dynamic Balance: A continual process that involves regulation with ongoing feedback to maintain comfort or balance in a living system.

Flourishing: A continual process of emergence that occurs to maintain the overall well-being in psychological, emotional, and physical domains for individual living systems long-term.

Learning Community: A complex adaptive system in which individuals work together as a system to achieve a purpose and set boundaries as they relate to each other in ongoing processes to support meaningful learning experiences.

Learning Sanctuary: A space to promote connectedness and learning readiness within a learning environment where learners feel comfortable to be their authentic selves. Belongingness is an attribute of a learning sanctuary.

Chapter 2
Promoting Flourishing in the Digital Age:
The Interplay of Well-Being, Lifelong Learning, and Success

Ranjit Singha
https://orcid.org/0000-0002-3541-8752
Christ University, India

Surjit Singha
https://orcid.org/0000-0002-5730-8677
Kristu Jayanti University, India

ABSTRACT

The digital era has changed learning, communication, and success. This chapter examines the complex link between thriving, lifelong learning, and success in the digital era, emphasizing flourishing's significance. Wellness is the cornerstone of digital life in many ways. In an age of continual technological change and unpredictable job markets, lifelong learning empowers people to adapt, flourish, and find fulfilment. Educational institutions and organizations pursuing digital well-being projects are given a set of digital success tips. Personal development requires a growth attitude and lifelong learning with digital technologies. Responsible digital citizenship and honest online connections foster a pleasant online environment. Mindfulness, digital detox, and digital or non-digital activity limits are crucial to well-being. This holistic approach helps individuals, educational institutions, and businesses thrive digitally while retaining their well-being and values by recognizing the complicated relationship between technology and personal growth.

DOI: 10.4018/979-8-3693-0997-1.ch002

INTRODUCTION

The notion of flourishing assumes additional complexities within the contemporary digital environment, characterized by the swift and continuous technological advancements that have become integral to nearly every facet of our lives. The advent of the digital age has brought forth a period characterized by exceptional prospects and difficulties, fundamentally reshaping how we acquire knowledge, engage in communication, and ultimately, determine the parameters of achievement (Janicke-Bowles et al., 2023; Kantar & Bynum, 2021; VanderWeele, 2017). This chapter explores the intricate correlation between well-being, lifelong learning, and success within the framework of the digital era, elucidating the importance of fostering genuine relationships and growth among individuals engaged in the learning process. Flourishing is characterized by favourable elements enabling individuals to thrive and experience a sense of fulfilment. In the context of the digital era, the increasing convergence of the physical and virtual realms necessitates a heightened understanding of the concept of flourishing. The ever-evolving nature of technology requires a deeper understanding of its impact on our overall well-being and individual development. As society traverses the realm of digital technology, the significance of its capacity to facilitate both personal and communal well-being becomes paramount.

In the contemporary era of digital advancements, technology presents unprecedented prospects for education and interpersonal connectivity. However, it also presents a myriad of challenges and risks. Individuals face many challenges in today's digital age, including the excessive amount of information available, heightened worries regarding privacy, and the risks associated with developing a dependency on digital devices. These factors contribute to a complicated environment that can profoundly impact individuals' welfare. Recognizing and resolving these difficulties are of utmost importance in enabling students to make well-informed decisions and maximize the potential benefits of digital technology while minimizing its adverse consequences (Janicke-Bowles et al., 2023; Kantar & Bynum, 2021). The subsequent chapters of this literary work will probe more into the methodologies, methodologies, and discernments that empower educators, students, and stakeholders to traverse the era of digitalization effectively. Our primary objective is to utilize technology's transformative potential to improve the well-being of individuals and society as a whole, achieved through the promotion of flourishing, the cultivation of authentic relationships, and the facilitation of growth. Through an in-depth examination of these subjects, we intend to offer a comprehensive guide for effectively navigating the digital age while upholding the fundamental values and ideals crucial to our shared accomplishments. The purpose of this chapter is to achieve the following objectives. This study aims to analyze the dynamic notion of thriving within the context of the digital era, emphasizing the importance of positive well-being and the intricate interplay between well-being, ongoing learning, and achievement.

This chapter will explore digital media's various problems and risks. It will also assess the changing role of education in the digital age and provide practical ways for fostering learners' well-being, genuine relationships, and personal development. This chapter aims to provide individuals and institutions with the essential knowledge and resources to navigate the digital terrain effectively while safeguarding and improving their well-being and values.

The digital age has significantly transformed learning, communication, and the conceptualization of success. This essay explores the intricate correlation between flourishing, lifelong learning, and success within the framework of the digital era, with particular emphasis on the significance of flourishing. The fundamental basis of existence in the digital age revolves around wellness, which spans various dimensions. In contemporary society, marked by perpetual technological progress and dynamic labour markets, acquiring knowledge throughout one's lifetime has emerged as an imperative, enabling individuals to adjust, excel, and attain personal satisfaction. To facilitate optimal development and well-being in the context of the digital age, we present a comprehensive compilation of suggestions—incorporating digital well-being programs within educational institutions and organizations. Personal development involves cultivating a growth mindset and properly utilizing digital tools for lifetime learning. The establishment of a positive online environment is facilitated by the promotion of responsible digital citizenship and the cultivation of authentic online interactions. Prioritizing well-being through mindfulness techniques, regular digital detoxification, and constructing clear boundaries between digital and non-digital activities is paramount. The holistic approach acknowledges the intricate interplay between technology and personal growth, providing individuals, educational institutions, and organizations with the necessary tools to thrive in the digital environment while safeguarding their welfare and principles.

The objective of this chapter is to thoroughly examine the complex relationship between well-being, lifelong learning, and success within the framework of the digital era. This analysis explores the importance of flourishing as a fundamental component of personal and professional growth. This chapter explores the various aspects of well-being, the importance of continuous learning in a time characterized by rapid technological progress, and the combined impact of these factors on achieving success and personal satisfaction. This chapter utilizes multiple foundational theoretical frameworks to understand the subject matter at hand thoroughly. This chapter is grounded in the principles of positive psychology, specifically focusing on theories about well-being. The elements of well-being and thriving are examined by exploring concepts such as PERMA, which encompasses Positive Emotions, Engagement, Relationships, Meaning, and Accomplishment. The Self-Determination

Theory (SDT) offers valuable insights into the underlying motivation and drive that propel individuals towards engaging in lifelong learning. The chapter explores the concepts of intrinsic motivation and self-determination as essential factors for achieving ongoing personal development and success. The concept of growth mindset, as proposed by Carol Dweck, holds significant importance in comprehending how individuals can adopt a mindset that embraces difficulties, perceives failures as chances for personal development, and fosters an attitude that appreciates work and knowledge acquisition. Theoretical underpinnings in digital literacy and media studies emphasize the imperative of responsibly, critically, and ethically engaging with the digital environment. The discourse revolves around examining concepts about media literacy and the practice of responsible digital citizenship. The chapter integrates the principles of constructivism with adult learning theories to emphasize the significance of self-directed learning, critical thinking, and adaptation in the context of lifelong learning and personal growth. Theoretical frameworks about the adoption and utilization of technology contribute to our understanding of how individuals integrate digital tools and resources into their lifelong learning pursuits. This study explores into the theoretical foundations of online interactions, examining the various aspects that impact the development of genuine relationships in virtual environments and the overall well-being of individuals in the digital realm. This chapter provides a comprehensive and holistic perspective on fostering flourishing, authentic interactions and facilitating progress in learners within the context of the digital age, drawing upon several academic disciplines. The primary objective of this endeavour is to furnish readers with theoretical perspectives and practical suggestions that can facilitate success in the digital realm while emphasizing the importance of personal well-being and continuous learning.

BACKGROUND

In the digital age, the integration of technology into everyday life has reshaped how we learn, interact, and perceive success. The pervasive use of digital tools presents both opportunities and challenges, influencing various aspects of individual well-being, education, and personal development. This evolving landscape necessitates a deeper understanding of the relationship between digital engagement and personal flourishing. By examining how digital technology impacts well-being and lifelong learning, we can identify strategies to enhance educational outcomes and personal growth in the digital era.

The research is grounded in several theoretical frameworks that collectively inform the investigation of digital technology's impact on well-being and lifelong learning. Positive Psychology serves as a foundational theory, emphasizing how positive emotions, strengths, and overall well-being contribute to life satisfaction and personal growth. Complementing this, Lifelong Learning Theory underscores the significance of continuous education as essential for ongoing personal and professional development throughout life. Digital Literacy Theory is also crucial, as it highlights the competencies required to effectively navigate and utilize digital tools, thereby promoting responsible and informed online behavior. Finally, Gamification Theory provides insight into how elements of game design can be strategically employed in non-game contexts to boost motivation and engagement, thereby enhancing the learning experience. Together, these frameworks offer a comprehensive lens through which to examine the interplay between digital technology, well-being, and learning.

The conceptual framework delineates the dynamic relationship between digital technology, well-being, and lifelong learning. It posits that Digital Well-Being encompasses the mental, emotional, and physical health impacts resulting from digital interactions and screen time. Lifelong Learning is viewed as the ongoing pursuit of knowledge and skills throughout one's life, significantly facilitated by digital tools and resources. Success is defined by personal satisfaction, professional achievement, and the capacity to maintain a balance between digital engagement and offline activities. The framework suggests that enhancing digital well-being and fostering lifelong learning are integral to achieving success in the digital age, highlighting the interconnected nature of these elements in supporting overall growth and fulfillment.

The aim of this research is to investigate the relationship between digital technology, well-being, and lifelong learning, and to develop strategies for enhancing personal and educational outcomes in the digital age. The objectives include examining the impact of digital technology on individual well-being and mental health, evaluating the effectiveness of digital literacy programs and interventions in educational settings, exploring the role of gamification in boosting learner engagement and achievement, identifying strategies for balancing digital and offline activities to promote overall well-being, and assessing the contribution of digital tools to addiction recovery and personal growth. The research problem highlights the concerns arising from the increasing integration of digital technology into daily life, emphasizing the need to understand its effects on mental health, the efficacy of digital literacy programs, and strategies for maintaining a healthy balance between digital and offline activities. Additionally, it seeks to explore how digital tools can aid in addiction recovery and personal development. The scope of the study covers the impact of digital technology on well-being, the effectiveness of digital literacy programs, the application of gamification in education, strategies for balancing digital and offline engagements, and the role of digital tools in supporting addiction recovery and personal growth. The research will address various demographic groups and educational settings, offering comprehensive insights into how digital technology influences well-being and learning across diverse contexts.

UNDERSTANDING WELL-BEING AND LIFELONG LEARNING

In the course of our inquiry into the intricate connection between well-being and lifelong learning, we undertake an exploration that probes into the fundamental nature of human flourishing and the enduring need for knowledge and personal development. The concept of well-being is broad and holistic, encompassing numerous dimensions of an individual's life and reflecting their overall quality of life and level of satisfaction. In order to fully grasp the complexity and importance of well-being within the context of the digital age, it is crucial to consider the relevant definitions and aspects. As the analysis progresses, the intricate nature of these dimensions becomes evident. Physical well-being is fundamental to an individual's overall physical health and vitality. It includes various components such as physical fitness, diet, sleep quality, and general health. Mental health involves various aspects, such as emotional resilience, self-esteem, stress management, and an internal state of tranquillity. The concept of emotional well-being, intricately linked to mental well-being, centres on an individual's emotional condition, encompassing good emotions such as pleasure, joy, and contentment. Additionally, it underscores the ability to handle and regulate unpleasant emotions (Cao & Li, 2023).

Social well-being pertains to an individual's interpersonal connections and interactions within society, encompassing an analysis of the quality and extent of their bonds with family, friends, and the broader community. The cultivation of intellectual well-being facilitates the advancement of cognitive abilities and active engagement in acquiring knowledge throughout one's lifetime. This process fosters critical thinking, curiosity, and mental stimulation, which are crucial for individual growth and adapting to new circumstances. Occupational well-being encompasses evaluating various elements, including but not limited to job satisfaction, the equilibrium between work and personal life, and the unity between an individual's professional choices and their values and ambitions within the context of their work or chosen career trajectory. The notion of environmental well-being revolves around the interconnectedness between humans and their physical surroundings, embracing both proximate and expansive ecosystems. It includes ensuring access to a clean and secure environment, adopting sustainable habits, and cultivating a sense of duty towards the world. Spiritual well-being encompasses a broader scope than religious affiliations, emphasizing a deep-seated understanding of purpose, significance, and a connection to a higher entity, along with personal values, ethical principles, and inner contentment (Mayer, 2017; Fisher, 2011).

The various dimensions of well-being have a significant role in shaping an individual's overall quality of life and sense of thriving as they interact and influence one another in a complex and linked manner. In the era of digitalization, it is imperative to understand and foster these aspects of well-being, as they are not only desired but also crucial for personal satisfaction, effective adjustment to the constantly evolving technological environment, and the development of continuous education. In a period marked by ongoing change and advancement, these elements jointly delineate the trajectory towards individual growth, flexibility, and comprehensive achievement. The acquisition of knowledge and skills throughout an individual's lifespan has transitioned from being optional to becoming an essential and constantly evolving endeavour, especially in the rapidly changing era of digital technology. This factor's significance in influencing people's lives and attaining their goals cannot be exaggerated. In a period marked by swift technological progress and ongoing fluctuations in the employment market, pursuing lifelong learning empowers individuals with the requisite competencies and knowledge to manage these transformations adeptly. It allows individuals to sustain their professional significance, embrace novel obstacles, and capitalize on emerging prospects. Pursuing knowledge throughout one's life extends beyond professional growth, encompassing various technical and interpersonal abilities. These skills, such as effective communication, problem-solving, and critical thinking, are crucial for personal development and achievement in various aspects of life (Fischer et al., 2022).

It facilitates cognitive growth through the cultivation of intellectual inquiry, critical analysis, and the cultivation of intellectual curiosity. As a result, it contributes to mental agility while augmenting creativity and problem-solving abilities. The concept of lifelong learning extends beyond the confines of the workplace, transforming into a personal path of self-actualization that empowers individuals to pursue their passions and interests. This pursuit enhances their lives beyond their professional pursuits and significantly contributes to their well-being. This particular instrument possesses considerable efficacy within the realm of professional progression, as it serves as a means to access promotions, salary increases, and an expanded array of work prospects. The process of continuous learning serves as evidence to potential employers that an individual possesses proactive qualities, adaptability, and a solid dedication to self-improvement (Sternberg, 1997). It is observed that individuals often enhance their self-confidence when they engage in lifelong learning, leading to beneficial outcomes in several aspects of life, including personal relationships and decision-making processes. In an era marked by perpetual transformation and uncertainty, individuals who engage in lifelong learning cultivate resilience and adaptability, enabling them to effectively address setbacks, surmount hurdles, and provide innovative resolutions. In addition, pursuing lifelong learning enables individuals to enhance their personal growth across cognitive, affective, and interpersonal domains, promoting self-reflection, compassion, and a more expansive perspective, ultimately leading to significant individual metamorphosis. The concept of lifelong learning fosters a cognitive orientation marked by curiosity, personal growth, and a readiness to accept novel encounters. It fosters a profound purpose and an unrelenting commitment to ongoing self-enhancement. Individuals continuously learning throughout their lives often significantly contribute to their communities and society. They enhance the collective expertise and stimulate good transformations by sharing their knowledge, skills, and experiences.

Everlasting learning serves as more than a simply instrumental tool, but rather as a transformative voyage that enhances the quality of life for individuals in manifold manners. This program provides individuals with the essential skills to navigate, thrive, and attain personal satisfaction in the digital era. Consequently, it contributes to their personal growth, career achievements, and the advancement of society. In the contemporary era characterized by rapid societal changes, acquiring knowledge throughout one's lifetime has become an imperative rather than a discretionary pursuit (Benavot et al., 2022; Roche, 2018).

IMPACT OF DIGITAL MEDIA ON WELL-BEING AND LEARNING

The proliferation and various manifestations of digital media in the contemporary day substantially influence the overall welfare of persons. The impact of this phenomenon is multifaceted, encompassing both advantageous and disadvantageous consequences that contribute to individuals' overall satisfaction and quality of life. Digital media is an influential tool that enables individuals to acquire information and knowledge while promoting mental well-being through intellectual stimulation and curiosity. Moreover, it facilitates and fosters social contacts and relationships, boosting individuals' social well-being by surmounting geographical limitations and cultivating a profound sense of belonging. In addition, platforms facilitating creative expression offer avenues for individuals to express themselves and engage in creative endeavours, consequently fostering emotional well-being and bolstering self-confidence.

Regarding occupational well-being, digital media offers possibilities for flexible work arrangements, which can enhance work-life balance and facilitate career progression. Online support networks provide individuals with emotional support and understanding, thus promoting emotional well-being. Nevertheless, the ubiquity of digital media also yields adverse repercussions. The phenomenon of information overload, which arises from a continuous influx of content, has the potential to induce feelings of stress, worry, and cognitive exhaustion, thereby exerting detrimental effects on an individual's mental well-being. The overuse of screens and reliance on virtual interactions might lead to social isolation due to a decrease in in-person connections, ultimately resulting in a decline in overall social well-being. The excessive utilization of digital media, particularly on platforms with addictive features, has the potential to result in digital addiction, hence exerting detrimental effects on one's mental, emotional, and physical well-being. The occurrence of adverse online encounters, such as cyberbullying and harassment, has the potential to induce emotional distress and exert detrimental effects on an individual's overall state of well-being. The potential implications of data privacy and online footprint on individuals' mental well-being have been identified as a source of stress and worry, ultimately exerting a detrimental influence on overall mental health (Burr et al., 2020).

Achieving an equilibrium between digital media's advantageous and detrimental impacts is paramount. Attaining this state of equilibrium necessitates the utilization of digital platforms with mindfulness and prudence, cultivating digital literacy competencies, and executing tactics that optimize advantages while mitigating potential harm. Individuals must understand these consequences to enhance their well-being, enabling them to make educated decisions and effectively navigate the digital realm. The advent of digital media has had a profound impact on moulding the current learning landscape, leading to a significant educational revolution. Online platforms have revolutionized access to an extensive range of knowledge and educational materials, hence promoting the democratization of information on a worldwide scale. Adaptive learning platforms and online courses leverage data analytics to customize educational experiences according to the unique needs of individual students, resulting in enhanced levels of engagement, comprehension, and retention. Digital media promotes active engagement and enjoyment in the educational experience by including interactive elements such as multimedia content, simulations, and gamification. Online platforms enable collaborative learning by overcoming geographical limitations to connect learners and educators, thereby cultivating a feeling of community and broadening intellectual perspectives. Individuals can participate in online courses, webinars, and workshops, enhancing the accessibility of lifelong learning and fostering personal growth and adaptation in an ever-evolving global landscape. The diverse educational materials, such as video lectures, interactive quizzes, and electronic books, cater to various learning styles and interests.

The flexibility and convenience of digital media enable students to engage with instructional materials at their own pace, which benefits individuals with busy schedules (Audrin & Audrin, 2022; Cannon, 2018). However, it is imperative to acknowledge that the involvement of digital media in education also poses particular difficulties, including the potential for overwhelming amounts of information and diversions that may hinder acquiring knowledge efficiently. Educators and students should thus leverage the advantages of digital media while formulating tactics to alleviate its limitations, ultimately establishing an educational setting that optimizes the utilization of digital resources for educational advancement and overall welfare.

PROMOTING FLOURISHING IN THE DIGITAL AGE

In light of the extensive impact of digital media, the cultivation of well-being has the utmost significance within the context of the digital era. To enhance overall well-being, it is imperative to foster a culture that encourages individuals to engage in frequent intervals of respite from electronic screens and gadgets. This practice enables individuals to effectively address the challenges of excessive information consumption and the resulting exhaustion, sometimes referred to as "digital fatigue," using designated periods of "digital detoxification." Furthermore, the promotion of attentive and intentional consumption of digital content facilitates the critical evaluation of information sources and the assessment of their emotional ramifications. In conjunction with the limitation of screen time, promoting diverse offline activities, including physical exercise and interpersonal engagements, contributes to overall well-being. Individuals with digital literacy abilities, including media literacy and online safety, can safely navigate the digital environment. Promoting physical well-being through consistent exercise and engagement in external activities improves physical health and positively impacts mental and emotional well-being. Individuals possess the capacity to effectively navigate the emotional fluctuations that arise from engaging in digital interactions through the acquisition and implementation of self-regulation strategies. It is imperative to prioritize cultivating healthy sleep habits and promoting dedicated "unplugged" periods with loved ones, as these practices are crucial for enhancing physical and social well-being. The encouragement of self-reflection about the utilization of digital media facilitates the identification and resolution of stress-inducing or negative factors, therefore fostering a more wholesome connection with technology. The promotion of an atmosphere that facilitates open discussions regarding individuals' digital encounters, difficulties, and apprehensions serves to motivate them to actively seek aid and guidance when needed, upholding the primacy of well-being in the era of digitalization (Valkenburg, 2022; Büchi, 2021). These tactics facilitate individuals in effectively navigating the digital landscape while concurrently upholding a harmonious equilibrium between their bodily and emotional needs and the digital realm.

In contemporary society, the cultivation of genuine relationships and connections within virtual settings is vital for the promotion of social welfare and the facilitation of meaningful engagements. To achieve this objective, fostering active engagement and high-quality contributions within virtual communities and cultivating empathetic and courteous online behaviour is imperative. Promoting compassion and empathy can be facilitated by reminding individuals that virtual interactions involve real individuals with emotional experiences. The importance of sustaining both face-to-face and virtual relationships is underscored by placing equal emphasis on both online and offline interactions. The protection of emotional well-being and responsible online conduct can be achieved by emphasizing the significance of online support communities, the promotion of digital citizenship, and the education of persons regarding online privacy and enhancing the extent of virtual connections through the implementation of mentorship programs, cultivation of face-to-face interactions, and encouragement of active listening abilities. Finally, promoting online groups centred around shared interests fosters a sense of belonging and genuineness in virtual engagements. In unison, these tactics ensure social well-being as a paramount concern in the digital age, facilitating authentic and significant interactions inside virtual environments (Longa et al., 2022; Schroeder, 2002).

ENHANCING LIFELONG LEARNING AND SUCCESS

In the contemporary era of digital advancements, cultivating a growth mindset and acquiring self-directed learning skills have emerged as imperative factors in establishing an atmosphere conducive to perpetual personal and professional development. This approach needs to prioritize recognizing work, persistence, and knowledge gained from obstacles while emphasizing that abilities and intelligence can be cultivated through dedication and patience. Furthermore, an essential aspect of self-directed learning involves facilitating individuals' understanding of their distinct learning styles, aptitudes, and areas requiring further development. Self-awareness allows individuals to tailor their learning experiences to meet their needs and objectives. Establishing clear, achievable, and congruent learning goals offers learners the impetus and guidance to sustain their educational concentration. Cultivating a sense of curiosity and a desire for knowledge is paramount. The impetus for self-directed learning is rooted in curiosity, making it imperative to foster an environment that promotes individuals' autonomy in formulating inquiries, exploring novel subjects, and seeking resolutions. Furthermore, the instruction of efficient time management and organizational skills guarantees that individuals can allocate time for educational pursuits amidst their busy schedules, underscoring the importance of prioritizing education and cultivating a well-defined plan (Jiang et al., 2023; Eurboonyanun et al., 2023; Sadoughi et al., 2022).

Acquiring skills necessary for identifying and effectively utilizing a wide range of educational materials, including online courses, tutorials, books, and mentorship, is paramount. It is imperative to provide instruction on evaluating the quality and pertinence of these resources since this is essential for facilitating informed decision-making. The cultivation of critical thinking abilities is of utmost importance in analyzing information, addressing intricate challenges, and arriving at well-informed conclusions, particularly when evaluating the integrity of digital content. Finally, it is beneficial to motivate individuals to actively solicit feedback regarding their learning process and engage in regular self-reflection on their advancement. This practice enables them to enhance their learning approaches and adjust to evolving goals (Eurboonyanun et al., 2023; London, 2011). Implementing these tactics allows individuals to foster a growth mindset, embrace lifelong learning as a continuous journey of ongoing progress, and cultivate self-directed learning abilities that empower them to flourish in the ever-changing digital era.

In the contemporary digital era, properly using digital tools and resources is crucial for pursuing lifelong learning. Encouraging individuals to explore diverse options, such as respected online courses and Massive Open Online Courses (MOOCs) provided by esteemed educational institutions, can facilitate access to various subjects and abilities. Furthermore, promoting e-books and digital libraries provides a convenient and cost-effective way of accessing vast knowledge archives. Familiarizing persons with Learning Management Systems (LMS) commonly employed in educational and professional contexts is imperative in providing organized and flexible learning experiences. The significance of webinars and virtual seminars lies in their ability to foster interactive learning experiences, enabling real-time engagement and knowledge exchange (Thwe & Kálmán, 2023; Herodotou et al., 2019).

It is essential to promote the utilization of podcasts and applications that offer easily accessible and captivating educational opportunities, which may be effortlessly integrated into everyday schedules. Engaging in social learning networks and online communities facilitates collaborative learning. It cultivates a communal atmosphere, as individuals can establish connections with peers, exchange knowledge, and collaborate on various projects. Enabling individuals with the capacity to utilize Internet research tools and databases effectively empowers them to engage in research, stay up-to-date with information, and explore specific subjects in greater depth. It is imperative to instruct students in utilizing efficient digital note-taking and organization strategies, as these resources enhance the retention and application of knowledge (Boulos et al., 2006). They can embark on a personalized and ongoing learning experience by guiding individuals to utilize digital tools and resources. In the contemporary digital landscape, these resources offer convenience and empower individuals to pursue their educational and personal development goals efficiently.

CASE STUDIES

Case Study 1: Digital Well-being Initiatives in Educational Institutions

This case study examines the proactive measures used by a notable educational institution, specifically a recognized university, in response to the digital well-being issues encountered by its student body in contemporary times. The institution initiated a transformative endeavour after acknowledging the concerns around prolonged usage of electronic screens, the stress induced by digital platforms, and the potential adverse effects of social media on psychological well-being. To promote a healthier and more balanced lifestyle among students during test seasons, educational institutions have introduced a practice known as "Digital Detox Weeks." This initiative encourages students to disengage from electronic screens and instead participate in intellectually stimulating and beneficial offline activities. Art lectures, outdoor excursions, and mindfulness exercises were conducted during this period to foster overall well-being.

The institution has included compulsory digital literacy courses in its academic program, providing students with essential skills in critical thinking and appropriate behaviour in online environments. To prioritize students' psychological well-being, the educational institution has broadened its range of services to encompass tailored therapy options for individuals grappling with digital stress and addiction. Additionally, the college has established a helpline to aid those who encounter online abuse or cyberbullying. The "Balanced Tech Use" initiative aimed to advocate for responsible utilization of technology by offering educational seminars focused on effective time management, practical advice for digital detoxification, and ways for achieving a harmonious equilibrium between online and offline activities. The findings indicate that students experienced decreased stress related to screen usage during exam periods and enhanced critical thinking skills and online conduct following their participation in digital literacy courses.

There was an observed rise in the utilization of mental health support services for stress arising from digital activities and the adoption of healthier digital practices as a consequence of the campaign. This case study emphasizes the significance of proactive programs promoting digital well-being inside educational institutions. It underscores the value of tackling the problems posed by the digital era and offering support and education to cultivate a more wholesome and harmonious learning environment.

Case Study 2: Successful Integration of Digital Media in Lifelong Learning Programs

The present case study explores into the progression of a non-profit organization dedicated to providing adult education and promoting lifelong learning. In light of the considerable opportunities presented by the digital era, the individuals embarked on a mission to update the dissemination of their programs. The researchers employed a novel methodology that involved developing an intuitive web-based educational platform that catered to all users. This platform had a user-friendly interface and offered diverse multimedia-enriched courses. Implementing frequent webinars, which incorporate knowledgeable guest speakers and foster meaningful dialogues, has enhanced accessibility by enabling participants to engage anywhere. Promoting student engagement in online communities affiliated with their academic courses facilitates the cultivation of peer learning, constructive conversations, and the dissemination of knowledge. Significantly, the platform employed algorithms to suggest customized learning trajectories tailored to an individual's interests, progress, and goals, augmenting the self-directed learning experience. The achievements were noteworthy due to the significant rise in participation rates, the presence of a more varied audience heightened learner engagement, and the expressed pleasure with interactive webinars and social learning communities. The use of personalized learning paths has resulted in improved individual progress and the attainment of specific objectives. This case study demonstrates the potential impact of strategically incorporating digital media into lifelong learning programs, resulting in enhanced accessibility, engagement, and customization to meet the unique needs of individual learners. These initiatives are crucial in promoting continuous learning and achieving success in the dynamically evolving digital era.

Case Study 3: Digital Tools for Mental Health and Tobacco Addiction Recovery

The case study of SK, a 22-year-old individual employed in a professional capacity, is a compelling illustration of the potential of digital tools and applications in effectively addressing mental health challenges and conquering addictive behaviours. This transformative process ultimately enhances overall welfare, continuous personal growth, and increased occupational achievements. SK's decade-long struggle with tobacco addiction and the significant stress produced by her career had adversely affected her physical and mental well-being, hindering her overall personal and professional growth. Nevertheless, the commencement of her work period was marked by the encounter with mindfulness and meditation tools such as Headspace and Calm, which she subsequently integrated into her daily routine. The individual acquired the ability to manage stress and anxiety through these strategies, resulting in the development of emotional regulation and resilience, facilitating more effective navigation of work-related difficulties. However, it may be argued that the most remarkable aspect of SK's transformation was her battle with cigarette dependency, a challenge that had previously eluded her despite multiple attempts. SK was able to identify the necessary motivation and resources to effectively cease smoking with the use of digitally produced software tailored explicitly for addiction therapy. The application provided features such as progress monitoring, a platform for exchanging personal experiences, and daily prompts to facilitate smoking cessation.

Additionally, she sought solace and support inside online platforms designed for individuals recovering from tobacco addiction, where she encountered individuals undergoing comparable journeys.

As the individual, referred to as SK, continued to utilize these digital tools, she observed notable enhancements in her mental well-being. The individual's ability to thrive in their professional endeavours and pursue additional educational opportunities was facilitated by alleviating stress and enhancing mental well-being resulting from their decision to abstain from smoking, which allowed them to accumulate financial savings. The enhanced cognitive clarity and concentration experienced by SK facilitated not just her professional growth in her present role but also her engagement in online courses and seminars aligned with her career aspirations. The individual's unwavering commitment to self-care and continuous education propelled her to unprecedented achievements in her professional career. The experience of SK serves as a prime example of how digital tools can effectively enhance mental well-being, facilitate recovery from addiction, and foster achievement in one's professional endeavours. The individual experienced enhancements in her mental well-being and cultivated a sense of self-empowerment to embrace continuous education and unleash her complete capabilities within the context of the digital age. This was achieved through utilizing mindfulness and meditation applications for stress management and a dedicated application for tobacco addiction treatment, which provided her with the necessary assistance. This case study underscores the significant impact that digital technologies may have on promoting thriving lifestyles, shedding light on the intricate relationship between well-being, ongoing education, and eventual success.

Case Study 4: Gamification for Learning - Enhancing Engagement, Motivation, and Success

The utilization of gamification as a powerful tool in the digital era to enhance the learning experience is exemplified by the success stories of Duolingo and Khan Academy. Duolingo, a widely used platform for language learning, adeptly integrates gamification elements within its framework, offering learners a dynamic and engaging learning environment. Users who complete courses and exercises accumulate experience points (XP), gaining access to additional information and advancing to higher levels. The website employs streaks as a means to motivate users to maintain consistent daily practice habits while also fostering a sense of friendly competition through the utilization of leaderboards. In addition, Duolingo incorporates "Lingots," a virtual currency that can be utilized to obtain various rewards within the application. Incorporating gamified elements enhances the dynamism and entertainment value of the learning process, fostering a voluntary inclination among users to engage consistently, maintain their learning streaks, and engage in healthy competition with their peers. Consequently, this approach yields remarkable outcomes in the realm of language acquisition.

Khan Academy, an e-learning platform specializing in mathematics and science education, employs gamification strategies to enhance the learning experience. Students are awarded badges for successfully completing exercises and mastery of concepts, which fosters a sense of pride and motivation. Visual dashboards allow students to evaluate their progress and identify areas for improvement through the ability to track their degrees of competence. In addition, Khan Academy utilizes data-driven algorithms to provide personalized learning pathways, guaranteeing that students concentrate on subject matter pertinent to their specific needs. Using gamification techniques has enhanced learner engagement, as visual stimuli entice students significantly, and they are more inclined to dedicate additional time to comprehending challenging subject matter. The acquisition of badges and proficiency in many disciplines provides students with a feeling of achievement, while customized learning pathways enhance the significance and feasibility of the educational experience. The implementation of mastery-based gamification inside Khan Academy aligns effectively with the principles of deeper learning and comprehension, ultimately resulting in academic achievement and building a robust groundwork for subsequent scholarly pursuits. Duolingo and Khan Academy exemplify the efficacy of gamification in enhancing learner engagement, motivation, and achievement within the context of the digital era. These companies have developed educational experiences that are immersive and effective, promoting learner engagement by integrating gamification elements into their platforms. They emphasize the interconnectedness of well-being, lifelong learning, and achievement within the contemporary educational environment. Gamification is an innovative educational strategy that enhances the learning process's enjoyment, motivation, and eventual success.

RECOMMENDATIONS AND SOLUTIONS

Educational institutions should embed digital literacy into their curricula to equip learners with the skills necessary for navigating digital environments safely and effectively. This includes training in critical thinking, digital citizenship, and evaluating the credibility of online information. Schools and organizations should develop and implement digital well-being programs that include digital detox initiatives, mindfulness practices, and strategies for managing screen time. Programs should offer resources for stress management and healthy technology use. Encourage lifelong learning through accessible and diverse educational resources. Utilize online platforms, MOOCs, webinars, and digital libraries to provide continuous learning opportunities. Ensure that these resources are user-friendly and cater to various learning styles.

Cultivate a growth mindset among learners and professionals by emphasizing the value of persistence, effort, and adaptability. Create environments that celebrate learning from failures and encourage the pursuit of new challenges. Advocate for a balanced approach to digital and non-digital activities. Encourage regular breaks from screens and promote engagement in offline activities such as outdoor exercises, creative pursuits, and face-to-face interactions. Provide tools and resources that enable individuals to take charge of their own learning. This includes personalized learning paths, self-assessment tools, and access to a range of educational materials tailored to individual needs and goals.

Offer training in emotional regulation and resilience-building techniques. Mindfulness and meditation practices can help individuals manage stress and improve overall well-being. Create and support online communities and networks where individuals can connect, share knowledge, and collaborate on projects. This fosters a sense of belonging and mutual support.

Utilize gamification strategies to make learning engaging and motivating. Incorporate elements such as badges, leaderboards, and progress tracking to enhance learner participation and satisfaction.

Regularly assess the effectiveness of digital well-being and learning programs. Collect feedback from participants and use it to refine and adapt strategies to better meet evolving needs and challenges. By adopting these recommendations and solutions, individuals and institutions can effectively navigate the digital landscape, enhance personal growth, and achieve success while maintaining a balanced and fulfilling life.

FUTURE RESEARCH DIRECTIONS

Conduct long-term studies to examine the sustained effects of digital well-being interventions on mental health, academic performance, and overall life satisfaction Assess how different age groups and demographic factors influence the outcomes of such interventions. Investigate the effectiveness of digital literacy programs in various educational settings. Research how these programs affect students' critical thinking, online behavior, and academic achievement, and identify best practices for program implementation. Explore the impact of personalized learning technologies on lifelong learning. Study how adaptive learning platforms, which use algorithms to tailor content to individual needs, affect learner engagement, achievement, and satisfaction.

Examine the relationship between gamification elements and educational outcomes. Research how different gamification strategies (e.g., badges, leaderboards) influence motivation, retention, and performance across various subjects and age groups. Investigate effective strategies for promoting a balance between digital and offline activities. Study how different interventions, such as digital detox programs or offline enrichment activities, impact well-being, productivity, and social interactions. Research the efficacy of digital tools and applications designed to address digital addiction. Evaluate their effectiveness in reducing screen time, improving mental health, and supporting behavioral change.

Explore how cultural and societal factors influence digital well-being and lifelong learning. Study how different regions and cultural contexts impact the adoption and effectiveness of digital well-being programs and learning technologies. Examine the role of digital interactions in emotional regulation. Investigate how digital platforms and social media influence emotional well-being and resilience, and identify strategies for mitigating negative effects.Analyze emerging technologies, such as virtual reality (VR) and augmented reality (AR), and their potential impact on learning and well-being. Research how these technologies can be effectively integrated into educational and well-being initiatives.

Study the ethical and privacy implications of digital technologies in education and mental health. Research how to balance technological advancements with privacy concerns and ensure responsible use of digital tools. These future research directions aim to deepen the understanding of how digital technology intersects with well-being and lifelong learning, providing insights that can inform the development of more effective strategies and interventions in the evolving digital landscape.

DISCUSSION

The investigation of the correlation between pleasure, lifelong learning, and success unveils a multifaceted and interconnected relationship that holds particular significance in the contemporary era of digital advancements. The concept of well-being spans several dimensions of an individual's existence and is fundamental in fostering personal growth and accomplishment. Positive well-being in an individual has been found to enhance their propensity to participate in lifelong learning and effectively adapt to the various difficulties and possibilities that arise in the digital era. The concept of well-being extends beyond the mere absence of adversity, encompassing the existence of positive elements that facilitate the flourishing of persons. In the contemporary digitalization era, technology's smooth incorporation into various aspects of human existence profoundly impacts individuals' cognitive, affective, and physiological conditions, thereby heightening the importance of overall well-being. As a result, the cultivation of well-being emerges as both an individual pursuit and a prerequisite for successful learning and achievement. The perpetuation of education throughout one's lifetime is an essential element of this connection. In an era characterized by swift transformations in the digital realm, the ability to engage in perpetual learning is vital for individual and vocational advancement. Individuals possess the requisite skills, knowledge, and adaptability essential for effectively navigating the digital era using continuous learning throughout their lives. The abovementioned factors, including intellectual stimulation, curiosity, and resiliency, collectively foster well-being. In the contemporary digital landscape, success extends beyond traditional parameters. In addition to professional achievements, this encompasses personal satisfaction, flexibility, and the capacity to maintain equilibrium between the virtual and tangible realms. A strong correlation exists between positive well-being and the probability of attaining personal goals and experiencing a satisfying existence, indicating a close interconnection between the two.

The case examples presented in this chapter demonstrate the proactive measures that educational institutions and businesses can undertake to foster well-being, continuous learning, and success in digital technology. Digital well-being programs and the deliberate incorporation of digital media in perpetual learning programs exemplify the positive impact of emphasizing well-being on learning outcomes and personal development. The interplay between well-being, lifelong learning, and success in the digital era is characterized by a dynamic and mutually reinforcing interaction. Prioritizing one's health is not solely a matter of personal choice but also a strategic decision that amplifies an individual's ability to acquire knowledge and succeed in an ever-changing digital environment. Various stakeholders, including individuals, educational institutions, and businesses, have the opportunity to devise methods that enhance overall well-being, promote continuous learning, and facilitate significant achievements in the era of digital technology. These stakeholders actively engage in ongoing research and understanding of the complex dynamics between individuals and the digital age.

Understanding the mechanisms and elements contributing to thriving in the digital era is a multifaceted undertaking that necessitates a thorough understanding of the interplay between technology, well-being, and individual development. Several essential aspects influence success in the digital age. Digital literacy and technology-related skills are essential for individuals to effectively navigate online environments, protect their privacy, and leverage technology for personal and professional growth. How individuals utilize technology has a substantial impact on their overall state of well-being. Engaging in purposeful and valuable online activities has the potential to augment one's intellectual and emotional wellness.

Educational institutions and organizations are vital in promoting digital well-being by implementing various measures, including digital detox programs and digital literacy courses. The effective administration of screen time, the promotion of a harmonious equilibrium between digital and non-digital engagements, and the cultivation of emotional regulating abilities are paramount. Individuals, institutions, and organizations must acknowledge and address several key elements to thrive in the digital age. These include self-reflection, embracing lifelong learning, fostering supportive communities, practising responsible online behaviour, and attaining a harmonious equilibrium between digital and non-digital aspects of life. By recognizing and attending to these factors, one can effectively harness the capabilities of technology while safeguarding personal well-being and upholding societal values.

CONCLUSION

The advent of the digital era has resulted in significant transformations in the methods through which we acquire knowledge, engage in interpersonal interactions, and conceptualize achievement. In the context of the dynamic and evolving landscape, the cultivation of individual well-being and the pursuit of continuous learning have emerged as critical considerations. Within the framework of the digital era, an examination has been conducted on the complex interconnection between thriving, lifelong learning, and achievement, with a recognition of the profound importance of flourishing as an essential component within this equation. The concept of well-being, which includes several dimensions, such as physical, mental, emotional, social, intellectual, occupational, environmental, and spiritual components, serves as the fundamental basis for all other facets of life in the contemporary digital era. Flourishing is characterized by favourable factors that facilitate individuals' prosperity, adaptability, and attainment of satisfying lifestyles. In the contemporary era characterized by persistent technological progress and dynamic job markets, pursuing lifelong learning has transformed from a discretionary option to an imperative requirement. Individuals possess the requisite abilities and information for adapting, excelling, and attaining personal fulfilment within a dynamic and ever-evolving world. Lifelong learning facilitates various facets of personal development and accomplishment, encompassing growth and attainment, ranging from technical proficiencies to critical thinking and adaptability.

Implementing a comprehensive set of guidelines is necessary to foster the flourishing of individuals and successfully address the issues that arise within the digital learning environment. The guidelines mentioned above encompass providing digital literacy skills to individuals, promoting a harmonious balance between online and offline activities, and implementing digital well-being programs inside educational institutions and organizations. In contemporary society, cultivating a growth mindset and effectively utilizing digital resources for continuous learning are integral facets of individual personal growth. In addition, cultivating authentic online connections, establishing supportive groups, and promoting digital citizenship is crucial in building a constructive online milieu. Prioritizing well-being is of utmost importance through mindfulness techniques, regular digital detoxification, and the construction of clear boundaries between digital and non-digital activities. By embracing a comprehensive strategy and acknowledging the complex relationship between technology and personal growth, individuals, educational institutions, and organizations have the potential to not only succeed in the digital realm but also safeguard their well-being and uphold their ideals for a more promising future.

REFERENCES

Audrin, C., & Audrin, B. (2022). Key factors in digital literacy in learning and education: A systematic literature review using text mining. *Education and Information Technologies, 27*(6), 7395–7419. DOI: 10.1007/s10639-021-10832-5

Benavot, A., Hoppers, C. A. O., Lockhart, A. S., & Hinzen, H. (2022). Reimagining adult education and lifelong learning for all: Historical and critical perspectives. *International Review of Education, 68*(2), 165–194. DOI: 10.1007/s11159-022-09955-9 PMID: 35668894

Boulos, M. N. K., Maramba, I., & Wheeler, S. (2006). Wikis, blogs and podcasts: A new generation of Web-based tools for virtual collaborative clinical practice and education. *BMC Medical Education, 6*(1). Advance online publication. DOI: 10.1186/1472-6920-6-41 PMID: 16911779

Büchi, M. (2021). Digital well-being theory and research. *New Media & Society, 146144482110568*. Advance online publication. DOI: 10.1177/14614448211056851

Burr, C., Taddeo, M., & Floridi, L. (2020). The Ethics of Digital Well-Being: A Thematic Review. *Science and Engineering Ethics, 26*(4), 2313–2343. DOI: 10.1007/s11948-020-00175-8 PMID: 31933119

Cannon, M. (2018). Digital media in education. In *Springer eBooks*. https://doi.org/ DOI: 10.1007/978-3-319-78304-8

Cao, S., & Li, H. (2023). A scoping review of Digital Well-Being in Early Childhood: Definitions, Measurements, contributors, and Interventions. *International Journal of Environmental Research and Public Health, 20*(4), 3510. DOI: 10.3390/ijerph20043510 PMID: 36834204

Della Longa, L., Valori, I., & Farroni, T. (2022). Interpersonal affective touch in a virtual world: Feeling the social presence of others to overcome loneliness. *Frontiers in Psychology, 12*. Advance online publication. DOI: 10.3389/fpsyg.2021.795283 PMID: 35087455

Eurboonyanun, C., Petrusa, E., Eurboonyanun, K., McKinley, S. K., Phanphruk, W., Gee, D. W., & Phitayakorn, R. (2023). Relationship of high self-directed learning readiness and growth mindset among general surgery resident. *Global Surgical Education : Journal of the Association for Surgical Education, 2*(1). Advance online publication. DOI: 10.1007/s44186-023-00115-7

Fisher, J. W. (2011). The four domains model: Connecting Spirituality, Health and Well-Being. *Religions, 2*(1), 17–28. DOI: 10.3390/rel2010017

Herodotou, C., Sharples, M., Gaved, M., Kukulska-Hulme, A., Rienties, B., Scanlon, E., & Whitelock, D. (2019). Innovative Pedagogies of the Future: An Evidence-Based Selection. *Frontiers in Education*, *4*. Advance online publication. DOI: 10.3389/feduc.2019.00113

Janicke-Bowles, S. H., Buckley, T. M., Rey, R. T., Wozniak, T., Meier, A., & Lomanowska, A. M. (2023). Digital Flourishing: Conceptualizing and assessing positive perceptions of mediated social interactions. *Journal of Happiness Studies*, *24*(3), 1013–1035. DOI: 10.1007/s10902-023-00619-5

Jiang, Y., Liu, H., Yao, Y., Li, Q., & Li, Y. (2023). The Positive Effects of Growth Mindset on Students' Intention toward Self-Regulated Learning during the COVID-19 Pandemic: A PLS-SEM Approach. *Sustainability*, *15*(3), 2180. DOI: 10.3390/su15032180

Kantar, N., & Bynum, T. W. (2021). Global ethics for the digital age – flourishing ethics. *Journal of Information. Communication and Ethics in Society*, *19*(3), 329–344. DOI: 10.1108/jices-01-2021-0016

London, M. (2011). *Lifelong Learning: Introduction*. The Oxford Handbook of Lifelong Learning., DOI: 10.1093/oxfordhb/9780195390483.013.0013

Mayer, C. (2017). The holistic wellness model. In *Springer eBooks* (pp. 95–117). https://doi.org/DOI: 10.1007/978-3-319-59638-9_4

Roche, S. (2018). The contribution of lifelong learning to development – personal and communal. *International Review of Education*, *64*(1), 1–7. DOI: 10.1007/s11159-018-9706-1

Sadoughi, M., Hejazi, S. Y., & Lou, N. M. (2022). How do growth mindsets contribute to academic engagement in L2 classes? The mediating and moderating roles of the L2 motivational self-system. *Social Psychology of Education*, *26*(1), 241–261. DOI: 10.1007/s11218-022-09744-0

Schroeder, R. (2002). Social interaction in virtual environments: key issues, common themes, and a framework for research. In *Springer eBooks* (pp. 1–18). https://doi.org/DOI: 10.1007/978-1-4471-0277-9_1

Sternberg, R. J. (1997). The concept of intelligence and its role in lifelong learning and success. *The American Psychologist*, *52*(10), 1030–1037. DOI: 10.1037/0003-066x.52.10.1030 PMID: 9329294

Thwe, W. P., & Kálmán, A. (2023). Lifelong Learning in the Educational Setting: A Systematic Literature Review. *The Asia-Pacific Education Researcher*. Advance online publication. DOI: 10.1007/s40299-023-00738-w

Valkenburg, P. M. (2022). Social media use and well-being: What we know and need to know. *Current Opinion in Psychology*, *45*, 101294. DOI: 10.1016/j.copsyc.2021.12.006 PMID: 35016087

VanderWeele, T. J. (2017). On the promotion of human flourishing. *Proceedings of the National Academy of Sciences of the United States of America*, *114*(31), 8148–8156. DOI: 10.1073/pnas.1702996114 PMID: 28705870

KEY TERMS AND DEFINITIONS

Digital Age: The digital age, also known as the information age or digital era, is characterized by the widespread use of digital technology and the internet. This era has transformed how people communicate, access information, and conduct daily activities, influencing various aspects of modern life.

Digital Media: Digital media encompasses all forms of media content created, distributed, and consumed via digital platforms, such as websites, social media, and mobile applications. It includes text, audio, video, and interactive content delivered through digital channels.

Educational Outcomes: Educational outcomes refer to the measurable results or achievements of educational processes, including student learning, skill acquisition, and academic performance. They assess the effectiveness of educational programs and interventions in achieving desired learning objectives and personal development goals.

Flourishing: Flourishing refers to a state of optimal well-being where individuals experience high levels of happiness, fulfillment, and personal growth. It involves thriving in various areas of life, including emotional resilience, positive relationships, and meaningful achievements.

Lifelong Learning: Lifelong learning is the continuous, voluntary, and self-motivated pursuit of knowledge for personal or professional development throughout an individual's life. It emphasizes the importance of ongoing education and skill acquisition beyond formal schooling to adapt to changing circumstances and advancements.

Success: Success is the achievement of desired goals or outcomes, which can be defined differently depending on individual or societal values. It often includes professional accomplishments, personal satisfaction, and the ability to balance various aspects of life effectively.

Well-Being: Well-being refers to the overall state of an individual's health, happiness, and prosperity. It encompasses various dimensions including mental, emotional, physical, and social aspects. Positive well-being involves experiencing positive emotions, life satisfaction, and effective functioning in daily life.

Chapter 3
Cultivating Flourishing and Resilience in the Digital Age:
Addressing Digital Addiction With Multidimensional Addiction Behavior Scale

Ranjit Singha
https://orcid.org/0000-0002-3541-8752
Christ University, India

Surjit Singha
https://orcid.org/0000-0002-5730-8677
Kristu Jayanti University, India

ABSTRACT

This study investigates strategies to mitigate digital addiction while promoting flourishing and resilience in the digital age. Digital addiction, characterized by compulsive behaviours related to digital devices and platforms, poses significant challenges to physical health, mental well-being, and social relationships. Grounded in the biopsychosocial model of health and drawing upon theories of behavioural addiction, social learning, self-determination, and cognitive-behavioural therapy, this research explores the prevalence, impacts, and interventions of digital addiction across diverse demographics. The study aims to identify practical educational, policy, and community-based approaches to foster healthy digital behaviours and

DOI: 10.4018/979-8-3693-0997-1.ch003

enhance resilience. By addressing these issues, this study contributes to a deeper understanding of digital addiction and provides recommendations for promoting well-being amidst pervasive digital technologies.

INTRODUCTION

In the ever-evolving landscape of the digital age, the pervasive integration of technology into daily life has fundamentally reshaped how individuals interact, learn, and communicate. This transformation has ushered in unprecedented opportunities for accessing information, fostering global connectivity, and enhancing entertainment experiences. However, alongside these benefits, the ubiquitous nature of digital tools has brought forth significant challenges.

One such challenge is the emergence of digital addiction, a phenomenon characterized by compulsive and excessive use of digital devices and platforms. Digital addiction spans a spectrum of behaviors, from incessant social media scrolling and online gaming to compulsive internet browsing, all of which can lead to profound implications for individual well-being and societal dynamics. These behaviors often disrupt daily routines, impair interpersonal relationships, and undermine mental health by fostering anxiety, depression, and a diminished sense of fulfillment (Grant, 2024; Karakose et al., 2022).

Understanding the complexities of digital addiction is crucial not only for mitigating its adverse effects but also for fostering flourishing and resilience in individuals within this digital milieu. Flourishing encompasses holistic well-being, including emotional vitality, engagement in meaningful activities, positive social relationships, a sense of purpose, and personal accomplishment. Resilience, on the other hand, denotes the ability to adapt positively to adversity, bounce back from setbacks, and maintain stable functioning amid stressors.

This chapter aims to explore the multifaceted dimensions of digital addiction, examining its impacts on both flourishing and resilience. By introducing multidimensional addictive behavior scales, this chapter seeks to provide a structured approach for assessing and understanding the various facets of digital addiction. These scales offer insights into behavioral, emotional, cognitive, and social dependencies on digital technologies, thereby facilitating tailored interventions and strategies to promote healthier digital habits.

In essence, navigating the complexities of digital addiction requires a comprehensive understanding of its psychological, social, and behavioral underpinnings. By addressing these challenges effectively, we can harness the transformative potential of digital technologies while safeguarding individual well-being and cultivating resilient communities in the digital age.

BACKGROUND

The rapid integration of digital technologies into daily life has brought about unprecedented opportunities for communication, learning, and entertainment. However, alongside these benefits, concerns have arisen regarding the potential negative impacts of excessive digital use, commonly referred to as digital addiction. Digital addiction encompasses compulsive behaviors related to digital devices and platforms, leading to adverse effects on physical health, mental well-being, and social relationships. Understanding and addressing digital addiction are critical for promoting holistic well-being and resilience in individuals, particularly in the context of the digital age(Grant, 2024; Karakose et al., 2022).

This study aims to explore effective strategies for mitigating digital addiction while concurrently fostering flourishing and resilience among individuals in the digital age. The objectives of this research encompass investigating the prevalence and patterns of digital addiction across diverse demographic groups, examining its impacts on physical health, mental well-being, and social relationships, and identifying interventions to prevent and manage digital addiction effectively. Additionally, the study will explore the roles of education, policy frameworks, and community support in promoting healthy digital behaviors. It focuses on various digital devices and platforms, such as smartphones, social media, online gaming, and internet use broadly, examining their impact across different age groups and socio-cultural contexts. Utilizing both quantitative and qualitative approaches, this research seeks to provide a comprehensive understanding of digital addiction's implications for well-being and resilience, culminating in recommendations to enhance individual flourishing amidst the pervasive influence of digital technologies.

The conceptual framework of this study is grounded in the biopsychosocial model of health, which posits that health outcomes result from interactions between biological, psychological, and social factors. In the context of digital addiction, this framework helps in understanding how individual vulnerabilities (biological), cognitive and emotional processes (psychological), and social influences (social) contribute to the development and maintenance of addictive behaviors related to digital technologies.

The theoretical framework of this study integrates several prominent theories and models to comprehensively understand digital addiction within the context of behavioral dynamics and psychological processes. Behavioral Addiction Theory posits that digital addiction mirrors other behavioral addictions like gambling and substance abuse, characterized by reinforcement mechanisms, cravings, and loss of control. Social Learning Theory emphasizes the role of observational learning, where individuals adopt behaviors, including digital addiction, through modeling others and receiving social rewards. Self-Determination Theory underscores intrinsic motivation and autonomy, suggesting that deficits in fulfilling psychological needs for autonomy, competence, and relatedness may contribute to digital addiction. Cognitive-Behavioral Theory examines the interplay of thoughts, feelings, and behaviors, focusing on how maladaptive cognitions perpetuate addictive patterns and the role of cognitive restructuring in promoting addiction recovery. By synthesizing these theories, this framework provides a nuanced lens to explore the complexities of digital addiction and inform effective interventions and strategies for promoting healthier digital behaviors and enhancing resilience in the digital age. By exploring these frameworks and conducting empirical research, this study aims to contribute to the understanding of digital addiction and provide actionable insights for promoting flourishing and resilience in the digital age. Understanding the complexities of digital addiction within these frameworks will inform the development of effective interventions, policies, and educational strategies to mitigate its negative impacts and enhance well-being in individuals and communities.

UNDERSTANDING DIGITAL ADDICTION

Digital addiction refers to the compulsive use of digital devices such as smartphones, computers, and gaming consoles, which can interfere with daily life and well-being. This phenomenon shares similarities with other behavioral addictions, such as gambling or shopping, where the behavior becomes a primary focus of an individual's life, leading to negative consequences (Hartogsohn & Vudka, 2022).

Understanding digital addiction involves recognizing its pervasive impact on individuals' lives as they increasingly rely on digital devices like smartphones, computers, and gaming consoles. Similar to other behavioral addictions such as gambling or shopping, digital addiction manifests as a compulsive need to engage with digital content and platforms, often to the detriment of other responsibilities and activities. This compulsive behavior can disrupt daily routines, impair social interactions, and compromise physical and mental well-being. Key features of digital addiction include loss of control over usage, withdrawal symptoms when access is limited, and continued use despite negative consequences. Psychological mechanisms underlying digital addiction often involve reinforcement processes, where the immediate rewards of digital engagement reinforce repeated behaviors. Moreover, the pervasive accessibility and immersive nature of digital technologies contribute to their addictive potential, blurring boundaries between work, leisure, and personal life. Recognizing digital addiction as a complex behavioral phenomenon necessitates comprehensive approaches that combine education, support, and policy measures to mitigate its impact and promote healthier digital habits in individuals and communities.

THE MECHANISMS OF DIGITAL ADDICTION

Digital addiction is fueled by various psychological and neurological mechanisms. Key among these are the intermittent reinforcement provided by social media notifications, the immersive nature of digital games, and the perpetual novelty offered by the internet. These elements activate the brain's reward system, releasing dopamine and creating a cycle of desire and gratification (Chang & Lee, 2024; Montag et al., 2016).

Digital addiction is intricately fueled by several psychological and neurological mechanisms that underscore its compelling nature. One of the primary drivers is intermittent reinforcement, particularly prevalent in social media platforms. Notifications, likes, and comments provide unpredictable rewards, triggering the brain's reward system. This reinforcement mechanism enhances the addictive nature of digital engagement by maintaining users' interest through sporadic positive feedback (Firth et al., 2019; Tereshchenko, 2023).

The immersive nature of digital games also plays a significant role in digital addiction. Games often feature intricate narratives, challenging levels, and social interactions that captivate attention and prolong engagement. The interactive and competitive elements within games stimulate dopamine release, reinforcing repeated gameplay and fostering dependence (Potenza, 2013; Wang et al., 2023).

Additionally, the internet's perpetual novelty contributes to digital addiction. Access to vast amounts of information, entertainment, and social connections creates an environment where users constantly seek new stimuli. This continuous exposure to novel content triggers dopamine release, driving individuals to seek out and consume digital content compulsively (Goldman, 2021; Park, 2024).

These mechanisms collectively activate the brain's reward pathways, particularly involving dopamine release, which reinforces the behavior of using digital devices and platforms. Over time, these patterns can lead to tolerance, withdrawal symptoms when digital access is restricted, and difficulty in regulating usage despite negative consequences. Understanding these mechanisms is crucial for developing effective interventions and strategies to mitigate digital addiction and promote healthier digital behaviors.

THE IMPACT ON WELL-BEING

Excessive use of digital devices can lead to a range of adverse outcomes. Physically, it can result in poor posture, eye strain, and disrupted sleep patterns. Psychologically, it can cause anxiety, depression, and decreased ability to focus. Socially, it may lead to isolation and strained relationships. These impacts are antithetical to the concept of flourishing, which involves thriving in multiple dimensions of life, including emotional, psychological, and social well-being (Cham et al., 2019; Han et al., 2023).

The impact of excessive digital device use extends across various dimensions of well-being, reflecting its pervasive influence on individuals' lives. Physically, prolonged screen time contributes to poor posture, musculoskeletal issues, and eye strain, often exacerbated by the sedentary nature of digital activities. Disrupted sleep patterns are also common, attributed to the exposure to blue light from screens and the stimulation of late-night digital engagement, which can impair overall physical health and cognitive function (Kumar et al., 2023; Small et al., 2020).

Psychologically, digital addiction correlates with heightened levels of anxiety and depression. The constant connectivity and exposure to curated images of others' lives on social media platforms can foster feelings of inadequacy and comparison, exacerbating mental health challenges. Moreover, excessive digital consumption can diminish attention spans and concentration abilities, impacting productivity and academic performance (Small et al., 2020; Zarate et al., 2022).

Socially, the pervasive use of digital devices can lead to isolation and strained interpersonal relationships. Despite the illusion of connectivity through online platforms, face-to-face interactions and meaningful social bonds may be neglected or diminished. This can hinder the development of empathy, communication skills, and emotional intelligence, essential for nurturing healthy relationships and overall social well-being (Audrin & Audrin, 2023; Scott et al., 2016).

These adverse impacts on physical, psychological, and social dimensions of well-being are antithetical to the concept of flourishing, which encompasses thriving in multiple facets of life. Recognizing these consequences underscores the importance of adopting balanced digital habits, promoting mindfulness in digital use, and fostering resilience to mitigate the detrimental effects of digital addiction on individuals' overall well-being and quality of life.

FLOURISHING IN THE DIGITAL AGE

Flourishing is a holistic concept encompassing well-being, happiness, and a sense of purpose. In the context of the digital age, it is essential to balance the benefits of technology with the need to maintain overall well-being (Marciano & Viswanath, 2023; Ruggeri et al., 2020).

Flourishing in the digital age involves navigating the complexities of modern technology to achieve a balanced and fulfilling life. It integrates the benefits of digital advancements—such as enhanced communication, access to information, and opportunities for creativity and productivity—with the imperative to preserve and promote overall well-being (Ardelt & Kingsbury, 2024; Marciano & Viswanath, 2023).

Central to flourishing is the cultivation of digital literacy that goes beyond mere technical skills. It encompasses critical thinking about digital content, ethical considerations in digital interactions, and the ability to manage digital consumption effectively. Individuals who flourish in the digital age are adept at harnessing technology to enhance their personal and professional lives while maintaining boundaries that safeguard their physical, mental, and emotional health (Burr et al., 2020; Gouseti et al., 2024).

Moreover, flourishing involves leveraging digital tools to cultivate meaningful connections and support networks. Despite the potential for digital devices to contribute to isolation, they also enable diverse forms of social engagement and community building. Flourishing individuals in the digital age recognize the importance of balancing online interactions with face-to-face connections, nurturing empathy, mutual support, and shared experiences (Janicke-Bowles et al., 2023; Montgomery, 2018).

Furthermore, fostering resilience is crucial in navigating the rapid pace of technological change and the potential pitfalls of digital overconsumption. Resilient individuals adapt to challenges posed by digital distractions, misinformation, and addictive behaviors, drawing on strategies such as mindfulness, self-regulation, and intentional digital use (Grant & Clarke, 2020; Qi & Yang, 2024).

Ultimately, flourishing in the digital age requires a proactive approach to integrating technology into one's life in ways that enhance personal growth, foster genuine connections, and contribute positively to society. By embracing digital tools mindfully and cultivating resilience, individuals can maximize the benefits of technology while safeguarding their well-being and maintaining a sense of purpose and fulfillment in today's interconnected world.

RESILIENCE IN THE DIGITAL AGE

Resilience refers to the capacity to adapt and recover from adversity. In the digital age, resilience includes managing digital stressors and maintaining well-being despite the pervasive presence of technology.

Resilience in the digital age encompasses the ability to effectively navigate and overcome challenges posed by constant digital interactions and technologies. It involves developing strategies to manage digital stressors, maintain well-being, and thrive amidst the rapid evolution of digital landscapes (Mehedintu & Soava, 2022; Schäfer et al., 2024).

One key aspect of resilience in the digital age is the cultivation of digital mindfulness and self-awareness. This includes being conscious of one's digital habits, recognizing when digital interactions are becoming overwhelming or detrimental, and proactively taking steps to mitigate their negative impact. Practices such as setting boundaries for digital use, practicing digital detoxes, and prioritizing offline activities contribute to maintaining balance and reducing the risk of digital burnout (Abhari et al., 2021; Mitsea et al., 2023).

Additionally, resilience involves developing critical thinking skills to discern credible information from misinformation and navigate digital environments responsibly. This includes being aware of the potential risks of online interactions, such as cyberbullying, privacy breaches, and digital addiction, and taking proactive measures to protect oneself and others from these risks (Qi & Yang, 2024; Vargas-Nieto et al., 2024).

Furthermore, resilience in the digital age entails fostering supportive relationships and networks both online and offline. Building connections with peers, mentors, and communities provides emotional support, opportunities for collaboration, and a sense of belonging that can bolster resilience in the face of digital challenges (Abhari et al., 2021; Mirbahaeddin & Chreim, 2024)

Lastly, promoting resilience involves embracing lifelong learning and adaptation to technological advancements. This includes staying informed about digital trends, acquiring new digital skills as needed, and remaining flexible in adapting to changes in digital platforms and technologies (Lim et al., 2024; Motz et al., 2023).

By cultivating resilience in the digital age, individuals are better equipped to navigate the complexities of digital interactions, maintain well-being, and effectively harness the benefits of technology to thrive personally, academically, and professionally.

MULTIDIMENSIONAL ADDICTION BEHAVIOR SCALES

To effectively address digital addiction, it is essential to use comprehensive assessment tools. Multidimensional addictive behavior scales provide a detailed approach to evaluating and understanding digital addiction, unlike simpler measures that may focus solely on usage frequency or duration.

Dimensions of MABS

Psychological Factor
Biological Factor
Social and Environmental Factors

Cognitive and Behavioral pattern
Motivation and Readiness for Change

By utilizing these scales, researchers, clinicians, and educators can obtain a comprehensive profile of an individual's digital addiction tendencies. This holistic understanding facilitates personalized interventions and treatments tailored to address specific dimensions of digital addiction, thereby promoting healthier digital behaviors and overall well-being. Moreover, these scales contribute to advancing research by providing standardized measures that enable comparisons across different populations and settings, ultimately aiding in the development of evidence-based strategies to mitigate digital addiction in the digital age.

Case Study

Background: MJ, a 22-year-old undergraduate student in Bangalore, demonstrates signs of digital addiction, characterized by excessive gaming and frequent social media use. His digital habits are impacting his academic performance and face-to-face interactions with peers.

Assessment: Ranjit Singha, a research fellow at MJ's university, utilizes multidimensional addiction behavior scales to assess MJ's digital addiction. The results highlight high dependence, indicating a higher addictive behaviour.

Intervention Plan

- **Behavioral Dependence:** MJ is supported in creating a balanced schedule that incorporates both study and leisure time. Strategies include setting limits on gaming and social media, encouraging physical activities, and exploring offline hobbies to reduce digital device reliance.

Promoting Flourishing and Resilience

- **Educational Programs:** The university can integrate digital literacy and well-being modules into the curriculum, educating students about responsible digital use and promoting balanced lifestyles.
- **Parental Involvement:** Parents can be engaged through workshops and information sessions to better understand digital addiction and support their children in managing digital use.
- **Policy Development:** The university can implement policies to encourage balanced digital use, including setting screen time limits in academic and res-

idential settings, supporting digital detox initiatives, and providing resources for students seeking help.

- **Community Support:** A supportive community can be cultivated through peer support groups, wellness workshops, and extracurricular activities.

RECOMMENDATIONS AND SOLUTIONS

Addressing digital addiction while promoting flourishing and resilience in the digital age requires a comprehensive and multi-faceted approach. Integrating digital literacy into educational curricula is paramount in equipping students with essential skills to navigate the digital landscape responsibly and promote overall well-being. Comprehensive programs should educate students on recognizing signs of digital addiction and developing strategies for maintaining a healthy digital balance. Critical thinking modules are crucial, empowering students to critically evaluate digital content and understand the manipulative design features of some platforms. Additionally, promoting well-being practices such as mindfulness exercises, physical activities, and social-emotional learning (SEL) helps students manage stress and cultivate resilience in their daily lives. Offering opportunities for non-digital activities that foster creativity, problem-solving, and interpersonal skills further supports a balanced approach to technology use. Utilizing multidimensional addictive behavior scales in schools allows for regular assessment of students' digital habits, facilitating early identification of problematic use patterns. This assessment data can then inform tailored interventions and support services, addressing specific dimensions of digital addiction within the student population effectively. By integrating these strategies into educational frameworks, schools can play a pivotal role in nurturing responsible digital citizenship and promoting flourishing among students in today's digital age.

Parents play a crucial role in guiding their children's digital habits and promoting healthy relationships with technology. To support this, modeling healthy digital behavior is essential—parents should demonstrate balanced screen use and establish clear boundaries for screen time within the family. Engaging in open conversations about the impact of digital media on well-being encourages children to share their experiences and feelings, fostering awareness and communication. Creating a supportive home environment involves designating tech-free times and spaces, such as during meals and family activities, to promote meaningful interactions and reduce screen dependency. Offering alternative activities like outdoor play, reading, and hobbies further enriches children's development beyond digital engagement. Monitoring and guiding digital use through parental controls and age-appropriate content ensures a safe and constructive online experience, while encouraging educational and enriching digital content helps children engage productively with technology.

By implementing these recommendations, parents can effectively nurture responsible digital citizenship and support their children's holistic development in today's digital age.

Policymakers play a pivotal role in addressing digital addiction and promoting healthy digital behaviors within communities. To effectively tackle these challenges, policymakers should prioritize the development and enforcement of regulations that foster transparency from technology companies regarding the addictive potential of their products. This includes advocating for features that encourage responsible usage and mitigate addictive behaviors. Additionally, policymakers can support the integration of digital well-being education into school curricula by allocating funding and resources to these initiatives, ensuring that students receive comprehensive education on responsible digital use. Supporting research initiatives on the impacts of digital addiction and the effectiveness of interventions is crucial, enabling evidence-based policymaking that addresses emerging trends and challenges in digital behavior. Launching public awareness campaigns further enhances community understanding of digital addiction, promoting access to support resources and interventions. By implementing these recommendations, policymakers can create a supportive regulatory framework and educational environment that fosters healthier digital practices and enhances overall well-being in society.

Mental health professionals play a vital role in addressing digital addiction and supporting individuals in developing healthier relationships with technology. To effectively address these challenges, professionals can provide targeted interventions such as cognitive-behavioral therapy (CBT) and other evidence-based treatments tailored to individuals struggling with digital addiction. These therapies focus on identifying and reshaping unhealthy thought patterns and behaviors associated with excessive digital use. Additionally, promoting and developing digital detox programs is essential, offering structured periods of reduced or eliminated digital engagement to help individuals reset their habits and regain control.

Collaboration with educators and parents is also crucial. Mental health professionals can work closely with schools to provide training and resources that enable educators to recognize and address digital addiction among students. Similarly, partnering with parents involves offering guidance on establishing healthy digital boundaries at home and fostering open communication about digital use. Facilitating support groups and workshops can further enhance community support and resilience, providing a forum for individuals and families to share experiences and strategies for managing digital habits and promoting overall well-being. By implementing these recommendations, mental health professionals can play a proactive role in mitigating digital addiction and supporting healthy digital behaviors in their clients and communities.

Comprehensive solutions to address digital addiction and promote holistic well-being encompass a multi-faceted approach across education, community engagement, and technological innovation. First, designing holistic education programs is essential, integrating digital literacy with well-being practices to equip students with the skills and resilience necessary to navigate the digital age responsibly. Project-based learning that combines digital and non-digital elements fosters a balanced educational experience, encouraging critical thinking and creativity while promoting healthy digital habits.

Community initiatives play a crucial role in supporting individuals seeking to reduce digital dependency. Establishing community centers and programs that offer diverse activities and support services can provide alternatives to excessive screen time while promoting overall well-being. Encouraging volunteer opportunities and community service projects further enhances social connections and a sense of purpose beyond digital engagement.

Technological innovations also offer significant potential in mitigating digital addiction. Advocating for the development of digital tools and applications, such as screen time trackers, mindfulness apps, and platforms that facilitate meaningful social interactions, promotes healthy digital usage habits. Additionally, supporting research into emerging technologies that can aid in managing digital addiction and enhancing digital well-being is essential for developing effective interventions and tools. By integrating these comprehensive solutions, stakeholders can collaboratively address the challenges posed by digital addiction, foster healthier digital behaviors, and promote flourishing in individuals and communities in the digital age.

Addressing digital addiction while fostering flourishing and resilience in the digital age is a collective effort that requires the collaboration of educators, parents, policymakers, and mental health professionals. By implementing these recommendations and solutions, we can create a balanced and healthy digital environment where individuals can thrive. This holistic approach ensures that technology serves as a tool for enhancement rather than a source of detriment, ultimately promoting well-being and resilience in an increasingly digital world.

FUTURE RESEARCH DIRECTIONS

As the digital landscape continues to evolve, so too must our understanding and approach to managing digital addiction and promoting flourishing and resilience. Longitudinal studies tracking individuals' digital use patterns over extended periods offer critical insights into the complex dynamics of digital addiction. These comprehensive investigations aim to identify key risk factors contributing to the development of digital addiction, including specific behaviors and personal characteristics that predispose individuals to excessive digital engagement. Concurrently, such studies explore protective factors that mitigate addiction risk, such as robust social support networks and resilient personality traits. Moreover, longitudinal research delves into the long-term outcomes of digital addiction, assessing its impacts on physical health, mental well-being, academic achievement, and social relationships. By uncovering these multifaceted dimensions, longitudinal studies contribute essential knowledge to inform targeted interventions, policies, and educational strategies aimed at mitigating digital addiction and promoting healthier digital behaviors in individuals and communities.

Further research is imperative to assess the effectiveness of interventions aimed at mitigating digital addiction and enhancing well-being in individuals. This research agenda includes conducting comparative studies to evaluate the relative efficacy of diverse intervention types, ranging from cognitive-behavioral therapy (CBT) and mindfulness practices to digital detox programs and educational initiatives. Additionally, exploring tailored approaches that customize interventions based on individual differences such as age, gender, personality traits, and specific aspects of digital addiction will be crucial in optimizing treatment outcomes. Moreover, investigating the potential of technology-based interventions, including digital tools and applications, holds promise in promoting healthier digital habits and providing targeted support to individuals grappling with addiction. By systematically evaluating these interventions, future research can contribute to evidence-based practices that effectively address digital addiction and cultivate resilient digital behaviors in diverse populations.

Understanding the intricate relationship between digital media use and mental health is paramount for future research endeavors. A crucial focus should be on establishing causal links between digital addiction and prevalent mental health issues such as anxiety, depression, and attention disorders. This investigation aims to elucidate whether excessive digital engagement exacerbates these conditions or vice versa, providing clarity for targeted intervention strategies. Additionally, exploring the positive impacts of digital media on mental health is essential. This includes identifying how platforms facilitate supportive online communities, offer accessible teletherapy options, and deliver educational content that enhances mental well-being. Furthermore, research should delve into how digital addiction uniquely impacts vulnerable populations, including children, adolescents, the elderly, and individuals with preexisting mental health conditions. By comprehensively examining these facets, future studies can inform policies, interventions, and digital literacy initiatives that promote mental health resilience and mitigate the adverse effects of digital addiction across diverse demographic groups.

Future research must delve into the socio-cultural dimensions that shape digital addiction and its impact on well-being, highlighting several critical areas of inquiry.

Cross-cultural studies are essential to compare addiction patterns and intervention outcomes across diverse global contexts, identifying both universal factors and culturally specific nuances that influence digital behaviors. Moreover, exploring the socio-economic influences on digital addiction is crucial, examining how disparities in socioeconomic status impact access to digital devices, the prevalence of addiction, and the availability of support resources. Additionally, assessing the effectiveness of policy measures and regulations across different countries is imperative to understand how varying regulatory frameworks influence digital well-being. By investigating these socio-cultural factors comprehensively, future research can contribute valuable insights to develop tailored interventions, policies, and educational initiatives that effectively mitigate digital addiction and promote healthier digital engagement globally.

Advancing our understanding of digital addiction through neurobiological research is essential for developing targeted interventions and strategies. Brain imaging studies utilizing neuroimaging techniques offer a direct window into examining brain activity and structural changes associated with digital addiction, shedding light on how prolonged digital engagement impacts neural circuits and functioning. Investigating neurochemical processes, particularly the role of neurotransmitters like dopamine, provides insights into the reinforcing mechanisms underlying addictive digital behaviors. Furthermore, exploring developmental differences in how digital addiction affects the developing brains of children and adolescents versus adults is crucial. This research can illuminate critical periods of vulnerability and inform age-appropriate interventions and prevention efforts. By synthesizing findings from these neurobiological studies, researchers can elucidate the complex interplay between digital technologies and brain function, paving the way for innovative approaches to mitigate digital addiction and promote healthier digital behaviors across the lifespan.

Understanding the implications of emerging technologies like virtual reality (VR), augmented reality (AR), and artificial intelligence (AI) on digital addiction and overall well-being is crucial as these innovations continue to shape our digital landscape. Research should investigate adoption and usage patterns of these technologies to discern potential addictive behaviors and dependencies that may arise. Additionally, exploring the positive applications of VR, AR, and AI in promoting mental health and cultivating healthy digital habits is essential. These technologies have the potential to enhance therapeutic interventions, educational experiences, and social interactions, thereby contributing positively to well-being. However, it is equally important to address ethical considerations surrounding their use, including privacy concerns, data security risks, and the potential for misuse. By comprehensively studying these aspects, researchers can inform policies and guidelines that maximize the benefits of emerging technologies while minimizing the risks associated with digital addiction and safeguarding user well-being in the evolving digital age.

Investigating effective educational strategies and policy frameworks is crucial for combating digital addiction and fostering positive digital engagement. Future research should focus on developing and testing comprehensive digital literacy and well-being curricula that can be integrated into school systems globally, equipping students with critical skills to navigate the digital landscape responsibly. Understanding the role of parental involvement in preventing digital addiction and promoting healthy digital habits in children is equally important, as parents play a pivotal role in shaping early digital behaviors and habits. Moreover, analyzing the impact of existing policies and regulations on digital addiction rates and well-being outcomes will provide insights into effective policy interventions. By identifying best practices and areas for improvement, this research can inform evidence-based policies that support healthy digital environments and promote resilience in individuals of all ages. Addressing these research directions is essential for harnessing the benefits of technology while mitigating its potential harms, ensuring that digital tools contribute positively to overall well-being in the digital age.

DISCUSSION

The intersection of digital addiction, flourishing, and resilience in the digital age presents a complex yet crucial area for exploration. The pervasive integration of technology into every facet of life necessitates a deeper understanding of how digital tools impact well-being and how individuals can navigate these challenges to thrive.

The concept of digital addiction has garnered significant attention in recent years, reflecting widespread concerns about the potential for technology to dominate lives in detrimental ways. The addictive nature of digital platforms, driven by sophisticated algorithms designed to capture and retain user attention, raises questions about the ethical responsibilities of technology creators and the need for greater regulatory oversight. One key aspect of the discussion is the recognition that not all digital engagement is harmful. The challenge lies in distinguishing between healthy and unhealthy usage patterns. This nuanced perspective is essential for developing balanced approaches to managing digital consumption without demonizing technology.

Educational institutions play a crucial role in combating digital addiction and fostering flourishing among students by integrating essential skills into their curriculum. By incorporating digital literacy and well-being education, schools equip learners with critical tools to navigate the digital landscape responsibly. This comprehensive approach includes raising awareness about the signs and consequences of digital addiction, empowering students to critically assess digital content and identify manipulative design elements. Moreover, education on self-regulation offers practical strategies for managing screen time and digital consumption, promoting healthier habits and balanced use. Integrating well-being practices such as mindfulness and physical activity into daily routines further enhances students' resilience and mental well-being, fostering a holistic approach to navigating digital environments effectively. By integrating these components, educational institutions not only prepare students to engage responsibly with technology but also empower them to thrive in the digital age while maintaining overall well-being.

Multidimensional addictive behavior scales provide a comprehensive framework for understanding digital addiction. By examining behavioral, emotional, cognitive, and social dimensions, these scales offer a holistic view of an individual's relationship with technology. This approach acknowledges that digital addiction is not monolithic and varies widely among individuals.

However, the implementation of these scales requires careful consideration. Ensuring that assessments are culturally sensitive and adaptable to diverse populations is crucial. Additionally, educators and mental health professionals must be adequately trained to interpret results and design effective interventions.

Addressing digital addiction necessitates a multifaceted approach that goes beyond mere reduction of screen time, aiming instead to cultivate supportive environments conducive to overall well-being. Effective interventions include structured Digital Detox Programs, which offer periods of reduced or eliminated digital use to facilitate habit reset and promote healthier routines. Mindfulness and Stress Reduction techniques, such as meditation and yoga, are integral for managing emotional triggers associated with digital addiction, promoting self-awareness and emotional regulation. Cognitive-Behavioral Strategies play a crucial role in reshaping maladaptive thought patterns and behaviors linked to excessive digital use, facilitating cognitive restructuring and behavior modification. Additionally, fostering robust Social Support Networks is essential, encouraging meaningful connections with peers, family members, and the community to provide mutual support, encouragement, and accountability in maintaining balanced digital habits and overall well-being. Integrating these interventions creates a comprehensive framework for addressing digital addiction and promoting sustainable, healthy relationships with digital technology.

The ethical implications of digital addiction extend to various stakeholders, including technology companies, educators, policymakers, and parents. Technology companies must balance innovation with responsibility, designing products that promote healthy usage. Policymakers should consider regulations that protect users, especially vulnerable populations such as children and adolescents.

Parents and educators also bear responsibility for modeling healthy digital behaviors and setting appropriate boundaries. Open communication about digital use and its impacts can foster mutual understanding and cooperative efforts to manage technology's role in daily life.

The rapidly evolving digital landscape necessitates ongoing research and adaptation. Future studies should focus on the long-term impacts of digital addiction and the effectiveness of various interventions. Additionally, exploring the intersection of digital addiction with other mental health issues, such as anxiety and depression, can provide deeper insights into holistic approaches to well-being.

Technological advancements will continue to shape the ways individuals interact with digital media. As such, fostering resilience and flourishing in the digital age requires a dynamic and proactive approach, combining education, assessment, intervention, and policy to create a balanced and healthy digital ecosystem.

The discussion on digital addiction, flourishing, and resilience underscores the importance of a multidimensional approach to understanding and addressing the challenges posed by the digital age. By leveraging comprehensive assessment tools, promoting digital literacy, and fostering supportive environments, we can empower individuals to thrive amidst the pervasive presence of technology. As we navigate the complexities of the digital world, a commitment to well-being and resilience remains paramount, ensuring that technology serves as a tool for enhancement rather than a source of detriment.

CONCLUSION

Cultivating flourishing and resilience in the digital age requires a multifaceted approach that addresses digital addiction through comprehensive assessment and targeted interventions. By utilizing multidimensional addictive behavior scales, educators, parents, and mental health professionals can better understand and mitigate the risks associated with digital addiction, ultimately promoting a healthier and more balanced relationship with technology. In doing so, we pave the way for learners to thrive in an increasingly digital world.

REFERENCES

Abhari, K., Klase, M., Koobchehr, F., Olivares, F., Pesavento, M., Sosa, L., & Vaghefi, I. (2021). Toward a theory of digital mindfulness: a case of Smartphone-Based self-monitoring. In *Lecture notes in computer science* (pp. 549–561). https://doi.org/DOI: 10.1007/978-3-030-77750-0_35

Ardelt, M., & Kingsbury, J. (2024). Wisdom, Virtues, and Well-Being: An Empirical test of Aristotle's Theory of Flourishing. *Topoi*. Advance online publication. DOI: 10.1007/s11245-023-10002-x

Audrin, C., & Audrin, B. (2023). More than just emotional intelligence online: Introducing "digital emotional intelligence.". *Frontiers in Psychology*, *14*. Advance online publication. DOI: 10.3389/fpsyg.2023.1154355 PMID: 37205063

Burr, C., Taddeo, M., & Floridi, L. (2020). The Ethics of Digital Well-Being: A Thematic Review. *Science and Engineering Ethics*, *26*(4), 2313–2343. DOI: 10.1007/s11948-020-00175-8 PMID: 31933119

Cham, S., Algashami, A., Aldhayan, M., McAlaney, J., Phalp, K., Almourad, M. B., & Ali, R. (2019). Digital Addiction: Negative life experiences and Potential for Technology-Assisted Solutions. In *Advances in intelligent systems and computing* (pp. 921–931). https://doi.org/DOI: 10.1007/978-3-030-16184-2_87

Chang, M. L. Y., & Lee, I. O. (2024). Functional connectivity changes in the brain of adolescents with internet addiction: A systematic literature review of imaging studies. *PLOS Mental Health*. Advance online publication. DOI: 10.1371/journal.pmen.0000022

Firth, J., Torous, J., Stubbs, B., Firth, J. A., Steiner, G. Z., Smith, L., Alvarez-Jimenez, M., Gleeson, J., Vancampfort, D., Armitage, C. J., & Sarris, J. (2019). The "online brain": How the Internet may be changing our cognition. *World Psychiatry; Official Journal of the World Psychiatric Association (WPA)*, *18*(2), 119–129. DOI: 10.1002/wps.20617 PMID: 31059635

Goldman, B. (2021, October 29). Addictive potential of social media, explained. *Stanford Medicine*. https://scopeblog.stanford.edu/2021/10/29/addictive-potential-of-social-media-explained/

Gouseti, A., Ilomäki, L., & Lakkala, M. (2024). Re-thinking critical digital literacies in the context of compulsory education. In *Springer eBooks* (pp. 261–281). https://doi.org/DOI: 10.1007/978-3-031-30438-5_15

Grant, D. (2024). How recognized addiction models and our relationships with digital media intersect. In Rich, G. J., Kumar, V. K., & Farley, F. H. (Eds.), *Handbook of media psychology* (pp. 233–245). Springer., DOI: 10.1007/978-3-031-56537-3_12

Han, S.-J., Nagduar, S., & Yu, H.-J. (2023). Digital addiction and related factors among college students. *Health Care*, *11*(22), 2943. DOI: 10.3390/healthcare11222943 PMID: 37998435

Hartogsohn, I., & Vudka, A. (2022). Technology and addiction: What drugs can teach us about digital media. *Transcultural Psychiatry*, *60*(4), 651–661. DOI: 10.1177/13634615221105116 PMID: 35799499

Janicke-Bowles, S. H., Buckley, T. M., Rey, R., Wozniak, T., Meier, A., & Lomanowska, A. (2023). Digital Flourishing: Conceptualizing and assessing positive perceptions of mediated social interactions. *Journal of Happiness Studies*, *24*(3), 1013–1035. DOI: 10.1007/s10902-023-00619-5

Karakose, T., Tülübaş, T., & Papadakis, S. (2022). Revealing the Intellectual Structure and evolution of Digital Addiction Research: An Integrated bibliometric and science mapping approach. *International Journal of Environmental Research and Public Health*, *19*(22), 14883. DOI: 10.3390/ijerph192214883 PMID: 36429603

Kumar, M., Ingale, V. S., Kaur, A., & Bhatia, K. (2023). Consequences of brain health in the digital era. In Battineni, G., Mittal, M., & Chintalapudi, N. (Eds.), *Computational methods in psychiatry* (pp. 123–145). Springer., DOI: 10.1007/978-981-99-6637-0_6

Lim, Z. Y., Yap, J. H., Lai, J. W., Mokhtar, I. A., Yeo, D. J., & Cheong, K. H. (2024). Advancing Lifelong Learning in the Digital Age: A narrative review of Singapore's SkillsFuture programme. *Social Sciences*, *13*(2), 73. DOI: 10.3390/socsci13020073

Marciano, L., & Viswanath, K. (2023). Social media use and adolescents' well-being: A note on flourishing. *Frontiers in Psychology*, *14*. Advance online publication. DOI: 10.3389/fpsyg.2023.1092109 PMID: 37089739

Mehedintu, A., & Soava, G. (2022). A structural framework for assessing the digital resilience of enterprises in the context of the technological revolution 4.0. *Electronics (Basel)*, *11*(15), 2439. DOI: 10.3390/electronics11152439

Mirbahaeddin, E., & Chreim, S. (2024). Transcending technology boundaries and maintaining sense of community in virtual mental health peer support: A qualitative study with service providers and users. *BMC Health Services Research*, *24*(1). Advance online publication. DOI: 10.1186/s12913-024-10943-y PMID: 38658968

Mitsea, E., Drigas, A., & Skianis, C. (2023). Digitally Assisted Mindfulness in Training Self-Regulation Skills for Sustainable Mental Health: A Systematic review. *Behavioral Sciences (Basel, Switzerland)*, *13*(12), 1008. DOI: 10.3390/bs13121008 PMID: 38131865

Montag, C., Sindermann, C., Becker, B., & Panksepp, J. (2016). An Affective Neuroscience Framework for the molecular study of Internet Addiction. *Frontiers in Psychology*, *7*. Advance online publication. DOI: 10.3389/fpsyg.2016.01906 PMID: 28018255

Montgomery, B. L. (2018). Building and sustaining diverse functioning networks using social media and digital platforms to improve diversity and inclusivity. *Frontiers in Digital Humanities*, *5*. Advance online publication. DOI: 10.3389/fdigh.2018.00022

Motz, R., Porta, M., & Reategui, E. (2023). Building resilient educational Systems: the power of digital technologies. In *Lecture notes in educational technology* (pp. 370–383). https://doi.org/DOI: 10.1007/978-981-99-7353-8_28

Park, J. (2024). An examination of why smartphone use gradually leads to addiction. In *Communications in computer and information science* (pp. 394–398). https://doi .org/DOI: 10.1007/978-3-031-61963-2_40

Potenza, M. N. (2013). How central is dopamine to pathological gambling or gambling disorder? *Frontiers in Behavioral Neuroscience*, *7*. Advance online publication. DOI: 10.3389/fnbeh.2013.00206 PMID: 24391562

Qi, C., & Yang, N. (2024). Digital resilience and technological stress in adolescents: A mixed-methods study of factors and interventions. *Education and Information Technologies*. Advance online publication. DOI: 10.1007/s10639-024-12595-1

Ruggeri, K., Garcia-Garzon, E., Maguire, Á., Matz, S., & Huppert, F. A. (2020). Well-being is more than happiness and life satisfaction: A multidimensional analysis of 21 countries. *Health and Quality of Life Outcomes*, *18*(1). Advance online publication. DOI: 10.1186/s12955-020-01423-y PMID: 32560725

Schäfer, S. K., Von Boros, L., Schaubruch, L. M., Kunzler, A. M., Lindner, S., Koehler, F., Werner, T., Zappalà, F., Helmreich, I., Wessa, M., Lieb, K., & Tüscher, O. (2024). Digital interventions to promote psychological resilience: A systematic review and meta-analysis. *NPJ Digital Medicine*, *7*(1). Advance online publication. DOI: 10.1038/s41746-024-01017-8 PMID: 38332030

Scott, D. A., Valley, B., & Simecka, B. A. (2016). Mental health concerns in the digital age. *International Journal of Mental Health and Addiction*, *15*(3), 604–613. DOI: 10.1007/s11469-016-9684-0

Small, G. W., Lee, J., Kaufman, A., Jalil, J., Siddarth, P., Gaddipati, H., Moody, T. D., & Bookheimer, S. Y. (2020). Brain health consequences of digital technology use. *Dialogues in Clinical Neuroscience*, *22*(2), 179–187. DOI: 10.31887/dcns.2020.22.2/gsmall PMID: 32699518

Tereshchenko, S. Y. (2023). Neurobiological risk factors for problematic social media use as a specific form of Internet addiction: A narrative review. *World Journal of Psychiatry*, *13*(5), 160–173. DOI: 10.5498/wjp.v13.i5.160 PMID: 37303928

Vargas-Nieto, J., Zambrano, D., Montorio, I., & Sanabria, L. M. (2024). Efficacy of Digital Mindfulness-Based Interventions for Repetitive Negative Thinking: A Systematic review and Bibliometric analysis. *Mindfulness*, *15*(3), 523–538. DOI: 10.1007/s12671-024-02321-w

Wang, G., Simkute, D., & Griskova-Bulanova, I. (2023). Neurobiological Link between Stress and Gaming: A Scoping Review. *Journal of Clinical Medicine*, *12*(9), 3113. DOI: 10.3390/jcm12093113 PMID: 37176554

Zarate, D., Stavropoulos, V., Ball, M., De Sena Collier, G., & Jacobson, N. C. (2022). Exploring the digital footprint of depression: A PRISMA systematic literature review of the empirical evidence. *BMC Psychiatry*, *22*(1). Advance online publication. DOI: 10.1186/s12888-022-04013-y PMID: 35733121

KEY TERMS AND DEFINITIONS

Behavioral addiction: Conceptualizes addiction as a pattern of behavior involving repeated engagement despite negative consequences, similar to substance addiction.

Biopsychosocial model: Framework that considers biological, psychological, and social factors in understanding health and illness.

Digital addiction: Compulsive use of digital devices and platforms leading to negative consequences such as impaired functioning and reduced well-being.

Flourishing: State of thriving characterized by positive emotions, engagement, relationships, meaning, and accomplishment in life.

Multidimensional Addictive Behavior Scales: are comprehensive tools that assess various aspects of addictive behaviors, including behavioral, emotional, cognitive, and social dimensions, to provide a nuanced understanding of addiction.

Resilience: Capacity to adapt positively to adversity, trauma, or stress, maintaining stable functioning and bouncing back from setbacks.

Self-determination theory: Focuses on intrinsic motivation and the fulfillment of psychological needs for autonomy, competence, and relatedness in behavior regulation.

Social learning theory: Theory emphasizing learning through observation, modeling, and reinforcement of behaviors observed in others within social contexts.

Chapter 4
Creativity and Critical Thinking in Students Through Non-Traditional Teaching Methods

Mohit Yadav
https://orcid.org/0000-0002-9341-2527
JGBS, O.P. Jindal Global University, India

Pankaj Jain
SGT University, Gurugram, India

Rajeev Goyal
Sat Kabir Institute of Technology and Management, Bahadurgarh, India

Ajay Chandel
https://orcid.org/0000-0002-4585-6406
Lovely Professional University, India

Ta Huy Hung
https://orcid.org/0009-0008-6835-3036
International School, Vietnam National University, Hanoi, Vietnam

ABSTRACT

This study investigates the impact of non-traditional teaching methods on students' creativity and critical thinking. A case study approach was employed to delve into a specific educational context. Data were collected through interviews, observations, and document analysis. Qualitative and quantitative data were analyzed to explore the relationship between teaching methods and student outcomes. Findings

DOI: 10.4018/979-8-3693-0997-1.ch004

suggest that non-traditional approaches, such as project-based and problem-based learning, can significantly enhance students' creative and critical thinking abilities. However, successful implementation requires adequate teacher training and institutional support. Further research is needed to generalize findings to diverse educational settings.

INTRODUCTIONS

The educational landscape is shifting under their feet. A period of such technological change, kaleidoscopic pace of globalization, and increasing complexity of societal problems are elements that put many pedagogies on the spot. It's an age where developing creativity and critical thinking goes beyond educational ambitions; rather, they have become imperative skills for people to survive in a world of rising complexity. These cognitive competencies form the basic platform for problem-solving, innovation, and informed citizenship.

For this, education over the past few centuries has been based largely on teacher-centered instruction, rote memorization, and rather monolithic assessments (Elenany, 2023). These methods, while undoubtedly helpful in gaining knowledge, are far from doing enough to promote higher-order thinking. A focus on uniformity and compliance could inadvertently suppress creativity, while rigid adherence to laid-down curricula may thwart the fostering of critical analysis. Furthermore, a fast-changing world makes transmission of static knowledge increasingly obsolete (Vimbelo, 2023).

Creativity and Critical Thinking: The Stanchions of 21st Century Learning

Creativity can be referred to as the ability to come up with relevant unique ideas; it is the prime factor in any innovation or solution to a problem. It encompasses divergent thinking, imagination, and the penchant to challenge the traditional order of things. Critical thinking refers to systematic analysis of information and evidence followed by the formation of reasoned judgment (Graham, 2012; Forrester, 2009). It is a repertoire of problem-solving skills, decision-making, and metacognition. Both these cognitive skills are interdependent and self-reinforcing. They are the basic constituents of a flexible, adaptive, and resilient mindset.

The Role of Non-Traditional Teaching Methods

A paradigm shift in teaching methodologies is needed to foster creativity and critical thinking. Non-traditional teaching methods, that is, teaching methods which depart from the conventional lecture format, open promising avenues for developing these basic skills (París & Hay, 2019; Kaplan, 2019). Such methods can easily establish a learning environment that can enhance the aforementioned skills by allowing students to explore, question, and work together (Aznia et al., 2022; Anggraeni, 2020; Hutchison et al., 2020; Gusti & Ratnawulan, 2021).

THE RESEARCH GAP

While there has been a growing body of literature pointing out the importance of creativity and critical thinking, there is less researched evidence explaining what part non-traditional teaching methods have on these cognitive abilities. Much research focuses on interventions in isolation or age ranges and provides small generalizations. Again, it is requisite to make a strong case for further, more rigorous research in developing robust methodologies that could identify causal claims between student outcomes and non-traditional teaching methods.

Study Objectives

The current research endeavours to assess whether the non-traditional methods of teaching would bring about an increase in creativity and the rise of critical thinking in students.

Precisely, effectiveness will be researched about some non-traditional methods of teaching, such as project-based learning, problem-based learning, inquiry-based learning, and gamification, in terms of enhancing creativity and critical thinking; this research will also check how far such methods have a positive impact on students' motivation, engagement, and learning outcome. This study will identify the factors influencing successful implementation of the non-traditional teaching methods and provide educators with practical recommendations who wish to implement these in their classrooms. Such research questions would allow this study to contribute meaningfully to the new body of knowledge that views the non-traditional teaching method as positively related to creativity and critical thinking. The findings could help further policy and practice reformation towards more innovative and effective learning environments.

LITERATURE REVIEW

The place of creativity in enhancing critical thinking has been engaged in contemporary discourse within education. Creativity, as the capacity to come up with original, relevant ideas, is considered the cornerstone of innovation and problem-solving (Widiastuti, 2023). It provides the catalyst for one to come up with many solutions, generate divergent thinking, imagine, and challenge the status quo. On the other hand, critical thinking is the component of which systemic information analysis, evaluation of evidence, and formation of reasoned judgments form the rational bases for the decision-making and problem-solving processes (Prayogi, 2024). In fact, cognitive skills are not independent but interrelate and reinforce one another. Traditional pedagogical methods, so often based on teacher-centered practices that included rote learning and standardized assessment tools, have received ever-increasing criticism for the little that could be gained toward the ends of developing these higher-order thinking skills. A growing body of literature advocates for educational environments centered on the development of these very higher-order thinking skills; chief among these is Sternberg, 2008. In reaction, there has been recent spate interest in alternative pedagogical methods straying from the traditional lecture format (Tila, 2023). Such learning methods, which include project-based, problem-based, and inquiry-based learning, complemented by gamification, are some of the promising ways of developing creativity and critical thinking. For example, in project-based learning, Thomas & Brown, 2007, it is noted that students improve their problem-solving skills, creativity, and ability to collaborate. This method gives students hands-on involvement in real projects, enabling them to develop critical thinking where they are required to analyze information and give innovative solutions. Similarly, problem-based learning has been associated with enhanced development of critical thinking, problem-solving, and self-directed learning (Hmelo-Silver, 2004).

In this approach, students are introduced to problems that pre-exist in the real world. This will entice them to evaluate complex situations by making hypotheses and finding information to solve the problem at hand. Inquiry-based learning is student-centered discovery and inquiry and has been linked with enhanced creativity and critical thinking (Colliver, 2000). This approach assists learners in developing curiosity, analysis, and the ability to devise new ideas by allowing the learners to formulate their own questions and find answers independently. Gamification refers to the application of elements characteristic of game design in non-game contexts, which has been lauded as a tool that possesses the potential for increasing motivation, engaging students in learning, and enhancing problem-solving skills (Kaplan, 2019). Gamification can motivate students towards creative thinking, collaboration, and the will to keep at it in the face of an obstacle, due to the challenging and rewarding experience created for learning. Literature, on the other hand, shows that non-traditional teaching methods actually do work to foster creativity and critical thinking; however, several challenges and limitations exist on the way to their application. For instance, implementation of the above-mentioned methods requires extensive teacher training and support (Lin, 2011). Moreover, creativity and critical thinking are complex constructs that are difficult to measure objectively; hence, their assessment can become quite complicated. Moreover, the efficiency of non-traditional teaching methods may be influenced by different factors, such as students' characteristics, subject matter, and classroom context. Despite these challenges, the research evidence indicates that these non-traditional teaching methods have a role in enhancing creativity and critical thinking. These methods may help create learning environments in which innovation, critical analysis, and lifelong learning are nurtured because they provide learners with exploratory, inquiry, and problem-solving opportunities (Cremin et al., 2006). It is because educators continue to seek innovative ways through which students are to be prepared for the challenges of the 21st century; non-traditional teaching methods offer another way forward.

RESEARCH METHOD: CASE STUDY APPROACH

Research Design: Case Study

Given that the relationship between non-traditional teaching methods, creativity, and critical thinking is complex, a case study approach would be most suitable for this research. It will give a clear in-depth study of a certain education setting to clearly understand the phenomenon being studied. The research work will be confined to one particular school or classroom, which will make it possible to tease out nuances of implementation, challenges, and outcomes.

Case Selection

Several criteria are, therefore, going to guide the selection of the case:

- **Implementation of Non-Traditional Methods:** The school or classroom chosen for the study has to be one with a well-established record in the implementation of a number of non-traditional methods of teaching.
- **Institutional Support:** An institution with a supportive environment that allows innovation and experimentation will be selected.
- **Teacher Expertise:** There has to be a teacher or teachers who have strong pedagogical skills and adhere to student-centered learning.

- **Student Diversity:** The case should represent a diverse student population to enhance generalizability.

Methods of Data Collection

A mixed-method approach will be used to collect data.

Qualitative Data:

- **In-depth Interviews:** Semi-structured interviews will be conducted with teachers, students, and administrators on the concept of creativity and critical thinking, and their perceptions on non-traditional ways of teaching.
- **Observations:** Classroom observations will be conducted to capture the teaching and learning processes, focusing on the implementation of non-traditional methods and student engagement.
- **Document Analysis:** The document analysis would draw its sources from the lesson plans, students' work, and school policies. It will further enrich the context of the study.

Quantitative Data:

- **Creativity and Critical Thinking Assessments:** It will be administered to students. These tests would be standardized to assess creativity and critical thinking.
- **Student Achievement Data:** Student achievement data will be collected on academic performance to create a relationship with the outcome of non-traditional teaching methods.

DATA ANALYSIS

Thematic analysis will be conducted on qualitative data in an attempt to find patterns and themes, especially the effects, if any, related to creativity, critical thinking, and non-traditional teaching methods. Statistics will be done on quantitative data in order to find the relationships of variables. The credibility and trustworthiness of the findings will be improved through triangulation from multiple sources.

Ethical Considerations

The research process shall be done considering the stiff adherence to ethical guidelines. Participants shall be informed on the purpose of the study, procedures, and the likely risks and benefits. Informed consent shall be sought from all participants, and confidentiality assured through the use of pseudonyms.

The research will adopt a case study approach that combines both qualitative and quantitative methods with the objective of enhancing an in-depth understanding of how non-traditional teaching methods would relate to creativity and critical thinking.

Case Studies

Case Study: Green Valley High School

This paper provides a case study on how non-traditional teaching methods will be implemented to achieve creativity and critical thinking among students at Green Valley High School, a public school in a suburban setting. In the past three years, the school has moved toward the adoption of PBL, flipped classrooms, and experiential learning to ensure high engagement of students with better learning outcomes (Tanana, 2022). In this mixed-method study, quantitative and qualitative data were obtained from the surveys and academic performance metrics, and in-depth interviews were conducted with students, teachers, and parents.

It introduced project-based learning into science and humanities classes, where students worked on long-term projects focused on solving real-world problems by working in teams and making presentations on their findings. For example, a biology class tasked students with researching environmental problems that exist within their community, proposing solutions, and then making presentations of their projects to stakeholders in the community. In the flipped classroom, video lessons took the place of traditional lectures that learners watched at home, while class time was dedicated to discussions, problem-solving activities, and hands-on experiments mostly in mathematics and language arts courses (Vass, 2024). There were also experiential learning opportunities through field trips, internships, and service-learning projects, where students would gain practical experiences and help them develop critical thinking.

These resulted in huge improvements in academic performance and engagement Visible increases were noted in scores for standardized tests, especially in areas where non-traditional methods were in use. Average math scores increased by 15% within two years. Engagement metrics went up as well: a rise of 10% in attendance rates and a decline in disciplinary incidents of 20% indicate students' higher motivation. On the other hand, qualitative data indicate that students enjoyed learning and found it relevant; teachers observed an enhanced problem-solving ability and creativity among the learners; and parents noticed a change in attitude towards school and learning among their children (Huong, 2022).

Notwithstanding these positive results, a number of challenges were faced. The application of non-traditional methods was extraordinarily time- and resource-intensive in terms of both planning and teaching time, and the support of teachers was required for its implementation. The process of assessment for creativity and critical thinking was cumbersome, with the development of relevant assessment tools being a continuing challenge (Xu et al., 2017). Some teachers and learners initially also resiliently reacted to the new pedagogies; hence, constant professional development and support were required to overcome this form of resistance.

The example of Green Valley High School is very revealing about using non-traditional teaching methods. This helps in enhancing creativeness and critical thinking in children. There are also some challenges associated with the methods, but enhanced student engagement and improved academic performance, coupled with the nurturing of some key skills, make these methods very worthwhile (Khairnar, 2015). Recommendations include ongoing professional development of teachers, adequate allocation of resources, development and improvement of assessment tools, and involvement of stakeholders in planning and implementation to drum up support and reduce resistance. This case example shows how non-traditional teaching methods really can effect change in education and meet the students' needs for the 21st century.

Case Study: Innovative Teaching Methods at Lincoln Middle School

This case study, conducted in a very urban school with demographic changes at Lincoln Middle School, assesses the impacts of such innovative teaching methods on student creativity and critical thinking. The school introduced several non-traditional methods of teaching—inquiry-based learning, gamification, and interdisciplinary projects—within a two-year period. This study adopted both student and teacher surveys, analysis of students' academic performance, and classroom observations to generate data (Eli, 2021).

Two classes teach; inquiry-based learning is in both science and social studies. In inquiry-based learning, students will ask their questions, find answers, and delve into the subject through experiments with hands-on experience. An example would be during social studies; the students will examine historical events through primary source analysis and reenact major events for a deeper understanding and critical analysis. Mathematics and language arts were gamified through the incorporation of gaming activities (Dung, 2024). This was facilitated by the use of digital platforms, which served in enhancing the learning process by creating better engagement and interactivity. Students gained more points and rewards by completing the challenges, hence encouraged and enhanced participation.

Such ideas are incorporated into the interdisciplinary projects that the students are designed to challenge in the knowledge of several disciplines in a way of their integrated form and, therefore, their application in the context of everyday life which is a learning experience. An example of these projects was for students to design a sustainable urban space that would call for students' demonstration of a knowledge of mathematics, science, geography, and art (Subramanian & Kelly, 2018). Students could then take these projects into the school-wide exhibition whereby students' work can be shared and commented upon by other students and the community.

Quantitative data showed significant improvements in student performance and engagement. The science and mathematics test scores improved by an average of 12 percent, attendance rates by 8 percent. Disciplinary incidents had also lessened by 15%, so, presumably, the intervention might have impacted student behavior and the school climate. At the qualitative level, students reported that they enjoyed learning more than before and it was more meaningful. Many have also gained more confidence in their problem-solving and creative abilities (Zhou et al., 2020). Teachers reported increased student engagement and more acting on their own initiative, greater interest in learning. Parents agreed to the positive change of attitude in children and appreciated practical competencies achieved by those methods.

Despite all the successes, several challenges were faced. The shift to non-traditional methods required a great deal of professional development by the teachers to refocus instructional strategies. Gamification and digital tools also demanded extra resources and technical support. It was quite a challenge to assess the results of interdisciplinary projects and inquiry learning because traditional evaluation tools were not easily applicable (Keinänen & Kairisto-Mertanen, 2019). Moreover, some of the students had difficulties in choosing topics of their interest at first because they were more used to a higher level of direction and thus needed extra support and help in these areas.

The example of Lincoln Middle School will illustrate very clearly that through innovative teaching methods, a lot can be done to enhance creativity and critical thinking in students' minds (Du, 2023). Though much effort and resources are needed to make a changeover to such teaching modes, increased student engagement, improved academic performance, and development of critical 21st-century skills repay off the benefits. Some other key recommendations to be taken up further would be constant training of the teachers, investment in needed resources and technology, developing proper assessment tools, and support for students to adjust to new learning techniques (Guo, 2023). This case study exemplifies the transformational power of non-traditional teaching techniques in the education of students for future challenges and opportunities.

Case Study: Transformative Learning at Horizon High School

This case study identifies the implementation and effects of non-traditional teaching methods within Horizon High School, a rural public school that strives to increase creativity and critical thinking skills among its students (Du, 2023). Within the past three years, this school has adopted a few innovative practices, including blended learning, design thinking, and outdoor education, in order to make the environment within which learning takes place more engaging and effective. Data were gathered from an analysis of academic performance, student and teacher surveys, and interviews with key informants (Elbahri et al., 2018).

This meant that a blend of online and face-to-face instruction at the school level was developed with specific emphasis on STEM subjects. In this approach, students covered digital content and interactive modules at their own pace, while the classroom time was used for collaborative projects and teachers' personalized support. This provided for differentiated instruction and diverse ways of learning. In the design thinking process, students worked on complex problems where the solutions were not fixed, using a method with stages of empathy, ideation, prototyping, and testing. In the example of an art class, for instance, students designed and created functional sculptures that catered to the needs of the community, thus enhancing creativity and problem-solving skills (Bawuro et al., 2018).

Outdoor education was another key component, utilizing the school's rural setting to offer experiential learning. These included studies on ecology, team-building exercises, and agricultural projects that helped students relate classroom teachings to real-life situations. One such innovation was when students worked on initiating and constantly improving a school garden, thereby relating this to their biology, environmental science, and nutrition classes (Séin-Echaluce et al., 2019).

Quantitative results showed marked improvements in academic performance and student engagement. On average, test scores in STEM fields increased by 14 percent, with overall attendance rates up 9 percent. In addition, there was an 18 percent reduction in disciplinary incidents, which indicates a better school climate as well. At the same time, qualitative feedback emphasized that students described learning as more relevant and fun, with many of them having become more confident about improving creative and critical thinking. Teachers reported students to be more motivated and engaged, which was manifested through active participation in discussions and group work (Du, 2023; Guo, 2023). Parents have also seen, in turn, an improvement in attitudes towards school and an appreciation for the practical skills learned through these approaches.

On the other side, are challenges that come with the implementation of non-traditional methodologies. The shift towards blended learning entailed heavy investments in technology and infrastructure with constant technical support to match.

Bringing design thinking and outdoor education into the classrooms required quite a huge degree of professional growth and investment in teachers, while assessing the feedback of these more recent methodologies was also complex and needed to develop new evaluative tools and metrics. Some students found it hard to engage in self-directed learning entailed by the blended and experiential learning—especially if they weren't used to that level of autonomy—and thus needed further support and guidance on these matters.

The example of Horizon High School is an illustration that such non-traditional teaching methods can be very good for creativity and critical thinking at very high levels in school children, even in rural settings (Liu, 2023) This certainly calls for a lot of hard work and resources, but the benefits resulting from improved academic achievement, heightened student engagement, and the development of these 21st-century skills validate the investment. This includes recommendations for sustained professional development of teachers in the future, continued investment in necessary technology and infrastructure, development of robust assessment tools, and support structures for students adjusting to new learning paradigms. The case emphasizes how innovative methods of teaching can really make a difference in transforming learners to become better prepared for challenges and opportunities lying ahead (Li et al., 2021).

Case Study: Creative Learning at Maplewood Elementary School

This is a case study on the effect of non-traditional teaching methods on developing creativity and critical thinking at Maplewood Elementary School, a diverse urban school known for its interest in innovative education. In the past two years, it has adopted art integration, mindfulness practices, and maker spaces with an aim of making the learning environment much more dynamic and engaging. Data were obtained from academic performance indicators, student and teacher surveys, and observations in class performance.

Arts integration was taken to almost all subjects, wherein teachers integrated music, visual arts, drama, and dance. For example, in history class, students were asked to create theatre performances that had to show some historical content. This allowed them to engage themselves in a deeper understanding and involvement with whatever was being taught. In math, students used visual arts to represent some geometric concepts, which helped them create an even deeper understanding by expressing themselves through such means. It introduced mindfulness practices and ways of developing focusing, emotional regulation, and stress management skills. This involved daily mindfulness sessions that included breathing exercises and guided meditations for setting up a calm and conducive learning environment.

It introduced students to maker spaces that allowed them to engage hands-on in STEAM. The spaces are equipped with tools, materials, and technology that allow students to get involved in building robots, creating art installations, and designing simple machines. Experimentation, problem-solving, and collaborative learning characteristics of the maker spaces foster creativity and critical thinking (Du, 2023; Guo, 2023).

Quantitative data showed marked improvements in student performance and engagement. Test scores in subjects using arts integration increased 10 percent, and the overall attendance rate climbed 7 percent. On the other hand, disciplinary incidents were down by 15 percent, thus portraying a more affirmative and focused school climate. Students further responded to have found learning much more enjoyable and meaningful. Many said they gained confidence in creating and solving problems (Guo, 2023). The teachers reported that there was increased engagement, involvement, and interest shown by students, as well as a serious investment in their learning. Parents, too, reported changes in the attitudes of children towards schools and recognized the practical and creative skills gained from these methods (Zulkifli & Azman, 2021).

Notwithstanding, there were a good number of challenges faced: arts integration took extensive professional development on the part of teachers so that they could understand how to work arts intelligently into their lesson plans; establishing and maintaining maker spaces took a huge investment in resources, materials, and technology; introducing mindfulness practices took training for teachers and students alike to know how to execute these techniques in ways that would help the students realize the most benefit; assessment of their outcomes was challenging because it took the development of new tools to measure and evaluate.

The case of Maplewood Elementary School proves that creativity and critical thinking in children can be effectively enhanced by methods not traditional in teaching. Though the shift is very resource- and labor-intensive, additional advantages in terms of raising student interest and improving academic achievement, coupled with the development of crucial skills, make this approach very worthwhile. Some of the recommendations that would be foreseen in its future implementations are teacher professional development, further investment in needed resources and technology, development of robust assessment tools, and support for students and teachers adjusting to new practices (Bawuro et al., 2018). This case therefore highlights how innovative teaching methods can really make a difference in setting learners up to meet the challenges and harness opportunities of the future.

Case Analysis Combined

These four case studies, from Green Valley High School, Lincoln Middle School, Horizon High School, and Maplewood Elementary School, all point to non-traditional teaching methods as the catalysts needed in building creativity and critical thinking skills within each student. That is to say, although each school implemented very specific strategies to suit their unique context, there exist common themes and outcomes that help to shed light on both the effectiveness and challenges of such an innovative educational strategy.

Shared Approaches and Strategies

Project-Based Learning and Inquiry-Based Learning

Both Green Valley High and Lincoln Middle integrated project-based learning and inquiry-based learning. This was done to engage students with real-world issues, develop collaborative work, enhance critical thinking, and further develop creativity. In this way, students could gain ownership of their learning, apply knowledge in practice, and design solutions for complex problems (Forbes, 2021).

Blended Learning and Flipped Classrooms

Horizon High and Green Valley High ran blended learning and flipped classrooms where digital content was integrated with face-to-face instruction. It enabled differentiated instruction, serviced unique learning styles, and ensured maximum classroom interaction time for deeper explorations and problem-solving activities (Jalinus et al., 2017).

Experiential and Outdoor Education

Experiential learning, from outdoor education at Horizon High to make spaces at Maplewood Elementary, provided students with opportunities to engage firsthand in the application of theory learned within the classroom. Experimentation and creativity joined critical thinking as skills that were encouraged through practical experiences and group projects (Hanipah et al., 2019).

Arts Integration and Mindfulness Practices

Maplewood Elementary provided arts integration and mindfulness practices focused on the well-rounded development of the student. Through the practice of integrating arts into different subjects, there was a higher degree of engagement and insight into the curriculum. Mindfulness practices help students with their focus, feeling self-regulation, and a conducive learning environment (Kokotsaki et al., 2016).

Positive Outcomes

Improved Academic Performance

All four schools indicated that the students' improvement in academic performance was at a noticeable level, particularly where non-traditional approaches had been implemented. Test scores in math, science, the humanities, and arts significantly improved, thus showing the effectiveness of such methods in enhancing learning outcomes (Mamuaja, 2023).

Improved Student Engagement and Attendance

This was evident through increased attendance rates and reduced disciplinary cases in all schools. The students found learning more enjoyable and relevant; thus, they were more engaged and motivated.

Increased Creativity and Critical Thinking

Among the 21st-century skills acquired by the students were those of creativity, critical thinking, and problem-solving, among others. These skills were enhanced through hands-on projects and solving real-life problems and products that involved creative expression (Gao, 2012).

Issues and Solutions

Resource Intensiveness and Training

The methods and approaches of increasing non-traditional methodologies were very resource intensive. This includes technology, materials, and teacher professional development. Ways needed to be found for its continual support and training for its effective implementation and sustainability (Wanyama & Singh, 2015).

Assessment Complexity

Traditional methods of assessment were found to be insufficient to measure the creativity and critical thinking developed by students. New ways of evaluation tools and metrics needed to be developed to measure the new learning outcomes that the innovative approaches to teaching achieved (Spendlove & Best, 2018).

Resistance to Change

In particular, the slow movement of some teachers and students showed a gradual change associated with full support. Professional development, continuous stakeholder engagement, and clear communication were the means for the struggle against resistance and the building up of acceptance.

Recommendations

Manpower Development

With constant investment in professional development, the teachers will be imbued with the proper skills and knowledge that will allow them to adopt and eventually sustain the use of non-traditional teaching methodologies.

Resource Allocation

Innovative strategies in education require proper resources and infrastructure. Therefore, the schools should invest in technology, materials, and support systems so these new strategies are effectively applied.

Robust Assessment Tools

The development and refinement of assessment tools validly measuring creativity, critical thinking, and other essential competencies will help assess the quality of non-traditional methods and continuous improvement.

Engage Stakeholders

Bringing students, parents, and the general community into the planning and implementation process may be able to maximally bring out support while minimizing resistance. Clear communication with stakeholders and seeking their active engagement are essential for successful adoption and sustainability of a particular intervention.

In sum, it is clear that case studies reflect that non-traditional teaching methods raise creativity and critical thinking among students. Improved academic performance, increased students' engagement, and developing skills that are important for life justify the investment in such innovative approaches despite challenges. A school could both implement and sustain non-traditional pedagogies by addressing challenges via professional development, resource allocation, robust assessment tools, and stakeholder engagement. It would give students the capacity to navigate complexity and opportunity in the 21st century.

DISCUSSION

The findings of the current investigation had to recall the transformative capacity of non-conventional pedagogies to make students' creative and critical thinking come alive. Through the application of case studies, it was shown how PBL or project-based learning, inquiry-based learning, gamification, and experiential education can all contribute highly to the bestowing of 21st-century skills, namely, problem-solving, collaboration, and adaptive thinking skills on the students. These methods lead to better performance and more interesting and student-centered processes of learning, thus removing the handicaps of traditional teacher-centered pedagogy.

One of the most significant strategies for stimulating creative and critical thinking was project-based learning (PBL). PBL allows students to take a central role in real life-problems that require them to work cooperatively. PBL hence gives learners space for exploration of the diversity of possible solutions and contributes to the application of knowledge to the world outside the classroom. In schools such as Green Valley High, where PBL has been incorporated into the science and humanities curriculum, the students have shown tremendous improvement in problem-solving capacity and also in creative output. The learning pattern also helps the student to learn and take ownership of the subject he or she has been learning; this helped them get more deeply involved in the study of the subject and increase their motivation towards it.

Students who had been trained by inquiry-based learning method were at most times facilitated to critically at times to ask questions, do research and attempt to draw conclusions, based on evidence. This approach, used at Lincoln Middle School, allowed the student to take ownership of his study of subject matter through research and experimentation. An important mechanism in developing the culture of curiosity and reflection-beliefs that underpin critical thinking-it also helped in making students more analytical as they work through challenging problems.

Gamification inside the classroom created further engagement and motivation. Especially in mathematics and language arts subjects, gamification elements such as points, challenges, and rewards enabled an interactive learning climate that motivated learners to do their best for their tasks. At Lincoln Middle School, for example, the case study revealed that with gamified learning, students not only improved in grades but also in their behavior. The students were showing better interest in class material, and there were fewer cases of disruptive behavior.

Experiential education, particularly outdoor and field-based learning was shown to produce students who clearly held strong correlates between theory and practice. Horizon High School students engaged in outdoor education and design thinking projects. By working on open-ended real-world challenges, the processes of these skills allowed students to combine whatever they were learning in the classroom with practical applicability, thereby making learning more relevant and impactful. It further solidified the creative and critical thinking of the students.

Although these inventions have encountered success, there are also some problems inhibiting the implementation of new approaches. Firstly, the processes consume a lot of resources. Schools require substantial financial investments in order to offer the required infrastructure, technology, and materials. Moreover, there is significant professional development need for teachers when transitioning from the traditional approaches since many are not prepared for the challenges of the new pedagogies. Training and constant support act as the prerequisites to prepare teachers for dealing with non-traditional methods.

Creative and critical thinking is yet another assessment challenge as standardized test designs do not so well apply to the outcome assessment of these skills. More sophisticated and flexible tools for a better grasp of assessing complexity in skills, such as problem solving, innovation and collaborative thinking, will be important to create because tracking the development of students and determining the effectiveness of non-traditional teaching methods would go a long way.

While non-traditional teaching presents several challenges, the advantages of enriching creativity, critical thinking, and engagement stand higher than those difficulties. The resources schools can invest, improving teachers' training, and discovering new tools for assessing learning will provide academies with classrooms which, in turn, will help students be better prepared to face the complexity of the 21st century.

RECOMMENDATIONS AND SUGGESTIONS

1. Teacher Professional Development

Implementing the alternative forms of teaching would require great training for teachers, ensuring the attainment of skills needed to effectively embrace the alternative forms of teaching. Continuous professional development programs should be availed to target such methods as project-based learning, inquiry-based learning, gamification, and blended learning. Through this, the educators would continue to perfect their approaches and find ways of dealing with potential problems and become confident in innovative teaching practices.

2. Adequate Resource Allocations

Often, innovative teaching methodologies require resource inputs: technology, materials, and even infrastructural supporting systems. A school should appropriate resources to provide digital platforms for blended learning, materials for maker spaces, and experiential learning equipment. A school will establish such techniques only if there is an allocation of sufficient funds along with technical backup so that these innovative strategies are applicable and long-term sustainable.

3. Comprehensive Toolkit for Appraisal

The traditional evaluation methods tend to fall apart when creativity and critical thinking are involved. Thus, there is a need for sound evaluative measures that can assess these skills. So, schools and teachers need to come together to formulate more valid measures than the traditional test. These tools will prove helpful for a cross-section of subjects and contexts.

4. Stakeholder Support and Involvement

Introducing new modes of teaching requires the participation of various stakeholders: the parents, the administrators, and members of the broader community. Highlighting clearly how benefits in terms of goals are achieved can facilitate garnering support instead of resistance to change. Involving stakeholders in the preparation as well as application process can make them turn into positives concerning the changes that need to be made; the environment will be more welcoming to innovation.

5. Support and Counseling for Students

For instance, students need some time to settle into and become self-reliant in the more student-centered methods of learning like inquiry or project-based learning. More system support would be needed to anchor these transition periods. Providing scaffolding, mentoring, and guidance can provide the students with the comfort of their own skills while settling into more non-traditional approaches.

6. Perpetual Investment in Technology and Infrastructure

Blended learning, gamification, and other new digital-based teaching methods rely significantly on the technological infrastructure. Schools thus have to make long-term investments in state-of-the-art technology in order that students and their teachers are able to use proper digital tools and platforms. Proper technological support is also a precursor of an effective learning environment, which necessitates scheduled updates and technical support.

IMPLICATIONS

Theoretical Implications

The findings from four case studies add to extant educational theory by providing empirical evidence supporting the effectiveness of non-traditional teaching methods in enhancing creativity and critical thinking (Vass, 2024). These include project-based learning, inquiry-based learning, blended learning, arts integration, and experiential education. While all these are very much different from one another, as they comply with constructivist theories of learning about active and student-centered learning in the construction of knowledge through experience, successful implementation and positive results reinforce theories arguing for holistic and integrated approaches toward education against traditional teacher-centered paradigms. Moreover, the development of instruments for assessment underscores the need to extend theoretical constructs in education to include a way of measuring creative and critical thinking.

Practical Implications

The case studies provide concrete lessons for practitioners and school heads who might want to adopt these non-traditional approaches to teaching. Documented successes underscore the need for professional development, resources, and stakeholders' buy-in in an enabling environment. Schools can introduce blended learning and flipped classroom models to accommodate different styles of learning and to enable maximum interaction within the class setup. Arts and mindfulness practices may be introduced to focus the attention of children and toward the emotional well-being of children for providing a better learning environment (Anggraeni, 2020). Further, maker spaces and outdoor education can be created for providing hands-on and experiential learning in a way that bridges theoretical knowledge to grassroots application levels. These are, in most cases, practical strategies that can be tailored and adapted into different educational contexts to attain or realize similar positive outcomes.

Societal Implications

The enhancement of creativity and critical thinking through these non-traditionalist methods of teaching has deep implications for society. Indeed, as education systems all over the world strive to ready students for the increasingly complex and dynamic world, the fostering of such skills is imperative. Such creativity and critical skills will more readily equip learners to function in and be significant contributors to a fast-changing global economy (Huong, 2022). They will be more creative, adaptable, and able to solve complex problems—major attributes for future leaders, entrepreneurs, and professionals. Moreover, emphasis on holistic development—including emotional regulation and mindfulness—will set a proper base for the well-being of students, which would mean mental health and resilience. They can become the agents of change and innovation when they enter the workforce and society, iParamorially addressing some of the larger challenges to society with creative, critical solutions.

Managerial Implications

School managers and the policymakers could learn from the case studies in effectively implementing and sustaining non-traditional teaching methods in schools. The initiative would have to be strategically planned, resources should be carefully allocated, and sustained support should be given to teachers and students (Hutchison et al., 2020). At the same time, one has to make those much-needed investments in professional development so that teachers are better equipped. However, with regard to leadership, getting technology and infrastructure for these future models of schooling—blended and experiential—is indeed very important. In a way, there is also a need to develop new assessment tools that measure creativity and critical thinking to really know that these are indeed working and ways to continue the process of improvement. This will involve the engagement of stakeholders, such as parents, community members, and policymakers, in the innovation process to gain support and reduce potential resistance (Gusti & Ratnawulan, 2021). By adopting a more holistic approach to collaboration, the school manager is better placed in creating an enabling environment for innovative teaching methods that eventually lead to improved student outcomes.

Theoretical, practical, social, and managerial domains are fully imbued with the implications brought about by the implementation of non-traditional teaching methods. It is through these four case studies that have evidenced positive outcomes to demonstrate the role they can play in transforming education through enhanced creativity and critical thinking. Teachers and school heads can create a thrilling and participatory learning environment by working on the challenges and learning from the same, with much ability to enable the learners to navigate intricacies and possibilities of the future.

LIMITATIONS AND SCOPE FOR FURTHER RESEARCH

While the case examples demonstrated positive results, several limitations must be discussed. Firstly, non-traditional pedagogical practices are exceptionally resource-intensive, not only in terms of technology and materials but also in terms of extensive professional development for teachers. Secondly, assessment of creativity and critical thinking is complex and may be quite subjective. In this regard, such approaches may be quite difficult to replicate in schools with inadequate funding. As most of these skills cannot be measured by traditional standardized testing, more reliable means of evaluation have to be developed. It will need ongoing research in constructing and validating these assessment methods that actually measure this impact of innovative teaching practices.

These studies were only conducted in suburban, urban, and rural schools with different sets of student populations. It may not be very proper to generalize the results since different schools have different challenges and limitations that are unique to each school. Future research should study whether the practical application of non-traditional teaching methods in different schools, obviously including under-equipped and resourced schools, differs from the settings in these studies to generalize the findings of these approaches.

It will also involve longitudinal studies to test the long-term impact of these non-traditional pedagogies on students' creativity and critical thinking. While case studies showed immediate gains in academic achievement and engagement, it will be important to track if these advantages are sustained and generalized into effectiveness in higher education and careers (Kokotsaki et al., 2016). Moreover, research on the best combinations of non-traditional methods for different subjects and age groups needs to be made in order to recommend, in a more specific and relevant way, such relevant recommendations for educators.

Further research is finally required on the role of pre-service teacher education and in-service professional development. Better training programs and resource allocations will bring knowledge about the specific competencies and support systems needed to enable teachers to succeed in both running and sustaining non-traditional methods (Kokotsaki et al., 2016). An addressing of such limitations, along with a further scope of research developed within them, will help future studies to be fully insightful into how best to optimize educational practice for the fostering of creativity and critical thinking in students across diverse contexts.

CONCLUSION

Exploring the four different schools, namely Green Valley High, Lincoln Middle, Horizon High, and Maplewood Elementary, into non-traditional teaching methodologies very much proves to have much potential to improve creativity and critical thinking skills in their students. Adopting project-based learning, blended learning, arts integration, experiential education, and mindfulness practices, these schools have shown an improvement in student achievement, enhancement of student engagement, and developing the much-required 21st-century skills. The execution of such methods requires first of all considerable resources and professional development, with new and innovative assessment devices necessitating continuous investment and support (Bawuro et al., 2018).

These case studies underline the idea of looking at the system of education as a holistic and student-centric one, which addresses not only the academic achievement but the emotional and creative development of students at large. These positive impacts found in schools thus lend strong support to the case for greater adoption of non-traditional teaching methods. At the same time, however, identified challenges—not least those related to resources and the issue of effectively assessing creative and critical thinking—raise concerns that point out a need for more research and policy support (Elbahri et al., 2018).

Future research should be expanded to different educational contexts; measurement tools developed; and professional development for educators sustained over time. Schools can, therefore, better negotiate the challenges and leverage the benefits that exist within innovative teaching practices. What this means, in essence, is a final goal: vibrant, interesting, and supportive learning environments that the students come out with in a situation that rapidly changes across the global landscape. Examples show the foundation for continuous transformation within the education sector to empower learners with requisite skills for the future.

REFERENCES

Anggraeni, A. (2020). Blended humor and mind mapping in improving 21st century skills. *Jurnal Ilmu Pendidikan, 25*(1), 1. DOI: 10.17977/um048v25i1p1-5

Aznia, N., Utina, R., & Hamidun, M. (2022). Using jigsaw learning model to improve collaboration and communication skills of high school students on environmental change. *Jurnal Pendidikan Mipa, 23*(4), 1610–1619. DOI: 10.23960/jpmipa/v23i4.pp1610-1619

Bawuro, F., Danjuma, I., & Wajiga, H. (2018). Factors influencing innovative behaviour of teachers in secondary schools in the north east of nigeria. *Path of Science, 4*(3), 1007–1017. DOI: 10.22178/pos.32-9

Colliver, J. A. (2000). Effectiveness of problem-based learning curricula. *Academic Medicine, 75*(3), 259–266. DOI: 10.1097/00001888-200003000-00017

Cremin, T., Burnard, P., & Craft, A. (2006). Pedagogy and possibility thinking in the early years. *Thinking Skills and Creativity, 1*(2), 108–119. DOI: 10.1016/j.tsc.2006.07.001

Du, M. (2023). Research and effectiveness analysis of innovative teaching models of physical education in colleges and universities under convergent network architecture. *Applied Mathematics and Nonlinear Sciences, 9*(1). Advance online publication. DOI: 10.2478/amns.2023.2.01099

Dung, Q. (2024). Outdoor teaching aims to enhance the positive learning attitude of 6th-grade students in biology at tuyen quang school for excellence. *International Journal of Multidisciplinary Research and Growth Evaluation, 5*(1), 644–648. DOI: 10.54660/.ijmrge.2024.5.1.644-648

Elbahri, M., Soliman, A., Yliniemi, K., Abdelaziz, R., Homaeigohar, S., & Zarie, E. (2018). Innovative education and active teaching with the leidenfrost nanochemistry. *Journal of Chemical Education, 95*(11), 1966–1974. DOI: 10.1021/acs.jchemed.7b00973

Elenany, Y. (2023). A proposed framework for the classification of game-based learning in construction management. *European Conference on Games Based Learning*, 17(1), 799-806. DOI: 10.34190/ecgbl.17.1.1712

Forbes, R. (2021). Descriptions of learning and teaching innovations; using project-based learning to support clinical education. *Australian Journal of Clinical Education, 9*(1). Advance online publication. DOI: 10.53300/001c.25453

Forrester, J. (2009). Thinking creatively; thinking critically. *Asian Social Science, 4*(5). Advance online publication. DOI: 10.5539/ass.v4n5p100

Gao, Z. (2012). An arduous but hopeful journey: Implementing project-based learning in a middle school of china. *Frontiers of Education in China, 7*(4), 608–634. DOI: 10.1007/bf03396956

Graham, C. (2012). Developing creativity across cultures. Text, 16(Special 16). DOI: 10.52086/001c.31193

Guo, H. (2023). An innovative approach to teaching physical education integrating modern network technology. *Applied Mathematics and Nonlinear Sciences, 9*(1). Advance online publication. DOI: 10.2478/amns.2023.2.00433

Gusti, D. & Ratnawulan, A. (2021). Validity of student worksheetswith the theme of energy in daily life by problem based learning of integrated in 21st century learning. *International Journal of Advanced Research, 9*(02), 403–407. DOI: 10.21474/ijar01/12459

Hanipah, H., Jiea, P., Rosly, R., & Omar, S. (2019). Integrated 21st century science, technology, engineering, mathematics (stem) education through robotics project-based learning. *Humanities & Social Sciences Reviews, 7*(2), 204–211. DOI: 10.18510/hssr.2019.7222

Hmelo-Silver, C. E. (2004). Problem-based learning: What and how do students learn? *Educational Psychology Review, 16*(3), 235–266. DOI: 10.1023/b:edpr.0000034022.16470.f3

Huong, N. (2022). Innovating teaching methods at the university level: Necessity and problems issues for higher education. *Global Academic Journal of Humanities and Social Sciences, 4*(6), 207–212. DOI: 10.36348/gajhss.2022.v04i06.002

Hutchison, K., Paatsch, L., & Cloonan, A. (2020). Reshaping home–school connections in the digital age: Challenges for teachers and parents. *E-Learning and Digital Media, 17*(2), 167–182. DOI: 10.1177/2042753019899527

Jalinus, N., Nabawi, R., & Mardin, A. (2017). The seven steps of project based learning model to enhance productive competences of vocational students.. DOI: 10.2991/ictvt-17.2017.43

Kaplan, D. (2019). Creativity in education: Teaching for creativity development. *Psychology (Irvine, Calif.), 10*(02), 140–147. DOI: 10.4236/psych.2019.102012

Keinänen, M., & Kairisto-Mertanen, L. (2019). Researching learning environments and students' innovation competences. *Education + Training*, *61*(1), 17–30. DOI: 10.1108/et-03-2018-0064

Khairnar, C. (2015). Advance pedagogy: Innovative methods of teaching and learning. *International Journal of Information and Education Technology (IJIET)*, *5*(11), 869–872. DOI: 10.7763/ijiet.2015.v5.629

Kokotsaki, D., Menzies, V., & Wiggins, A. (2016). Project-based learning: A review of the literature. *Improving Schools*, *19*(3), 267–277. DOI: 10.1177/1365480216659733

Li, L., Ting-ting, Z., Liu, B., Wu, L., & Huang, H. (2021). Observation and thinking of innovative courses in colleges and universities.. DOI: 10.2991/assehr.k.210121.071

Lin, Y. (2011). Fostering creativity through education – a conceptual framework of creative pedagogy. *Creative Education*, *02*(03), 149–155. DOI: 10.4236/ce.2011.23021

Liu, Z. (2023). The influence of ai chatgpt on improving teachers' creative thinking. *International Journal of Learning Teaching and Educational Research*, *22*(12), 124–139. DOI: 10.26803/ijlter.22.12.7

Mamuaja, M. (2023). The role of m-learning in project-based learning models in elementary schools. *IJITE*, *2*(3), 118–132. DOI: 10.62711/ijite.v2i3.131

París, G., & Hay, P. (2019). 5x5x5=creativity: Art as a transformative practice. *International Journal of Art & Design Education*, *39*(1), 69–84. DOI: 10.1111/jade.12229

Prayogi, S. (2024). Inquiry vs. inquiry-creative: Emphasizing critical thinking skills of prospective stem teachers in the context of stem learning in indonesia. *Education Sciences*, *14*(6), 593. DOI: 10.3390/educsci14060593

Spendlove, Z., & Best, R. (2018). Innovation in assessment: Building student confidence in preparation for unfamiliar assessment methods. *British Journal of Midwifery*, *26*(3), 180–184. DOI: 10.12968/bjom.2018.26.3.180

Subramanian, D., & Kelly, P. (2018). Effects of introducing innovative teaching methods in engineering classes: A case study on classes in an indian university. *Computer Applications in Engineering Education*, *27*(1), 183–193. DOI: 10.1002/cae.22067

Tanana, S. (2022). Innovative format of organization teaching of foreign languages in the professional preparation of future teachers-philologists. *European Humanities Studies State and Society*, (2), 138–150. DOI: 10.38014/ehs-ss.2022.2.08

Tila, D. (2023). Open pedagogy, renewable assignments, and course content creation in economics. *Creative Education, 14*(12), 2394–2404. DOI: 10.4236/ce.2023.1412153

Vass, V. (2024). The coherence between innovative teaching methods and formative assessment in higher education. *International Journal of Advanced Corporate Learning (Ijac), 17*(3), 108–116. DOI: 10.3991/ijac.v17i3.45657

Vimbelo, S. (2023). Current pedagogical practices employed by technical vocational education and training college's mathematics lecturers. *South African Journal of Higher Education, 37*(4). Advance online publication. DOI: 10.20853/37-4-5292

Wanyama, T., & Singh, I. (2015). Laboratory based project for experiential learning in plc systems integration and plc systems data access. *Proceedings of the Canadian Engineering Education Association (Ceea)*. DOI: 10.24908/pceea.v0i0.5866

Widiastuti, I. (2023). Implementing problem-based learning to develop students' critical and creative thinking skills. [Jurnal Pendidikan Indonesia]. *Jpi, 12*(4), 658–667. DOI: 10.23887/jpiundiksha.v12i4.63588

Xu, R., Li, J., & Zou, Y. (2017). Research on the innovation of teaching method and the cultivation of innovative undertaking talents in colleges.. DOI: 10.2991/icemc-17.2017.176

Zhou, S., Lin, L., Shu, Y., & Xiong, N. (2020). The construction and practice of computer network course driven by innovative thinking. Matec Web of Conferences, 309, 05017. DOI: 10.1051/matecconf/202030905017

Zulkifli, H., Tamuri, A. H., & Azman, N. A. (2022). Understanding creative teaching in twenty-first century learning among Islamic education teachers during the COVID-19 pandemic. *Frontiers in Psychology, 13*. Advance online publication. DOI: 10.3389/fpsyg.2022.920859

Chapter 5
Emancipatory Education in Higher Education
A Transformative Approach

Pam Epler
https://orcid.org/0000-0001-5655-369X
Grand Canyon University, USA

ABSTRACT

This chapter introduces the reader to emancipatory education within the institute of higher education. Emancipatory education is an approach that empowers learners by promoting critical thinking, autonomy, and social justice. Its principles energize students by having them actively engage in their learning process and question norms and structures. It liberates minds by having students practice prioritization of historically marginalized perspectives and drives social justice efforts involving collaboration with communities to transform educational systems. Emancipatory education goes beyond traditional teaching methods. It encourages students to critically examine their experiences, societal structures, and power dynamics. By fostering awareness, it emboldens them to challenge injustice. Emancipatory education aims for liberation—both personal and collective. It seeks to transform oppressive systems and create a more just society. Teaching methods that emancipatory education supports include dialogic teaching, problem-posing, and participatory action research. These approaches prioritize dialogue, collaboration, and student voice.

INTRODUCTION

The renowned anthropologist Margaret Mead once said, "Never doubt that a small group of thoughtful, committed, organized citizens can change the world; indeed,

DOI: 10.4018/979-8-3693-0997-1.ch005

it's the only thing that ever has" (Bowman-Kruhm, 2003, p. 34). Although Mead may not have been specifically referring to *emancipatory education*, she certainly captured the essence of the concept. Emancipatory education is a powerful framework that challenges traditional educational norms and seeks to empower learners. In the context of higher education, it aims to liberate minds, foster critical consciousness, and promote social justice using small groups of students and university faculty. This chapter will explore its key principles, prospects, and impact.

BACKGROUND

Definition of Emancipatory Education

Emancipatory education has been defined in the literature in a variety of ways. According to Davis (2019), it is "encouraging students to question and examine their world using self-reflection as a keyway of learning and gaining knowledge" (para. 3). Nouri and Mahdi Sajjadi (2014) noted that emancipatory education is defined as "identifying and redressing the injustices, inequalities and myths of an often-oppressive world" (p. 78). According to Rule (2015), Paulo Freire defined emancipatory education as a way for schools to "regain humanity and respect students' experiences and their culture" (p. 50) through problem-solving and an interactive dialogue between the educator and the students. We Rise Up (n.d.) defined emancipatory education as an approach that aims to free individuals from oppressive structures, thereby enabling them to critically analyze their surroundings, challenge inequalities, and actively participate in shaping their own lives. It emphasizes personal and collective liberation and fosters critical thinking, self-awareness, and social consciousness. Alhadeff-Jones (2016) defined emancipatory education using two different viewpoints: (a) the personal, which highlights intellectual liberation, critical thinking, personal growth, and (b) the political, which focuses on freeing oppressed groups and transforming all of society. As all these definitions suggest, if a pupil and teacher problem-solve the issue together, both will be intellectually engaged and empowered and take pride in the fact that they derived a potential solution on their own. They will also understand how the issue affects their lives on a local, state, national, and world level (Nouri & Mahdi Sajjadi, 2014).

History of Emancipatory Education

The term *emancipation* emerged in 17th-century Britain. Initially, it related to religious tolerance, such as the easing of restrictions on Catholics and other minority religions (Moore, 2001). In the 18th century, it became associated with freedom from slavery, and later with women's liberation from societal conventions. The term was greatly popularized by the *Emancipation Proclamation* set forth in the United States in 1863, which freed enslaved African Americans, and President Lincoln was hailed as the *Great Emancipator* (Alhadeff-Jones, 2016).

The *Enlightenment Ideal* was a European intellectual movement during the 17th and 18th centuries that influenced emancipatory education (Moore, 2001). It synthesized ideas about God, reason, nature, and humanity into a worldview that gained widespread acceptance in the West. Enlightenment thinkers celebrated reason as the primary source of authority and legitimacy (Moore, 2001). They believed humans could understand the universe and improve their condition through rational inquiry. Like emancipatory education, they advocated for liberty, progress, tolerance, fraternity, constitutional government separation of church and state, protection of rights, equality, improved education, and minimizing state and religious interference (Alhadeff-Jones, 2016). The Enlightenment emphasized reason, individual rights, and societal progress—ideas that shaped art, philosophy, and politics in profound ways.

Many of the classic thinkers, like John Dewey, Paulo Freire, Henry Giroux, Peter McLauren, and Ira Shor (among many others), molded the Enlightenment ideal of emancipatory education (Alhadeff-Jones, 2016). Although they stayed true to Enlightenment ideals, they democratized the concepts by emphasizing equality and freedom and questioning some aspects of the concept. Because of these enlightened scholars, the pursuit of emancipatory education continues to empower learners and challenge oppressive structures.

Influencers of the Emancipatory Education Movement

Currently in U.S. postsecondary school systems, teachers are revered as having great knowledge and information to lavish on their students. The pupils then take in this knowledge and parrot it back to the educator in the form of an assessment to see if learning has occurred. This method was seen by some—Dewey, Freire, Giroux, McLauren, and Shor—as a repressive and discordant system, and they set out to change education by introducing emancipatory education.

John Dewey

John Dewey, an American philosopher, psychologist, and educational reformer, advocated for a more experiential and student-centered approach to education (Attick, 2006; Brehony, 1997; Gibbon, 2019; Piedra, 2018; Sekulović & Rajković, 2024; Talebi, 2015). His influential work challenged traditional models of schooling and emphasized active learning, critical thinking, and problem-solving. In his classic discussion about education goals, Dewey highlighted the emancipatory dimension

(Attick, 2006; Brehony, 1997; Gibbon, 2019; Piedra, 2018; Sekulović & Rajković, 2024; Talebi, 2015). He believed education should emancipate the young from outdated ideas and enable them to think more clearly about equality and freedoms while encouraging their growth and self-discovery. Dewey emphasized that learning should come from nature, contradictory lessons, and experiences to impact students' minds and behaviors, which will in turn influence their social environment (Attick, 2006; Brehony, 1997; Gibbon, 2019; Piedra, 2018; Sekulović & Rajković, 2024; Talebi, 2015).

Paulo Freire

Paulo Freire is considered the true founder of the emancipatory educational movement (Nouri & Mahdi Sajjadi, 2014). Mies (1973) reported that Freire was asked by the Brazilian government to educate poor, illiterate workers. He started in the traditional way of providing them with everyday vocabulary words but quickly found that this did not satisfy their needs. The workers wanted to know how to get themselves out of poverty and provide better lives for their children (Mies, 1973). Armed with this insight, Freire decided that to have a democratic society, students needed to be participants in their own education—needed to interact with it based on their own experiences and background—not simply sit in a seat and have a teacher talk to them. Freire felt that if the workers could develop their own problem-solving skills, they could assist with identifying and perhaps alleviating the transgressions and inadequacies of the unjust living environment in which they existed (Nouri & Mahdi Sajjadi, 2014). He identified this phenomenon as *cultural awareness* and insisted that for change to occur, a revolution had to happen so that the opposition were heard and recognized (Mies, 1973).

Henry Giroux

Henry Giroux was influenced by Freire and is given credit for coining the phrase *critical pedagogy* (Costandius & Bitzer, 2015). Giroux defined this term as educational perceptions, standards, rituals, and doctrines that support critical thinking (Costandius & Bitzer, 2015). He argued that differences and diversity among the masses should be celebrated because they are a part of society's collective history and can be seen within the daily struggles of the common people (Costandius & Bitzer, 2015).

He, like Freire, felt that the current educational environment should be adjusted so that teachers are not the driving force behind a lesson. Giroux suggested that students should think and act critically, thereby not only transforming themselves but also society (Costandius & Bitzer, 2015). He felt that current educational curricula support deliberate inequality and injustice and should be transformed so that students are at liberty to express themselves without fear of retribution (Costandius & Bitzer, 2015). He felt school curricula, both in the K–12 education environments as well as postsecondary institutions, should move more toward decentralization so that students might gain an understanding of how skills, influence, and support may influence justice and equality in local, state, national, and international societies (Costandius & Bitzer, 2015).

Peter McLauren

After Freire and Giroux, Peter McLauren entered the emancipatory educational movement (although he, like Giroux, referred to it as critical pedagogy) by insisting that teachers assist their students when they provide an understanding of schools' inner political workings and power schemes. He felt that classrooms tend to support diversity when all participants' ideas are respected, even when there are differences (Chalaune, 2021). The classrooms should also demonstrate collaboration and a desire to improve society through "antiracism, antisexist, and antihomophobic practices" (McLauren, 2012, p. 209). McLauren felt that educators should empower their students by making them aware of the inequalities within social institutions and schools (Aliakbari & Faraji, 2011). He also felt that students within their own educational environment should be taught to become critics of society in order to assist them when they are making decisions that may affect politics and their economic status (Aliakbari & Faraji, 2011).

Ira Shor

Finally, Ira Shor examined the inner workings of the typical classroom and determined that teachers spend a lot of time talking to students and not enough time listening to their pupils' voices or opinions (Chalaune, 2021). Shor felt, like his predecessors, that there must be a balance of equality between teacher authority and student input (Chalaune, 2021). Shor also felt that students benefited from an in-depth dialogue between educators and pupils but also could profit from discussing life conditions in a variety of contexts (Edling & Mooney Simmie, 2018). Shor stated that these practices should not only occur through interactions within the classroom environment but within social media and the reading of literature and political texts (Edling & Mooney Simmie, 2018).

Although Dewey, Freire, Giroux, McLauren, and Shor may vary slightly in their definitions of what constitutes emancipatory education, they all have in common the belief that teachers and their pupils should have a better understanding of the social, political, environmental, and fiscal occurrences that affect their daily lives. Their philosophy is that emancipatory education seeks liberation, critical awareness, and empowerment within historical and philosophical contexts (Alhadeff-Jones, 2016). From their perspective, once educators and students are provided with this knowledge, both should be able to act and think critically and creatively about humankind.

CURRENT ISSUES, CONTROVERSIES, AND PROBLEMS

Emancipatory Education Today

Despite originating over 3 centuries ago, emancipatory education has not changed in its philosophy and continues to be at the forefront of educators' deliberations. Instructors still want to empower their pupils to foster critical thinking and challenge oppressive structures. They continue to encourage students to question power dynamics, engage in theory and practice, and become active agents in their learning process (Krstić et al., 2024). Educators who support emancipatory education want to promote the empowerment of marginalized groups, address social justice issues, and promote equity (Lackovic et al. 2024). Advocates of emancipatory education want to uphold inclusive practices that accommodate diverse learners, including those with disabilities, different cultural backgrounds, and varying learning styles, because inclusion fosters empathy, understanding, and a sense of belonging[REMOVED HYPERLINK FIELD] (Krstić et al., 2024). Academic scholars want to continue to offer opportunities for personalized learning, global collaboration, and access to information using digital tools and technology (Lackovic et al. 2024). Educators want to create safe spaces for dialogue, self-reflection, and action[REMOVED HYPERLINK FIELD] (Lackovic et al. 2024) and seek to decolonize curricula, challenge Eurocentric perspectives, and incorporate diverse voices by acknowledging historical injustices, empowering learners, and promoting cultural understanding[REMOVED HYPERLINK FIELD] (Krstić et al., 2024). These movements of emancipatory education can influence campus policies, curriculum, and institutional practices as well as have students worldwide advocate for change and address issues like climate change, racial justice, and mental health (Lackovic et al. 2024).

Emancipatory Education in Higher Education

Contemporary movements in emancipatory education can drive positive changes in higher education by promoting empowerment, social justice, and transformative learning. Colleges and universities can endorse empowerment through their hiring protocol, campus climate, and support services to bolster diversity, equity, and inclusive practices (Krstić et al., 2024; Lackovic et al. 2024). Institutions of higher education can advance their social justice practices by allowing scholars to explore emancipatory research methodologies, amplify marginalized voices, and challenge dominant paradigms (Krstić et al., 2024; Lackovic et al. 2024). Finally, postsecondary schools can support transformative learning by including emancipatory approaches that lead to revised curricula that prioritize critical thinking, social justice, and interdisciplinary perspectives, and educators must adopt student-centered, participatory methods that encourage dialogue, experiential learning, and community engagement (Krstić et al., 2024; Lackovic et al. 2024).

Emancipatory education within the U.S. higher educational system addresses persistent patterns of campus inequality driven by rapid demographic shifts, reduced public spending, and a polarized political landscape (Krstić et al., 2024; Lackovic et al. 2024). These movements aim to create more equitable systems that distribute social benefits across race, gender, class, identity, and abilities. Emerging from the pandemic, these actions are a response to the ongoing structured racism, Black Lives Matter, climate activism, and gender equality movements that colleges and universities currently face (Krstić et al., 2024). Student-led activism and advocacy are pushing for change. They demand representation, curriculum reform, and social justice. The students want their educators to embrace emancipatory education by emphasizing dialogue, empowerment, and social transformation through experiential learning, community engagement, and global perspectives (Lackovic et al. 2024). Student-powered contemporary movements seek to make higher education more inclusive, just, and responsive to societal challenges.

Advantages of Emancipatory Education in Higher Education

There are numerous advantages to emancipatory education within a higher education institution. According to Aleheg Sewagegn and Diale (2019), emancipatory education encourages students to question norms, engage in dialogue, and explore diverse perspectives. It empowers them to become active agents of change. This form of learning encourages students to develop critical thinking by examining societal issues, power dynamics, and historical contexts. They learn to challenge dominant narratives and seek alternative viewpoints (Gasman, 2023; Joubert, 2019). Emancipatory education aligns with social justice goals. It equips learners to address systemic inequalities, advocate for marginalized groups, and work toward a more just society (Aleheg Sewagegn & Diale, 2019). Beyond academic content, emancipatory education promotes holistic learning by emphasizing personal growth, empathy, and ethical responsibility (Gasman, 2023; Joubert, 2019). Finally, students are liberated from passive roles, becoming co-creators of knowledge and active participants in their education (Gasman, 2023; Joubert, 2019).

For an emancipatory education culture to occur, the current educational environment must become more humanized by allowing students and teachers to become aware of the world and conditions surrounding them. Nouri and Mahdi Sajjadi (2014) described the following benefits to accomplishing that goal:

- Emancipatory education offers students the opportunity to think critically about their own lives and, based on this knowledge, encourages them to advocate for and make changes to the status quo. By doing so, students will become better aware of the inequalities within their immediate surroundings and how they affect their local community, state, nation, and the world (Nouri & Mahdi Sajjadi, 2014).
- Collaboration is stressed within emancipatory education not only among educators and students but also with others, such as community leaders, state representatives, and organizational directors. This type of education stresses open dialogue among the masses and encourages mutual respect among all involved (Nouri & Mahdi Sajjadi, 2014).
- By connecting real-life experiences to academic content, emancipatory education allows students and teachers to enlist in problem-solving activities that improve and enhance comprehension of the material learned (Nouri & Mahdi Sajjadi, 2014). Students will be more likely to participate in an activity that they have experienced or are interested in learning more about.
- Emancipatory education allows students and teachers to share their own experiences with social injustice, discrimination, and inequality issues (Nouri & Mahdi Sajjadi, 2014). By sharing this knowledge, they are more likely to want to take action to eradicate injustice and advocate for change.

Davis (2019) added that not only must students think critically, they must also be taught to identify and assess their thinking. To do so, he suggested the following:

- Engaging in emancipatory educational thinking should be completed with a pragmatic and compelling purpose (Davis, 2019).
- Students should think about the questions to ask for clarification on the issue prior to engaging in problem-solving activities. If needed, additional queries can be requested, or the original queries can be broken down into smaller subquestions. In addition, investigations into whether the original question has only one solution or can be answered from multiple viewpoints should also be considered (Davis, 2019).

- Prior to the students stating their point of view on the issue, assumptions should be discussed and evaluated to determine if they are valuable. This action will lead to students being more open-minded (Davis, 2019).
- Before thinking critically about an issue, information about the topic should be collected from a reputable, reliable, peer-reviewed resource. The data collected should relate directly to the issue being analyzed. Students and teachers should verify each other's information for accuracy (Davis, 2019).
- Once all the information is gathered and verified, students should take turns sharing their information with their peers and allowing their classmates to offer alternative ideas. Both positive and negative sides of each issue should be presented (Davis, 2019).
- Students should also use their personal experiences from their culture and background to assist with understanding the issues. In doing so, they contribute their unique perspective to the issue (Davis, 2019).

If done correctly, emancipatory education fosters critical awareness, empowerment, and social transformation within higher education contexts. Teachers can also secure a positive relationship with their students by learning more about them. The educator can use this information to teach their pupils about the values and expectations within the school and their community and motivate them to learn more about themselves (Davis, 2019). Emancipatory education will also provide students with the ability to use and depend on their judgments by tearing down the unjust barriers between the pupils and their educators. Once this is accomplished, students can depend on their intellect for academic and social success (Nouri & Mahdi Sajjadi, 2014).

Impact and Outcomes

Emancipatory education significantly influences student empowerment and engagement. Through empowerment, it fosters critical thinking, self-awareness, and social consciousness. Students become active agents challenging oppressive structures and advocating for change (Galloway, 2012). They evaluate their own lives, identities, and roles in society, which leads to personal growth (Krstić et al., 2024). Through the use of engagement, emancipatory education practices involve students in co-creating knowledge and shaping their learning experiences (Nouri & Mahdi Sajjadi, 2104). By connecting education to real-world issues, students engage more deeply and apply learning to address community challenges, thereby promoting active citizenship (Krstić et al., 2024).

Emancipatory education empowers students to transform themselves and their communities, fosters meaningful engagement in learning and social change, and plays a crucial role in driving broader social change. By celebrating marginalized spaces and fostering counter-leadership discourses, it generates actions of liberation and progressive transformation (Nouri & Mahdi Sajjadi, 2014). Unlike mainstream educational systems that may reinforce oppression, emancipatory education empowers individuals to challenge exclusion and actively participate in positive community regeneration. Through critical pedagogy, dialogue, and praxis, it redefines education as a practice of emancipation, contributing meaningfully to peaceful struggles for social justice (Mandal, 2023).

Challenges to Implementing Emancipatory Education in Higher Education

Implementing emancipatory education in higher education can be challenging, but it is essential for fostering equity and social justice. Overcoming barriers requires intentional effort, collaboration between the faculty and the governing powers, and a commitment by the college or university to meaningful change. If these obstacles exist, emancipatory education will not become a reality.

According to Lattimer and Pizarro (2021), large, complex organizations tend to maintain institutional inertia and follow the status quo. Shifting policies, practices, and culture requires overcoming entrenched systems and structures that perpetuate inequities that they are not particularly interested in ending. It is common for institutions of higher education to have limited, if any explicit, comprehensive policies that address past and ongoing inequities (Lattimer & Pizarro, 2021). Institutions often use terms like *social justice* and *equity* without translating them into actionable policies; as a result, aspirational claims remain disconnected from the actual practices (Cappiali, 2023).

Since many faculty and staff align with social justice principles, institutions must actively confront these issues, which they may not be prepared to do (Cappiali, 2023). Postsecondary education courses should include emancipatory education in their syllabi. However, traditional curricula are rigid and lack cross-collaboration among disciplines, thus hindering the integration of emancipatory approaches (Roth et al., 2023). In addition, university leaders, instructors, staff, and professors may lack expertise and training in emancipatory pedagogy. Although training programs should focus on sustainable teaching approaches that promote social justice (Bananuka, 2023), shrinking budgets and limited resources, such as finances, space, and time, can hinder experimentation with new learning environments that align with emancipatory principles (Bananuka, 2023).

However, the biggest barrier may simply be resistance to change. Conversations about culture, policies, and practices are challenging, and institutions avoid necessary introspection and fail to address inequities. The college or university's culture may hinder progress toward social and racial justice (Cappiali, 2023). Resistance from stakeholders who benefit from the status quo can also impede progress. Overcoming such resistance requires strategic leadership and collective commitment (Lattimer & Pizarro, 2021). Institutions must actively confront past inequities and prioritize equity. Addressing these barriers involves intentional action, collaboration, and a commitment to transformative change. Once committed to change, institutions will find that emancipatory education can be a powerful tool for promoting equity and empowering marginalized voices in higher education (Bananuka, 2023; Cappiali, 2023; Lattimer & Pizarro, 2021; Roth et al., 2023).

Critics of emancipatory education being used in a higher educational institution argue that it overemphasizes individualism and focuses solely on individual empowerment, which may lead to overlooking systemic issues and not addressing broader structural inequalities (Galloway, 2012). Some opponents view emancipatory theories as idealistic and challenging to implement in real-world classrooms and feel that practical constraints, standardized testing, and specific curriculum pressures can hinder the full implementation of emancipatory education within a postsecondary environment (Nouri & Mahdi Sajjadi, 2014). Those critics who have analyzed emancipatory education feel that it may not fully account for cultural, social, or historical variations and question whether one model will fit all contexts (Mandal, 2023). Emancipatory education does focus on student-led learning, but critics feel that this is overemphasized, and pupils may neglect the valuable experience educators bring to the classroom. Attempting to balance teacher guidance, expertise, and authority with student autonomy can be complex and challenging (Nouri & Mahdi Sajjadi, 2014). Due to how the current, traditional, higher education institutions classes are structured, there is resistance to any radical change. Faculty are not openly willing to change how they present knowledge to their students or the way they assess students since measuring critical conscience, empowerment, and social justice remains a challenge (Krstić et al., 2024). Although emancipatory education offers transformative potential, addressing these disadvantages is essential for it to have a meaningful impact.

Overcoming the Challenges

For higher educational institutions to overcome the challenges of emancipatory education, they must take initiative and collective action so that meaningful change can occur. To accomplish this goal, the following actions are suggested:

- Leadership Commitment—The heads of the colleges and universities must recognize historical inequities and center marginalized voices. They must prioritize equity in policies and practices, eventually moving from words to tangible change (Lattimer & Pizarro, 2021).

- Comprehensive Policies—Students and faculty must engage in conversation to foster dialogue on social justice, equity, and anti-racism and establish practices that actively address inequities and promote racial justice (Clack, 2022). Each campus must assess its climate and policies regarding emancipatory education to ensure alignment with the institution's mission and values. Every institution must commit to and advocate for policies that promote diversity, equity, and social justice (Clack, 2022).
- Faculty Development—Perhaps one of the main reasons emancipatory education is not currently occurring on college campuses is due to the lack of professional training on the topic. Workshops on inclusive teaching practices must be required of all faculty and instructors, and learning communities must be established in which educators can come together and discuss their challenges and successes in implementing emancipatory education within their classrooms (Nouri & Mahdi Sajjadi, 2014). Faculty development requires educating not only faculty but also staff, instructors, students, counselors, and others working on a college or university campus about emancipatory education and its implementation. All stakeholders should be equipped to create inclusive, transformative learning experiences. Colleges and universities should also create spaces for both educators and students to share experiences, resources, and strategies (Krstić et al., 2024).
- Student Involvement—The president, board members, and faculty members should ensure that student voices relating to emancipatory education are heard and that they are involved in all decision-making processes. Collaboration with students will assist with shaping and changing curriculum and policies (Tibbitts & Keet, 2023).

Emancipatory education in higher education has both positive and negative aspects. The positive aspects include the following:

- Critical Thinking—Emancipatory education encourages students to think critically, question assumptions, and engage actively with content.
- Empowerment—Learners gain confidence and become active agents of change in their own lives and society.
- Social Justice—it promotes equity, inclusivity, awareness of social issues, intrinsic motivation, and a deeper love for learning.

The negative aspects of emancipatory education in higher education are as follows:

- Resource Constraints—Implementing emancipatory education can be challenging due to limited resources, large class sizes, and institutional barriers.
- Resistance—Some educators and institutions resist change because they prefer traditional methods.
- Assessment Challenges—Standardized testing may not fully capture the benefits of emancipatory practices.
- Time Intensive—Creating inclusive, dialogic classrooms requires time and effort.

In summary, while emancipatory education offers transformative potential, overcoming challenges and fostering widespread adoption remains essential.

Curriculum Design

Emancipatory education can be integrated into the postsecondary educational curriculum, but it will require ongoing reflection, adaptation, and collaboration among faculty, students, and administrators, as well as involve intentional design and implementation. Here are some practical steps:

- Curriculum Design—College and university faculty and instructors should embed into their classes opportunities for students to critically reflect on their own experiences, values, and societal contexts. All programs should ensure that inclusive content, diverse perspectives, voices, and histories are represented in course materials. Every assignment should be designed to encourage students to pose questions, explore complexities, problem-solve, and engage with real-world issues (Groenke, 2009; Smith & Seal, 2021).
- Pedagogical Approaches—Classroom teaching should be dialogue-based, which fosters open dialogue, active listening, and respectful debate. Postsecondary faculty and staff should provide a learning environment in which students feel safe to challenge assumptions. Through internships, students should have an opportunity to participate in experiential learning in which they can connect theory to practice through community service or research projects. These pedagogical approaches should encourage collaborative learning and promote group work, peer teaching, and cooperative problem-solving (Groenke, 2009; Smith & Seal, 2021).
- Assessment Strategies—University and college faculty and staff need to move beyond traditional exams and focus more on authentic assessments such as the use of portfolios, presentations, and projects that address real-world problems. Students should also be encouraged to self-assess and evaluate their learning process, growth, and critical consciousness (Groenke,

2009; Smith & Seal, 2021). Across all college campuses, faculty should work in collaboration with students to develop assessments that measure emancipatory education practices. These assessment tools should evaluate student empowerment and critical thinking skills. The exams should also align with the specific university's emancipatory education goals (Krstić et al., 2024).

Emancipatory education in higher education focuses on empowering learners, challenging oppressive structures, and promoting social justice. There are many key points related to curriculum design within this framework. First, it is a learner-centered approach that prioritizes student involvement, critical thinking, and active engagement, and learners actively participate in shaping their educational experiences. Second, the curricula include content that challenges dominant narratives, encourages reflection, and addresses societal inequalities, and all specific content topics related to equity, diversity, and social change are central. Third, teaching methods emphasize dialogue, collaboration, and real-world application, and instructors create inclusive learning environments that value diverse perspectives. Fourth, emancipatory curricula involve social transformation aimed at preparing graduates who can contribute to positive societal change. Students learn to advocate for justice, challenge inequities, and engage with global issues. In summary, emancipatory curriculum design prioritizes critical consciousness, empowerment, and transformative learning.

Educators' Role in Postsecondary Emancipatory Education

Freire (1968) explored the principles of emancipatory education. He felt that it should promote active learning, critical awareness, and social transformation. According to Freire, emancipatory education should also align with empowerment and liberation by challenging traditional norms, questioning authority, and promoting critical consciousness. He felt that the teacher should be a facilitator rather than an authority figure and that the focus should be on collaborative learning in which teachers and students engage in dialogue and mutual exploration to make meaningful change. Freire also believed that learning should be a social process, and all involved must be active participants. He wanted educators to help their students see the relevance of their education beyond the classroom by connecting classroom learning to real-world contexts. In addition, he wanted to empower learners to challenge power structures and patterns of inequality. Rather than maintaining the status quo, Freire asked learners and educators through emancipatory education to seek to transform culture and institutions, to become aware of one's oppression, and to work toward social change.

Teaching Methods

To accomplish Freire's emancipatory education within higher education institutions, teaching methods that promote critical thinking and empower students must be employed. The following are some effective strategies that can apply to emancipatory education in higher education.

- Active Learning—Engages students in the learning process, moving beyond passive listening. There are a variety of ways this teaching method can be employed:
  - Debates—Encourage students to discuss current events or controversial topics.
  - Case Studies—Analyze real-world scenarios, thus fostering problem-solving skills.
  - Simulations—Create immersive experiences related to course content.
  - Self-monitoring—Students actively assess their learning progress.
  - Peer-Generated Quizzes—Construct quizzes collaboratively.
  - Reflection—Encourage students to think deeply about covered topics.
  - Expert Interviews—Connect with professionals in their field (Jaffe, 2024).
- Cooperative Work—Group projects enhance critical thinking and teamwork. Students learn from diverse perspectives and develop interpersonal skills (Gravani et al., 2024).
- Problem-Based Learning (PBL)—Students solve real-world problems by applying knowledge to practical situations. Through this teaching method, students develop skills such as critical thinking, research, and collaboration (Aleheg Sewagegn & Diale, 2019).
- Project-Based Learning (PjBL)—Like problem-based learning, project-based learning requires students working collaboratively on extended projects that are often interdisciplinary. This teaching method encourages creativity, autonomy, and deeper understanding (Gasman, 2023).
- Case Studies—Exploring complex issues through detailed scenarios. This teaching method can be applied to small groups or to the entire class. In small groups, students can be given different case studies to compare with the others. Students in classrooms that use this teaching method develop analytical skills, decision-making, and empathy (Clack, 2022).
- Oral Presentations—Students deliver presentations on course topics either individually or as a small group. Through this teaching method, students learn to enhance communication, research, and critical thinking and fine-tune their oral demonstration (Edling & Mooney Simmie, 2018).

- Real-World Activities—In this teaching method, students learn to apply and connect what they have learned in the classroom to practical contexts. It can be an issue on the community, state, national, or international level. This teaching method shows students the impact of their voices by demonstrating relevance and applicability (Álvarez-Huerta et al., 2023).

Although each strategy can be used independently, a combination of these methods can create an engaging, student-centered learning environment that fosters critical thinking and empowerment in higher education.

In emancipatory education within higher education, the teacher's role is multifaceted and transformative. They act as a facilitator and guide by shifting from a traditional authority figure to a mentor and listener. They create spaces for critical dialogue, reflection, and active learning. The educators empower students by valuing their voices, experiences, and agency and encourage learners to question norms, challenge oppressive structures, and advocate for justice. The college and university faculty and staff model social justice principles, address inequities, promote inclusivity, and prepare students to engage in societal change. In summary, teachers in emancipatory education foster critical consciousness, agency, and a commitment to equity.

MODELS OF EMANCIPATORY EDUCATION IN HIGHER EDUCATION

There are two prominent models of emancipatory education within postsecondary institutions. The first, CARES, was developed by Lattimer and Pizarro in 2014 at San Jose State University (SJSU), and the other, the Five E, was established by Janak in 2019. A description of each is below.

CARES Model

The CARES model of emancipatory education in higher education is a framework that aims to transform educational institutions by focusing on equity, justice, and social change. This model invites students and educators to move beyond words and embrace actions that dismantle oppressive structures in higher education. It has three key components—*critical reflection*, *agency and advocacy*, and *reframing engagement* (Lattimer & Pizarro, 2014).

- Critical Reflection—This component plays a crucial role in fostering transformative learning by encouraging and empowering educators and students to critically evaluate existing systems and structures of oppression within educational institutions. By examining power dynamics, biases, and inequities, critical reflection lays the foundation for transformative action. Critical reflection is not merely an event or skill; it is an ongoing process. It involves looking back on one's actions, pondering their impact, and learning from what worked or did not work. Good practitioners of critical reflection continually learn, develop, and grow their abilities by studiously examining their assumptions, knowledge, beliefs, and values. Instructors and pupils of critical reflection analyze assumptions and reflect on the underlying assumptions that shape not only their actions and decisions but also society's. They are also skeptical of existing knowledge and question and challenge established norms. Teachers and students within higher education who use the CARES model attain social awareness by considering the broader context—both for themselves and the people who use services—and alternative ways an event might have unfolded. Critical reflection empowers educators and students to question, learn, and grow. It is a vital component of emancipatory education that allows individuals to access their innate intelligence and dismantle barriers of inequity (Lattimer & Pizarro, 2014).

- Agency and Advocacy—According to Lattimer and Pizarro (2014), this component also plays a pivotal role in the CARES model because it empowers individuals to act against injustice and foster social change. Students and educators become advocates for change by challenging discriminatory practices and promoting equity. The agency component refers to an individual's capacity to act intentionally and make choices—thus empowering students to take purposeful action. Students and instructors become active agents in their learning, advocating for justice, equity, and transformative change. By recognizing their agency, learners engage critically with their environment and contribute to dismantling oppressive structures. The other portion of this component, advocacy, involves speaking up for oneself or others, especially in the face of injustice, and encourages students to advocate for marginalized groups, challenge discriminatory practices, and promote social justice. Advocacy also extends beyond the classroom; it can influence policies, institutions, and broader societal norms. Importantly, it aligns with the goal of liberation and equitable opportunities for all (Lattimer & Pizarro, 2014).
- Reframing Engagement—This final critical component of the CARES model challenges traditional notions of student involvement and shifts the focus from passive participation to active engagement. It emphasizes that student and community engagement should extend beyond the academic curriculum and become vehicles for social transformation. Rather than viewing student engagement as passive participation in prescribed activities, the CARES model

encourages a shift to active engagement that emphasizes critical thinking, agency, and transformative action. Students and instructors are invited to engage beyond the classroom, connecting their learning to real-world contexts and social change efforts. Collegiate stakeholders become authentic partners who collaborate with community members, organizations, and practitioners. They put the policy to practice by bridging theory and action and exploring how policies impact practice and vice versa. University faculty and learners also recognize diverse cultural backgrounds and integrate them into educational practices (Lattimer & Pizarro, 2014). Reframing engagement empowers students and teachers to be active agents of change by connecting their learning to meaningful, real-world contexts.

The Five E Model

The Five E model of emancipatory education in higher education is as widely recognized a framework as the CARES model; importantly, their principles intersect with emancipatory goals in higher education. Even though the Five E model may not directly align with the CARES framework, the two models' pursuit of excellence, equality, and emancipation remains relevant in the broader context of transformative education (Janak, 2019). The Five E components in this model represent *excellence, equality, expansion, expertise,* and *emancipation* (Janak, 2019).

- Excellence—While not part of the original Five E model, high-quality education and excellence in math and science education were emphasized from 1954 to 1983 in colleges and universities. The pursuit of excellence aimed to elevate educational standards and outcomes. Institutions today should still strive for excellence in teaching, research, and student outcomes (Janak, 2019).
- Equality—Equality was another trend during the 1954 to 1983 period. The focus was on equal access and opportunities regardless of race, sex, language, or ability. Efforts aimed to reduce disparities and promote fairness in education (Janak, 2019).
- Expansion—This component refers to the growth of educational institutions into growth industries and their need to expand to adapt to changing needs and demographics and to accommodate increasing student populations. The expansion trend reflects the need for accessible education for all (Janak, 2019).
- Expertise—This component contributes to the Five E model by emphasizing the development of diverse leadership and administration bodies. Inclusion and the growth of diversity in administration lead to increased expertise.

Diverse leadership and a variety of perspectives contribute to decision-making and policy development (Janak, 2019).

- Emancipation—The pursuit of emancipation involves freeing education from local control and historical inequities. It aims to challenge existing norms and empower learners to critically engage with their own experiences and contexts. Emancipation also advocates for social justice, anti-racism, and liberation (Janak, 2019).

Other Frameworks

In addition to the CARES and Five E models, other frameworks related to emancipatory education include *democratic pedagogies*, *critical pedagogies*, *liberatory research*, and *emancipatory pedagogy in practice* (Bananuka, 2023; El Amin & Brion Miesels, 2024; Nouri & Mahdi Sajjadi, 2014). These models intersect and evolve in response to contemporary challenges and crises as emancipatory education continues to be a dynamic field that promote equity, freedom, and social transformation.

- Democratic Pedagogies—These methods emphasize active participation, collaboration, and student-centered methods. They promote dialogue, collaboration, and critical thinking. The goal is to create a just and democratic society in which student voices are considered equal to those of educators. The challenges with implementing democratic pedagogies are resource constraints and increasing student enrollment. Institutions must balance student-centered methods with limited resources. Democratic pedagogies foster active learning, critical consciousness, and student agency, contributing to a more equitable and liberating educational experience (Bananuka, 2023; El Amin & Brion Miesels, 2024; Nouri & Mahdi Sajjadi, 2014).
- Critical Pedagogies—This framework is a powerful approach that challenges traditional teaching methods, aims to empower learners, denounces oppressive structures, encourages dialogue, and promotes social justice. Critical pedagogies aim to transform both individuals and society through education. A critical pedagogy provides a theoretical framework for examining power dynamics in the classroom. It encourages educators to face and challenge biases and oppressive structures that hinder learning and alienate students. Instructors can create more inclusive and equitable learning environments by critically analyzing these issues. Critical pedagogies prioritize student participation by encouraging learners to engage with content and question dominant narratives actively. They seek to address societal inequalities by fostering critical consciousness and promoting social change. Critical pedagogy emphasizes open dialogue wherein learners and educators collaboratively

explore ideas and challenge assumptions. In higher education, critical pedagogy encourages educators to recognize diverse backgrounds and identities, question authority, and promote social awareness by addressing real-world issues and advocating for justice. When applied effectively, critical pedagogy enhances learning outcomes, encourages empathy, and prepares students to engage meaningfully in society. Critical pedagogy invites educators to rethink teaching practices, dismantle biases, and create inclusive classrooms in which all learning thrives (Bananuka, 2023; El Amin & Brion Miesels, 2024; Nouri & Mahdi Sajjadi, 2014).

- Emancipatory Research—This model encompasses various frameworks rooted in critical theory (e.g., critical feminist, disability, race, and queer theory). Emancipatory research seeks to redefine who the researcher is, values diverse forms of knowledge, and advances social justice for marginalized communities. Emancipatory research aims to empower minorities or the historically disadvantaged and challenges traditional research practices that may perpetuate inequities. It attempts to minimize the potential for marginalized individuals or groups to remain voiceless or marginalized in research inquiries. Unlike other research approaches, emancipatory research requires prominent transparency. Researchers actively involve participants, share information openly, and prioritize their voices. Emancipatory research aligns with social justice goals because it seeks to dismantle oppressive structures and promote equity and empowerment. Emancipatory research is a powerful tool for amplifying marginalized voices and advancing social change within higher education and beyond (Bananuka, 2023; El Amin & Brion Miesels, 2024; Nouri & Mahdi Sajjadi, 2014).
- Emancipatory Pedagogy in Practice—This framework aims to create a just and democratic society that includes humanization, critical conscientization, and problem-posing education. Emancipatory pedagogy centers on the belief that education should empower learners. Its main goals include fostering a sense of dignity, agency, and critical awareness; encouraging learners to question and transform oppressive structures; and moving beyond rote learning to engage with real-world issues. Like the other frameworks, emancipatory pedagogy in practice encourages student-centered learning in which students are active participants who collaborate and critically engage with content. Emancipatory pedagogy encourages open dialogue, reflection, and questioning. It addresses inequalities, promotes equity, and prepares students for active citizenship. Emancipatory pedagogy requires overcoming resource constraints and adapting to diverse contexts. However, it has the potential to transform education, empower learners, and create positive societal change. Emancipatory pedagogy goes beyond traditional methods, emphasizing criti-

cal thinking, agency, and justice (Bananuka, 2023; El Amin & Brion Miesels, 2024; Nouri & Mahdi Sajjadi, 2014).

The models and frameworks related to emancipatory education in higher education encompass three areas: emancipatory education, critical emancipatory pedagogy, and human rights within higher education. Emancipatory education is an umbrella term that includes various research frameworks rooted in critical theory (e.g., critical feminist, disability, race, and queer theory). It emphasizes objectives such as redefining the researcher-researched relationship, valuing diverse forms of knowledge, and advancing social justice for marginalized groups. Critical emancipatory pedagogy seeks to create learner-centered, liberating educational experiences; empowers graduates to be independent-minded, adaptable, and socially conscious; challenges oppressive structures; and emphasizes marginalized voices. Finally, the human rights within higher education framework explores applying human rights principles to university settings and considers how a framework grounded in liberation and justice can inform teaching practices and ways of working. In summary, these models and frameworks promote equity, critical consciousness, and transformative learning within higher education.

SUCCESSFUL EMANCIPATORY EDUCATION PROGRAMS

Institute of Emancipatory Education at San Jose State University

The Institute of Emancipatory Education (IEE) at SJSU, the National Association of Secondary School Principals (NASSP), and the Addition Technology Transfer Center (ATTC) Network are examples of programs or initiatives that have been successfully implemented and are actively incorporating emancipatory principles into their educational practices.

The IEE at SJSU is committed to radically transforming educational systems. Recognizing that many P20 students face marginalization based on race, class, gender identity, and other factors, the IEE challenges existing frameworks. It prioritizes community-engaged research and advances emancipatory pedagogies from preschool through postsecondary education. IEE strives for equitable and inclusive educational systems that empower students and promote social justice. By centering historically marginalized perspectives, the IEE aims to nurture creativity and brilliance in all learners, thus fostering an equitable and inclusive society (SJSU, 2024).

The IEE at SJSU is dedicated to radically transforming educational systems and advancing emancipatory educational practices through emancipatory teaching. To accomplish this goal, the IEE equips students with tools to identify and challenge oppressive systems. By fostering freedom and critical thinking, the students can then contribute to more humanistic personal care. Students at SJSU in the IEE college are empowered to actively engage in their learning process. They do so by using critical thinking and learning to question, analyze, and challenge existing norms and structures. This process fosters a deeper understanding of content and promotes independent thought. Students explore topics and seek answers, which enhances their motivation and love for learning. The students within the IEE program also engage in dialogue, reflection, and cooperative work. These actions not only enrich their understanding but also build social skills. Finally, instead of rote memorization, students explore questions, conduct research, and construct knowledge. This approach aligns with the idea that education should create critical thinkers who can apply skills across various contexts (SJSU, 2024). Emancipatory practices benefit both academic success and personal growth. By tapping into students' innate intelligence and fostering their ability to reason, the IEE breaks down barriers and promotes equity in education.

The IEE at SJSU also facilitates community-engaged research that supports the redesign of learning from preschool through postsecondary education. They prioritize historically marginalized perspectives and nurture creativity in all learners. Through their research, they aim to develop equitable and inclusive educational systems that nurture the creativity and brilliance of all learners. Their mission is to develop educational systems that empower students and promote social justice. By challenging existing norms and prioritizing community partnerships, the IEE aims to create equitable and inclusive environments in which all learners can thrive. The IEE hosts workshops on topics like critical race theory and abolition in the context of emancipatory education. These events foster dialogue and critical reflection, which contribute to transformative change (SJSU, 2024).

National Association of Secondary School Principals

The NASSP recognizes the importance of emancipatory education. It emphasizes the importance of creating a stimulating atmosphere in which students can draw from their understanding. It advocates for critical thinking, self-reflection, and allowing students to access their innate intelligence (Davis, 2019). This approach aims to empower students as critical thinkers and masters of their learning. It encourages self-reflection, inquiry-based instruction, and cooperative work. By allowing students to access their innate intelligence, emancipatory practices tear down barriers and promote equity in education (Davis, 2019).

According to Davis (2019), the NASSP provides tools and resources to effectively lead school communities. While navigating state and federal expectations, school leaders can embrace emancipatory practices by facilitating learning and encouraging teachers to promote learning rather than merely disseminate information. This shift allows students to access their innate intelligence and become critical thinkers. The NASSP also promotes student-centered techniques like inquiry-based learning and STEM skills. These methods align with critical thinking pedagogy and emancipatory education and foster cooperative work and dialogue. School leaders must balance meeting academic standards with promoting equity. Emancipatory practices enhance critical thinking, thereby positively impacting both learning outcomes and test scores.

Alternative Education Movements

Groups like the ATTC Network promote alternative education to challenge the monopoly of knowledge held by traditional institutions. They emphasize the importance of emancipatory education, and their goal is to spread it across all levels of society (ATTC, 2024). They challenge commercialization by stating that emancipatory education opposes the increasing commercialization of universities worldwide. As institutions prioritize profitability, some courses face closure due to a lack of economic value. However, these very courses often encourage critical thinking and autonomy (ATTC, 2024). Also, the ATTC (2024) feels that a broader education is necessary within schools. Unlike training focused solely on job-related skills, emancipatory education provides a broader understanding of society, power structures, and social groups' methods to push their interests. It aims to create active citizens who can shape democratic systems. In addition, ATTC proposes that emancipatory education should be inclusive and accessible to everyone regardless of age or financial background. It extends beyond professional interests and fosters lifelong learning and critical reflection. Groups like the ATTC Network support alternative educational movements rather than the traditional higher educational learning environment and demonstrate that institutions like universities should not monopolize knowledge. Instead, they should contribute to spreading emancipatory education across all levels of society (ATTC, 2024).

Emancipatory education in higher education involves transformative models and methods that empower learners, challenge oppressive structures, and promote social justice. Emancipatory education should foster research on applying critical, anti-oppressive, or liberatory research frameworks, even while redefining the researcher-researched relationship, valuing diverse forms of knowledge, and advancing social justice. Emancipatory research should aim to center marginalized voices, address power dynamics, and examine socialization processes in graduate education. Emancipatory education within postsecondary institutions should apply human rights principles to their university or college and focus on liberation, justice, ways of working, and teaching practices in higher education. Finally, higher educational institutions that employ emancipatory education should consider a decolonial approach when rethinking their curriculum, pedagogy, and institutional structures in order to incorporate diverse knowledge systems, amplify marginalized perspectives, and promote epistemic justice. In summary, these programs must aim to create inclusive, transformative educational experiences that empower learners and advance social change.

PROSPECTS OF EMANCIPATORY EDUCATION IN HIGHER EDUCATION

The future of emancipatory education in higher education holds promise and significant prospects for transformative change. Emancipatory education enriches teaching practices, empowers students, and contributes to a more just and inclusive society that empowers students and challenges oppressive norms. The key prospects to consider include the following:

- Transformational Pedagogical and Shifts—Universities around the world need to shift their thinking from teacher-centered and student-centered model classrooms and replace them with more holistic approaches. Postsecondary learning institutions need to broaden their academic goals to include students' well-being and emancipatory aspirations. Colleges need to integrate these perspectives to challenge power imbalances and center marginalized voices (Cappiali, 2023).
- Diverse Educational Settings—Universities are increasingly diverse, with students from varied backgrounds and life paths. This diversity must be embraced, but it will require innovative teaching methods that empower all learners (Cappiali, 2023).
- Scientific Relevance and Exploration—Transformative pedagogy is an activist approach to teaching and learning that combines elements of constructivist and critical pedagogy and deserves more attention in both practice and research. Since this approach aims to transform not only individual learners but also the broader educational system and society, it should be recognized as a powerful tool for social change and liberation within higher educational institutions (Khedkar & Nair, 2020). Research and exploration in this area should include (a) building on constructivist and critical pedagogies and how they empower students to critically examine their beliefs, values, and knowledge; (b) developing a reflective knowledge base that considers multiple perspectives; and (c) cultivating a sense of critical consciousness (awareness of social issues) and agency (the ability to act; Khedkar & Nair, 2020). Transformative

pedagogy should also recognize that education can be a powerful tool for understanding social change and liberation, and educators should be encouraged to center students' well-being and emancipatory goals while at the same time challenging oppressive structures in academia (Cappiali, 2023).

- Human Rights Framework—Applying a human rights lens to higher education can foster liberation and justice. It encourages critical engagement and transformation within educational practices (Cappiali, 2023). The Human Rights Framework emphasizes principles such as equality, nondiscrimination, participation, empowerment, and accountability. It recognizes education as a fundamental human right; advocates for inclusive, equitable, and just educational practices; and provides a normative framework for assessing educational policies, practices, and outcomes (Tibbitts & Keet, 2023). Emancipatory education draws on human rights values and recognizes education as a pathway to liberation. It aligns with human rights principles by challenging discriminatory practices, promoting inclusion, and empowering marginalized groups. The integration of human rights within emancipatory education contributes to a more just and equitable educational landscape (Tibbitts & Keet, 2023).
- Global Perspectives—Emancipatory education bridges global north and south perspectives. It encourages dialogue between human rights approaches and other transformative paradigms, such as decolonization, anti-racism, diversity, and inclusion (Cappiali, 2023). It also involves applying it across a variety of cultural, historical, and geographic contexts as well as engaging with diverse viewpoints and addressing present challenges (Krstić et al., 2024; Lackovic et al., 2024).
- Student Activism—Emancipatory practices center the humanity of student activists. Pedagogy becomes a form of resistance against neoliberalism by promoting critical thinking and social change (Tibbitts & Keet, 2023). Within higher education, student activism involves learners taking deliberate actions to create change related to social, political, and economic issues; challenge existing norms; advocate for justice; and promote equity (Cole & Heinecke, 2020). It often occurs outside institutional channels and aims to address broader societal issues. Techniques to stimulate student activism within a higher educational institution include mobilizing groups, coalition building, and actions that lead to social change (Martinez Benyarko et al., 2023). Student activists challenge dominant narratives, advocate for marginalized groups, and promote critical consciousness (Cole & Heinecke, 2020; Martinez Benyarko et al., 2023). By engaging in activism, students contribute to transforming both themselves and the educational system. Student activism plays a crucial role in advancing emancipatory goals within higher education and fostering

social change and equity (Cole & Heinecke, 2020; Martinez Benyarko et al., 2023).

- Gender-Based Violence—Within the context of emancipatory education in higher education, gender-based violence refers to acts of violence, discrimination, or harm based on an individual's gender identity or expression. It encompasses various forms, including physical, sexual, psychological, and economic violence (Marine & Lewis, 2024). In educational settings, it can manifest as sexual harassment, intimate partner violence, or discriminatory practices and perpetuates as a power imbalance restricting an individual's well-being (Makhene, 2022). Gender-based violence undermines the principles of emancipatory education, which seeks to liberate learners from oppressive structures. When students experience gender-based violence, their ability to engage critically, reflect, and advocate for justice is compromised (Makhene, 2022; Marine & Lewis, 2024). Universities must serve as sites of protection against gender-based violence to create safe, inclusive learning environments that promote emancipatory goals and ensure equitable, respectful learning spaces (Tibbitts & Keet, 2023).

CONCLUSION

The main point of emancipatory education in higher educational institutions is to empower learners by fostering critical thinking, self-awareness, and social consciousness. It challenges oppressive structures, encourages dialogue, and promotes active participation in shaping one's life and society. Emancipatory education is not merely an educational theory; it is a transformative force. Empowering students, fostering critical consciousness, and promoting social justice reshape higher education. As a more equitable and inclusive future is envisioned, embracing emancipatory principles becomes essential. Advocating for education that liberates minds, challenges norms, and empowers learners to create positive change must continue to move educators beyond rhetoric and actively create equitable, just learning environments. Because the future of higher education is essential, prioritizing empowerment, critical thinking, and social transformation is non-negotiable.

ADDITIONAL READINGS

Apple, M. W. (2004). *Ideology and curriculum*. Routledge.

Brookfield, S. D., & Preskill, S. (2005). *Discussion as a way of teaching: Tools and techniques for democratic classrooms*. Jossey-Bass.

Butin, D. W. (2010). *Service learning in theory and practice: The future of community engagement in higher education*. Palgrave Macmillan.

Dey, A. K. (2024). The CARE model: Reimagining education through an emancipatory framework that disrupts coloniality in school systems. *Canadian Journal for New Scholars in Education, 15*(1). https://journalhosting.ucalgary.ca/index.php/cjnse/article/view/78965

Giroux, H. A. (1988). *Teachers as intellectuals: Toward a critical pedagogy of learning*. Bergin & Garvey.

Hachem, H., & Westberg, J. (2022). On older learners' naïveté: An examination of the emancipatory function of critical older adult education. *International Journal of Lifelong Education, 42*(1), 101–116. DOI: 10.1080/02601370.2022.2152117

Kincheloe, J. L. (2008). *Critical pedagogy primer*. Peter Lang.

McLaren, P. (2003). *Life in schools: An introduction to critical pedagogy in the foundations of education*. Allyn & Bacon.

Melo, V. (2019). Emancipatory education and youth engagement in Brazil: A study bridging the theory and practice of education for social transformation. *Education Sciences, 9*(23), 1–14. https://files.eric.ed.gov/fulltext/EJ1211912.pdf

REFERENCES

Addition Technology Transfer Center (ATTC). (2024). *Education resources: Group work*. https://attcnetwork.org

Aleheg Sewagegn, A., & Diale, B. M. (2019). Empowering learners using active learning in higher education institutions. In Brito, S. M. (Ed.), *Active learning—Beyond the future*. Intechopen., DOI: 10.5772/intechopen.80838

Alhadeff-Jones, M. (2016). *Time and the rhythm of emancipatory education: Rethinking the temporal complexity of self and society*. Routledge., DOI: 10.4324/9781315727899

Aliakbari, M., & Faraji, E. (2011). Basic principles of critical pedagogy. *International Proceedings of Economics Development and Research, 17*, 77–85. https://www.researchgate.net/publication/266224451_Basic_Principles_of_Critical_Pedagogy

Álvarez-Huerta, P., Muela, A., & Larrea, I. (2023). Disposition towards critical thinking and student engagement in higher education. *Innovative Higher Education, 48*, 239–256. DOI: 10.1007/s10755-022-09614-9

Attick, D. (2006). John Dewey and the decline of American education [Review of the book *John Dewey and the decline of American education: How the patron saint of schools has corrupted teaching and learning*, by H.T. Edmondson III]. *Education and Culture, 22*(2), 87–91. https://www.jstor.org/stable/42922595

Bananuka, T. H. (2023). The pursuit of critical-emancipatory pedagogy in higher education. In Daniel, B. K., & Bisaso, R. (Eds.), *Higher education in Sub-Saharan Africa in the 21st century* (pp. 69–86). Springer., DOI: 10.1007/978-981-99-3212-2_5

Bowman-Kruhm, M. (2003). *Margaret Mead: A biography*. Bloomsbury Academic.

Brehony, K. J. (1997). An "undeniable" and "disastrous" influence? Dewey and English education (1895–1939). *Oxford Review of Education, 23*(4), 427–445. https://www.jstor.org/stable/1050860

Cappiali, T. M. (2023). A paradigm shift for a more inclusive, equal, and just academia? Towards a transformative-emancipatory pedagogy. *Education Sciences, 13*(9), 876. DOI: 10.3390/educsci13090876

Chalaune, B. (2021). Paulo Freire's critical pedagogy in educational transformation. *International Journal of Research, 9*, 185–194. DOI: 10.29121/granthaalayah.v9.i4.2021.3813

Clack, J. (2022). Can we fix education? Living emancipatory pedagogy in higher education. *Teaching in Higher Education, 27*(2), 141–154. DOI: 10.1080/13562517.2019.1704724

Cole, R. M., & Heinecke, W. F. (2020). Higher education after Neoliberalism: Student activism as a guiding light. *Policy Future in Education, 18*(1), 90–116. https://journals.sagepub.com/doi/10.1177/1478210318767459

Costandius, E., & Bitzer, E. (2015). Henry Giroux on critical pedagogy and engaged curricula. In E. Costandius & E. Bitzer (Eds.), (2015). *Engaging in higher education curriculum.* Sun Press.

Davis, K. (2019). Emancipatory education. *Principal Leadership*, *20*, •••. https://www.nassp.org/publication/principal-leadership/volume-20/principal-leadership-november-2019/emancipatory-education/

Edling, S., & Mooney Simmie, G. (2018). Democracy and emancipation in teacher education: A summative content analysis of teacher educators' democratic assignment expressed in policies for teacher education in Sweden and Ireland between 2000-2010. *Citizenship. Social and Economic Education*, *17*(1), 20–34. DOI: 10.1177/2047173417743760

El Amin, A., & Brion Meisels, G. (2024). Emancipatory inquiry in educational research: Models and methods for transformational learning. *Frontiers in Education*, *9*. Advance online publication. DOI: 10.3389/feduc.2024.1396662

Freire, P. (1968). *Pedagogy of the oppressed*. Continuum International.

Galloway, S. (2012). Reconsidering emancipatory education: Staging a conversation between Paulo Freire and Jacques Rancière. *Educational Theory*, *62*, 163–184. DOI: 10.1111/j.1741-5446.2012.00441.x

Gasman, M. (2023). *Eight tips for teaching to empower all students.* National Education Association. https://www.nea.org/advocating-for-change/new-from-nea/eight-tips-teaching-empower-all-students

Gibbon, P. (2019). John Dewey: Portrait of a progressive thinker. *Humanities (Washington)*, *40*(2). https://www.neh.gov/article/john-dewey-portrait-progressive-thinker

Gravani, M. N., Slade, B., Brown, M., Jõgi, L., & Borg, C. (2024). From learner-centered education (LCE) to emancipatory learner-center education (ELEC): A comparative case study of language education for adult migrants in four European countries. *Prospects*, *54*, 175–190. DOI: 10.1007/s11125-023-09633-0

Groenke, S. L. (2009). Social reconstructionism and the roots of critical pedagogy: Implications for teacher education in the neoliberal era. In Groenke, S. L., & Hatch, J. A. (Eds.), *Critical pedagogy and teacher education in the neoliberal era: Explorations of educational purpose* (pp. 3–17). Springer., DOI: 10.1007/978-1-4020-9588-7_1

Jaffe, L. (2024). *Cultivating critical thinking skills for higher education* [blog]. Higher Learning. https://higherlearninghub.com/cultivating-critical-thinking-skills-in-higher-education/

Janak, E. (2019). Education in the five E's period (1954–1983). In *A brief history of schooling in the United States. The cultural and social foundations of education* (pp. 65–82). Palgrave Pivot., DOI: 10.1007/978-3-030-24397-5_5

Joubert, S. (2019). *The benefits of active learning in higher education.* https://graduate.northeastern.edu/resources/active-learning-higher-education/

Khedkar, P. D., & Nair, P. (2020). Transformative pedagogy: A paradigm shift in higher education. *International Journal of Research and Scientific Innovation, 4*(1), 332–337. https://www.rsisinternational.org/3ICMRP-2016/332-337.pdf

Krstić, P., Nikolić, O., Lacković, N., & Cvejic, I. (2024). On the relationship between education and emancipation. In Lacković, N., Cvejic, I., Krstić, P., & Nikolić, O. (Eds.), *Rethinking education and emancipation* (pp. 1–22). Palgrave Macmillan., DOI: 10.1007/978-3-031-47044-8_1

Lackovic, K., Cvejic, I., Krstić, P., & Nikoloc, O. (2024). *Rethinking education and emancipation.* SpringerLink. https://link.springer.com/book/10.1007/978-3-031-47044-8

Lattimer, H., & Pizarro, M. (2021). *Building a framework for transformation in higher education: Leadership lessons in emancipatory education.* IGI Global.

Makhene, A. (2022). Gender-based violence in higher education: An integrative review. *Open Journal of Social Sciences, 10*, 234–247. DOI: 10.4236/jss.2022.103017

Mandal, M. M. (2023). Paulo Freire's pedagogy of liberation: A critical analysis and contemporary perspectives. *International Journal of Research Publication and Reviews, 4*(7), 2328–2337. https://ijrpr.com/uploads/V4ISSUE7/IJRPR15548.pdf

Marine, S., & Lewis, R. (Eds.). (2024). *Collaborating for change: Transforming cultures to end gender-based violence in higher education.* Oxford University Press., DOI: 10.1093/oso/9780190071820.001.0001

Martinez Benyarko, M., Lerna Jones, Y., & Tullier, S. (2023). Activism trends in higher education: Snapshots from 2018–2021. *Journal of Campus Activities Practice and Scholarship, 5*(3). Advance online publication. DOI: 10.52499/2023026

McLauren, P. (2012). The future of the past: Reflections on the present state of empire and pedagogy. *Counterpoints, 422*, 184–212. https://www.jstor.org/stable/42981759

Mies, M. (1973). Paulo Freire's method of education: Conscientisation in Latin America. *Economic and Political Weekly, 8*(39), 1764–1767. https://www.jstor.org/stable/4363063

Moore, C. A. (2001). Victor and Constance Daniel and emancipatory education at the Cardinal Gibbons Institute. *Journal of Catholic Education.* Advance online publication. DOI: 10.15365/joce.0403092013

Nouri, A., & Mahdi Sajjadi, S. (2014). Emancipatory pedagogy in practice: Aims, principles, and curriculum orientation. *The International Journal of Critical Pedagogy*, *5*(2), 76–87. https://libjournal.uncg.edu/ijcp/article/view/228/671

Piedra, A. M. (2018). *The tragedy of American Education: The role of John Dewey*. The Institute of World Politics. https://www.iwp.edu/articles/2018/02/01/the-tragedy-of-american-education-the-role-of-john-dewey/

Roth, K. R., Kumah-Abiwu, F., & Ritter, Z. S. (Eds.). (2023). *Emancipatory change in US higher education*. Palgrave Macmillan.

Rule, P. N. (2015). Paulo Freire and emancipatory education. In *Dialogue and boundary learning* (pp. 43–54). Springer., DOI: 10.1007/978-94-6300-160-1_4

San Jose State University. (2024). *Institute for Emancipatory Education.* https://www.sjsu.edu/education/community/iee/index.php

Sekulović, M., & Ilić Rajković, A. (2024). Ways and sideways of emancipation: Dewey's reception in different political eras of an other-than-western context. In Lacković, N., Cvejic, I., Krstić, P., & Nikolić, O. (Eds.), *Rethinking education and emancipation* (pp. 65–84). Palgrave Macmillan., DOI: 10.1007/978-3-031-47044-8_4

Smith, A., & Seal, M. (2021). The contested terrain of critical pedagogy and teaching informal education in higher education. *Education Sciences*, *11*(9), 497. DOI: 10.3390/educsci11090476

Talebi, K. (2015). John Dewey: Philosopher and educational reformer. *European Journal of Education Studies*, *1*(1). https://files.eric.ed.gov/fulltext/ED564712.pdf

Tibbitts, F., & Keet, A. (2023). *Emancipatory human rights and the university: Promoting social justice in higher education*. Routledge.

We Rise Up. (n.d.). *Emancipatory education for all.* https://we.riseup.net/emancipating-education-for-all/how-we-define-emancipatory-education-and-why-it-is

KEY TERMS AND DEFINITIONS

Critical Thinking: being able to analyze information and form judgments by questioning, interpreting, and evaluating information based on reliable resources.

Dialogic Teaching: an ongoing conversation between a teacher and student as well as among students themselves to enrich classroom practice and learning outcomes.

Emancipatory: actions, either verbal or physical, that free one from restraint, control, or oppressive influences.

Empowerment: enabling students to take control of and actively shape their learning journey. In higher education, this means fostering autonomy, critical thinking, and self-efficacy.

Inclusivity: promotion and embrace of equity and diversity regardless of race, gender, class, sexuality, disability, or other factors that foster a sense of belonging for all persons.

Inequalities: in education, unequal distribution of academic resources, such as school funding, qualified teachers, books, and technologies.

Injustice: in education, factors that significantly impact a quality education, such as funding, policies, and institutional practices.

Liberation: breaking free from oppressive structures. In higher education, it means engaging in a dialogue that seeks social change.

Oppressive: in education, any cultural or structural obstacles that affect or inhibit effective teaching and learning.

Praxis: applying a theory or an action to practice.

Self-Awareness: being aware of one's actions, thoughts, and values and how they influence one's behavior in a variety of circumstances.

Self-Reflection: thinking deeply about one's learning progress and using this knowledge to self-regulate, monitor progress, and actively plan.

Social Justice: addressing inequalities, advocating for marginalized groups, and creating an inclusive environment. In higher education, it refers to promoting equity, diversity, and fairness through policies and daily practices.

Transformative Learning: acquiring new knowledge while evaluating past understandings and concepts.

Chapter 6
Pedagogy of the Impressed:
Classroom Reflections Toward a Neocalvinistic Teaching Framework

Jeremiah Paul Giron Manuel
https://orcid.org/0000-0001-6597-1295
Sekolah Pelita Harapan, Indonesia

ABSTRACT

Human flourishing is the end of education, mandating institutions to put an emphasis on the psychological and psychosocial health of the students. In a way, Neocalvinism forms a nexus with schools, demanding humanity to perform at its best to contribute to the flourishing of children. This study revolves around the self-reflection of the teacher-researcher who professes this system as a presupposed ideology in his professional practice, believing that it advances the well-being of children. Through thematic analysis, key patterns are identified and analyzed towards a distinct teaching framework. This study contributes to the present discourses on the influence of religion and spirituality in education, particularly from the perspective of professional development and classroom performance toward human flourishing.

BACKGROUND OF THE STUDY

Flourishing is a theme in the academic world that emphasizes humanity's need to thrive and evolve to better stances, including happiness, meaning and purpose, mental and physical health, and life satisfaction (Vanderweele, 2017). De Ruyter

DOI: 10.4018/979-8-3693-0997-1.ch006

and Wolbert (2020) presented education as a means to human flourishing. Accordingly, education aims to optimize humanity's well-being, setting schools as avenues for children's flourishing. While a specific pedagogical approach, positive education has impacted the educational community, leading explorers to visualize communal flourishing among its students. Most significantly, flourishing is related to optimizing a learning child (Wolbert et al., 2021), and schools are implicated in its exploration and considerations (Kristjansson, 2016). One of the religious movements that formed a nexus with education was Neocalvinism, regarding flourishing as an essence of human life.

Neocalvinism is an ideological system that capitalizes on the sovereignty of God in all areas of life, mandating humanity to flourish in all aspects (Joustra & Joustra, 2022; Brock & Sutanto, 2023; van der Kroef, 2009). Accordingly, the ideological enterprise was heavily influenced by Kuyper and Bavinck's theological thoughts, encompassing the influences in the reformed seminaries in the Netherlands. The world needed more time to accommodate Neocalvinism, accepting university-sent influencers from the West. The positive reception enjoyed by this system was approved by its adherents, confiding in its capacity to create harmonious international constructs (Harinck, 2014; Ong, 2018; Harinck, 2021). As general as it may be for this worldview to thrive in schools, studies have been conducted in educational settings (Taylor, 1999; Vandervliet, 2020; Dykstra, 1982; Low, 2014). This worldview implicates schools as they serve as channels of flourishing. The teacher influences students to perform optimally, preparing their skills and personality for societal contribution. Considering this, the teacher's role in creating such a grand theater in their respective classrooms greatly facilitates human advancement. Postholm (2008) postulated that teacher reflections are integral to professional practice, importing thoughts and concepts to effect classroom maximal production (Cimer et al., 2013; Matthew et al., 2017). Liu (2015) provided a framework that allowed teachers to critically reflect on their transformative learning, begetting a vocation in a similar category, transformative. Such advancements in the field of reflection allowed educators to pursue pedagogical enhancements through this approach. Moreover, Farrell and Ives (2014) advocated including personal beliefs as anchors of professional practice, demonstrating their vital influence on one's class performance.

Unfortunately, religious presuppositions are only sometimes recognized well in non-ecclesiastical agencies. The crusade of Baker et al. (2020), insinuating the dichotomy of faith and Science, demanded that faith-based materials should be included in schools due to the growing prominence of Science-based elements, implying that there are fewer religious materials than Scientific ones. As Brooks et al. (2024) observed, religion and Science elicit polarizing views, as if the two possess antithetical ends. This puts faith-based pedagogies as a stumbling block to the flourishing of the students, demanding unnecessary choices between religion and Science. This paper seeks to address this issue, demonstrating that flourishing is possible under the rubric of religion, specifically within the tenets of Neo-Calvinism.

The reflections presented in this material are founded on the presupposition that religious beliefs can be utilized for the well-being of the students. In this case, the teacher reflected on his Neocalvinistic tendencies to organize his pedagogical arsenal. While the long-standing tenets of this principle have been accepted as a valid framework for human flourishing, the area demands a specific framework for educators, especially in today's generation. This paper is interested in this temporal gap as well. The teacher-researcher confidently offers a teaching framework based on Neo-Calvinism, supposing the ideology's premise towards human flourishing in school settings. This will be essential material in helping teachers reflect on their stances and produce optimized classroom engagements.

This chapter capitalizes on the self-reflection of the teacher-researcher, who has heavily influenced the philosophies of Kuyper, Bavinck, and the present scholars in the field. His two decades of professional practice form a nexus with his Neo-calvinistic principles, providing an avenue for breakthroughs and advancements. Believing that his presupposition boosts his vocation, it permeates his reflections and presents valuable insights. Specifically, it inquires about:

1. the specific practices of the teacher-researcher after the principles of Neo-Calvinism;
2. the reflections of the teacher-researcher relative to his ideological persuasion and professional practice and
3. what teaching framework promotes human flourishing can be shaped from these insights.

LITERATURE REVIEW

Flourishing in the Schools

Butler and Kern (2016) defined flourishing as the best psychosocial state created in an environment that prioritizes psychological well-being. With this definition, student flourishing should be at the center of schools, prioritizing the well-being of students across disciplines and activities (Eckert, 2022). As Kandasamy et al. (2018) and Murray (2018) demonstrated, flourishing children in schools possess positive mental health, safe and secure neighborhoods, and even enough sleep in their daily lives. Van Zyl and Stander (2019) regarded the flourishing of children as avenues for positive work and life outcomes, anticipating social contribution for enriching humanity. This coincided with the findings of Zeng et al. (2016), demonstrating the potency of a positive growth mindset as a predictive factor to good psychological well-being. Noble and Mcgrath (2015) developed the PROSPER, a tool that utilizes positive education for the well-being and achievement of the students. These materials present that flourishing is a school theme that should be emphasized. In a way, teachers' professional flourishing advancement relates this theme to the students, hence the continuing development of materials for the teachers' well-being (Cherkowski, 2018).

An Overview of the Neocalvinism Movement

Brock and Sutanto (2022) recently published an introductory book on Neo-Calvinism, postulating that Christians have a role in fulfilling the world in a transformative and flourishing manner. This movement maintains the five nuances specific to its program: God's sovereignty, grace restoring nature, the goodness of creation, creational redemption, and the fact that Christianity is a public story (Vanderwoerd, 2015). Similarly, van der Kooi (2021) provided six dimensions of the system: gospel and culture, the sovereignty of God, humanity being elected to be active, God owning the world, Trinitarian foundations, and the call to ensure faith, hope, and love. Gordon Spykman, a scholar in this field, developed a tripartite framework of God's revelation: creational Word, inscripturated Word, and personified Word (Bishop, 2024). Herman Dooyewerd devoted his teaching to integrating Science and faith, distinguishing fifteen (15) law spheres in his proposed individuality and modal structures (Choi, 2018). Considering that this ideology considers theology a foundation of all spheres, it is unsurprising that its public aspect is subject to multidisciplinary advances (Tseng, 2022; Jong, 2019). Sutanto (2015) posited that the sovereignty of God implicates the natural operation of the multifaceted dimensions of the creaturely order, calling Christians to maintain a positive cultural engagement as their primary vocation (Roth, 2021). By actively contributing to society, the Christian enriches the world's thinking, ensuring the positive trajectory of human flourishing (Bishop, 2017; Boersma, 2017).

The transformative thoughts of Neo-Calvinism developed its seminal ideas from the theological and modern ideas of Abraham Kuyper and Herman Bavinck (Willson, 2016). Contrasting the reductionist worldview prevalent during the Enlightenment era, Kuyper fiercely set an opposing view, elevating the role of God's sovereignty above the natural sciences (Hubner, 2021). He reiterated that the smaller social spheres, such as family, business, art, and sciences, are contingent on the authority of God's rule. Reechoing Kuyper, studies demonstrated that humanity was deployed on the planet to work, maintain, investigate, and advance into a state that may be offered back to God (Holdahl, 2023; Skaff, 2015). Considering this mandate to man, human flourishing becomes a mandated task for everyone.

Neocalvinism in Education

The fame of Enlightenment in the 18th to 19th century forced the Dutch and English reformed churches to recover the schools (Choi, 2016). The tension of the contrasting paradigms during these years strengthened the conviction of the Christians to reclaim the schools, securing funding for both private and public schools at the time. Since then, Neocalvinistic crusades have penetrated educational systems to ensure the recovery of godly children-rearing.

Kuyper has enormously influenced the scholarship of Cochran (Caudill, 2019), promoting three prominent thoughts: sphere sovereignty, dualism/ antithesis, and common grace. His tenure as a professor has strong roots in these trilogical Neocalvinistic assumptions. Christians like Cochran and Kuyper understood schools as a place for social transformation. With the Enlightenment concepts getting attention, thousands of Christians built primary schools and universities to allow multiformity in society (Vanderwoerd, 2015). Since 1870, these thoughts have substantially reformed the school and family culture, updating traditional Calvinism with the modern developments of the time (Sturm & Groenendijk, 1998). America did not escape this influence as the Dutch immigrants encultured its primary schools, embracing Neocalvinistic thoughts within their academic operations (Oppewel, 1963). These Dutch migrated to the USA because they were dissatisfied with the ever-growing modernity of the primary schools in the Netherlands. However, Bavinck's idea on the presence of modernity in schools deviates from Kuyper's antithetical attitude towards it.

Bavinck believed Science should be contingent on true faith (De Jong, 2015). Sutanto (2018) pressed on this idea and posited that Bavinck recognized modernity and Science as valid disciplines but never in separation from the truth. Neo Calvinism, in Bavinck's nuances, calls Christians to pursue discipleship even in educational settings, maintaining a solid foundation of faith in the Sciences (Clausing, 2016). He dedicated two chapters related to pedagogy and classical education in his Essays on Religion, Science, and Society (Bolt, 2004). He tied pedagogy and education to theology and insisted that schools must continually address questions on human origin, purpose, and essence, granting rational answers solely from religious and philosophical thoughts.

Taylor (1999) posited that the Christian Schools International (CSI) in Canada, one of the most significant Christian school associations, strongly ties educational philosophy to one's community. As a social transformationalist, CSI based its worldview on Neocalvinistic presumptions, deploying educators in its system with the elements of the Kuyperian system present in their foundations: religion as a foundation in education and the cultural affirmation and transformational aspects of the Christian worldview. Sturm (2006) distinguished his description of Neocalvinistic education as modern, bourgeois, and secular. While there are truths to this claim that this type of schooling favors a specific fortunate group, it does not take away its preconceived notion that God is the foundation of all academic disciplines.

Competing Worldviews

Kuyper began his revolutionary education as a response to the growing influence of modernity in the halls of universities and academies (Hubner, 2021). Modernity, the bastard son of the reformation, resulted from the Enlightenment's redirection of epistemological focus and ontological shift (Reisner, 2019). At some point, one can agree with Vanhoozer's (2003) idea that modernity eclipsed the reformation. Both movements criticize the present traditional practices and beliefs at the moment but deviate from frodeviatether's source of authority, with modernity anchoring on an overwhelming estrangement act (Horton, 2011) and the reformation of the authority of God revealed in the Scriptures. Modern education stimulates and amplifies humanistic potential apart from external authorities, gearing existence to a higher plane of the ontological stage (Bobbit, 1941), ergo, human flourishing. At some point, modern education was credited to the revolution of different disciplines, allowing humanity to achieve a higher plane of existence in terms of ease and technology. In the Kuyperian worldview, this nuanced statement must be carefully stated so that the impression of deification may be easily denied immediately. This posed a problem among the orthodox believers as they have unnecessarily placed a dichotomic chasm between modernity and Christianity that such Enlightenment is labeled atheistic, even in superficial explanations (Aloni, 2002).

Modernity had its high time, changing the faces of universities from God-contingent interests to humanistic endeavors apart from God. Unfortunately, just as it diminished the reformation's philosophical and pedagogical tenures, its slippery slope gave birth to its child, postmodernity. As Kahraman (2015) observed, modernism is heavily linked to postmodernism. However, to distinguish, the postmodern paradigm capitalizes on individualistic reflections and self-referential emphasis, allowing the decentralization of concepts, unbound structures, and infinite meaning-making (Rikowski & McLaren, 2002). Both modernity and postmodernity possess commendable ends, such as human flourishing and freedom. However, the absolutism of truth loses its battle as both put a premium on relativistic sources, the self.

Teacher Self-Reflection

Erdemir and Yesilcinar (2021) recognize reflective practices as integral in one's professional training in a teaching career, recommending a model for teachers to consider. Concurring with this idea, studies have long showcased the necessity of this practice to stimulate academic growth (Pedrosa-de Jesus et al., 2016; Zahid & Khanam, 2019). Multiple methodologies have been developed to capacitate teachers to implement reflective practices toward their growth, such as e-portfolios (Slepcevic-Zach & Stock, 2018), role-playing (Kilgour et al., 2015), strategic resource use (Chen et al., 2017), and online feedback videos (Odo, 2022). These practices presume academic growth and provide substantial production for students. Novozhenina and Lopez Pinzon (2018) concluded that professional development programs positively impact students' performance.

This literature review highlighted a wide gap in many aspects: temporal, theoretical, methodological, and empirical gaps. As one may observe, this exploration contains materials published a century ago, proving the wide temporal gap in the field. The recent explorations of Neo-Calvinism as a more religious field may be observed in that its affinity with classroom presuppositions seems unattended. While this material possesses limitations, disallowing it to engage all the mentioned gaps, it provides beneficial insights into the nexus of this foundational thought and education, as both aspire for humanity to advance in its existence.

THEORETICAL FRAMEWORKS

This study anchors its conduct on the foundations of the living educational theory (Whitehead & Huxtable, 2024), flourishing in school (Kristjansson, 2019), and Neo-Calvinism (Kuyper, 2008).

The principles of the living educational theory emphasize one's epistemological presupposition, influencing one's practice toward social impact (Gumede, 2020). Living educational theory, adherents consider their practices as a fusion of epistemology, praxis, and ontology (Mellet, 2020; Vaughan, 2019). As Whitehead (2008) presented initially, this supposes the impact of one's learning to fundamental thinking, rationalizing the presentations of one's practice towards human advancement. Beginning with the desire to improve, this principle heralds an enhanced version, precisely that of professional advancement, disambiguating confusions that lead to better classroom outputs. The substance of this principle includes four essential concepts:

- Constructing reasonable inquiries
- Improving practice through reflection
- Clarifyingrinciples in knowledge acquisition via action reflection cycles
- Enhancingional influences in learning through validation group feedback

Kristasson (2019) developed the idea that flourishing is the aim of education. Alluding to Aristotle's *eudaimonia,* schools should emphasize the good life, well-being, productivity, and overall quality of life inside the classrooms. This implicates how the teachers managed their classes, mandating the urgency of putting the children's perspective in a flourishing setting. Moreover, it also describes how schools visualize the future of other children's future mission statements that support the children's psychological states.

Neocalvinism also played a role in analyzing the data in this paper. As this study showcased the motivation of the teacher-researcher coming from his religious considerations, the principles of Neo-Calvinism, as a running processor of his practice, influenced the expression of his pedagogical approaches. This study's analysis section emphasizes the contingency of the sciences to the religious domain, the importance of God in the formation and advancement of education and its related disciplines, and how men ought to contribute to the efficient operation of God's creation. While there were no definitive subKuyperian nuances to attach to his discussion, a general Neocalvinistic flavor may be easily classified in the presentation of his data.

Inclusive of the researcher's practice and reflections, his integrated foundations amongst the classified themes were considered to formulate a specific pedagogical framework. The teaching framework developed and proposed assumes that human flourishing is the end of one's professional service. The projected Neocalvinistic teaching framework would be a feasible guide for Christian teachers whose career is empowered by a flourishing humanistic agenda.

RESEARCH METHODOLOGY

The flow of this study followed a qualitative design, following a reflective model with a framework as an end in mind. Primary data is the story and reflective thoughts of the teacher-researcher who has been in the profession for two decades, associating his practice with his foundational presuppositions. Influenced by the Kuyperian principle that everything is founded on God's revelatory condescension, the teacher-researcher empowers his practice with guiding ideas from Neocalvinism. Moreover, his post as an educator in a Christian institution with firm reformed persuasion has allowed him to articulate his preferred guidelines for optimizing children in his class. The belief that schools are social transformation agents for humanity to thrive and flourish is an essential motif in his career track. The data included narratives of his practices reflecting his beliefs and rationalizing his actions and choices as he provided instructions, demonstrations, and even assessments to his grade school learners. The presentation was deliberately written in the first person to emphasize the authenticity of the data collected. An arbitrary selection of specific instances was included in the narration, securing the most significant events that are strongly related to the theme of this study. The materials that he organized and presented in this chapter were coded to generate themes, informing the development of the end of this paper, a Neocalvinistic teaching framework.

REFLECTIONS: A NEOCALVINIST TEACHER

The Impressed Religion

My Christian roots were from a modern Presbyterian church. While conceived in our articles of faith, the reformed doctrines needed more exposure to the system. My first encounter with the doctrines of grace was in the middle of the 2000s, thanks to the Christian social media, Christianster. The reformed took little time to mold my Christian foundations, reading every possible resource I could access among my connections. The free online course offered by Third Millenium Ministries at Birmingham Theological Seminary, the video lectures that Covenant Theological Seminary provided, and the social media exchanges I had were instrumental in molding the reformed persuasion in my heart.

Moreover, the websites of Ligonier, Monergism, and Desiringgod were my go-to sites to satisfy my reformed cravings. John Piper, the author of Desiring God, was my gateway drug to reformed theology, leading me to the incomparable insights of the reformed confessions. Confessional Presbyterianism finally landed on my claimed stance years before the pandemic arrived. In 2021, my family was on its way to embracing the Westminster confessions, catechisms, and all in a more robust manner.

One of the things that Presbyterianism impressed on my religious awareness is its firm conviction to engage the culture positively. My initial impression of the reformed tradition was that it was monolithic, disallowing distinctive nuances considered orthodox or heterodox among Christians. Moreover, my first exposure to Christian culture engagement was that of Dr. Horton of the White Horse Inn, Radical Two Kingdoms (R2K). To be consistent with my belief, I did not start my classes with prayer, which is believed to have betrayed my philosophy. It was not until 2018 that a Bavinck scholar named Dr. Nathaniel Gray Sutanto presented a different tradition. Nuanced by the phrase "borrowed culture," my cultural sensitivities were challenged, especially since the R2K position renders general revolution firmly detached from the church. At least, in my perception, the church had to do sacred stuff while the world was secular machinery. This exposure led me to explore a different tradition in the reformed camp, the Kuyperian approach to culture.

I was already hearing back then that one of the professors of Westminster Seminary California, a strong influencer of my Christian journey, held this principle.

Then-president Dr. Robert Godfrey was unashamedly professing adherence to Kuyper. At some point, I knew it was a tradition fenced within the confessions. On the other hand, I had the wrong notion that Kuyperianism was automatically labeled under postmillennialism. Hence, my allergy to the system was justified. My "truly reformed" behavior flagged Abraham Kuyper as almost a heretic.

Nevertheless, the conference in 2018 made me rethink my stance. Kuyper was a church treasure, and in the same year, I bought a printed copy of his lesson at the Stone Lectures. Calvinism became more than a soteriological concept but a life system. Through this exposure, I valued life more, calling people to give weight to their psychological health.

Soon enough, I shared quotes from Kuyper, Bavinck, and Sutanto on cultural activity. I bought books on Neo-Calvinism, principles of Kuyperian theology, and other titles that implicate societal transformation and human flourishing. N.T. Wright, I realized that my professional practice was also empowered, shattering my former belief in my dichotomized societal views. Prayer in the classroom became a norm instead of an option, knowing that God uses even the most evil towards human advancement. My ideals after my bachelor's graduation returned to my heart, head, and hands. It also coincided with the fact that my graduate classes started in the same year. I was so encouraged to fulfill my God-mandated duty as a teacher. I strongly desired to improve because I realized I was a channel for human flourishing, emphasizing my students' well-being and optimal performance.

The Impressed Profession

Neocalvinism has revitalized my teaching career. From someone who used to engage the classroom at a minimum, merely waiting for Jesus to return for a paradisiacal experience, I began teaching with a strong awareness that I was glorifying and enjoying God amid my instructions. The level placement was never an issue. I would teach any classroom I was demanded of, whether it was kinder, grade schoolers, or even a substitute administrator. Every classroom I was assigned to, regardless of the period and level, was an opportunity for me to perform. In my head, an optimized class performance leads to a maximal experience for the children. It would bring a positive outcome to the students' end. It also ignited a desire to be a knowledge explorer as I tried to fill gaps in research fields.

The impression of this worldview was so prevalent in the teaching career that I put God as a foundation for everything: Science, arts, music, language, literacy, and P.E. If not hymns and Christian songs; my classroom reechoes the goodness and grace of God in morning devotion or homeroom sharing. Old Testament stories and the New City Catechism were utilized to share God's Word and message, challenging the seemingly depleted knowledge of the children about the concealed material in the Torah and the Prophets. Homeroom period in the morning was also a moment for values recalibration, engaging the children's values and emphasizing God's mandate and grace of making us behave socially. Moreover, posters of Westminster's shorter catechism questions and answers colorfully fill my classroom. At a glance, one would know that the teacher was reformed and intended to color his classroom with Kuyperian principles.

In Physical Education (P.E.), I created a framework that guided my activities: happy, healthy, and heavenly. These were the essential agreements that I had with my students. "Happy" refers to the deliberate participation of the students to ensure that the activities run smoothly. Similarly, the expectation from students was that they would avoid anything that may disrupt the happiness of the class. "Healthy" meant the importance of safety within P.E. classes. The children were asked to follow instructions carefully to ensure that getting hurt would be avoided. "Heavenly" implies positive relationships among the class members, teachers, and students. This reminded the children of honesty, respect, care, and responsibility, mimicking what heaven supposedly is regarding relationships. The aim to produce excellent sportspeople and athletes permeated the curriculum and implementation, providing instructions with the most recent research advancements and considerations.

Literacy development is another setting of my multifaceted roles as a school teacher. Using the most recent advances in educational neuroscience, multiculturalism, early literacy, pedagogy, and andragogy, I integrated these findings into my practice, appropriating whatever intervention is tailored to my children's needs. My exposure to these varieties of approaches towards functional literacy in graduate school has helped me test and run tools, optimizing the experiences of my students through appropriate interventions and advancing their literacy progress. The multicultural aspect of my classes, setting up an international set of kids, contributed to another layer of challenge in my instructional delivery. However, the recent means programmed to maintain progressing literacy levels have assisted my way, allowing children to flourish in this area.

Envisioning the future is one of my favorite add-ons and class kickers. Using this activity, I probe the class with what they aspire to be and how they would contribute to the planet's rotation and revolution of life. Children would gladly share their usual influences in the family or social media, what they do, and how they want to practice these vocations. Students were directed to social impact instead of mere wealth and social status acquisition. I organized activities that made the pupils realize that they should contribute to their communities and that everyone is a social worker. Those who spoke of their dreams to be teachers, engineers, doctors, and other vocations were processed to help them understand that the complexity of life and the mandate of God are linked and that we are commanded to help advance the cause of humanity and the planet. In a way, the enthusiasm of these children to be social citizens was born out of a stable psychological state, understanding that their schooling means serving their communities for their satisfaction and advancement.

Professional advancement became normative, emphasizing my passionate pursuit of lifelong learning. I realized that to optimize my professional service, I had to catch up with the innovations of the time. On top of my graduate and postgraduate advances, I took advantage of the Massive Online Open Courses (MOOC) opportunities on multiple platforms. While most of these offerings were free, some applications required subscription fees or payment to produce the certificates. There were materials that I had to spend on to maximize my immersion in such themes, allowing my professional stance to grow beyond my current level. It is good that people and agencies were interested enough to help me fund my professional advances. While I must admit the limitations of my exposure, they were enough to stimulate a hunger to discover beyond what the courses offered.

The impact of this worldview on my teaching career may not have been exclusive to these instances. The paradigm shift caused an internal change in how I viewed my profession, leading me to manage my pedagogical tools accordingly. How I perceived the children, the class activities, and my workplace informed my attitude that instead of looking out for short-term results from my students, I invested my time in their long-term impact on society. Moreover, I considered optimizing their learning process by capitalizing on their psychological well-being and happiness in class.

The Impressed Reflections

The nexus of my foundational thoughts and classroom practices has shaped most of my reflections. Looking back, I realize that my passion right after my bachelor's graduation was at the same level as my current passion. Admittedly, both were driven to please God; regardless of my theological convictions, I knew that serving the community may be equated to serving Himself. However, the level of my foundation-driven acts was different, boosting my career more when Neocalvinism became the backbone of my ideals. While the results were inconsistent regarding my students' academic performance, my desire to influence the children toward societal functional presence was observable in my mini-lectures in the class. Also, I ensured the children were delighted with my presentations, ensuring they were happy and enjoying the activities.

The visionary aspect of my Neocalvinistic efforts had little effect on my previous institution, having a bigger student populace and a broader role on my end to accomplish. However, the seed of delight in integrating socially transformative themes in my small academic tasks, such as journalistic and athletic endeavors, permeated my vocation. Children became surprisingly looking forward to how they could contribute to the school's little operations, such as keeping our rooms clean, being socially sensitive to interrelationships, and performing well in programs and competitions. However, I was given a better potential in expressing my theory-based practice when I transferred to an international Christian school. The expected student outcomes of this institution strongly present its Neocalvinistic tendencies: flourishing learners, truth seekers, world changers, confident communicators, and servant leaders. These objectives demonstrate the school's strong affiliation to Christianized ideals, expecting students to beget socially functioning acts in their community.

Our school observes daily devotions and chapel services. One of my roles is to deliver messages on these programmed tasks, and it has helped me assume more opportunities to subject the children to flourishing and encouraging messages. These transforming messages reverb their way back to me and help me approach my other tasks with similar vitality. It is entertaining because it is contagious, and its broadening aspect expands beyond me, influencing the people around me to seek optimized and efficient performance at the school. I remember one of the basketball coaches who emphasized that while we compete with all our heart, we gratefully acknowledge God's bestowal of athletic gifts to us, playing our all for God's glory. The principle of God's ownership within the school halls seemed to saturate the thinking of the school, adding some relief to my passionate delivery.

As I complete my daily school chores, the percolation of these thoughts in my head redirects my focus whenever frustrating scenarios disrupt my temper. As a human teacher, imperfect and only contingent on God's restraint, disappointments still appear and affect my instructions. On the bright side, it makes me return to the cross and realize that such deviations are:

- *Part of God's grand design.*
- *Permitting difference to arise from the ashes.*
- *Hence, the wonders of creativity are before my eyes.*

While it may not look perfect, it possesses valuable insights that inform my way of building rapport with my children, reinforcing whatever links I may have with them. With these variables, I am tempered to modify personalized instructions. It also presents the multiformity of God's works, expanding beautiful design beyond my criteria and taste.

Concepts relating to human flourishing got stuck in my head, especially from the perspective of a Neocalvinist. Relatively, this system allows a multi-perspectival approach to religious stances, giving freedom for religious differences to work, even anti-religious movements. In light of this movement's inclusive aspect, how I dealt with non-Christians was modeled after that of Kuyper, giving human dignity despite our differences. While I would want Christians to practice reflections on God's revelations through His creation or the bible, I have gone out of the cage of disallowing Christian nuances. The ramifications of my actions have led to the actual ideals of my work, building more connections and collaborating with non-Christians to maximize students' exposure to tasks that encourage human advancement. This dignity is due to these people encouraging me to express my vision for flourishing students by making the activities enjoyable. In the same way, I ensured that my students were engaged, leading them intentionally out of boredom in case I observed them falling on one.

The reflective narratives included in this paper were arbitrarily posted here by the teacher-researcher, choosing significant meditations over his philosophy and practice. While it may not be exhaustive and exclusive in scope and content, the data presented possess substantial material for analysis.

FINDINGS AND ANALYSIS

The nomenclature of the neo-Calvinism-contingent professional considerations of the teacher-researcher consists of three themes: God-dependent human advancements, God-dependent behavior management, and God-dependent professional practice.

God-Dependent Human Advancements

Human advancements may be attributed to modernity, enlightening the human mind to access feasible areas of development for life ease and flourishing. Bobbit (1941) observed the fallout of the phenomenal arrival at the epistemological field that caused advancements in the development arena of humanity. Its vital influence in the budding universities back then reinforced the idea of human flourishing. However, the telos of this program progressed slowly as autonomous epistemology broke the pieces of its weak foundations, and religious foundations had to step in and take back their formative bricks. As Neocalvinism claims, Christianity is a public story, and men also have an active role in building a story that benefits the public (Vanderwoerd, 2015). Van der Kooi (2021) concurred with this concept that humanity ought to be active in the Creational Word (Bishop, 2005) that God owns, enriching the pathway of humans to flourish (Bishop, 2017; Boersma, 2017). Unlike modernity, the Neocalvinistic worldview attributes the foundation to God, allowing religious presuppositions to intrude into the humanistic endeavors of the schools and academies (Groenendijk, 2006).

This theme analyzed in the data of the teacher-researcher reflects his idea of pursuing excellent practice, leading children to mimic the same passion. As his narration displays, he motivates students to pursue non-spiritual disciplines such as vocations and careers, exhibiting a grand performance in whatever field glorifies God.

Roth (2021) posited that Christians are called to keep a good engagement with the culture using their God-given vocation. Examples of the teacher-researchers' specific practices are that he bases various subjects on God, and each of these contributes to the planet's operation, specifically one's contribution through their livelihood or vocation. Moreover, he constructed the Triple H framework, the happy, healthy, and heavenly, as a guiding principle in his class administration in physical education. In light of the data he provided and the equivocal definitions awarded to these terms, he permeated his instructions with ideas of cultural considerations for better communal relationships and functions. The Neocalvinistic ideology strongly issues mandates on man as a governor of the creation, putting the burden on the crowned creature to keep its line flourishing alongside the recovery of the groaning-created dwelling place (Harinck, 2014; Ong, 2018; Harinck, 2021).

Framing this under the living educational theory links the impact of one's learning and concepts to fundamental practice. In the context of this study, the teacher-researcher anchors his ideas on Neo-Calvinism, specifically its emphasis on social transformation (Taylor, 1999). Motivating children to pursue vocations and careers in intentionally contributory manners is a valid expression of a Kuyperian philosophy. As Tseng (2022) and Jong (2019) observed, the importance of religious awareness boosts the multidisciplinary operation of Neocalvinistic considerations. The teacher-researcher, strongly advocating to pursue even Scientific advances in the educational field and related disciplines such as brain-based learning, utilization of technology, and personalized instructions, exemplifies this humanistic agenda. One true humanist exists in a Neocalvinist. One who advances human flourishing in the rubric of God's sovereignty hails this Christian tradition (Brock & Sutanto, 2023) and is a believer and respecter of true humanism.

Because God Himself establishes Science and other human advancements, students can rest assured that they can utilize these without reservations, contrasting the false dichotomy of Science and Faith (Baker et al., 2020; Brooks et al., 2024). Teachers could utilize these innovations and have children optimize their learning processes. One can also include how these children are used to using gadgets, endorsing a more relaxed means of learning through these materials. After all, education is a means to the flourishing of these children inside the school halls (Vanderweele, 2017). One can assume the delight that children enjoy when they utilize what they usually commit to entertainment only.

God-Dependent Behavior Management

Unlike in the postmodern philosophy, wherein values are interpreted relatively (Rikowski & McLaren, 2002), the teacher-researcher capitalized on religious ethics as the basis of his student's behavioral management. As per his story, he recalibrated the assumed norms of his children and posted them against the absolutes of God, observable as well in one of the tenets, "heavenly" of his pedagogical framework, "Triple H." In this presentation, he framed the expected classroom norms as founded on God's mandate, leading to socially accepted behavior. The call to exhibit faith, hope, and love in the presentation of Van der Kooi (2021) filters the excesses of the student's disposition in the classroom, hoping that it would also go a long way and endow their characters. The refocusing from wealth acquisition to societal contribution accentuates this character formation among the pupils, too. Enculturating society in the norms of God's law amplifies human flourishing (Bishop, 2017; Boersma, 2017).

They established the significance of Christian ethics in practicing the premises of the educational living theory in action. Whitehead (2008) considered the underpinnings of a particular concept as the driving engine of one's output. In the context of the teacher-researcher, his Neocalvinistic background provided the pillar for helping the students assume their character. The reformation of school and family cultures implicated the formation of values among the children (Sturm & Groenendijk, 1998), providing absolute moral sets for the Neocalvinists. Moreover, Holdahl (2023) and Skaff (2015) postulated that one of the human tasks was maintaining, implying that certain community norms are to be kept to ensure flourishing. Gumede (2020) posited similar thoughts in which conceived ideas are integral to social transformation, in this case, Neo-Calvinism as the bedrock of learned assumption. Children who possess confidence in God-begotten social norms will contribute to the advancement of their community, much more if a framework capable of being replicated in multiple communities may subject their own towards norm appropriation, ergo, this development. Choi (2016) mentioned that the early phenomenon of academy recovery from the Neocalvinistic side was for godly children rearing.

A school that supposes faith in behavioral management also assumes a positive means of managing the children's behavior in class. In a way, this helps the children to find positive characterization in a flourishing manner, finding the school safe and secure even amid their errors and imperfections (Kandasamy et al., 2018; Murray, 2018). This implies that teachers should deal with their students whenever they are caught in any mistakes or errors, considering withdrawing from punitive manners when working with these children.

God-Dependent Professional Practice

The development of the Triple H, the teacher-researchers classroom guidelines of happy, healthy, and heavenly, the character formation through morning devotions, the utility of educational advances as a professional tool such as multicultural approaches, and educational neuroscience, and educational investments with graduate and postgraduate school are career moves that may be defined under the Neocalvinistic lens. Sutanto (2015) and Roth (2021) indicated substantial implications for assuming that the creational order is multifaceted and that humans should align themselves to these vocational advancements, contributing to the creation's flow towards its end. The unvalidated Triple H may need expert and content validation at the moment. However, the research-based consideration of the teacher-researcher showcased how research values are integrated into his work. This may also be observed in his importation of educational neuroscience materials that assist him in dealing with his students. The idea that God provides advancements in education for maximal performance may be analyzed in the findings of Caudill (2019), as he capitalized on common grace as an essential part of Kuyper's thoughts. Common grace allowed the continuing life of creation despite the fall, allowing humanity to flourish in many disciplines and fields.

With God as the cornerstone of the teacher-researcher's belief, Neocalvinism must have been informing his vocation. He mentioned that he looked up to his theological subscription as a life system, not just a mere "save-me-from-hell" channel. His dealings with his professional advancement in his master's and doctorate degrees were boosted by his faith, believing that his advancement would benefit the public. This also allowed him, like Bavinck, to utilize modern educational tools, technology, and neuroscience, recognizing that these developments were also from God and were given to humanity to help creation move from one place to another, leveling up but not deifying itself in contrast to what Dr. Horton mentioned (2011). When thinking is influenced by a legitimate task to improve one's creatureliness and not a deified ontological change, flourishing becomes an ethical end.

Cherkowski (2018) supported the professional advancements of teachers aimed at the pupils' flourishing. While the teacher-researcher's framework is still developing, the "happy" section meant a lot on the agenda of promoting flourishing learners among the children. Moreover, the morning devotions also processed emotional concerns that helped the children maintain a better psychological state throughout the classes. Kristjansson (2016) implied the necessity of teachers continuing to explore how it could serve as a place for flourishing children, providing the mandate for professional learning to include this theme in its mechanism.

The teacher-researcher reflected on various things but made arbitrary choices to include selected thoughts for this material. Three themes were developed from his reflections in his professional practice.

For the Lord

The data reveals the undying commitment of the teacher in his career, explicitly articulating his drive for service to God. This relieves him as he faces the unlikely events and phenomena in his professional career. Contributing factors to this perspective could be his immersion in the Christian faith, which he articulated in his narration, his theological subscription, and the culture he belongs to, assuming that his community puts a premium value on the Christian faith. Considering how vocations are God's instruments of human flourishing, his passion for teaching is rationalized as serving the Lord (Brock & Sutanto, 2022). Similarly, his acceptance of how the world does not always work as he assumed it demonstrates a fiducial faith in God's sovereign operation for its societal growth, a foundational principle in Neocalvinism (Harinck, 2014; Ong, 2018). The idea that God has sovereign power, choice, and wise actions is prevalent in the minds of Neocalvinists despite their scholastic nuances (Joustra & Joustra, 2022; Vanderwoerd, 2015; van der Kooi, 2021).

A motivating pillar in one's career produces a game-changing passion in one's practice. Quoting directly from the teacher-researcher's narration, "*concepts relating to human flourishing got stuck in my head, especially in the perspective of a Neo-Calvinist,*" his cause of impacting society through his students made a mark. A teacher who drags his feet to work will possess a different drive. Much like the perspectives in both modernity and postmodernity, which have the best intentions toward humanity (Kahraman, 2015), a Neocalvinist propels his career with the fuel to enhance humanity's present state. While this may look like it is geared towards a humanistic agenda, it distinguishes itself from the two atheistic frameworks with the assumption of God as creator, sustainer, and owner of the world (Sutanto, 2015; Hubner, 2021). One can deduce that such a service, even with its societal impact, is done for the Lord's pleasure (Holdahl, 2023; Skaff, 2015). The teacher-researcher serves his community as an educator in the name of God.

Moreover, the nexus Neocalvinism crossed to the educational agencies provided an avenue for flourishing and finding a space to fill, especially in one's dedication to His God. As the system assumes, humanity is expected to take active responsibility for societal functions (van der Kooi, 2021). In a school setting, it calls the teachers to build a pedagogical mechanism that heavily considers the flourishing of the students. As Kahraman (2015) explained, one's service to God must develop an intent to improve humanity. One way of doing this is by helping the children find a good life within the limits of the school operation. In a way, keeping an atmosphere conducive to the flourishing of the children is a service to God.

Figure 1. Flow Concept

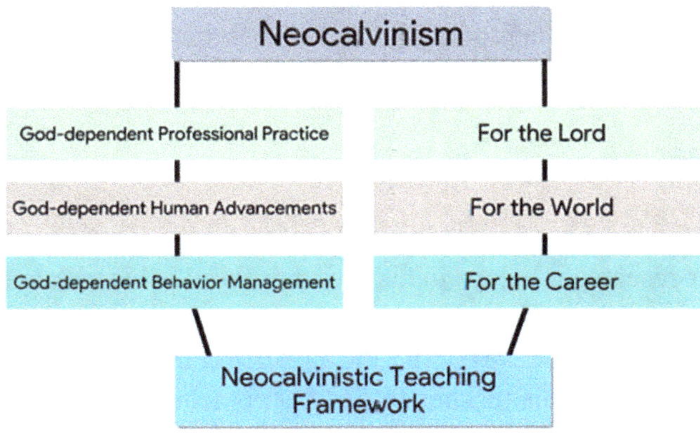

For the World

"Serving the community may be equated to serving God Himself... " the teacher-researcher speaks. He confidently believes that he is giving his all for his community. The deliberate framing of his pedagogical practices, whatever discipline it may be, showcases his desire to help children maximize social concerns to develop a functional presence in their adult lives. In light of his practice, which has social implications, it may be safe to assume that reflective thoughts are processed among his students. Accordingly, these are helpful to their academic growth (Pedrosa-de Jesus et al., 2016; Zahid & Khanam, 2019). The educational living theory supports this seed placement among the children as it will blossom into actual human flourishing themes in the children's service should the concept be processed in their future social exposures (Whitehead, 2008). In addition, the teacher-researcher utilizes multidisciplinary approaches, such as journalism and athletics, to embed the need to further enhance the present state of humanity in terms of technology, ease, economics, and other spheres. Considering that Neocalvinism configures the world as a setting of multiple and equal spheres, harnessing opportunities to expose children to these different disciplines expresses its system (Roth, 2021). Having a Neocalvinistic framework at the head of the implementer of these activities helps seek such a long-term agenda. In this case, the teacher-researcher claims that stance and serves his God through his vocation that advances the world.

Adding to this, the perspective of flourishing children, including communal development as a pattern in behavioral consideration, possesses vital insights into the nexus of school and faith. Neocalvinism calls for teachers to emphasize optimized service, even influencing the younger generation to steadily strengthen their grip on this belief. On the other hand, it also assumes that as teachers present maximal performance, a learner-centered itemization of their outlook mandates the psychological states of their students.

For the Career

Professionally, teaching has its institutional demands. One of the critical roles that the teacher-researcher enjoys in his present school is his task to deliver chapel messages. It may be surmised that even his messages are saturated with material from his theological perspective. Unlike the modern theme of "quiet quitting" among the employed populace, this teacher actively approaches his tasks (van Der Kooi, 2015). With neoliberalism supporting human flourishing, a career boost is essential to achieve optimized levels of the spheres. This coincides with the teacher's direction to project a better version of himself through professional advancements. Whitehead (2008) provides a framework that intellectual imports serve as foundations of one's praxis; the gleanings from such progress are essential for career optimization. With Neocalvinism framing his career projection, maximized production on his end may be anticipated.

Career-directed efforts are worthwhile, especially as they are God-bestowed educational opportunities and have presuppositions in religious stances (Taylor, 1999). De Jong (2015) affirmed this idea and concluded that all the other sciences operate on God's gracious wisdom. Given his Neocalvinistic foundations, the teacher invests in his career and works optimally. At some point, this system has a mechanism for production and preparation, allowing and even demanding workers to submit themselves to a system that capacitates them to grow better so they can serve better.

Moreover, career-based developments place a high premium on one's value, whether personal or professional. Zeng et al. (2016) linked a positive mentality to the well-being of one's constituents. In a way, promoting Neo-Calvinism to encourage continuing development among professionals cascades to the classroom, maintaining its upbeat atmosphere and leading to the students' commendable psychological and psychosocial states.

The Neocalvinistic Teaching Framework

The data processed from the teacher's practices and reflections were analyzed towards a teaching framework. The Neocalvinistic Teaching Framework (NTF) comprises both these materials, which led to the composition that may help teachers whose presuppositions are similar to these concepts. Three feasible pedagogical considerations were gleaned from these and utilized towards the constructions of the NTF: starting with God, performing optimally through God's gifts, and molding God-assumed behavior.

Figure 2. The Neocalvinistic Teaching Framework (NTF)

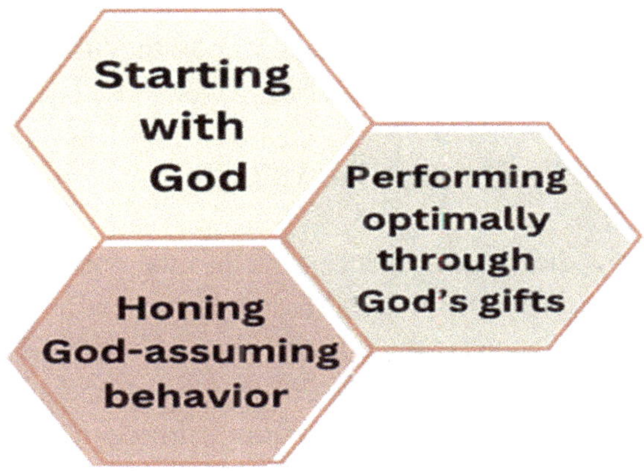

Starting with God

The basic premise of the NTF is that teaching ought to be founded on a theistic premise, the Christian one, to be specific. In contrast with the modern and post-modern frameworks, the NTF assumes God as the foundation of all learning and human flourishing (Brock & Sutanto, 2022). Placing God as the cornerstone of one's teaching ideology disallows the impoverishment of any discipline, enhancing equally as each sphere contributes to the overall operation of God's creation. For instance, the data gathered from the narrative in this project showcased the utility of different disciplines to inculcate insights into children, specifically in athletics and journalism. Moreover, having God as the core of one's presupposition leads to maximal production, at least in the Neocalvinistic system, as it also serves as an offering to God Himself (Holdahl, 2023; Skaff, 2015). A teacher with God as His guiding principle demonstrates a deliberately influential approach, especially in human flourishing, as this system supposes such a mandate from God Himself (Sutanto, 2015; Hubner, 2021). As discussion themes, specific practices may include homeroom prayers, class devotions, and interactions with the Bible and God. Integrations that highlight God as the source of everything in this creaturely world, including the arts and Science, are equally beneficial to this cause. Even amid atheistic presentations such as modern and postmodern themes, a teacher can recalibrate these advances by emphasizing God's creatorship and ownership of this world. This implies that all disciplines advance due to His persevering grace to everyone.

This pedagogical consideration pulls the necessity for the teacher to emphasize the well-being of the children, understanding that regardless of race, gender, and even faith, one has value based on the imprint of Imago Dei to everyone. Classroom activities framed with the idea of starting with God allow the teacher to emphasize one's value, calling for equality and respect that boost the flourishing of the children, hence their academic performance.

Performing Optimally Through God's Gifts

The unnecessary dichotomy between modernity and Christianity, assumed because of a misconception of faith and Science, was addressed in this principle. As literature reveals, Science is only possible through religious foundations (Choi, 2018; Tseng, 2022; Jong, 2019; Hubner, 2021). The advancements in the different disciplines have been utilized in modern and postmodern ideologies as partners in pedagogy. However, the Neocalvinistic foundation insists that the possibility of Scientific advancements only works in a theistic model (Joustra & Joustra, 2022; Brock & Sutanto, 2023). This includes educational tools such as multiculturalism approaches, technology enhancements, and educational neuroscience that are now being utilized in classrooms for better academic production. With these tools, teachers can perform their best to help the children find a pathway to flourishing plates. The teacher-researcher who used these materials has helped him develop relative success in optimizing his students toward better academic learning.

On the other hand, the utility of these materials demands teachers to train for better use. For instance, educational neuroscience would require deep immersion in the literature, actual exposure to the practice, and, at some levels, a form of unlearning of the traditional considerations and frameworks that ignore the modern findings of this discipline. Similarly, the intricacies of educational technology require teachers to keep training, assuming that the ever-evolving innovations in this field have yet to rest. These are some gifts that God has provided humanity to help them flourish in many ways, in this case, educational advancements!

Honing God-Assuming Behavior

Placing God as the foundation of education explicitly provides a rubric for behavior modification. Regardless of how weak one's exposure is to Christian values, the assumption that one knows the norms accepted in Christian circles is often generalized. In contrast to modern and postmodern values, these are based on theistic authority and not on autonomous values (Rikowski & McLaren, 2002).

Faith, hope, and love are general but effective platforms for socially valid norms, especially since this language is biblical (Van der Kooi, 2021). While God has specific mandates that Christian institutions have been adamant about, teachers may condense these into comprehensible and practical statements. By doing so, human flourishing is given an opportunity as one of the outward impacts of these values is strong communal consideration, having to love one's neighbor after God. Putting these formative tools in the classroom and exposure to the concepts will help the children remember. On top of these, it would help if the local community of its implementation, such as the school or a state like Iowa, whose significant population professes the reformed faith, firmly adheres to these theistic values. Teachers can also strengthen these values and hone one's students towards the affirmation and practice of these by keeping a consistent practice before their students. Regular bible stories or devotions on the social norms of Christians are also helpful to help students exhibit God-assuming behavior. Human flourishing is not far, for society has capitalized on these as integral aspects of their communal life.

CONCLUSION AND FUTURE DIRECTIONS

This book chapter focused on the narrative of a teacher whose theological presupposition is Neocalvinism and how he framed his practice towards the flourishing of his students. Using the educational living theory, flourishing in the school, and the tenets of Neo-Calvinism itself, data was analyzed from his narration of reflective practices. To supplement the inquiries of this paper, a short overview of how Neocalvinism impressed him was included, tracking its influence on his life and profession. Three themes were composed in his professional practice: God-dependent professional practice, God-dependent human advancements, and God-dependent behavior management, and three were also developed in his reflections: for the Lord, the world, and the career. These themes were examined against the literature explored and led to the formulation of the Neocalvinistic Teaching Framework (NTF). It includes a tripartite approach to pedagogical considerations, which starts with God, performing optimally through God's gifts, and honing God-assuming behavior, understanding that through this framework, children's well-being shall be emphasized in the school.

The NTF provides substantial material for further development across multiple disciplines. Future research could be the development of a particular model that adheres to this system in the different levels of education and how flourishing in the school, considering the teachers and students, could be better implemented. Moreover, considering that innovations keep appearing in technology, neuroscience, and multiculturalism, expanding the framework to more novel ideas in these disciplines could provide significant insights that will help its further development. Strengthening the collaborations among Neocalvinists in flourishing education may also lead to innovative models and adaptations of this framework.

STATEMENT OF DECLARATION

This study did not receive any funding concerning the research proper, access to resources, and publication. No commercial or financial interests conflict with its production. The author declares that no A.I. platform was utilized in the development of this paper. Ethical considerations were emphasized in its conduct, and while the data mostly came from the teacher-researcher himself, those implicated in the study remained anonymous.

I dedicate the completion of this book chapter to my wife, Cheri Manuel, who observes the Klinean work-rest framework and tells me, "Do this and live."

REFERENCES

Aloni, N. (2002). Enhancing humanity. *The philosophical foundations of humanistic education. Bos.* https://link.springer.com/book/10.1007/978-1-4020-6168-4

Baker, J. O., Perry, S. L., & Whitehead, A. L. (2020, September). Crusading for moral authority: Christian nationalism and opposition to science. In *Sociological Forum* (Vol. 35, No. 3, pp. 587-607). DOI: 10.1111/socf.12619

Bavinck, H. (2013). Essays on Religion, Science, and Society. Bolt, John (Ed). Baker Academic. Chapters 9 and 10. Original work published in 1921.

Bishop, S. (2017). Understanding legitimacy: political theory and neo-Calvinist social thought, Philip D. Shadd. *Journal for Christian Scholarship= Tydskrif vir Christelike Wetenskap, 53*(1-2), 331-333. https://hdl.handle.net/10520/EJC-86a05b35a

Bishop, S. (2024). Everything Matters: Gordon Spykman-A Neo-Calvinist Theologian. *Pro Rege, 52*(3), 1-15. https://digitalcollections.dordt.edu/pro_rege/vol52/iss3/1

Boersma, H. (2017). Blessing and Glory: Abraham Kuyper on the Beatific Vision. *Calvin Theological Journal, 52*(2), 205-241. https://www.hansboersma.org/articles-1/blessing-and-glory-kuyper-beatific-vision

Bolt, J. (2004). From Princeton to Wheaton: The Course of Neo-Calvinism in North America. In *Vicissitudes of Reformed Theology in the Twentieth Century* (pp. 163-184). Brill. DOI: 10.1163/9789004389168_010

Brock, C. C., & Sutanto, N. G. (2023). *Neo-Calvinism: A theological introduction*. Lexham Academic. https://books.google.co.uk/books?hl=en&lr=&id=eLANEQAAQBAJ&oi=fnd&pg=PT5&dq=neocalvinism+sutanto&ots=Nqo55L3tK3&sig=qAVuLdxUbgowE_XI8y5-Dp_hIzM&redir_esc=y#v=onepage&q=neocalvinism%20sutanto&f=false

Brooks, W. S., Deweese, J. E., & Wilson, A. B. (2024). Faith and facts: Exploring the intersection of religion and science among anatomy educators. *Anatomical Sciences Education*. Advance online publication. DOI: 10.1002/ase.2400 PMID: 38409570

Butler, J., & Kern, M. L. (2016). The PERMA-Profiler: A brief multidimensional measure of flourishing. *International Journal of Wellbeing*, *6*(3). https://www.internationaljournalofwellbeing.org/index.php/ijow/article/view/526

Caudill, D. S. (2019). The Dutch Effect: Kuyper and Neo-Calvinism in Professor Cochran's Scholarship. *Pepp. L. Rev.*, *47*, 419. https://heinonline.org/HOL/LandingPage?handle=hein.journals/pepplr47&div=23&id=&page=

Chen, P., Chavez, O., Ong, D. C., & Gunderson, B. (2017). Strategic resource use for learning: A self-administered intervention that guides self-reflection on effective resource use enhances academic performance. *Psychological Science*, *28*(6), 774–785. DOI: 10.1177/0956797617696456 PMID: 28447894

Cherkowski, S. (2018). Positive teacher leadership: Building mindsets and capacities to grow wellbeing. *International Journal of Teacher Leadership*, *9*(1), 63–78. https://eric.ed.gov/?id=EJ1182707

Choi, J. (2018). Chapter twelve science and faith: from conflict to integration. *Christian Mind in the Emerging World: Faith Integration in Asian Contexts and Global Perspectives*, pp. 268-285.

Choi, Y. J. J. (2016). *Research on the Christian Philosophy of Education in the Netherlands: a historical approach*. Faith and Learning. DOI: 10.30806/fs.21.2.201606.231

Çimer, A., Çimer, S. O., & Vekli, G. S. (2013). How does reflection help teachers to become effective teachers. *International Journal of Educational Research*, *1*(4), 133–149. https://www.researchgate.net/publication/337992327_How_does_Reflection_Help_Teachers_to_Become_Effective_Teachers

Clausing, C. (2016). Bavinck on the Christian Life: Following Jesus in Faithful Service. *European Journal of Theology*, *25*(2). https://bavinckinstitute.org/.well-known/sgcaptcha/?r=%2F2015%2F09%2Fannouncing-bavinck-on-the-christian-life-following-jesus-in-faithful-service-by-john-bolt%2F&y=ipr:194.61.41.35:1723894769.632

De Jong, M. (2015). *The Heart of the Academy: Herman Bavinck in Debate with Modernity on the Academy, Theology, and the Church. The Kuyper Center Review* (Vol. 5). Church and Academy.

de Ruyter, D., & Wolbert, L. (2020). Human flourishing as an aim of education. In *Oxford research encyclopedia of education*. DOI: 10.1093/acrefore/9780190264093.013.1418

Dykstra, G. (1982). *Basic concepts for art curricula development in neo-calvinistic education* (Doctoral dissertation, University of British Columbia). http://hdl.handle.net/2429/23288

Eckert, J. (2022). *Just teaching: Feedback, engagement, and well-being for each student*. Corwin Press. https://uk.sagepub.com/en-gb/eur/just-teaching/book282609

Erdemir, N., & Yeşilçınar, S. (2021). Reflective practices in micro teaching from the perspective of preservice teachers: Teacher feedback, peer feedback and self-reflection. *Reflective Practice*, *22*(6), 766–781. DOI: 10.1080/14623943.2021.1968818

Gumede, J. T. (2020). Living Educational Theory Development of a Black African (Zulu) Male Educator. *Educational Journal of Living Theories, 13*(1). https://ejolts.net/node/354

Harinck, G. (2014). 'We must no longer restrict our horizon to one country': Neo-Calvinism and Internationalism in the Interbellum Era. In *European Encounters* (pp. 225–245). Brill., DOI: 10.1163/9789401210775_014

Holdahl, E. (2023). The Earth as an Altar: Understanding Humanity's Place and Duty in Creation through Neo-Calvinism. *Pro Rege, 51*(4), 26-31. https://digitalcollections.dordt.edu/pro_rege/vol51/iss4/4?utm_source=digitalcollections.dordt.edu%2Fpro_rege%2Fvol51%2Fiss4%2F4&utm_medium=PDF&utm_campaign=PDFCoverPages

Horton, M. (2011). *The Christian faith: A systematic theology for pilgrims on the way*. Zondervan Academic.

Hübner, J. A. (2021). Anti-reductionist christian philosophy in the twentieth century. Owen Barfield and Neo-Calvinists. *Pro Rege., 49*(3), 25-40. https://vl.lcc.lt/object/elaba:105963484/

Jong, M. D. (2019). *The Church is the Means, the World is the End: The Development of Klaas Schilder's Thought on the Relationship between the Church and the World* (Doctoral dissertation). https://theoluniv.ub.rug.nl/337/

Joustra, J. R., & Joustra, R. J. (Eds.). (2022). *Calvinism for a secular age: a twenty-first-century reading of Abraham Kuyper's Stone lectures*. InterVarsity Press. https://books.google.co.uk/books?hl=en&lr=&id=T1I2EAAAQBAJ&oi=fnd&pg=PT5&dq=calvinism+is+life+system+kuyper&ots=3kljDaY1Tj&sig=9xjCPBqcuBUF-yUYxSc5iA_Lxm8&redir_esc=y#v=onepage&q=calvinism%20is%20life%20system%20kuyper&f=false

Kahraman, A. D. (2015). Relationship of modernism, postmodernism and reflections of it on education. *Procedia: Social and Behavioral Sciences, 174*, 3991–3996. DOI: 10.1016/j.sbspro.2015.01.1146

Kandasamy, V., Hirai, A. H., Ghandour, R. M., & Kogan, M. D. (2018). Parental perception of flourishing in school-aged children: 2011–2012 National Survey of Children's Health. *Journal of Developmental and Behavioral Pediatrics, 39*(6), 497–507. DOI: 10.1097/dbp.0000000000000559 PMID: 29521665

Kilgour, P., Reynaud, D., Northcote, M. T., & Shields, M. (2015). Role-playing as a tool to facilitate learning, self-reflection and social awareness in teacher education. *International Journal of Innovative Interdisciplinary Research, 2*(4), 8–20. https://www.academia.edu/81758080/Role_Playing_as_a_Tool_to_Facilitate_Learning_Self_Reflection_and_Social_Awareness_in_Teacher_Education

Kristjánsson, K. (2016). Flourishing as the aim of education: Towards an extended, 'enchanted' Aristotelian account. *Oxford Review of Education, 42*(6), 707–720. DOI: 10.1080/03054985.2016.1226791

Kuyper, A. (2008). *Lectures on calvinism*. Hendrickson Publishers. Originally published in 1931. https://books.google.co.uk/books?hl=en&lr=&id=-OMa70AxqvAC&oi=fnd&pg=PR7&dq=calvinism+is+life+system+kuyper&ots=0STFPosxaS&sig=CyBGYxMaPioQam_XePep4qPX8Fs&redir_esc=y#v=onepage&q=calvinism%20is%20life%20system%20kuyper&f=false

Liu, K. (2015). Critical reflection as a framework for transformative learning in teacher education. *Educational Review, 67*(2), 135–157. DOI: 10.1080/00131911.2013.839546

Low, R. (2014). 'Fulfilling Their God-given Talents': Neo-Calvinist 'Parent-controlled' Schooling and Neo-liberal Education Policy. *Crucible, 6*(1). chrome-extension://efaidnbmnnnibpcajpcglclefindmkaj/https://www.crucibleonline.net/wp-content/uploads/2016/08/Low-Fulfilling-their-God-given-talents-Crucible-6-1-November-2014.pdf

Murphy Odo, D. (2022). An action research investigation of the impact of using online feedback videos to promote self-reflection on the microteaching of preservice EFL teachers. *Systemic Practice and Action Research, 35*(3), 327–343. DOI: 10.1007/s11213-021-09575-8 PMID: 34248347

Murray, J. (2018). Early childhood pedagogies: Spaces for young children to flourish. In *Early Childhood Pedagogies* (pp. 1–18). Routledge., https://www.taylorfrancis.com/chapters/edit/10.4324/9781315473536-1/early-childhood-pedagogies-spaces-young-children-flourish-jane-murray

Noble, T., & McGrath, H. (2015). PROSPER: A New Framework for Positive Education. *Psychology of Well-Being*, *5*, 2. DOI: 10.1186/s13612-015-0030-2

Novozhenina, A., & López Pinzón, M. M. (2018). Impact of a professional development program on EFL teachers' performance. *How, 25*(2), 113-128. DOI: 10.19183/how.25.2.406

Ong, A. (2018). Neo-Calvinism and Ethnic Churches in Multiethnic Contexts. *Journal of Reformed Theology*, *12*(3), 296–320. https://brill.com/view/journals/jrt/12/3/article-p296_6.xml

Pedrosa-de-Jesus, H., Guerra, C., & Watts, M. (2016). University teachers' self-reflection on their academic growth. *Professional Development in Education*, *43*(3), 454–473. DOI: 10.1080/19415257.2016.1194877

Postholm, M. B. (2008). Teachers developing practice: Reflection as key activity. *Teaching and Teacher Education*, *24*(7), 1717–1728. DOI: 10.1016/j.tate.2008.02.024

Reisner, P. (2019). Modernity and the Early Modern: Fifty Years of Reformation Scholarship. *The Sixteenth Century Journal*, *50*(1), 29–36. DOI: 10.1086/SCJ5001004

Rikowski, G., & McLaren, P. (2002). Postmodernism in educational theory. *Marxism against postmodernism in educational theory*, 3-13. https://www.researchgate.net/publication/344154923_Postmodernism_in_Educational_Theory_Education_and_the_Politics_of_Human_Resistance

Roth, D. (2021). Neo-Calvinism for the Nations: Reviewing Part 2 & 3 of Reformed Public Theology. https://digitalcollections.dordt.edu/faculty_work/1356/

Skaff, J. (2015). Common Grace and the Ends of Creation in Abraham Kuyper and Herman Bavinck. *Journal of Reformed Theology*, *9*(1), 3–18. DOI: 10.1163/15697312-00901003

Slepcevic-Zach, P., & Stock, M. (2018). ePortfolio as a tool for reflection and self-reflection. *Reflective Practice*, *19*(3), 291–307. DOI: 10.1080/14623943.2018.1437399

Sturm, J., & Groenendijk, L. (1998). Gender Education and the Transformation of Calvinism in the Netherlands, 1870-1970. *Journal of Beliefs & Values, 19*(1), 83–96. DOI: 10.1080/1361767980190107

Sturm, J. C. (2006). Education between indoctrination and emancipation. *Religious Education (Chicago, Ill.), 88*(1), 40–51. DOI: 10.1080/0034408930880104

Sutanto, N. G. (2015). Neo-Calvinism and the French Revolution. James Eglinton and George Harinck (Eds). DOI: 10.1093/jts/flv082

Sutanto, N. G. (2018). Organic knowing: the theological epistemology of Herman Bavinck. https://era.ed.ac.uk/handle/1842/31241

Taylor, D. M. (1999). Education in the neo-Calvinist Reformed Christian tradition, the meaning of a religious worldview and philosophy for the practice of education. https://mspace.lib.umanitoba.ca/handle/1993/2327

Tseng, S. K. (2022). Emerging Neo-Calvinistic Barth Interpretation in Sinophone Scholarship: Its Significance for Sino-Christian Theology. *Journal of Chinese Theology, 1*(aop), 1-23. https://brill.com/view/journals/jct/10/1/article-p97_5.xml

Van der Kooi, C. (2021). The Relevance of Neo-Calvinism for Church and Theology. *European Journal of Theology, 30*(2). Advance online publication. DOI: 10.5117/EJT2021.2.004.KOOI

Van der Kroef, J. M. (2009). Abraham Kuyper and the rise of neo-Calvinism in the Netherlands. *Church History, 17*(4), 316-334. Originally published in 1948. DOI: 10.2307/3160320

Van Zyl, L. E., & Stander, M. W. (2019). Flourishing Interventions 2.0: A Practical Guide to Student Development. In Van Zyl, L., & Rothmann, S.Sr., (Eds.), *Positive Psychological Intervention Design and Protocols for Multi-Cultural Contexts.* Springer., DOI: 10.1007/978-3-030-20020-6_20

VanderVliet, C. F. (2020). Negotiating a Gendered Neo-Calvinist Pillar: Immigrant Loss, Transformation, and Lifelong Learning. http://hdl.handle.net/10464/14613 accessed July 11, 2024.

VanderWeele, T. J. (2017). On the promotion of human flourishing. *Proceedings of the National Academy of Sciences of the United States of America, 114*(31), 8148–8156. DOI: 10.1073/pnas.1702996114 PMID: 28705870

Vanderwoerd, J. R. (2015). All things new: Neo-Calvinist groundings for social work. *Social Work & Christianity*, *42*(2), 121. Retrieved August 15, 2024, from https://www.researchgate.net/publication/301553141_All_Things_New_Neo-Calvinist_Groundings_for_Social_Work

Vanhoozer, K.J. (2003). Scripture and Tradition in Modernity: From Reformation to Enlightenment. *The Cambridge Companion to Postmodern Theology*, 149.

Vaughan, M. (2019). Learning who I am: The exploration of my guiding values through a Living Theory methodology. *Educational Journal of Living Theories,* vol. 12 issue 1, pp. 62-80. https://ejolts.net/node/336

Whitehead, J. (2008) Using a living theory methodology in improving practice and generating educational knowledge in living theories. Educational Journal of Living Theories. Vol 1. Issue 1. pp. 103-126. https://ejolts.net/node/80

Whitehead, J., & Huxtable, M. (2024). *Living Educational Theory Research as an epistemology for practice: the role of values in practitioners' professional development*. Taylor & Francis. DOI: 10.4324/9781003429074

Willson, C. B. (2016). *Poetics of everyday work: A neo-Calvinist approach to vocational discipleship in local churches*. Fuller Theological Seminary, Center for Advanced Theological Study. https://www.proquest.com/openview/0f653db331773c65a8004754940f4129/1?pq-origsite=gscholar&cbl=18750

Zahid, M., & Khanam, A. (2019). Effect of reflective teaching practices on the performance of prospective teachers. *Turkish Online Journal of Educational Technology-TOJET, 18*(1), 32-43. https://eric.ed.gov/?id=EJ1201647

Chapter 7
Virtue as Applied to Digital Learning:
Observations From a Faith-Based Institution

Megan Reister
Franciscan University, USA

Liz Allgood
https://orcid.org/0009-0003-5135-7261
Franciscan University, USA

ABSTRACT

This chapter analyzes opportunities students, in digital environments, have to grow in and apply virtue. The authors of the chapter, who work at a faith-based institution, share their observations and insights as they have actively sought to assist with the promotion of flourishing and growth in learners at their university within the Digital Age. The beginning of the chapter will provide readers with an overview of terms used within the chapter (e.g., virtue, flourishing, personal vocation) as connected to postsecondary outcomes or goals. Next, we will highlight information about technology and the impact it can have on virtue building followed by a section on personal vocation. We will then provide a reflection on encouraging students to be critical consumers as they engage in prudence with regards to use of technology in the learning environment and will conclude the chapter with a call to action.

DOI: 10.4018/979-8-3693-0997-1.ch007

INTRODUCTION

Digital learning environments uniquely influence virtue development within students. Through sharing our observations in this chapter, the hope is that professionals, scholars, and students will consider ways in which the impacts of digital learning can be influenced by virtue. Likewise, we encourage the reader to think about ways in which digital learning environments provide students opportunities to grow in virtue. This, in turn, enables learners to flourish, not only as a learner, but as an individual. The chapter is grounded in Tinto's theory of classrooms as communities as we seek to describe ways in which students are able to flourish by growing in virtue within digital learning environments. Additionally, we make connections to Miller's concept of personal vocation in terms of moral development and as we encourage readers to think about how they can assist students with considering who they are as online students and how their actions within the digital learning environment from their identities. We will now define two terms of importance within this chapter.

Virtue

We define virtue as a good habit and a strong decision to do what is right. To cultivate a virtue takes constant practice to strengthen the virtue and virtue grows through education, deliberate acts, and perseverance in struggle.

Flourishing

When one hears the term, flourishing, chances are any number of the following words might come to mind: thriving, vigorous and healthy growth, actively working toward a goal, satisfaction, or success. In our experiences at our faith-based institution, when thinking about how virtue can be applied to digital learning, we define flourishing as ways in which our students grow. This growth can occur within the academic realm and also personally through the encounters the students have in their digital learning experiences. The hope is they will be able to thrive, learn, and contribute to the classroom environment while also growing in virtue through how they conduct themselves in the online environment using the digital tools.

To flourish as a human being, both as a person and a student, the student may experience transformation, sacrifices, and have a willingness to grow. If an individual is feeling burnt out or unable to navigate competing demands on one's time, flourishing as a human will not be able to occur. There is a time for work and a time for rest. Students may need direct instruction on how to navigate schedules, independent learning, and other supports to succeed as new or returning college students. Within the research conducted on First-Year Experiences (FYE), we know that a student thrives and flourishes as a result of implementing relational practices that focus on attentiveness to the well-being of others in the immediate learning community (Collier, 2017). This may include working to encourage, support, or include other students, especially those who are marginal, and being aware of their needs. It may include learning to navigate cultural differences that may impede learning. It may include working to help another student learn. A focus on building a connection with others helps to lead students toward flourishing, and also allows for the formation of a hospitable community (Ladson-Billings, 2021).

We believe if students engage in flourishing as they work toward their goals, flourishing will help them fulfil their vocations or purposes in life at the higher education level as measured by students successfully completing programs of study and graduating. Students acquire wisdom as they discover their calling, develop critical and creative thinking skills, and mature into faithful, socially aware world citizens who are prepared to serve, solve problems, and be agents of transformation in the communities in which they live and work (Tinto, 1993; Tinto, 1997). Since we are focusing on the digital learning environment, which is a type of classroom community, we will now take a look at Tinto's theory of a sense of belonging as applied to classroom communities in higher education.

Tinto (1993) has determined that college students are more likely to remain enrolled at that institution if they feel as if they belong to or are connected to the social and academic life of that college, university, or institution. Students who become integrated into a university by developing connections to individuals, participating in clubs, or engaging in academic activities, are more likely to persist than those who remain on the periphery (Braxton et al., 2004). Students who are isolated, or who do not engage in social interactions within the university, are less likely to persist in the Institution, according to these same researchers.

Tinto (1993) highlights that student integration into an institution happens in two ways: academic and social. Academic integration occurs when students become attached to the intellectual life of the college. Social integration occurs when students create relationships and connections outside of the classroom through both formal and informal systems within Institutions that may or may not be informed by academic or classroom processes (Tinto, 1997). The more connected a student feels, the more likely that student will flourish and be able to fulfill his or her vocation. Based on the importance of making connections within social and academic supports, we will now describe examples of what we have observed at our institution.

Examples of social supports for online learners at our institution are weekly small group book studies comprised of online students, faculty, and staff who get together over Zoom. They may discuss a book the group is reading, or host virtual happy hours that encourage online students to mingle and network. Academic supports at our institution involve providing students with access to trainings on how to navigate Canvas, the university's Learning Management System (LMS). We encourage faculty to offer virtual office hours to students and encourage students to make use of these office hours. Our Online Academic Counselors monitor student progress in their courses and reach out to students who may be falling behind or otherwise struggling. The Online Academic Counselor inquires if help is needed with logging into the university's LMS, if students are struggling with contacting the faculty member teaching their course, or if they are struggling to obtain class resources in the digital learning environment. Then the Online Academic Counselor and student engage in problem-solving approaches to overcome struggles the student may be facing in their learning. Finally, our Online Academic Counselors take time to build relationships with students by listening to their struggles and committing to pray for them.

Faculty are encouraged to collaborate with the Center for Success to provide accommodations and support as needed. Recently, at our institution, students, staff, and faculty have been encouraged to complete an online form anytime there is a concern about a student's emotional well-being or academic performance. As a result of the online form submission, (i.e., CARE Report), the staff in the Center for Success reach out to the student in question and offer support and resources. Other connections that are made are to match up our alumni to our current students through an online alumni and student networking site. This online mentoring and networking platform is designed to help bridge the gap between classroom and career. Alumni who choose to participate are then connected with students who have an interest in the career path the alumni currently work in and are involved. Additionally, the alumni are provided with a connection to other alumni who share their same background. These examples of both academic and social support allow students to grow in virtue, grow in attachment to the institution, grow in good use of technology, and engage in meaningful communication rather than scrolling through social media.

As demonstrated above, this comprehensive approach to student support takes place through viewing all aspects of student life and determining how we may be of assistance in a holistic manner. Our faith teaches us that each person is a unique, unrepeatable individual with a set of talents and gifts bestowed by Our Creator (Burgis & Miller, 2023). One way our faith-based institution has lived out this belief is through including all students, including online-only students, as members of the university community. However, we must not wait until these students are enrolled in the university to consider postsecondary outcomes. Preparing for postsecondary outcomes earlier in a student's life has benefits as we will describe in the next section of this chapter.

GUIDING SCHOOL-AGED STUDENTS TOWARD POSTSECONDARY OUTCOMES

Starting discussions early with elementary, middle, and high school students in anticipation of preparing them for whatever it is they will grow up to be reaps many benefits. While some students have a clear career path in mind, even from a young age, others are left without inspiration for their career path. As institutions of higher education, it is never too early to inspire students to pursue higher education. Whatever the postsecondary outcome is for an individual, it is never too early to begin thinking of how we can promote flourishing in our students. One way of doing this is to offer programs that invite students to imagine themselves as a student at an institution of higher education. Programs that offer school field trips to a local university campus (Dulany et al., 2022) are important. During such visit days, or field trips, the school-aged students can take part in interactive programs that might tap into their interests, hobbies, or what they are learning at school. These programs for potential students might well plant the seed for what they may want to do as an adult.

Faculty and staff participating in planned, collaborative, ongoing, and inquiry-based professional development leads to professional growth and improved instruction (Vacca et al., 2014). This professional growth supports programs designed for potential students during an Education Day visit. A campus visit on Education Day provides children with the opportunity to set foot on campus and take part in a variety of educational learning opportunities (e.g., through collaborating with the Math, Engineering, Education, and other departments at the Institution of Higher Education (IHE)).

All of these taken together, in a comprehensive manner of providing education, training, and support, will improve postsecondary outcomes as the students transition from high school to college at the IHE and as younger elementary-aged students consider their own postsecondary outcomes when they are older (Wehmeyer & Palmer, 2009). Our university also offers high school students the opportunity to get a head start on their postsecondary outcomes while still enrolled in high school. This Fast Track option for high school students is a way to support high school students as they transition to becoming college students at our institution. Should the high school students choose to go elsewhere, the credits they earned in our online classes will transfer to other colleges.

Building off Tinto's theory of belonging and classroom communities, our institution has worked to support these high schoolers and to have them feel assimilated and part of the university. One way of integrating these online students is to bring the campus to them by including digital pictures of the campus into the LMS. Additionally, within the courses, from a spiritual standpoint, one thing our institution is trying to do as courses are refreshed, is to have prayers recorded by friars inserted within the course content at certain points in the semester. Praying before exams is one way to help bring the faith-based portion to the classes and a way to help the students grow. While something like praying before an exam can seem so small to those who do that regularly, for someone still growing in faith, doing so can be a teachable moment when fostering virtue. The next section of the chapter will consider how virtue development can occur with technology use.

Technology and Virtues

This section will reflect on ways we, as teachers, can help students be good users of technology. Additionally, in addition to the observations we will share, we will enrich the narrative with student voices to provide authenticity for the reader and practical relevance. The student quotes, obtained from written reflective essays college students submitted after attending an annual interprofessional collaboration conference at our institution that centered on the topic of vocation, provide contextual information. Additionally, as you read this section, it may be helpful to stop and reflect on ways your institution utilizes technology and how you, or your students, grow in virtue through the use of these tools.

Within our faith-based institution, we believe we are stewards of what has been created and given to us and that involves our working on virtues within ourselves. The following quote from a college student studying to be a teacher reflects this notion of the importance of embracing the present moment while also striving toward obtaining a college degree and teacher license one day,

> *Our vocation as individuals is to love right where we are. The uniqueness of who we are allows us to love others in such a personal way right now, not down the road when our degree is complete or when we get the job we want or have the family of our dreams. It's about using the gifts and experiences we have right now. This extends to how we utilize the tools and resources provided to us, such as, online discussion boards, websites we reference when working on assignments, and using examples we may find through the Internet when working on learning activities for our students. As college students, we need to recognize the teachable moments that come up through stretching ourselves and engaging in the learning activities even if we might find a shortcut online. For example, when completing an online test, I should strive to grow in the virtue of wisdom and fortitude and not fall back on searching for answers online because an answer key likely has been posted already. My engaging in the learning process and being honest when taking the online test is a way I can live out my vocation as student and show respect to my professor and peers by not cheating.*

Being a good steward includes our use of technology as the above student quote reflects. Salkeld (2023) reminds us that while technology can give humans power and can assist us with overcoming obstacles, we must take care to recognize technology allows us, as a people, to work with creation rather than work against it. For instance, editing software can help students write stronger papers but what good is that technology if students overly rely on that software, and do not refine their own writing and editing skills as they polish their rough drafts? A professor, adjunct instructor, teacher, faculty member, or teaching assistant (from this point forward, we will refer to this grouping as teachers) may utilize digital lectures to reach students in a virtual classroom, but students may feel disconnected if the only interaction with the teachers in that class is via recorded lectures and not through live conversations. Having healthy and productive online relationships takes work, discernment, and virtues (Salkeld, 2023).

Likewise, growing in discipline or habits of virtue takes work and practice as the below quote from a college student who reflected on what she learned from a panel she attended reveals. The panel, comprised of four professionals discussing vocation, struck a chord with the college student as she reflected on the importance of truly listening and engaging with others,

> *There is always something you can learn. Even if you do not agree with that person's contributions to the task at hand, there is still something you can learn from the person. This really struck me because I find that if I meet someone and do not necessarily feel connected to the person right off the bat, I write that person off and feel that person can not help me much – whether in my personal life or within my career. I need to remember that everyone has something that I can learn and that I need to be open to receiving advice from others. I hope to be more open and willing to listen. This is especially important in the online forum because communication is so key for sharing of ideas and views when interacting with others online.*

As the above quote highlights, the learning process never stops. Similarly, growing in habits of virtue is important in both traditional on the ground and in remote learning environments and also never ends.

An example of virtue-building in this context is that our students must demonstrate prudence as applied to making the right choice in digital learning environments. For instance, do students utilize online resources for a good purpose rather than turning to them as a form of cheating? A reflection submitted by a college student studying to be a social worker emphasizes the importance of virtue development when it comes to behaviors and choices that he makes,

> *To lead with my actions is the most important way I can minister to others in my life, such as, friends, roommates, teammates on the tennis team, family, and others. The way I act, carry myself, act when others are not looking, and by my speech can all be non-direct ways of how I can minister to those around me. Thinking more on this path I am on and where I hope to go, I need to think a little*

deeper about what I bring to the table and how I can improve myself. Improving myself in these actions, I can become a better person for not only myself, but also for those around me.

It is not always just purely up to the student when it comes to making good choices in digital environments. When teachers require students to use Respondus Lockdown Browser to take an online exam, for instance, this may assist with taking away the temptation for the students of using outside resources while taking an online exam (due to the browser being locked down) because, as we know, we are all still human. It is crucial to recognize that we can start to help our students to cultivate and grow in virtue, by taking away temptations, to try to teach the students to make the right decision/choice. A university may want to consider having policies in place that force students to practice virtue, such as requiring students to use Respondus Lockdown Browser when taking online exams. Through this policy, the students may become accustomed to taking exams without referring to outside resources, which may help them to grow in virtue as well.

Another area to consider when helping students to make wise decisions with regards to use of technology is to consider what sort of training the online students receive. Some teachers offer orientations to classes and how to use Canvas within that particular course. When thinking about meeting the needs of online students, it can be quite difficult to find a common time to schedule an orientation for the training. Faculty can help students with navigating the LMS and engaging in recommended practices through providing an orientation or course tour of where to find items in courses. This then trains students to utilize the LMS and unpack the way the courses are laid out each semester.

Our institution provides an orientation for online students, helping them to get familiar with the LMS and other online features, such as, the university's portal and online dashboard. First, students are introduced to our Charisms: Conversion, Encounter, and Community. Students are then presented with an interactive campus map that allows them to virtually meet with a friar, join a live-streamed mass, connect with the Center for Success, register or pay for classes, sign up to meet with their advisor, or join an online student group. This map shows online students the layout of the on-ground campus. For example, the "livestream mass" link is shown over the image of our chapel. Finally, students build a community with other new online students via a discussion board where they answer questions such as:

- Where are you from?
- What are you studying?
- Share a bit about God's call for you. How do you hope to serve Him through your studies?
- What are some of your interests or hobbies?

- How can your fellow classmates be praying for you?

It is our hope that building this community will help students to thrive and flourish by creating relationships that last their entire career here. Additionally, our Institution has an online student handbook that is shared with online students at the start of their time with us. The orientation not only informs about campus resources, but also speaks of the proper tools to equip students for success. Students are walked through how to upload assignments, download Respondus Lockdown Browser, download the Office 365 Suite, locate a professor's office hours, and other helpful hints for navigating the digital learning environment.

To design our online courses in the most meaningful way, our institution utilizes the "backwards" design model when working with faculty. This means that we begin with the objectives of the course and the faculty choose materials to help students meet those objectives. Then our Instructional Designers work to ensure that courses across all disciplines are similarly laid out in weekly modules to lessen the stress associated with taking an online course, allowing students to instead focus on their course content. Our Instructional Designers work to ensure all course content meets accessibility standards, providing all students the same opportunity to learn. Within each course, we challenge professors to think of ways to bring meaningful Catholic content into the course. One example of this is having students read a Catholic reading related to the discipline and reflect upon how they can apply the reading to their current or future career. Then, they comment on their peers' posts, furthering the ideas that peer originally presented. This provides students with many opportunities to practice or grow in virtue.

Practicing habits of virtue as applied to digital learning or utilizing educational technology tools (e.g., LMS, video calls, electronic office hours) enable a student to succeed in higher education through promotion of professional dispositions in many ways. For instance, a commuter student, online student, hybrid student, or student enrolled in traditional on the ground classes can utilize a teacher's online calendar to schedule a last-minute appointment or seek out advising as needs arise. Utilizing online video conferencing with a teacher is a benefit for students unable to meet in person. Grades that are posted via a digital grade center is another way to allow students to increase in professional dispositions because they can monitor their progress and performance in the courses as they go. Tools like online attendance (e.g., Qwickly) are able to be automatically tracked and monitored by multiple individuals at the university in efforts to support the students.

There are many opportunities within education to foster and cultivate habits of virtue that lead to success as students and, more importantly, as human beings. We have learned from ancient philosophers' perspectives and would do well to bear some of those in mind as we consider how to promote habits of virtue as applied to digital learning (Nichols, 2023). The teachings of Socrates and Aristotle, for instance, can still be applied to today's learners. Socrates considered virtue as being knowledge and a method of interacting with one another. The Socratic Method is built around dialogue, asking and answering questions, and reflecting on individuals' beliefs through collaboration and communication with others. Aristotle believed that the more one carries out or engages with virtuous acts, the more it becomes a habit and way of living for the individual.

Therefore, teachers would be wise to include many opportunities within the learning environment for students to engage in cultivating virtuous behaviors that would then lead to living good lives. This holds true for any learning environment and speaks to the importance of teachers modeling and demonstrating for students the habits of virtue they can apply to their learning. Consider how a teacher may explain expectations for participation within the digital classroom. Perhaps the teacher will spend time discussing social netiquette and what is acceptable or not within his or her classroom when setting expectations (Vacca et al., 2014). Growing in virtue can lead to human flourishing as students grow in their skills and values while increasing in resilience, which will serve them well, in the online world and on the ground. Given the digital age in which we live, now more than ever, do students need to cultivate habits of virtue as they seek to live and interact, contributing to society among an ever increasingly interconnected world (Kemmery et al., 2014; Nichols, 2023; Vacca et al., 2014).

In summary, actionable recommendations for teachers and institutions to advance virtue in digital learning environments that have been presented in this chapter are provided in Table 1.

Table 1. Recommendations for teachers and institutions to advance virtue in digital environments

Conduct weekly small groups using a digital platform.
Provide trainings to students on how to navigate the Learning Management System (LMS) and online course tours to help students become familiar with navigation of the online classes.
Offer virtual office hours and share other online resources and supports that are available to the students.
Employ online academic counselors, instructional designers, and academic coaches to assist students as needed.
Utilize discussion boards for online students to chat and network.
Complete and submit online submission forms to share concerns or worries that might arise regarding student progress or performance in the course to alert Center for Success or other support staff so they can provide services.
Make alumni connections and facilitate introductions between graduates and current students.
Provide online mentoring and networking opportunities within the online community.
Embed digital pictures of campus in the LMS along with an interactive campus map.
Record prayers and provide access to live-streams of masses for online students to view.
Utilize Respondus Lockdown Browser for online exams to help reduce temptations for students.
Insert live sessions for classes to supplement recorded lectures.

Contemporaries of today would also agree with the suggestions we have outlined thus far in this chapter. Dr. Jordan Peterson, psychologist and lecturer, in reflecting on purpose and motivation has been known to say, "The purpose of life, as far as I can tell… is to find a mode of being that's so meaningful that the fact that life is suffering is no longer relevant". One of his rules he has promoted that leads to a life of purpose is to compare yourself to who you were yesterday, not to who someone else is today. By taking stock of talents, interests, and gifts, a person can leverage his or her abilities to cultivate and create the life he or she desires (Peterson et al., 2019). In other words, through cultivating habits of virtue in our students, the goal is, as they work toward their dreams and life goals, they become fulfilled, put in the work, and are willing to work through suffering and hardships knowing it is worth it to actualize their purpose in life. Another way to look at virtue development within digital learning environments is to think of what it is the student is working toward or what is the student's vocation in life? Dr. Joshua Miller, a colleague at our faith-based institution, has devoted his life's work to answering these questions and pondering what supports can be provided to help individuals achieve their personal vocations. See Table 2 for a brief review of definitions of key terms we analyzed thus far and as applied to personal vocation.

Table 2. Key terms and definitions when thinking about virtue and flourishing in this chapter

Authentic assessment – applying knowledge from a lesson to a real-world situation.
Flourishing - thriving, vigorous and healthy growth, actively working toward a goal, satisfaction, or success.
Learning management system (LMS) - a university's online learning management system, such as, Canvas that is used to disseminate course content via digital means.
Personal vocation - a person's unique calling that only that person can carry out and fulfill.
Postsecondary outcomes - goals an individual has for after completing schooling whether it be to go on for additional schooling or to enter directly into the workforce.
Prudence – making the right choice.
Self-efficacy – "I can" belief in self.
Virtue - a good habit and a strong decision to do what is right.

We will now spend some time considering the meaning of personal vocation in the next section of this chapter.

Personal Vocation

The university where we work has drawn from the work of Dr. Miller in staff and faculty collectively working together to help all students identify their unique gifts and gain tools for living their personal vocations on a daily basis and throughout the course of their lives (Payne et al., 2023). When describing vocation with regard to our students and their purpose, we are building off the work of our colleagues in describing vocation as both the what and why of one's life and work, that is, the everyday work people do and the motivations behind their efforts (Payne et al, 2023; Vance, 2022). Personal vocation is defined as the unique and personal call that is singular and unique to each individual (Burgis & Miller, 2023). Extending beyond just thinking of vocation as a career choice, or state in life, we take on a broader view of personal vocation which has been shown to be particularly important to new college students given the finding that over 80% of first-year college students report finding meaning and purpose in life was a reason they chose to go to college (Gallup & Bates College, 2019; Payne et al., 2023).

Dr. Miller facilitates the Living Your Personal Vocation Seminar online. During this seminar, students complete the CliftonStrengths assessment. This assessment helps students discover their talents and discern their personal vocation. Personal vocation is a person's unique calling that only that person can carry out and fulfill. Students meet one-on-one with a qualified coach to deepen their understanding of their top five strengths and how they should utilize these strengths to live authentically fulfilling lives. Students can opt for additional sessions to learn more about their weaknesses and how they can flourish not only as students, but as professionals in the workforce by focusing more so on their strengths and leveraging those strengths both inside and outside the classroom to be successful.

While living out their personal vocation, honesty can be described as one of the most important virtues a student can develop. With Artificial Intelligence (AI) readily available, online students are more tempted to cheat than their on-ground counterparts, who may not have easy access to online materials. We can assist students in being more virtuous through the types of assessments faculty design. When we design authentic assessments that relate back to real world examples, we are preparing them, in essence--not to be tempted. We can require them to be more engaged with content through presenting, rather than just taking objective quizzes. Authentic assessments take the learning to a deeper level. One way to take the learning to a deeper level is to utilize performance-based assessments in which students demonstrate their learnings through a hands-on way rather than simply filling in multiple choice answers. Another way we can take learning to a deeper level is to require citations on discussion board responses. Utilizing these types of assessments hopefully transforms student learning and allows students to put their learnings into their own words through engaging in applied knowledge (e.g., SAMR model of digital learning).

Another instance of this is to utilize rubrics when grading. By outlining clear expectations from the start, faculty convey to students what the criteria for successful assignment completion is. Students can score themselves as they engage in self-evaluation, checking their work against the predetermined requirements of the assignment as they determine if they satisfactorily met the requirements of the assignment. Fostering these habits of virtue, as described above, can lead to preparation for lifelong learning and success which, in turn, contributes to human flourishing. According to Payne et al. (2023), people who effectively fulfill their vocations are those who have a deep commitment to God, a clear discipline in their lifestyle and behavior, and a clear sense of apostolic calling and service for their fellow human beings. Regarding considering the influence of others who practice or foster habits of virtue and the impact they can have on others watching them, mentorship has been shown to be beneficial (Reister, 2023). Additionally, benefits of mentorship are manifested through students feeling strongly that such mentorship serves as more than just operational advice and enables them to improve their discernment and response to their own personal vocation (Payne et al., 2023). Furthermore, these researchers share that students can link their efforts in curricular and co-curricular activities and achieve a greater sense of importance in their decision-making, daily efforts, and life trajectory.

Time management is crucial in every aspect of life and the temptation to procrastinate is present within the digital learning environment. A teacher might insert a suggested deadline within the weekly module to alert students to the suggested pace of the week. Students should be encouraged to turn on notifications that send automated reminders as assignments are due. At the start of the semester, students should be encouraged to block off time on a calendar for working within their courses, especially with online or hybrid courses. Other ways to set up for success are to silence notifications and limit distractions, such as closing out windows, emails, and determining when the most productive time is for achieving success. For example, for a particular student, he or she may ask if working in the early morning hours might be better than working in the evening? For one student it might but for another, working at a different time during the day may lead to more productivity for that individual.

Taking note of due dates, both long and short-term, and recognizing when course content is made available by a teacher will assist students with practicing discipline if they utilize good time management to stay on top of course requirements and assignments. Online students are guided in adding their class calendar to their personal calendar during the online orientation course. They are presented with example schedules from 7a-10p Monday-Sunday. These schedules build in time for class, mass, chores, mealtime, extra curriculars, work, and time with friends and family. Then, the students are guided through thinking of other parts of their schedules as applied to their studies. They are asked to consider their responses to the following questions:

- When will you work on assignments?
- Where will you study?

- What factors might get in your way?

Our university has academic coaches for online and on-ground students through the Center for Success. These academic coaches set up one-on-one weekly meetings with students to help them develop time-management and study skills.

It is through these supports, as we have described here, that we hope our students will grow and flourish as learners within their learning environments. The result of engaging in flourishing leads to students feeling a greater self-awareness as well as greater ability to set and achieve goals. Students tend to engage further in course material and community, and students can unite these efforts toward career planning and development (Payne et al., 2023). New possibilities arise for meaningful student engagement when we can set up our students to flourish and reach their full potential, both in digital learning environments and on the ground. One such way, in the digital environment, for students to engage is through use of an online LMS (e.g., Canvas, Blackboard). At our Institution, for example, students majoring in Education can increase self-knowledge and/or self-understanding through the online group in which the faculty and staff of the Education Department share announcements, resources, and support. Their goal is to assist Education majors in successfully meeting transition point milestones as they study to become a teacher.

Through the use of the Education Majors Group on Canvas, social media posts and reels, and electronic student bulletins, the education majors increase in well-being, courage, and resilience (e.g., fostering a sense of connection, access to supports, mentoring). Furthermore, through use of the LMS, Education majors are encouraged to seek out professional development, to contribute to the dialogue, and engage in ways they can transform themselves as pre-service teachers so they can better meet the needs of their future or current students (Reister & Rook, 2021). The Education Majors Group that was designed on the university's LMS of Canvas is used to create a community around online resources and tools. In a sense, this group is helping to rebuild and shape the students' first-year experiences by providing them with more resources that they can utilize during the first year and refer to repeatedly (Dulany et al., 2022). Providing these resources is a great service to the online students. However, the students must also utilize the virtue of prudence as they consume and refer to these resources which will be discussed in the next section.

Critical Consumers and Using Prudence

How do students in higher education evaluate digital resources available at their fingertips? Within our educator preparation program, we review a framework for evaluation of online materials as pre-service teachers (Vacca et al., 2014). First, the students examine for any possible bias within the online material or website. Second, they determine how reliable the source is and third, they look at the accuracy. Finally, as a fourth step, the students work to synthesize information in a meaningful way (Reister & Rook, 2021). This directly connects to the development of an active, critical consciousness towards digital media (and more broadly, technology).

How do faculty in higher education keep the resources they have created safe? It is important to be aware of how to prevent a student from taking the work of a faculty member and presenting it as their own. Through settings on OneDrive, for example, downloads can be prevented. Our video platform, Yuja, allows us to prevent download of our online lectures. Engaging in dialogue with the class allows a faculty member to describe expectations of how materials and resources are to be utilized within the course.

How can students feel safe when submitting their work online? Canvas can only be accessed with a username and password generated by the Institution. Our Yuja videos can only be accessed within the LMS unless a specific link is generated for public viewing. This link can only be generated by the owner of the video.

What is plagiarism? Teachers can have differing expectations within and across courses regarding submission of original work. For example, one teacher might allow assignments or previous work to be submitted again in a different course if that work meets the criteria of the current rubric or assignment instructions. Other teachers are against recycling work in any way, shape, or form. Similar to attendance policies, different teachers have different policies in place regarding submission or reuse of prior assignments that could be perceived as plagiarizing by another teacher in a different course. Professors should cover these policies on the first day of class, so students are aware

Another area to consider is accessibility. During the peak of the pandemic and remote learning, we were made aware of the disparities that existed regarding access to technology, internet, and technical skillsets when we were all forced online. Some online learners may be at a disadvantage compared to their peers due to lack of access. We should not take for granted all our students will have access to the same tools needed for successful learning in the digital classroom.

In our experience, we have noticed older online students tend to be less likely to know how to log into the LMS or troubleshoot issues whereas recent high school graduates are a bit more adept at navigating a LMS. A gap exists. On the other hand, some of our older learners exhibit a willingness to persevere and overcome challenges to be successful. Perhaps it is having lived through prior experiences or through gaining maturity over time, these individuals engage in an "I can" belief or in self-efficacy in attempting to navigate the digital classroom. Other differences we have seen in our students lie in the sources of motivation. Some learners are driven by a sense of an internal or intrinsic motivation (e.g., feeling a sense of satisfaction over work that is completed), while others are driven by an external or extrinsic motivation (e.g., seeking approval or praise from others).

The desire to learn tends to be the primary motivation for some of our nontraditional older online students who are enrolling in classes to grow personally and professionally after retiring or for their own professional development. This may impact how they approach the digital learning environment as well. Within our younger online students, we have observed they are able to better connect with the course content if they are able to see how it adds value or is able to be applied to their major.

This, in turn, affects how they gain and manipulate the academic content as well. Generational differences exist on how to "do school" given the opportunities that lie in wait to access information in the digital format when compared to how information is obtained via traditional schooling means. Online learners face different challenges. For some, perhaps due to life experiences or age, there is a lack of exposure or use of technology which then impacts the learning experience. Older students may be less likely to utilize the digital tools due to lack of knowledge or awareness of these tools whereas younger students have more exposure to technology and fewer opportunities to practice waiting and patience as applied to instant vs. delayed gratification. For example, when doing research for a paper in the past, older students made use of encyclopedias and print-based resources compared to those from more recent years who were able to find tons of information with the click of a few buttons.

On the flip side, older students may have more opportunities to grow in virtue, such as, fortitude, perseverance, and humility in not only learning the academic content but also the learning platform. It is through becoming more engaged and critical as consumers of technology as students in higher education, that all students (regardless of age) can grow in "good judgment" and become flourishing citizens in their communities (e.g., of learning). Students can become fluent in multimodal elements of new literacies, or digital resources, such as print, graphic design, audio, video, gesture, and continuous interaction (Vacca et al., 2014).

Technology is most certainly transforming scholarly practice as author Martin Weller (2011) describes in his book on digital scholars. Even if individuals are not directly part of technological changes, technology still has an impact. The three major changes, according to Weller, are the quantity of information that is online has increased tremendously compared to when information first started becoming available in the online format, the role of social network and the significance of online network within the writing process, and the range and variety of content that is readily available online. Today's learners are faced with a distributed, global peer network that links to resources, commentary on issues, extended debate, and invaluable resources which can be a tremendous asset to learning but can also lead to overwhelm. There are many different types of information sources, such as, books, articles, blogs, videos, draft publications, conference presentations, and discussion thanks to technological advances and the digital repository that our current students have access to with ease in most instances.

Weller coined a term: techno-angst as applied to the rapidly evolving pace of information becoming available via digital means. Will a certain piece of information stay? Will it go? What will follow it? We are learning what role digital tools play in our lives and, as with anything, tools will be misused and there will be mistakes. Weller (2011) believes to counter this, we must actively plan for and use technology every day. He encourages us all to become digital scholars through engaging with, experimenting with, reflecting on, and sharing technology and tools. We have seen at our faith-based institution that once students (and sometimes faculty) know eLearning exists, they are too quick to call eLearning rather than trying things on their own or engaging in problem solving. However, on the flip side, it has been observed some students are the opposite. Some students decide they will not call eLearning until they have done everything possible. They spend an hour on a problem that can be solved in two minutes. Students need to find the balance of knowing when to reach out and knowing when to persevere and overcome challenges.

How do we empower our students to utilize digital tools to allow them to thrive and flourish as students in higher education and to not succumb to learned helplessness in challenging situations (e.g., learned helplessness as applied to utilizing a LMS, and/or navigating a hybrid or online class, and tips for succeeding as a college student through use of an LMS and other digital tools to help them flourish and as preparation for lifelong learning and success)? Learned helplessness is defined as a tendency to be a passive learner who depends on others for decisions and guidance (Cervantes et al., 2001). At our faith-based institution, like many other institutions, we all want to set our students up to succeed in the classroom whether it be fully online or remote, hybrid, or on the ground. Decades of research have shown the method, rather than modality or media, is what directly influences student learning whereas modality does improve access (Greenhow et al., 2022). Students will have varying abilities and levels as well as varying exposure to digital learning environments and all that entails. We, as teachers, must consider this when planning learning experiences for our students. If a student feels unable to do something, there is a risk of the student losing interest and feeling frustration within the learning experience. Many of our younger students are growing up in a society that embraces both instant gratification due to the speed information is exchanged, and information overload due to the sheer amount of information that is available with the click of a mouse. One could argue that this way of living contributes to learned helplessness, or a sense of being unable to solve a problem.

Individuals who have struggled and perceive their actions as not having an impact on their learning may operate from an external locus of control, having given up responsibility for their actions (especially academic actions) and they often view their lives as being controlled by external forces (Case et al., 2001). Three theories at play here relate to cognitive motivation, social learning, and attribution. When considering cognitive motivation, an individual's beliefs determine behavior rather than solely being driven by punishment or rewards. Within social learning, expectations of reinforcement, beliefs, affect behavior and judgments are made on past actions. Looking at attribution, individuals want to know why something happened and judgments are based on information in present task at hand. A learned response is responsible for learned helplessness. Additionally, students may strive for unattainable goals, procrastinate, or may set out to complete tasks that do not require much effort on their part which results in self-defeating strategies being employed.

Ways to overcome learned helplessness are to work with the students in helping them realize how their thoughts affect what happens. The students' root beliefs and the distorted perceptions that are viewed are what can cause self-defeating deficits to occur. Part of working through learned helplessness is to change the destructive thoughts when failure or setbacks occur. Children usually form the way they explain to themselves why something happened by the 3rd grade, so some of these beliefs or thoughts may be deeply rooted in the students we encounter (Burns & Seligman, 1991).

When looking at the explanatory style in students who are experiencing learned helplessness, three areas must be considered: permanency, pervasive, and personalization. Some students may view failures or circumstances that caused failure as being permanent. In contrast, while a lack of reading ability can be a permanent condition, lack of effort is a changeable condition that can remediate or exasperate the impact of poor reading ability. Some students may apply one particular failure to everything else in life or to other areas thereby attributing that failure as being pervasive. For instance, a student may say, "I'm bad at reading so I will not be good at math or history, too". Within personalization of learned helplessness, a student may experience low self-esteem and depression, and label himself a failure. For instance, a student may say, "I'm dumb" or "Online learning is not for me".

How do we change explanatory styles to overcome the challenges as described in the previous paragraph? Cognitive behavioral training and learning how to use problem-solving strategies to deal with and overcome challenges and adversity are two ways to tackle learned helplessness. Seligman's ABCDE Method has been proven an effective form of cognitive therapy in changing perceptions. Engaging in language experience stories, multisensory reading approaches, and role playing through case studies, analogies, and questioning techniques helps students change their perceptions. Through metacognitive tasks and awareness, problem solving, modeling, taking stock of self-talk, engaging in self-regulation, and conducting self-evaluation, individuals who work through the ABCDE Method can shift their perceptions.

The steps of cognitive therapy in this context of working with students who may feel challenged when it comes to utilizing technology tools or taking part in the digital classroom environment are: teach the student to recognize the automatic thoughts going through his or her mind especially when feeling badly then teach the student to dispute the automatic thoughts by gathering evidence to the contrary. Next, teach the student to make different explanations called reattributions and use them to dispute the automatic thoughts that come to mind. Then, teach the student to distract himself from the thoughts that are depressing. Finally, teach the student to change unrealistic, demanding assumptions to realistic, flexible ones.

When incorporating Seligman's ABCDE Method, the A represents adversity. Adversity can be almost anything and for a student, it might be a low grade on a test or something negative a group project member might say. The B represents beliefs. These are how the adversity is interpreted by the student. They are the automatic thoughts that go through our minds when an adversity, or something we think to be an adversity, has happened to us. It is not the adversity itself, but the student's perception of the threat and failure expectations they bring. The C represents consequences. It is here where the student records how he or she felt and what was done about it. The student ought to write as many feelings and actions he or she is aware of in this step. It is at this point, the student is taught how to see the distortions, to refute them, and then to argue with self to change the thoughts (Gordon, 2004). The D represents dispute and occurs when the student argues with self to change way of reacting or believing about something. In other words, the student holds up the thought and asks if it is a rational or an irrational thought. The E represents the energize step. It is during this step the student is moved to act in a different way or energized into changing the outcome.

In closing, what are ways to prevent learned helplessness in online learning, and instead to help students flourish? Consider teaching multisensory through using a variety of methods to reach diverse learners. Monitor students' progress regularly and talk with students about what and how they are feeling. There are moments that may, at first, seem as if they are unteachable moments. However, with reframing and practice, students can persist and overcome these challenging moments in their learning encounters. They can anticipate and prepare for these moments through how they choose to respond and reflect. Sensoy and Diangelo (2014) say our goal, in teaching and learning, is to create opportunities for students to practice vocabulary, concepts, and skills that move the students into humility, openness, and analysis rather than certainty, rebuttal, or refusal. We will now consider implications as we begin to conclude the chapter.

IMPLICATIONS

As shown throughout this chapter, digital learning environments uniquely influence virtue development within students. We have provided examples and suggestions for ways in which teachers can provide students opportunities to grow in virtue in their digital learning environments to assist students with flourishing inside and outside the classroom. Other institutions may want to examine enrollment numbers of online students and analyze whether or not there are more older online students than traditional counterparts after considering what we shared we observed at our institution (e.g., increase in all ages within our online learners in recent years). Consistency is also needed for flourishing to occur so teachers may want to engage in creating rubrics to explicitly state for learners what the expectations are of the online coursework. An institution may want to investigate and compare the type of courses created with and without an instructional designer. We hope the ideas suggested in this chapter can serve as a call to action as readers consider ways they can promote virtue development and help their students to flourish in their digital learning environments.

REFERENCES

Braxton, J. M., Milem, J. F., & Sullivan, A. S. (2004). The influence of active learning on the college student departure process: Toward a revision of Tinto's theory. *The Journal of Higher Education, 71*(5), 569–590.

Burgis, L., & Miller, J. (2023). *Unrepeatable: Cultivating the unique calling of every person*. Emmaus Road.

Burns, M., & Seligman, M. E. P. (1991). *Explanatory style, helplessness, and depression. Handbook of Social and Clinical Psychology*. Pergamon Press.

Case, L., Harris, K., & Mamlin, N. (2001, Winter). A methodological analysis of research on locus of control and learning disabilities: Rethinking a common assumption. *The Journal of Special Education*, •••, 11–15.

Cervantes, J. M., Craik, L., Kreil, D., Wiest, D., & Wong, E. (2001, Spring). Intrinsic motivation among regular, special, and alternative education high school students. *Adolescence, 5*(4).

Collier, P. J. (2017). Why peer mentoring is an effective approach for promoting college student success. *Metropolitan Universities, 28*(3), 9–19. DOI: 10.18060/21539

Dulany, A., Rook, R., Reister, M., & Utz, B. (2022, September). Forming the Student Experience from Start to Finish: Education Day: Enabling potential students to see themselves at our Institution of higher education. *Best Practices in Christian Higher Education Conference*, Abilene, Texas.

Gordon, R. M. (2004). *The GRAM: Learned helplessness and school failure*. Retrieved July 8, 2004 from http://www.ldaca.org/gram/gordon.htm

Greenhow, C., Graham, C. R., & Koehler, M. J. (2022). Foundations of online learning: Challenges and opportunities. *Educational Psychologist, 57*(3), 131–147. DOI: 10.1080/00461520.2022.20903644

Kemmery, M., Appenzeller, M., & Gardiner-Walsh, S. (2014, January). Creating new collaboration…One car ride at a time! *North Carolina Council for Exceptional Children*, Pinehurst, NC.

Ladson-Billings, G. (2021). Three decades of culturally relevant, responsive, & sustaining pedagogy: What lies ahead? *The Educational Forum, 85*(4), 351–354. DOI: 10.1080/00131725.2021.1957632

Nichols, M. (2023, April 14). Cultivating virtue in education: Insights from Socrates and Aristotle. https://www.linkedin.com/pulse/cultivating-virtue-education-insights -from- socrates-mark-nichols

Payne, C., Plaus, V., Reister, M., Miller, J., Frezza, S., Jauregui, J., & Pilsner, J. (2023). Toward a comprehensive approach to personal vocation. *Christian Higher Education, 22*, 3–4. DOI: 10.1080/15363759.2023.2223163

Peterson, J. B., Doidge, N., & Van Sciver, E. (2019). *12 rules for life: an antidote to chaos* [London]. Penguin Books.

Reister, M. (2023). Teachable Moments: What can we learn from peer mentors and teacher workshops? *Teaching and Teacher Education, 135*. Advance online publication. DOI: 10.1016/j.tate.2023.104330

Reister, M., & Rook, R. (2021). Perceptions of preparedness for online teaching due to the COVID-19 pandemic as a graduate of an education program at a university in the Midwest. *Journal of Digital Learning in Teacher Education*. Advance online publication. DOI: 10.1080/21532974.2021.1908920

Salkeld, B. (2023). *Educating for eternity: A teacher's companion for making every class Catholic*. Our Sunday Visitor.

Sensoy, Ö., & Diangelo, R. J. (2014). Respect differences? Challenging the common guidelines in social justice education. *Democracy & Education, 22*, 1.

Tinto, V. (1993). *Leaving college: Rethinking the causes and cures of student attrition* (2nd ed.). University of Chicago Press.

Tinto, V. (1997). Classrooms as communities: Exploring the educational character of student persistence. *The Journal of Higher Education, 68*(6), 599–623.

Vacca, R. T., Vacca, J. A. L., & Mraz, M. (2014). *Content area reading: Literacy and learning across the curriculum* (11th ed.). Pearson.

Wehmeyer, M. L., Little, T. D., & Sergeant, J. (2009). Self-determination. In Lopez, S. J., & Snyder, C. R. (Eds.), *Oxford handbook of positive psychology* (2nd ed., pp. 357–366). Oxford University Press.

Weller, M.J. (2011). The digital scholar: How technology is changing academic practice.

Chapter 8
Social and Digital Media:
Promoting Rationality, Self-Knowledge, and Self-Understanding in Higher Education

Surjit Singha
https://orcid.org/0000-0002-5730-8677
Kristu Jayanti University, India

ABSTRACT

Higher education needs social and digital media in the digital age. This chapter examines how these tools help students develop logic, self-awareness, and self-understanding. Strategic integration allows educators to build a dynamic learning environment that gives pupils modern-day abilities. Students develop rationality through critical thinking, different perspectives, and digital debates. The wealth of knowledge helps them make decisions and solve challenges. Students can document their experiences and growth on social media. It increases self-awareness and personal growth. A well-planned approach is needed to integrate social and digital media into higher education. It requires integrating technology with educational goals, choosing appropriate platforms, stressing digital literacy, and encouraging reflection and cooperation. Methods are evaluated and updated to stay current, accessible, and sustainable. Social and digital media in higher education are helpful and essential in an age of digitalization.

DOI: 10.4018/979-8-3693-0997-1.ch008

INTRODUCTION

Within the dynamic realm of higher education, the emergence of social and digital media has initiated a paradigm shift, fundamentally altering how students interact with information, other students, and the broader global context. The rapid expansion of digital platforms, social networks, and online resources has not only facilitated unparalleled access to knowledge. Still, it has also created a distinctive prospect for nurturing personal and intellectual development. In the present dynamic milieu, our chapter undertakes an endeavour to examine the significant influence of social and digital media in the realm of higher education, with a particular emphasis on their potential to foster rationality, self-knowledge, and self-understanding (Li & Wong, 2020). The initial segment of our investigation focuses on the profound transformations that social and digital media have instigated inside higher education. The increasing use of digital tools in educational settings, such as classrooms, lecture halls, and research activities, is causing significant shifts in the fundamental approaches to teaching and learning. The advent of extensive knowledge repositories and the interconnected global community has significantly transformed how students and educators engage with educational materials and one another. This paradigm shift extends beyond mere convenience, as it fundamentally alters the essence of education by changing the processes through which students get, evaluate, and employ information. Educators, administrators, and students must comprehend the significance of this alteration. Amid this significant shift, it is crucial to acknowledge the importance of cultivating attributes such as rationality, self-knowledge, and self-understanding in our students. With the increasing integration of digital media into the educational process, the ability to participate in critical thinking, make well-informed judgments, and partake in meaningful self-reflection becomes increasingly crucial yet more demanding. Within the given framework, the objective of our chapter is to provide a comprehensive understanding of the influence exerted by social and digital media in fostering these essential qualities among students. This influence extends beyond mere information consumption and sharing, as it empowers students to develop critical thinking skills and engage thoughtfully in their educational pursuits.

This chapter examines the convergence of technology, higher education, and human growth. This study seeks to thoroughly analyze the impact of social and digital media, as well as their capacity to improve rationality, self-knowledge, and self-understanding. The objective is to provide educators, learners, and researchers with a more profound comprehension of how to effectively utilize these tools to enhance the educational experience for all parties involved. Amid the unexplored terrain of the digital era, our objective is to elucidate a trajectory that fosters the development of thriving, genuine connections and substantial advancement in individuals seeking knowledge. This introduction serves as the basis for an intellectually stimulating and enlightening exploration of the digital realm within the context of higher education and its potential to enhance or degrade human attributes. The main objective of this chapter is to conduct a comprehensive examination and analysis of the significant impact of social and digital media on higher education. The aim is to explore the profound implications of these technologies in teaching and highlight their capacity to foster distinct attributes in students, including rationality, self-awareness, and self-comprehension. The primary goal is to elucidate the appropriate utilization of social and digital media to enhance the comprehensive educational experience and facilitate students' personal growth.

The investigation begins by examining the profound influence of social and digital media on higher education. This statement emphasizes the transformative impact of modern technologies on students knowledge acquisition and social connections with peers and the wider society. The enhanced availability of information and the interconnected global community are essential factors in defining modern schooling. The scope of analysis expands beyond the first examination to encompass integrating digital technologies into educational settings such as classrooms, lecture halls, and research activities. The primary emphasis lies in the transformative impact of these instruments on the fundamental principles of pedagogy and educational processes. It is imperative to emphasize that this paradigm shift goes beyond mere convenience; it extends to the essence of education, significantly impacting information acquisition, analysis, and application methods. The chapter explores the significance of rationality, self-knowledge, and self-understanding. It examines how social and digital media contribute to developing these features in learners. It is essential to recognize that in a time characterized by integrating digital media into the educational process, the capacity for critical thinking, informed decision-making, and meaningful self-reflection has assumed heightened difficulty and indispensability.

The chapter thoroughly analyses technology, higher education, and human growth. This study offers a comprehensive perspective on the potential of social and digital media in promoting rationality, self-knowledge, and self-understanding among students. The primary objective is to provide educators, learners, and researchers with a comprehensive comprehension of effectively utilizing social and digital media to enhance the educational experience for all stakeholders. Amid the unexplored territory of the digital era, the objective is to elucidate a trajectory that fosters the development of thriving, genuine connections and significant advancement in individuals seeking knowledge. This study considers both the possible advantages and difficulties that come with the ever-changing digital environment. This chapter's primary focus and objective revolve around understanding the influence of social and digital media on higher education, with a particular emphasis on their potential to foster critical thinking and self-awareness among students. The primary goal is to enhance pupils' personal and cognitive development within the ever-evolving and technology-driven digital era.

This chapter incorporates a comprehensive theoretical and contextual framework that includes various theories and backgrounds. These approaches establish a robust basis for comprehending the significant impact of social and digital media on higher education and their role in fostering rationality, self-knowledge, and self-understanding among learners. The analysis of the effects of social and digital media on higher education is guided by the concept of Technological Determinism. According to Hällström (2020) and Oliver (2011), this theory asserts that technology plays a significant role in shaping and influencing societal and educational transformations. It allows for examining the underlying changes in how students interact with knowledge, their peers, and the world.

The concept of Social Constructivism plays a crucial role in the examination of knowledge formation, emphasizing the importance of social interactions. The abovementioned theory contributes to the discourse on how social and digital media support collaborative learning, peer relationships, and the shared building of knowledge within higher Education (Cilliers, 2021). The concept of digital literacy holds significant importance when examining the influence of digital media on schooling. The comprehension of this theory facilitates the evaluation of the aptitudes and proficiencies necessary for students to navigate the digital environment efficiently, augmenting their educational encounters (Audrin & Audrin, 2022). The debate surrounding enhancing cognitive development, critical thinking, and problem-solving skills among students is informed by many cognitive development theories, such as those proposed by Piaget, Vygotsky, and Bruner. These theories contribute to understanding how digital media can facilitate these cognitive processes. According to Vedechkina and Borgonovi (2021), these ideas provide a framework for comprehending how these technologies can promote cognitive development.

The Media Ecology Theory, as postulated by Marshall McLuhan, offers significant insights into the interdependent connection between media and society. The study by Islas and Bernal (2016) highlights the significance of examining the role of social and digital media in the educational setting. This research emphasizes the impact of these media platforms on the dissemination and consumption of knowledge. EdTech acceptance Models, such as the Technology Acceptance Model (TAM) and the Unified Theory of Acceptance and Use of Technology (UTAUT), offer insights into the factors influencing the acceptance and use of educational technology, including digital media. The models above provide valuable insights into how instructors and students incorporate these technologies within the context of the learning process (Ursavaş, 2022). Understanding the historical context of higher education enables one to gain a deeper understanding of how traditional educational practices have transformed and adapted within the digital realm. This text offers crucial contextual information regarding the underlying objectives and inherent obstacles associated with integrating technology into educational environments.

The utilization of social and digital media in education has prompted conversations on the ethical frameworks and privacy considerations, which serve as a crucial backdrop. These considerations encompass a range of ethical and privacy concerns that need to be considered when employing such media in educational settings. Examining these debates holds significant importance in comprehending the ramifications of technology on students (Marín et al., 2022; Duran, 2022). The field of Learning Analytics emphasizes the use of data and analytics in monitoring and assessing student advancement and involvement. The context above provides a foundation for investigating how digital media facilitates educational institutions in gathering and utilizing data to enhance the educational experience (Lee et al., 2020). By integrating various theoretical perspectives and historical contexts, the chapter develops a comprehensive academic and contextual framework for conducting a thorough analysis of the transformative impact of social and digital media on higher education. These viewpoints and ideas offer valuable contributions to understanding how these technologies can enable students to cultivate rationality, self-knowledge, and self-understanding within the dynamic digital environment, promoting a comprehensive comprehension of the subject matter.

THE POTENTIAL OF SOCIAL AND DIGITAL MEDIA IN HIGHER EDUCATION

Within the ever-evolving realm of higher education, the fusion of social and digital media has emerged as a potent catalyst for augmenting the development of critical thinking abilities among students. These innovative tools provide a comprehensive strategy for fostering the ability to critically analyze information, empowering students to develop the skills necessary to evaluate and produce knowledge. Social and digital media play a significant role in fostering critical thinking skills among students by granting them unparalleled opportunities to engage with a diverse range of viewpoints, ideas, and information. Online platforms allow students to converse with peers with unique backgrounds and reside in various geographical areas. It fosters the development of intellectual curiosity and enhances their capacity to critically analyze complicated issues from multiple perspectives. In addition, digital media facilitates the development of interactive learning environments that encourage students to engage in critical thinking. According to Jahn and Kenner (2017), using online forums, collaborative projects, and virtual simulations promotes active engagement and the development of problem-solving skills, hence facilitating the practical application of critical thinking in real-life situations.

In the current era characterized by abundant information, digital media provides students with the means to develop proficiency in verifying facts and assessing the credibility of sources. These skills are crucial for academic pursuits and the cultivation of responsible digital citizenship. Furthermore, using digital media frequently entails examining and interpreting data, fostering critical thinking skills as students analyze results, formulate conclusions, and provide recommendations based on empirical evidence (Brodsky et al., 2021). Educators are crucial in facilitating students' social and digital media utilization to cultivate their critical thinking abilities. The resources above offer instruction on the proficient execution of online research, critical assessment of sources, and developing positive online discourse. Educators enhance students' intellectual growth by designing assignments and activities that foster critical thinking and effective communication in the digital domain. This pedagogical approach cultivates students with comprehensive knowledge in their respective disciplines and proficient essential thinking skills. Incorporating social and digital media within higher education presents a fertile ground for augmenting critical thinking abilities and equipping a cohort of students with the skills needed to effectively navigate the intricacies of the digital era (Cheng et al., 2022).

Within higher education, incorporating digital and social media transcends the mere augmentation of critical thinking abilities; instead, it serves as a potent catalyst for fostering self-reflection and self-awareness among students. Digital learning settings provide students with a distinct opportunity for self-reflection, contributing substantially to their personal development and self-awareness. Digital platforms such as e-portfolios and reflective journals provide students with digital mediums to record their educational experiences and personal reflections. E-portfolios allow students to amass substantiating documentation of their academic progression, thereby exhibiting their developmental trajectory. Reflective journals serve as confidential platforms wherein students can articulate their thoughts and emotions regarding their educational encounters, thus facilitating self-reflection and the discernment of personal growth opportunities (Otto et al., 2023; Kümmel et al., 2020; Nīmante et al., 2022; Brika et al., 2022).

Furthermore, the utilization of digital media provides students with the ability to create narratives regarding their educational experiences and self-identity. Students can use personal blogs and digital storytelling to explore how their educational journey influences their self-perception and self-awareness. These narratives serve as platforms for students to articulate their records and contemplate how their experiences have shaped their personal development (Mantulenko & Goryachev, 2020; Pumptow & Brahm, 2020; Li & Wong, 2020). Peer feedback and online communities are essential components of digital learning. Students are motivated to self-reflect as they evaluate peer feedback and critically appraise their efforts. The practice of enhancing self-awareness in the digital learning community not only contributes to personal development but also cultivates a sense of belonging, hence fostering a supportive atmosphere (Simonsmeier et al., 2020; Loureiro & Gomes, 2023; Brika et al., 2022).

Ethical and privacy considerations must be balanced when promoting self-reflection in digital environments. Students must experience a sense of security and receive adequate support while engaging in self-exploration. According to Bhattacharya et al. (2022), digital learning settings must uphold the principles of individual privacy and boundaries while providing the requisite support and materials for fostering responsible self-reflection. Digital learning environments are indispensable resources for promoting self-reflection and self-awareness within higher education. Students engage in self-reflection and individual development by utilizing e-portfolios, reflective journals, narrative construction, peer evaluation, and online communities. These platforms allow students to construct their educational narratives, enhancing their self-awareness and assisting them in navigating their roles in the digital era. When digital learning environments are implemented with a conscientious regard for ethical and privacy considerations, they offer a conducive and transforming platform for students to participate actively in introspection and personal growth.

LEVERAGING SOCIAL AND DIGITAL MEDIA FOR RATIONAL THINKING

In the contemporary era of digitalization, characterized by the unrestricted and copious dissemination of information, the cultivation of evidence-based thinking and the advancement of information literacy emerge as essential proficiencies for students in higher education. Social and digital media are precious instruments in this endeavour, offering students a platform to develop and refine their critical thinking skills and ability to make informed judgments. Promoting evidence-based reasoning entails instructing students to analyze and evaluate information sources, enabling them to discern between reliable, extensively supported sources and those lacking credibility. It entails acknowledging the significance of peer-reviewed scholarly journals, reputable online sources, and authoritative expert viewpoints. Including critical thinking and fact-checking exercises within the educational process is of utmost importance, as they play a crucial role in encouraging students to develop a propensity for questioning the material they come across and fostering a well-founded scepticism.

Furthermore, students are provided with vital digital research abilities, including proficient search techniques and adept database navigation, enabling them to participate in research-oriented tasks with assurance effectively. Ethical issues are also highlighted to promote responsible use of information, correct citation of sources, and respect for intellectual property rights among students. Through cultivating these abilities, educators empower students to effectively navigate the extensive realm of information by exercising discernment and critical thinking. It expands their influence beyond the realm of academia but also equips them with the capacity to make well-informed judgments in both their personal and professional spheres. It gives individuals the necessary skills and knowledge to assume their responsibilities as educated and conscientious members of society, particularly in an era marked by the swift and widespread circulation of information.

In the contemporary digital age, characterized by the plentiful flow of information, acquiring media literacy and fostering critical consuming skills about online content has become imperative for students pursuing higher education. The competencies above serve as the basis for cultivating responsible digital citizenship, enabling students to navigate the digital terrain effectively by exercising discernment and making well-informed assessments of the encountered content (Erdem et al., 2022; Audrin & Audrin, 2022). An essential aspect of fostering media literacy among students involves facilitating their understanding of digital media's various techniques and strategies, encompassing persuasive tactics, framing, and story creation. The comprehension above enables students to develop the ability to distinguish the impact of media on perceptions and the formation of opinions, hence enhancing their capacity to evaluate online information (Tran-Duong, 2022) critically.

Equally crucial is the capacity to identify misinformation and counterfeit news, competencies that instructors instil in their students. By instructing kids on how to discern untrustworthy sources and evaluate the reliability of information, they are better prepared for academic pursuits and develop the capacity to be conscientious digital citizens capable of differentiating between factual and fictional content (Pappas, 2021). Moreover, the promotion of ethical and responsible information sharing is prioritized in the pursuit of cultivating media literacy. Students understand the ramifications of disseminating unverified or deceptive content, thereby recognizing the significance of verifying information before publishing it. The practices above foster a heightened awareness of accountability and ethical conduct in individuals' online engagements, enhancing their capacity to fulfil the obligations associated with being conscientious participants in the digital realm (Audrin & Audrin, 2022; Kümmel et al., 2020).

As an integral component of the educational journey, students cultivate essential habits of critical consumption, encompassing practices such as engaging in reflective thought before disseminating content, actively seeking out a wide range of perspectives, and diligently verifying the accuracy and reliability of information. These behaviours safeguard against disinformation and enhance their contributions to a more knowledgeable and accountable digital community. Culturing media literacy and promoting critical engagement with content are integral facets of higher education in the contemporary digital world. According to Mauriz et al. (2020), these competencies enable students to appropriately interact with digital media content, identify biases, and distinguish between credible and inaccurate sources. In addition to facilitating academic achievement, these institutions equip students with the necessary skills and knowledge to become knowledgeable, ethical, and accountable participants in the digital realm. This preparation ensures that students actively contribute to the responsible generation and utilization of online information.

FACILITATING SELF-KNOWLEDGE AND SELF-UNDERSTANDING THROUGH SOCIAL AND DIGITAL MEDIA

Within higher education, incorporating self-reflection tools and digital platforms has introduced a paradigm shift in how students engage with personal development and self-awareness. These digital platforms provide a distinctive environment in which individuals can engage in introspection, promoting self-awareness and a more profound comprehension of oneself. Digital journals and reflection platforms offer students a secure and confidential means to record their thoughts, experiences, and personal development efforts, enabling ongoing self-reflection. This approach motivates individuals to recognize their aptitudes, limitations, and opportunities for growth, fostering personal growth and self-consciousness (Basilotta-Gómez-Pablos et al., 2022; Ebil et al., 2020). In addition, digital platforms allow students to establish and monitor individualized personal and academic objectives, presenting a well-organized framework for cultivating self-discipline and fostering personal development. Through delineating dreams, formulating a series of stages towards attainment, and diligently monitoring progress over time, students get profound insights into their underlying motivations, personal values, and aspirational goals. According to Carrigan and Jordan (2021), this particular procedure facilitates improving individuals' comprehension of themselves, establishing a firm basis for personal growth.

Active participation in online communities and utilizing peer feedback systems are equally crucial in cultivating self-awareness and facilitating individual development. In digital environments, students can engage with peers and mentors, facilitating the reception of constructive feedback and the acquisition of novel viewpoints about their strengths and growth areas. Incorporating external input, in conjunction with introspection, enhances the development of a holistic comprehension of one's capabilities and potential for personal progress (Simonsmeier et al., 2020; Vrieling-Teunter et al., 2022). Nevertheless, upholding ethical considerations when employing self-reflection tools and platforms is paramount. It is imperative to provide students with the choice to maintain the confidentiality of their self-reflection while also ensuring the safeguarding of personal data and adherence to ethical principles to protect the privacy and security of individuals (Perez et al., 2023; Kawai, 2021). The utilization of self-reflection instruments and digital platforms within higher education serves as a potent catalyst for fostering personal development and enhancing self-awareness. By utilizing digital journals, engaging in goal-setting activities, providing and receiving peer feedback, and actively participating in online communities, students engage in self-reflection, fostering the growth of self-awareness and personal development. These tools offer an organized and supportive setting for students to augment their comprehension of their own identities, objectives, and ambitions. Maintaining ethical concerns and responsible digital conduct plays a crucial role in effectively harnessing this potential while also demonstrating respect for the privacy and security of persons (Timotheou et al., 2022; Falloon, 2020).

Participating in virtual communities and networks to investigate a range of viewpoints is a transformative endeavour within higher education. This activity not only expands the intellectual boundaries of students but also cultivates a more profound comprehension of the intricate and interrelated global landscape that encompasses our existence. In the contemporary period characterized by the ubiquity of digital connectivity, online platforms play a crucial role in facilitating meaningful student interactions. These platforms serve as vital spaces where students may engage with their classmates, professionals, and persons from diverse backgrounds, thereby gaining access to various perspectives. One of the notable advantages lies in the potential for intercultural interaction, which enables students to be exposed to a diverse range of perspectives, customs, and ideologies (Falloon, 2020). It facilitates the development of cultural competency and fosters a deeper comprehension of the global society.

Moreover, integrating interdisciplinary perspectives from persons with varied academic and professional experiences fosters a cognitive orientation among students, enabling them to tackle intricate issues from a comprehensive and diversified standpoint. These exchanges can expose students to ideas and opinions that diverge from their own, so presenting opportunities to question preconceived conceptions fosters personal development and a receptive mindset. Engaging in collaborative projects and activities within online communities can strengthen problem-solving and communication skills, equipping students with the necessary abilities to thrive in the collective dynamics prevalent in the contemporary workforce. Moreover, engaging in interactions with persons from other backgrounds facilitates the development of empathy and a more profound comprehension of the experiences of others, thereby cultivating a heightened feeling of compassion and social accountability. However, it is imperative for students to actively participate politely and ethically while following established norms that encourage productive discourse, foster a favourable online community, and develop crucial digital citizenship abilities (Ferrer et al., 2020; Nkomo et al., 2021). In conclusion, this educational involvement effectively equips students with the necessary knowledge, open-mindedness, and sense of responsibility to become well-informed global citizens capable of navigating the intricate dynamics of our linked world.

ADDRESSING CONCERNS AND RISKS

In the contemporary era of technology, students enrolled in higher education institutions have significant obstacles due to the prevalence of digital distractions and the overwhelming abundance of information. Although social and digital media offer various advantages, they also present potential distractions that can impede academic achievement. The presence of distractions can take on different manifestations, including multiple forms, such as notifications from social media platforms and enticing entertainment applications. These distractions frequently divert students' focus and concentration in various educational settings, including lectures, study sessions, and assignments (Pérez-Juárez et al., 2023; Flanigan et al., 2023). Furthermore, the proliferation of digital resources presents students with an overwhelming abundance of information, posing a challenge in determining the relevance of content to their academic pursuits. Excessive information might result in perplexity and dissatisfaction, hindering the discerning reliable sources. Adopting a comprehensive approach to tackle these issues is imperative, as highlighted by previous research (Zalat et al., 2021; Rötzel, 2018).

One practical approach to address the challenges posed by digital distractions and information overload is the implementation of strategies such as advocating for digital detoxification and employing time management techniques, such as the Pomodoro method, to enhance concentration and productivity. The provision of digital literacy education enables students to develop the capacity to utilize technology conscientiously, effectively regulate notifications, and curate digital workplaces that facilitate productivity. Educators can create online courses incorporating captivating methodologies, while educational establishments can provide supplementary offerings such as workshops on time management and counselling services. Effective communication of expectations for technology use, the formulation of technology policies, and the provision of education on digital etiquette are other factors that contribute to creating an optimal learning environment (Mirbabaie et al., 2022; Miranda et al., 2018; Yang, 2017). Acknowledging the significance of mitigating digital distractions and managing information overload is imperative to enhance the overall higher education experience. The tactics mentioned above not only serve to empower students in efficiently navigating the digital landscape but also facilitate the maintenance of attention and productivity. It, in turn, ensures that students can maximize the educational opportunities afforded by digital tools (Flanigan et al., 2023; Pérez-Juárez et al., 2023). Privacy, the establishment of online identity, and the difficulties associated with self-revelation are of utmost importance in the contemporary era of technology, particularly within higher education. The utilization of social and digital media platforms raises a multitude of concerns about the safeguarding of personal information, the establishment of one's online identity, and the intricate dynamics involved in sharing content inside digital environments (Jahankhani et al., 2023).

The boundaries of privacy become indistinct in digital environments. Students may encounter apprehensions regarding the individuals or entities that can obtain their personal information, the level of protection around their data, and the degree to which their online actions are subject to surveillance. Privacy breaches can potentially result in detrimental consequences such as identity theft, the improper use of data, or the inadvertent disclosure of personal information. Developing an online persona holds considerable importance within a student's virtual existence. Students are faced with determining which facets of their lives to exhibit and which to maintain as private. Striking a delicate equilibrium between cultivating a professional internet presence and preserving an individual's personal and genuine identity presents a formidable task. The task of maintaining a coherent and attractive digital identity might engender feelings of stress and worry among students. Online platforms facilitate the act of self-revelation, whether it be through social media updates, interactive forums, or individual weblogs.

Nevertheless, the degree to which students feel at ease disclosing personal information differs. Individuals may be reluctant to freely articulate their opinions, owing to apprehension regarding potential criticism, negative repercussions, or safeguarding personal information. Individuals may encounter difficulties with excessive disclosure, potentially jeopardizing their online security and overall welfare (Safaei & Shahrokhi, 2019). Integrating digital citizenship education into higher education curricula can provide students with the necessary information and abilities to effectively and ethically navigate online environments. It encompasses comprehending privacy settings, identifying phishing efforts, and adhering to secure online conduct. Promoting the efficient utilization of privacy settings on digital platforms among students permits them to exert control over the accessibility of their personal information. Educators possess the ability to offer valuable advice about the protection of personal data.

Emphasizing the ethical utilization of information is vital. It is imperative to provide students with comprehensive education regarding the appropriate practices of citation, the need to respect copyright laws, and the necessity of adhering to ethical principles when disseminating content on digital platforms. Promoting a harmonious equilibrium between students' online and offline identities is imperative, ensuring their digital personas are congruent with their values and aspirations. Providing students with the necessary skills to engage in critical thinking when consuming and disseminating online content is imperative. It is crucial to comprehend the ramifications of self-disclosure and the potential outcomes of excessive sharing. Privacy, online identity, and the difficulties associated with self-disclosure are complex elements of the digital landscape within higher education. Addressing these concerns necessitates implementing digital citizenship education, establishing ethical principles, and empowering students to exercise control over their online privacy settings. Implementing a comprehensive approach guarantees that students can take advantage of the various opportunities presented by digital media while protecting their privacy and ensuring their overall well-being in the online realm.

CASE STUDIES

Case Study 1

Technology is imperative to augment the educational process in higher education's dynamic and ever-changing realm. This case study examines a novel higher-education course strategy for collaborative and reflective learning using social media platforms. This study investigates these platforms' potential in enhancing student engagement, collaborative work, and self-evaluation. The case study focuses on a higher education institution where professors identified social media's potential to engage students effectively. The course under consideration pertains to a discipline that derives advantages from collaborative learning, critical thinking, and self-assessment, rendering it a prime choice for experimental exploration. The educators opted for various social media platforms like discussion forums, wikis, and a bespoke course-specific platform. The assortment of tools provided multiple options to accommodate different collaborative endeavours. Throughout the course, students were tasked with various projects that necessitated collaborative efforts, fostering the development of critical thinking skills, creativity, and problem-solving abilities. Social media platforms functioned as primary channels for students to engage in communication, collaborative idea generation, and resource dissemination.

Reflection and self-assessment were a fundamental component of the course design. The students were encouraged to chronicle their personal and group educational experiences on social media, engaging in introspection over their advancements, obstacles faced, and knowledge acquired.

One of the primary challenges that needed to be addressed was the assurance of privacy and the establishment of a secure learning environment, particularly in the context of public social media platforms. It was necessary to develop strategic techniques to promote fair participation among students with varying levels of digital literacy. These strategies addressed potential diversions and off-topic debates on open platforms. The utilization of social media platforms has facilitated the advancement of collaborative learning, fostering substantive discourse and the exchange of resources. Through reflection and self-assessment, students could cultivate critical thinking abilities and attain a more profound comprehension of the subject matter. The enhanced interactivity in social media platforms has positively impacted student engagement, resulting in notable improvements in learning outcomes.

Identifying best practices includes providing explicit standards for utilizing social media in educational contexts, consistently monitoring the online learning environment, and providing support as necessary. Constructive feedback was secured by integrating grading criteria for collaborative projects and incorporating reflective exercises. This case study exemplifies the effective incorporation of social media inside a higher education course, promoting joint and reflective learning. Despite various problems, the advantages associated with engagement, critical thinking, and practical cooperation underscore the potential of these tools in fostering interactive and reflective experiences within higher education. The knowledge and perspectives presented in this case study might serve as valuable guidance for educators and institutions seeking to implement comparable methodologies in their educational programs.

Case Study 2

Within the ever-evolving realm of higher education, self-awareness and individual maturation are significant in conjunction with conventional scholarly endeavours. This case study explores the utilization of digital storytelling platforms as a means to facilitate self-reflection, self-expression, and the creation of personal narratives within the student population. Digital storytelling is an effective medium that integrates many multimedia elements, including photographs, videos, and descriptions, to foster self-awareness and facilitate the expression of one's artistic abilities. This case study focuses on a course within a forward-thinking higher education institution. The university is dedicated to offering a well-rounded educational experience that goes beyond traditional classroom learning. The course itself is designed to explore personal growth, emotional intelligence, and self-awareness. This course provides an optimal basis for integrating digital storytelling into its educational framework. The careful selection of digital storytelling platforms is crucial in strategically implementing this strategy. The instructors carefully selected widely recognized outlets for their ease of use, availability, and effective integration of various media components. The options considered encompassed Adobe Spark and StoryMapJS and the development of customized websites explicitly designed for the task at hand.

The students went on an educational endeavour characterized by a series of storytelling prompts intricately intertwined with their personal experiences, various challenges, and thought-provoking subjects. The carefully crafted prompts provided a catalyst for students to engage with the narratives of their lives, examine pivotal moments, and contemplate the significant impact of these experiences on their self-awareness and personal development. This methodology's core is rooted in the students' innovative utilization of various multimedia components, including visuals, films, written content, and audio, to construct and distribute their tales. The interactive nature of this engagement fostered the ability to express oneself creatively and catered to a wide range of individual learning preferences. The core of the strategy revolved around incorporating collaboration and peer engagement. Students were actively encouraged to share their tales with their peers, cultivating a dynamic and lively exchange of stories and stimulating intellectually stimulating dialogues. This methodology fostered a sense of communal engagement and revealed avenues for knowledge exchange among peers.

Notwithstanding the presence of various obstacles, these issues were successfully mitigated by the execution of meticulously planned efforts. Establishing a secure and nurturing atmosphere for kids to share personal or sensitive narratives openly was emphasized. Furthermore, pupils requiring support in utilizing multimedia tools were provided with the necessary advice.

The enormous merits derived from this new method were significant. The students experienced a process of increased self-awareness, where they explored their personal experiences and examined the complexities of personal development, expressing their findings through investigation and communication. The formation of empathy and a thorough awareness of the different experiences of their peers was also of equal significance. The utilization of multimedia components to articulate their narratives functioned as a medium to enhance their creative and communicative abilities, which are essential in contemporary globalized society. To optimize the approach's effectiveness, it was supported by established methodologies, such as establishing a secure and supportive setting for exchanging personal narratives and incorporating explicit evaluation standards, facilitating students' reception of valuable and constructive critique. Integrating digital storytelling platforms within higher education is a potent tool for fostering introspection, self-consciousness, and the construction of individual narratives. Recognizing the inherent difficulties of privacy and digital literacy, it is essential to note that the inclusion of this technique within the realm of higher education holds considerable value due to its notable advantages in terms of personal development, empathy cultivation, creative aptitude, and communication proficiency. This case study provides valuable insights for educators and institutions aiming to enhance the educational experience by encouraging students to engage in introspection and contemplate their narratives. Both case studies offer significant illustrations of the effective integration of social and digital media in higher education, intending to foster collaborative learning, reflection, and personal growth among students. These studies provide valuable insights into these techniques' pragmatic implications and advantages and the obstacles and factors educators and institutions should consider when incorporating such strategies.

DISCUSSION

Social and digital media use within higher education offers numerous advantages that greatly enhance the promotion of rationality, self-knowledge, and self-understanding. These platforms are potent catalysts for improved communication, providing students and instructors immediate access to deeper discussions, meaningful feedback, and efficient information exchange. Social and digital media also serve as effective platforms for connecting individuals from various backgrounds and geographic regions, facilitating the exchange of diverse perspectives and valuable insights. The presence of diversity in educational settings not only enhances the quality of the learning experience but also promotes the development of critical thinking skills and the expansion of students' perspectives on the world. Collaborative learning flourishes in digital environments, facilitating student engagement in collective project work, interactive discourse, and effortless resource sharing. The fostering of critical thinking and problem-solving abilities is facilitated within this collaborative setting, which is vital to developing a comprehensive education. Moreover, social and digital media platforms serve as catalysts for promoting reflective practices among students, as they provide dedicated venues for documenting personal experiences and the process of personal development. Students can explore their inner selves through self-assessment and introspection, leading to a heightened comprehension of their learning paths.

Another significant aspect to consider is the development of digital literacy skills, which are essential in the contemporary technologically-driven society. Students adeptly navigate digital environments, proficiently assess online material, and skillfully utilize multimedia components to facilitate compelling and reasonable communication. Nevertheless, it is crucial to recognize that although these platforms provide many advantages, they also present significant constraints. The presence of digital distractions has the potential to divert the attention of pupils, resulting in reduced levels of focus and concentration during both classroom instruction and individual study periods. Privacy considerations are essential, particularly in promoting self-disclosure and personal reflection. The potential for data breaches or the inadvertent disclosure of personal information continues to be a significant concern. The abundance of information accessible through digital platforms can be overwhelming, resulting in confusion, dissatisfaction, and challenges in identifying reliable sources. Furthermore, it is essential to acknowledge that kids possess diverse levels of digital literacy, leading to potential disparities in their engagement and comprehension.

Consequently, students may necessitate supplementary support and instruction. To properly leverage the complete capabilities of social and digital media in the context of higher education, educators must formulate and execute strategies and best practices that specifically target and overcome the inherent limitations associated with these platforms. These tactics will empower instructors to establish a learning environment characterized by support and engagement, enabling students to optimize the advantages while mitigating the difficulties connected with these digital technologies.

In the ever-evolving realm of higher education, the successful implementation of social and digital media relies on a carefully constructed framework encompassing strategic approaches and optimal methodologies. Commencing with a precise specification of learning objectives that connect with the course material, educators set the stage for a purpose-driven integration of these resources. The meticulous choice of suitable platforms, customized to meet the specific requirements of students, guarantees a harmonious alignment between the selected media and the course's objectives. Recognizing students' diverse proficiency levels and striving for fair and inclusive engagement, providing digital literacy instruction is deemed essential. The prioritization of privacy and ethical issues is of utmost importance, as it fosters responsible conduct in the digital realm and safeguards individuals' data. Promoting active interaction and participation on these platforms using interactive assignments facilitates the cultivation of meaningful learning experiences. Implementing efficient monitoring and moderation strategies in online discussions serves to sustain a conducive atmosphere that promotes respectfulness and adherence to the topic—the integration of evaluation criteria and the provision of prompt feedback foster student advancement. The recognition of diverse student cohorts necessitates the inclusion of flexibility as a crucial element. By fostering collaboration and promoting the exchange of ideas among students, the educational environment may effectively harness the benefits of collective learning. The exhibition of the practical applicability of social and digital media competencies equips students with the necessary preparation for prospective professional endeavours. Establishing a secure and inclusive atmosphere is fundamental, enabling students to freely articulate their thoughts and opinions. Faculty development programs aim to enhance instructors' proficiency in efficiently utilizing online platforms and understanding the ethical aspects of online communication. Social and digital media utilization is enhanced through continuous research and assessment, further informed by valuable insights from students. The prioritization of accessibility for all students, including those with disabilities, is paramount. It is essential to emphasize sustainable methods that can be consistently upheld to utilize these tools entirely. By adopting these tactics and adhering to established principles, educators are well-positioned to optimize the advantages of social and digital media in higher education. It will enhance the overall learning experience and adequately equip students to confront the digital complexities of contemporary society.

CONCLUSION

Incorporating social and digital media into higher education is not only a choice but a must in the contemporary era characterized by pervasive digitalization. The capacity of these instruments to cultivate rationality, self-awareness, and self-comprehension among pupils is significant. Through social and digital media, instructors can establish an enhanced educational setting that empowers students with essential competencies for effectively navigating the intricacies of the contemporary era. The cultivation of rationality is enhanced when students actively employ critical thinking skills, examine a range of perspectives, and engage in lively dialogues provided by these educational platforms. The vast availability of knowledge allows pupils to make well-informed judgments and effectively address real-world situations.

Self-knowledge and self-understanding are cultivated by engaging in self-reflection and constructing personal narratives. Social and digital media platforms serve as a medium for students to record their experiences, express their personal development, and disseminate their reports. These techniques facilitate a more profound comprehension of one's being, nurturing self-awareness and supporting personal growth. To effectively include social and digital media within the context of higher education, it is imperative to adopt a strategic strategy. It integrates technology with educational goals, carefully choosing suitable platforms, emphasizing the development of digital literacy, and fostering an environment that promotes critical thinking and cooperative learning. Additionally, it involves the ongoing assessment and adjustment of techniques, focusing on practical applicability, guaranteeing inclusivity, and upholding long-term viability.

Ultimately, these educational techniques equip students with the necessary skills and knowledge to thrive in a technologically advanced and globally networked society. Through intentional methodologies and optimal approaches, integrating social and digital media within higher education assumes a significant role as indispensable resources. This integration cultivates a cohort of students who demonstrate exceptional academic aptitude and possess the necessary proficiencies for personal development and triumph in the contemporary era.

REFERENCES

Audrin, C., & Audrin, B. (2022). Key factors in digital literacy in learning and education: A systematic literature review using text mining. *Education and Information Technologies*, *27*(6), 7395–7419. DOI: 10.1007/s10639-021-10832-5

Basilotta-Gómez-Pablos, V., Matarranz, M., Casado-Aranda, L., & Otto, A. (2022). Teachers' digital competencies in higher education: A systematic literature review. *International Journal of Educational Technology in Higher Education*, *19*(1). Advance online publication. DOI: 10.1186/s41239-021-00312-8

Bhattacharya, S., Murthy, V., & Bhattacharya, S. (2022). The social and ethical issues of online learning during the pandemic and beyond. *Asian Journal of Business Ethics*, *11*(1), 275–293. DOI: 10.1007/s13520-022-00148-z

Brika, S. K. M., Chergui, K., Algamdi, A., Musa, A. A., & Zouaghi, R. (2022). E-Learning Research Trends in Higher Education in light of COVID-19: A Bibliometric analysis. *Frontiers in Psychology*, *12*. Advance online publication. DOI: 10.3389/fpsyg.2021.762819

Brodsky, J. E., Brooks, P. J., Scimeca, D., Todorova, R., Galati, P., Batson, M., Grosso, R., Matthews, M., Miller, V. B., & Caulfield, M. P. (2021). Improving college students' fact-checking strategies through lateral reading instruction in a general education civics course. *Cognitive Research: Principles and Implications*, *6*(1). Advance online publication. DOI: 10.1186/s41235-021-00291-4

Carrigan, M., & Jordan, K. (2021). Platforms and Institutions in the Post-Pandemic University: A Case Study of Social Media and the Impact Agenda. *Postdigital Science and Education*, *4*(2), 354–372. DOI: 10.1007/s42438-021-00269-x

Cheng, L. J., Fang, G., Zhang, X., Lv, Y., & Liu, L. (2022). Impact of social media use on critical thinking ability of university students. *Library Hi Tech*. Advance online publication. DOI: 10.1108/lht-11-2021-0393

Cilliers, E. J. (2021). Reflecting on social learning tools to enhance the Teaching-Learning Experience of Generation Z learners. *Frontiers in Education*, *5*. Advance online publication. DOI: 10.3389/feduc.2020.606533

Duran, M. (2022). Legal and ethical issues in educational technology. In *Springer eBooks* (pp. 89–122). https://doi.org/DOI: 10.1007/978-3-031-18111-5_6

Ebil, S., Salleh, S. M., & Shahrill, M. (2020). Using E-portfolio for self-reflection to promote learning: A case of TVET students. *Education and Information Technologies*, *25*(6), 5797–5814. DOI: 10.1007/s10639-020-10248-7

Erdem, C., Oruç, E., Atar, C., & Bağcı, H. (2022). The mediating effect of digital literacy in the relationship between media literacy and digital citizenship. *Education and Information Technologies*, *28*(5), 4875–4891. DOI: 10.1007/s10639-022-11354-4

Falloon, G. (2020). From digital literacy to digital competence: The teacher digital competency (TDC) framework. *Educational Technology Research and Development*, *68*(5), 2449–2472. DOI: 10.1007/s11423-020-09767-4

Ferrer, J., Ringer, A., Saville, K., Parris, M. A., & Kashi, K. (2020). Students' motivation and engagement in higher education: The importance of attitude to online learning. *Higher Education*, *83*(2), 317–338. DOI: 10.1007/s10734-020-00657-5

Flanigan, A. E., Brady, A. C., Dai, Y., & Ray, E. (2023). Managing Student Digital Distraction in the College Classroom: A Self-Determination Theory Perspective. *Educational Psychology Review*, *35*(2). Advance online publication. DOI: 10.1007/s10648-023-09780-y

Hällström, J. (2020). Embodying the past, designing the future: Technological determinism reconsidered in technology education. *International Journal of Technology and Design Education*, *32*(1), 17–31. DOI: 10.1007/s10798-020-09600-2

Islas, O., & Bernal, J. (2016). Media Ecology: A complex and systemic meta discipline. *Philosophies*, *1*(3), 190–198. DOI: 10.3390/philosophies1030190

Jahankhani, H., Jamal, A., Brown, G., Sainidis, E., Fong, R., & Butt, U. (2023). AI, Blockchain and Self-Sovereign Identity in Higher Education. In *Advanced sciences and technologies for security applications*. https://doi.org/DOI: 10.1007/978-3-031-33627-0

Jahn, D., & Kenner, A. (2017). Critical Thinking in Higher Education: How to foster it using Digital Media. In *Springer eBooks* (pp. 81–109). https://doi.org/DOI: 10.1007/978-3-658-19925-8_7

Kawai, T. (2021). A theoretical framework on reflection in service learning: Deepening Reflection through Identity Development. *Frontiers in education*, p. *5*. https://doi.org/DOI: 10.3389/feduc.2020.604997

Kümmel, E., Moskaliuk, J., Cress, U., & Kimmerle, J. (2020). Digital Learning Environments in Higher Education: A Literature Review of the Role of Individual vs Social Settings for Measuring Learning Outcomes. *Education Sciences*, *10*(3), 78. DOI: 10.3390/educsci10030078

Lee, L., Cheung, S. T., & Kwok, L. F. (2020). Learning analytics: Current trends and innovative practices. *Journal of Computers in Education*, *7*(1), 1–6. DOI: 10.1007/s40692-020-00155-8

Li, K. C., & Wong, B. (2020). Social media in Higher Education: A Review of Their uses, benefits and Limitations. In *Communications in computer and information science*. https://doi.org/DOI: 10.1007/978-981-33-4594-2_21

Loureiro, P., & Gomes, M. J. (2023). Online Peer Assessment for Learning: Findings from Higher Education Students. *Education Sciences*, *13*(3), 253. DOI: 10.3390/educsci13030253

Marín, V. I., Carpenter, J. P., Tur, G., & Williamson-Leadley, S. (2022). Social media and data privacy in education: An international comparative study of perceptions among pre-service teachers. *Journal of Computers in Education*. Advance online publication. DOI: 10.1007/s40692-022-00243-x

Mauriz, B. P., Anaya, P. B., & Bargiela, I. M. (2020). A Systematic Review on E-learning Environments for Promoting Critical Thinking in Higher Education. In *Springer eBooks* (pp. 345–362). https://doi.org/DOI: 10.1007/978-3-030-36119-8_15

Miranda, P., Isaías, P., & Pífano, S. (2018). Digital literacy in higher education. In *Lecture Notes in Computer Science* (pp. 71–87). https://doi.org/DOI: 10.1007/978-3-319-91152-6_6

Mirbabaie, M., Stieglitz, S., & Marx, J. (2022). Digital Detox. *Business & Information Systems Engineering*, *64*(2), 239–246. DOI: 10.1007/s12599-022-00747-x

Nīmante, D., Kalniņa, D., & Baranova, S. (2022). Towards an Inclusive Digital Learning Environment in Higher Education: Opportunities and Limitations Gleaned from Working Students' Remote Learning Experiences During COVID-19. In *Springer eBooks* (pp. 213–226). https://doi.org/DOI: 10.1007/978-3-031-14775-3_14

Nkomo, L. M., Daniel, B. K., & Butson, R. (2021). *Synthesis of student engagement with digital technologies: a systematic literature review*. PubMed., DOI: 10.1186/s41239-021-00270-1

Oliver, M. (2011). Technological determinism in educational technology research: Some alternative ways of thinking about the relationship between learning and technology. *Journal of Computer Assisted Learning*, *27*(5), 373–384. DOI: 10.1111/j.1365-2729.2011.00406.x

Otto, S., Bertel, L. B., Lyngdorf, N. E. R., Markman, A. O., Andersen, T. F., & Ryberg, T. (2023). Emerging Digital Practices Supporting Student-Centered Learning Environments in Higher Education: A Review of Literature and Lessons Learned from the Covid-19 Pandemic. *Education and Information Technologies*. Advance online publication. DOI: 10.1007/s10639-023-11789-3

Pappas, S. (2021). Fighting fake news in the classroom. https://www.apa.org. https://www.apa.org/monitor/2022/01/career-fake-news

Pérez-Juárez, M. A., González-Ortega, D., & Aguiar-Pérez, J. M. (2023). Digital Distractions from the Point of View of Higher Education Students. *Sustainability, 15*(7), 6044. DOI: 10.3390/su15076044

Pumptow, M., & Brahm, T. (2020). Students' Digital Media Self-Efficacy and Its Importance for Higher Education Institutions: Development and Validation of a survey instrument. *Technology, Knowledge, and Learning*, *26*(3), 555–575. DOI: 10.1007/s10758-020-09463-5

Rötzel, P. (2018). Information overload in the information age: A literature review from business administration, business psychology, and related disciplines with a bibliometric approach and framework development. *Business Research*, *12*(2), 479–522. DOI: 10.1007/s40685-018-0069-z

Safaei, N., & Shahrokhi, M. (2019). Relationship between teacher self-disclosure and teaching style: Perception of EFL teachers. *Cogent Education*, *6*(1), 1678231. DOI: 10.1080/2331186x.2019.1678231

Simonsmeier, B. A., Peiffer, H., Flaig, M., & Schneider, M. (2020). Peer feedback improves students' academic Self-Concept in higher education. *Research in Higher Education*, *61*(6), 706–724. DOI: 10.1007/s11162-020-09591-y

Timotheou, S., Miliou, O., Dimitriadis, Y., Sobrino, S. V., Giannoutsou, N., Cachia, R., Martínez-Monés, A., & Ioannou, A. (2022). Impacts of digital technologies on education and factors influencing schools' digital capacity and transformation: A literature review. *Education and Information Technologies*, *28*(6), 6695–6726. DOI: 10.1007/s10639-022-11431-8

Tran-Duong, Q. H. (2022). The effect of media literacy on effective learning outcomes in online learning. *Education and Information Technologies*, *28*(3), 3605–3624. DOI: 10.1007/s10639-022-11313-z

Ursavaş, Ö. F. (2022). Unified Theory of Acceptance and Use of Technology Model (UTAUT). In *Springer eBooks* (pp. 111–133). https://doi.org/DOI: 10.1007/978-3-031-10846-4_6

Vedechkina, M., & Borgonovi, F. (2021). A review of evidence on digital technology's role in shaping children's attention and cognitive control. *Frontiers in Psychology*, *12*. Advance online publication. DOI: 10.3389/fpsyg.2021.611155

Vrieling-Teunter, E., Henderikx, M., Nadolski, R., & Kreijns, K. (2022). Facilitating peer interaction Regulation in online settings: The role of social presence, social space and sociability. *Frontiers in Psychology*, *13*. Advance online publication. DOI: 10.3389/fpsyg.2022.793798

Yang, D. (2017). Instructional strategies and course design for teaching statistics online: Perspectives from online students. *International Journal of STEM Education*, *4*(1). Advance online publication. DOI: 10.1186/s40594-017-0096-x

Zalat, M. M., Hamed, M., & Bolbol, S. A. (2021). The experiences, challenges, and acceptance of e-learning as a tool for teaching during the COVID-19 pandemic among university medical staff. *PLoS One*, *16*(3), e0248758. DOI: 10.1371/journal.pone.0248758

ADDITIONAL READING

Frazier, D. (Ed.). (2023). *Teaching Humanities with Cultural Responsiveness at HBCUs and HSIs* (pp. 1–270). IGI Global., DOI: 10.4018/978-1-6684-9782-1

Singha, S. (2023). Exploring the Role of Social Media in Enhancing K-12 Economics Education. In Scott, B., & Fox, M. (Eds.), *Cases on Economics Education and Tools for Educators* (pp. 160–182). IGI Global., DOI: 10.4018/978-1-6684-7583-6.ch007

Younis, R. A. (2005). Integral reality, digital cultures, digital divides. *Postcolonial Studies*, *8*(2), 219–226. DOI: 10.1080/13688790500196744

KEY TERMS AND DEFINITIONS

Critical Thinking: The ability to analyze information objectively and make a reasoned judgment.

Digital Media: Electronic media that uses digital codes, encompassing websites, social media, online videos, and more.

Higher Education: Post-secondary education offered by universities, colleges, and other institutions awarding academic degrees.

Rationality: The quality of being based on or following reason or logic.

Self-Knowledge: Understanding of oneself, including one's desires, motives, and emotions.

Self-Understanding: A deeper comprehension of one's character, feelings, and motivations.

Social Media: Platforms and applications that enable users to create, share content, and engage in social networking.

Chapter 9

Digitalization and the Impact of Facebook Usage on University Students' Academic Performance

Md. Ashrafuzzaman
https://orcid.org/0000-0003-2100-9998
University of Frontier Technology, Bangladesh

Sabbir Ahmed
https://orcid.org/0009-0005-8118-9873
University of Frontier Technology, Bangladesh

ABSTRACT

This study investigates the impact of Facebook usage on the academic performance of university students, particularly during the COVID-19 pandemic. The study surveyed 220 students from public and private universities in Bangladesh using a mixed methodology, removing invalid responses. Results show that students use Facebook for communication, entertainment, and educational activities like collaborations, live classes, and teacher interactions. However, challenges like distraction, harassment, unverified content, and spam hinder its effective use for educational purposes. Most students still have a positive opinion of Facebook despite these problems, even though 73% think that excessive socializing and distractions are harmful for their academic performance. Facebook is a helpful teaching tool, but excessive use might

DOI: 10.4018/979-8-3693-0997-1.ch009

negatively affect students' academic performance. According to the study, students can use Facebook more effectively for academic success if they receive additional support in the form of financial aid, emotional counseling, and clear guidance.

1. INTRODUCTION

This is the age of Information Communication Technology and modern education systems are reshaped with technological developments (Büyükbaykal, 2015). Over recent years, web 2.0 tools including social media platforms, wikis, blogs, folksonomies, video sharing sites, and web applications have undeniably garnered significant popularity. User observations have shown the transformative impact of these technologies on work processes and interpersonal dynamics (Moghavvemi et al., 2017). Popular social networking sites namely Twitter, Myspace, Facebook, etc. have addressed the urge to express one's feelings which is a basic human tendency. Consequently, the use of social networking sites has been associated with both beneficial and detrimental impacts on different areas of people's lives (Ravichandran, 2019). Social media networks like Facebook were originally for private communication but now share photographs, stories, and news. People now communicate and sustain social connections differently (Vardi, 2024). However, Facebook is very popular in Bangladesh among students since they can upload pictures, and videos, share feelings, play games, and publish scores. Besides, students can get their necessary academic information from friends, teachers, pages, and groups. Unfortunately, once students log in to Facebook for an academic activity, they get involved in different unnecessary tasks that are rather distracting. Most of the students who have net accessibility and Facebook id spend a lot of time using this. Guardians are very worried about their children. They think Facebook is diverting students' focus to otherwise. On the other hand, it is true that learners can get their necessary academic information from that.

The research investigates the motives for using Facebook, which include spending time, managing loneliness, socialization, information, entertainment, shopping, relaxation, educational purposes, and online business. Facebook has helped greatly the promotion of students' motivation for learning for instructional purposes and has played a significant role in improving students' social presence (Samad et al., 2019). In contrast, Valkenburg (2022) used nine meta-analyses, nine systematic reviews, and nine narrative reviews to emphasize social media's effects on well-being and ill-being. Few research studies in developed countries have investigated the impact of Facebook on academic achievement, social life, academic motivation, and social adjustment (Wohn & LaRose, 2014; Ainin et al., 2015). Therefore, it will be imperative to conduct an investigation if the academic success of university students is significantly correlated with their usage of Facebook. Since the university level is an important phase of student life and there is little research on this subject in Bangladesh, it is worth conducting research on this subject to fill the gap.

This study aims to examine the relationship between university students' academic achievement in Bangladesh and their use of Facebook. It seeks to address the concerns of teachers, administrators, researchers, and guardians regarding Facebook usage. The research will provide important guidance to students on how to use Facebook responsibly. Additionally, teachers will receive clear guidelines on effectively managing Facebook use in the classroom.

1.1 Objective and Research Question

The study seeks to evaluate how university students' academic performance is impacted by their personal use of Facebook. This research aims to address the following research questions:

a) What do university students think about using Facebook?
b) What are the educational purposes for which university students are using Facebook?
c) What difficulties do university students face when exploring the educational applications of Facebook?
d) To what extent does Facebook influence the academic achievements of university students?

2. LITERATURE REVIEW

2.1 Perceptions and challenges of Facebook usage for educational purpose

Research has shown that higher education students, together with the wider societal population, are frequent users of Facebook (Bicen & Cavus, 2011). Students use Facebook to enhance communication and collaboration by keeping in touch with old high school acquaintances as well as developing and establishing new friendships on their campuses (Al-Hail et al., 2024).

By combining Facebook with traditional teaching methods, it is feasible to break down the four classroom walls and give students a space to connect and increase their learning. However, students and academics may experience work overload because of Facebook; it is difficult for them to distinguish useful information from useless information, and Facebook encompasses too many distractions (advertisements, games, etc.), emotional distress, and difficulties in sharing content, which can hinder their learning experiences (Mauludina et al., 2024; He, 2024).

The ability to engage with friends and teachers is a well-known benefit of using Facebook for higher education purposes (Hamid et al. 2015). Facebook's algorithms elevate low-quality content during major events like the 2020 US election, lowering user information quality. Critical content quality evaluation is crucial in education (Bandy & Diakopoulos, 2023).

However, the algorithms employed by Facebook play a crucial role in determining the content to which users are exposed, thereby influencing educational experiences. Educators should facilitate students' understanding of the societal and political implications associated with algorithmic processes (De Groot et al., 2023). Furthermore, Educational information like fact-checking videos is affected by Facebook's News Feed algorithm. Educators must grasp how algorithm changes affect content visibility and interaction (Dafonte-Gómez et al., 2023).

Aside from the educational benefits of Facebook, specific issues were identified, including distraction, poor collaboration and communication, information accuracy, and cyberbullying. It was also discovered that this skepticism can impede the efficacy of social media as a learning instrument, as users may doubt the credibility of the material disseminated (Martindale et al., 2024). Educational institutions regularly accidentally post students' personally identifiable information on Facebook, underscoring the need for stronger data ethics and privacy standards (Rosenberg et al., 2022).

Although many students acknowledge the benefits of convenient availability and sharing of educational resources, they may have reservations regarding the genuineness and dependability of content shared on Facebook. Nevertheless, while utilizing Facebook for instructional purposes, students are easily diverted and captured by irrelevant material, which supports the conclusions found in previous studies (Cassidy, 2006; Wise et al., 2011). Another major difficulty is that students face anxiety regarding data privacy, fearing breaches of personal information via Facebook (Kumi–Yeboah et al., 2023). Cultural disparities and diverse legal systems throughout nations shape perceptions of social media utilization in education, including the management of privacy and trust concerns (Marín et al., 2022).

Social network analysis (SNA) indicates a correlation between student connectivity and academic performance, especially in collaborative environments (Crossette et al., 2023). Facebook may integrate features akin to those found in academic social networks, including scholar recommendations and collaboration tools, to assist students and academics in identifying appropriate partners for research and projects (Yuan et al., 2021). Facebook has the potential to incorporate tools that enable students to collaboratively annotate and discuss academic content, thereby improving their engagement and comprehension (Cui & Wang, 2023). Facebook can promote true academic interactions, but privacy and academic misbehavior must be addressed. Honor codes and platform ethics can reduce these threats (Elkhatat, 2023).

Finally, due to some periodic stumbling blocks, using Facebook for educational reasons may be challenging. As the Facebook social networking site becomes more commercialized, some students are having trouble recovering prior posts or are becoming irritated by spam/irrelevant posts. Furthermore, as emphasized by Catanzaro (2011) and Willems & Bateman (2011), Facebook might contribute to the worsening of school bullying by subjecting victims to discrimination that extends beyond the physical sphere to encompass the digital realm as well. Furthermore, promoting resilience and social support may alleviate certain negative impacts linked to social media usage (Fruehwirth et al., 2024). The collective experience of navigating uncertainties can strengthen community and authenticity among members, as they engage together in learning and discovery (Wolbert & ínlüsoy, 2023).

2.2 Influence of Facebook usage on university students' academic performance

The results of research that examines the relationship between academic achievement and Facebook usage have been diverse. Pasek et al. (2009) found that there was no link between using Facebook and doing well in school. On the other hand, Kirschner and Karpinski (2010) discovered that Facebook users had a lower average GPA than people who didn't use Facebook and studied less each week than people who didn't use Facebook. Also, students can share what they know through Facebook, which helps them do better in school by letting them work together to learn (Alsarayreh & Aljaafreh, 2023). Effective utilization of these platforms can enhance collaborative learning and facilitate access to educational resources (Shafiq & Parveen, 2023). On the other hand, for instance, Black/African American students using Facebook for news reported lower GPAs, highlighting the importance of content type in determining the impact on academic outcomes (Zavala et al., 2023). Facebook use can lead to internet addiction, which hurts academic achievement. This emphasizes social media balance and mindfulness (Jiang et al., 2024). Throughout the COVID-19 pandemic, Facebook emerged as a crucial means of maintaining communication with friends and family, therefore indirectly contributing to the well-being and academic achievements of students (Van Huan et al., 2024). Mobile learning and academic performance are mediated by social media, including Facebook, demonstrating that when utilized wisely, these platforms can improve learning experiences and outcomes (Amjad et al., 2024).

Through a study undertaken by Mazman and Usluel (2010), it was found that five specific characteristics had a notable influence on Facebook adoption. These characteristics, Specifically, the factors of usefulness, accessibility, social influence, facilitating conditions, and community identity also had a favorable effect on the adoption of the product. Among these factors, the most important predictor was found to be usefulness. In addition, the three factors of social relations, work-related activities, and daily activities all had a big impact on the goals of Facebook use, with social relations being the most important. Figure 1 demonstrates that communication, working together, and sharing materials and tools all play a role in how Facebook is used for education in a similar way.

Figure 1. The objectives of utilizing Facebook and the adoption of Facebook (Mazman and Usluel, 2010)

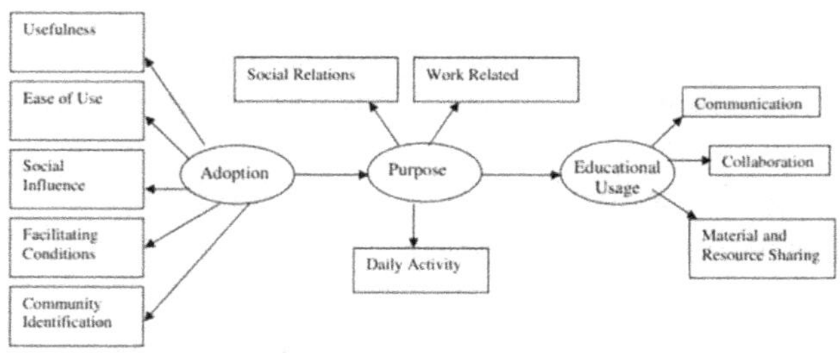

In terms of the relationships between the three key elements of this model, it was discovered that the purposes of Facebook users and their adoption of the platform are closely intertwined, suggesting that an individual's perception of Facebook significantly influences their usage patterns. Furthermore, there was a link between Facebook adoption and educational usage (Nguyen, 2017).

2.3 Positive impact of Facebook usage on university students' academic performance

Academic performance is frequently discussed in educational and educational psychology studies. Different perspectives on academic performance are offered by two basic approaches (Rouis et al. 2017). The most typical method of evaluating academic success is to approach a certain goal, but avoiding negative outcomes gives an option (Valle et al., 2009). Facebook helps students, professors, and classmates communicate. According to the conceptual paper on social media usage in Sabah, this communication is essential for collaborative learning and can be integrated into face-to-face, blended, and e-learning settings (Hasan et al., 2022).

The TAM and ISSM reveal that students find Facebook useful and easy to learn. This attitude boosts academic performance and pleasure by encouraging student interaction with peers and platform material (Al-Rahmi et al., 2021). From a broader perspective, research has shown that students tend to utilize Facebook as a platform for building educational connections and engaging in educational initiatives (Al-rahmi et al., 2014). This is also corroborated by the Loralai division study, which demonstrates a beneficial effect of social media usage for academic and socialization objectives on the academic performance of students (Javeed, 2023).

A study conducted by Hurt et al. (2012) on 107 university students revealed that students who utilized Facebook Groups as a learning forum attained superior learning results in comparison to those who used traditional LMS platforms like Blackboard Vista and e-Learning Commons. Kashif (2013) found that most students articulated a favorable disposition toward utilizing Facebook. In the Bahawalpur region study, Facebook and YouTube were identified as aiding students in their search for academic materials, thereby enhancing their academic performance (Shams et al., 2022).

An analysis was conducted by Tananuraksakul (2015) to examine the impact of using Facebook groups on students' language learning in a Thai context. The findings of the study indicated that the Facebook Group might provide individuals with a sense of convenience, simplicity, and relaxation, as well as lessen the cultural power distance between them and the instructor. Using multimodal learning analytics, students who prioritized Facebook peer learning had higher course marks. Facebook may be useful for collaborative learning if used properly (Liao & Wu, 2022).

The study's results illustrated that students had good attitudes toward using Facebook for online engagement with classmates. Furthermore, the data show a link between students' perceptions of online contact via Facebook and academic success (Al-Dheleai & Tasir, 2017).

2.4 Negative effects of Facebook usage on university students' academic performance

As a social network, Facebook offers the usual social interaction and entertainment features that Tang et al. (2015) describe as significant factors in attracting users. According to Dyson et al. (2014), an investigation revealed that the usage of Facebook in the educational process did not lead to any significant improvement in knowledge or student involvement. Facebook addiction is common among college students and lowers academic performance. Addiction increases anxiety and sadness, which worsens academic performance (Dule et al., 2023). Social media addiction also reduces academic engagement since students spend more time on Facebook and less time studying (Mou et al., 2024).

Facebook addiction is significantly linked to lower academic achievements, anxiety, and depression among students (Dule et al. 2023). The study conducted by Junco (2012) revealed a negative association between the duration of Facebook usage and the duration of class preparation. One issue that arises from Facebook's massive data is the potential insufficient critical reasoning. This can result in misunderstandings and the dissemination of incorrect information among students (Klomsri et al., 2013).

Studies conducted by Kirschner & Karpinski (2010) and Junco (2015) have discovered a possible association between the use of Facebook and academic achievement. However, Facebook addiction has a severe impact on self-control, which in turn reduces students' GPAs, emphasizing a harmful loop (Ning & Inan, 2023).

Finally, various research has revealed the prevalence of cyberbullying among undergraduates. An increase in cyberbullying spurred by social media, particularly Facebook, was discovered during a comprehensive literature review on the topic of indirect bullying of teenage girls in different countries (Catanzaro, 2011). Also, loneliness, sometimes aggravated by excessive social media use, might lower students' academic self-efficacy and performance because they lack social support and motivation.

2.5 Conceptual framework of the study

The purpose of this study is to look into how university students' use of Facebook affects their academic achievement. The "conceptual basis for Facebook use and academic achievement" was developed in the research through an exhaustive analysis of current literature. The study identified key features, which are illustrated in Figure 2.

Figure 2. Conceptual Framework of the Study

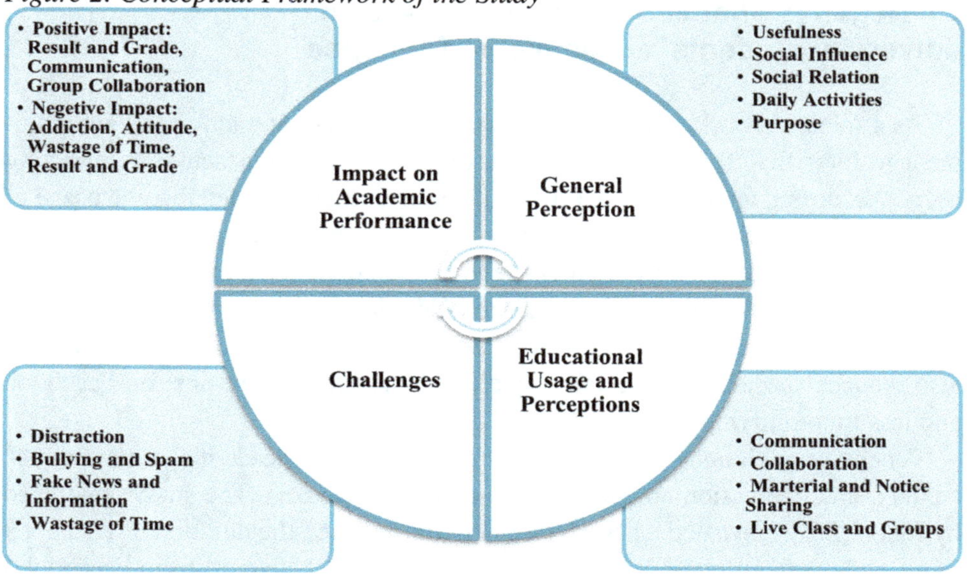

This study aims to determine the correlation between online Facebook usage and the academic performance of university students in Bangladesh. Hence, the researcher examines the incentives and perspectives of individuals who use Facebook for both general and educational intentions, together with the challenges associated with using Facebook for educational purposes. Consequently, the objective of this study is to examine and assess the correlation between academic performance and Facebook use by university students

3. METHODOLOGY OF THE STUDY

The study was conducted using a quantitative approach, supplemented with some qualitative information, to provide a comprehensive description of the students in public and private universities in Bangladesh. The research is guided by constructivist and pragmatic perspectives. The study employed a quantitative method that was both statistical and descriptive in nature. Additionally, a qualitative method was utilized, which involved an analytical and narrative approach. These methods were chosen to gain a comprehensive understanding of the Effects of Facebook usage on university students' academic performance.

3.1 Tools for collecting data

The secondary research data were collected by means of a document survey that encompassed journal articles, previous studies, books, periodicals, websites, and thesis papers that were pertinent to the subject at hand. This was done to acquire a comprehensive understanding of the research area and the existing research and research in this field. Additionally, web-based surveys provide significant design flexibility, the advantage is in its speed, cost-effectiveness, and ease of completion within a few hours.

In this study, we developed and utilized Google Forms for the purpose of online data collection. We relied on various related literature sources (Duhoki, 2017; Kashif, 2013) to guide our approach. The researcher generated questionnaires on various topics related to university students' perceptions and usage of Facebook. These topics included perceptions of Facebook use, both for personal and educational purposes, as well as the pedagogical application of Facebook. The questionnaires also explored the perceived usefulness of Facebook, the challenges that university students face when using Facebook for educational purposes, and the influence of Facebook usage on scholastic achievement. Lastly, the questionnaires investigated the positive impact of Facebook usage on university students' academic results.

3.2 Sampling methods

The research population was chosen through convenience sampling, which involves selecting participants at random, providing each member has an equal probability of being selected. Online questionnaire surveys were deployed to gather responses from public and private universities in Bangladesh during the pandemic. The total response from 220 respondents was tabulated and analyzed from a different perspective during this study.

3.3 Piloting and data collection

The questionnaire's initial version was presented to my colleagues for constructive criticism, leading to the implementation of several significant enhancements. Following that, the survey was accessed online through the Google Forms application and assessed by a cohort of 10 undergraduate students from BDU and DU participating in a pilot study. After making all necessary changes, the prepared questionnaire was sent to possible participants by email and Facebook platforms.

At the conclusion of the survey session, a total of 240 replies had been obtained. Following the completion of the online survey, the data was saved from Google Forms imported into a Microsoft Excel file, and organized into categories. Once all invalid replies were removed, the final data sample for the online questionnaire was 220. Since it takes 25 to 30 minutes to complete all the questionnaires and submit survey forms, the response rate was low.

3.4 Data analysis

The study employed an online questionnaire as the instrument for gathering primary data, enabling the examination of data that is both quantitative and qualitative. Data manipulations and statistical analysis were performed using Microsoft Excel. The data from the online poll has been downloaded into a Microsoft Excel spreadsheet and organized into various categories. Nearly all of the statistical functions required for data analysis in this study may be accessed in Excel. The initial task was to transform the string data type structure into a numerical data type format. Following the data conversion, the subsequent task is to classify the data into summaries stored in tabular format. Subsequently, further functions are implemented based on the specific data needed to thoroughly analyze the outcomes. To communicate the facts, both descriptive and quantitative methods were applied. Quantitative frequency studies were conducted utilizing demographic data and survey metrics. Analysis of the questionnaire data was conducted using Excel and thereafter displayed in the form of graphs, tables, and pie charts. A narrative structure was used to provide the descriptive data. Analysis of the survey responses was conducted using statistical computations, and comparisons of results were employed as an additional method of data analysis.

The primary topics guided the organization and analysis of the data, including Demographic information about the respondents, Facebook usage patterns, perceptions of university students about Facebook usage, perceptions of Facebook usage for educational purposes, challenges faced by university students when using Facebook for education, effects of Facebook usage on academic performance, both positive and negative effects of Facebook usage on academic results.

4. ANALYSIS OF THE DATA

4.1 Tendency of using Facebook among university students

All the respondents (100) use Facebook at home and in other places such as universities (68%) and outings (70%), while meeting up with friends (60%) and at social gatherings (46%) and everywhere (26%). They primarily use smartphones to access Facebook; however, some also use laptops, tablets, and desktop computers. Figure 3 illustrates that (73%) of respondents use Facebook daily, whereas (19%) use it hourly.

Figure 3. Tendency of using Facebook for university students

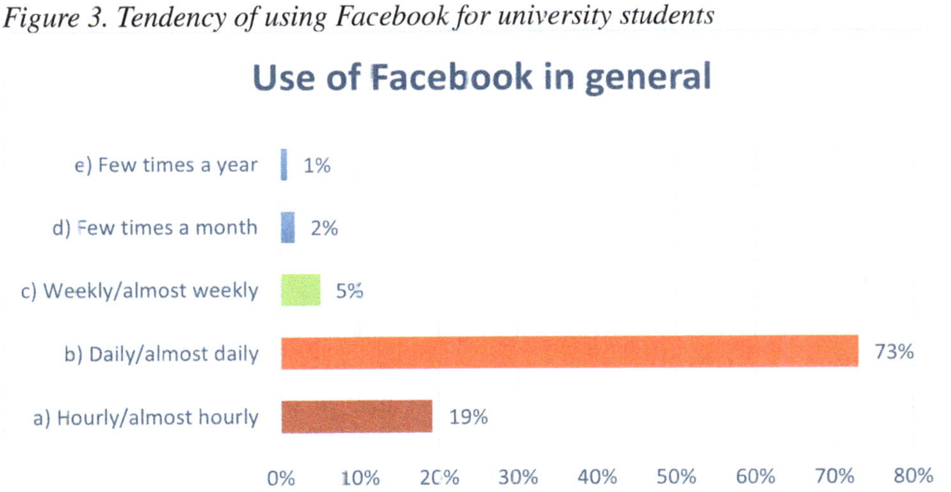

4.2 University student's perception about Facebook usage

This study focuses on tertiary level students' perceptions. The researcher has created a series of questions that lead to responses using a 5-point Likert scale. The order is strongly agree, agree, neutral, disagree, and strongly disagree.

Figure 4. University students' perception towards the use of Facebook

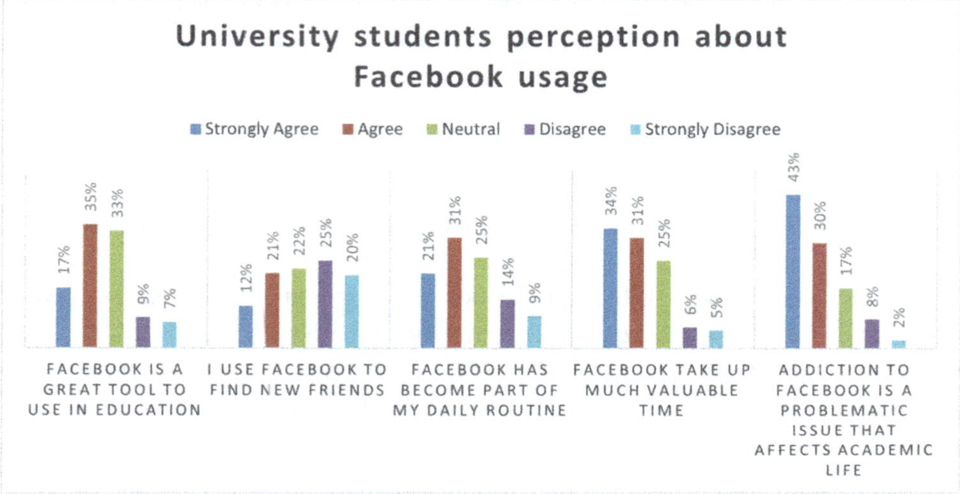

Figure 4 reveals that 52% of university students "agree" that Facebook is a great tool that can be used in education, while 16% disagree, and 33% are undecided. Students use Facebook to make new friends; 33% agreed, 45% disagreed, and 22% were undecided. According to 52% of students, it has become a part of their daily routine, while 23% disagree, and 25% are unsure. a lot of time is wasted on Facebook, say 65% of students, while 11% disagree and 25% are unsure. Facebook is causing a problem that is affecting their academic lives as well; 73% of students support this, while 10% disagree and 17% are unsure.

Most students believe that the most well-known social networking site is Facebook for sharing and receiving information and news daily. Respondents chose Facebook because it is free and simple to use. There are also plenty of other features and options that encourage students to utilize Facebook. For students, the features of Facebook that appeal to them the most are communication, and connection; news, entertainment, exchanging ideas, knowledge gathering and sharing, and up-to-date information are all key components of Facebook (Lee & Dioso, 2023).

Most respondents claimed that the benefits of using Facebook include communication with friends and family, news and information, staying active outside of class, getting the latest news, purchasing online, joining numerous study groups, and using a low-cost marketing sharing platform, as well as social awareness, study-related information, and removing stress.

On the other hand, many students are deeply worried about the security of their personal information as they find themselves spending a substantial amount of time consumed by their addiction to Facebook. Facebook Addiction is a new disorder, according to the responders. Facebook's major drawbacks include the transmission of fake news and rumors, an increase in social crime, adverse criticism, misleading individuals, the distribution of prohibited materials, photographs, and videos, gadget addiction, loss of time, sleeping disorders, relationship problems, data leaks, false profiles, and phishing. Increased sexual harassment and bullying through Facebook are also drawbacks of the social media platform.

Facebook stories and timelines, amusing posts and videos, games, chatting, news, sexual content, viral content, friendship and love affairs, time passing, news and information, live courses, and videos, according to respondents, are the causes of student Facebook addiction.

A respondent reported that Facebook, a widely used social networking platform, has been utilized by individuals of all age groups and occupations for diverse objectives. Its application in the field of medical education is experiencing very rapid growth. Simultaneously, the advantages and disadvantages of Facebook usage among health science students have captured the interest of educators. Documentation of the data pertaining to the use and impact of this technology on the lives of Nepalese health science students is still lacking. Hence, this study aims to assess the impact of Facebook usage on the social interactions, behavior, academic performance, and health of students admitted to a medical college in Nepal.

4.3 Motivations that drive students to use Facebook

Mostly, students use Facebook for the purposes of communication, leisure, and amusement, as well as for publishing posts and updates, and for sharing thoughts, experiences, photographs, videos, and feelings. Sharing material, playing games, watching funny video clips, staying up to date on news and information, chatting with friends, connecting with other websites and groups, maintaining relationships, removing depression and frustration, and educational purposes are all common activities.

Figure 5. Motivations that drive students to use Facebook

They believe it is a beneficial way to contact friends and that they may discuss any problem with friends or teachers, as well as learn a lot about social media sites such as e-commerce, Facebook groups or pages, websites, and so on. They also believe that

Facebook aids their knowledge and keeps them informed about what is going on in the world. Because Facebook is free and simple to use, it has become a habit for this generation. The following are the incentives that motivate students to regularly utilize Facebook. Now, it is just a habit for this generation to use Facebook because It is free and simple to use. Those are the motivations shown in Figure 5 that drive students easily to use Facebook.

4.4 Educational Usage of Facebook

Figure 6 illustrates the utilization of Facebook by students for several academic objectives, including collecting and sharing academic information, group work, collaboration, receiving updated notice, class and examination information, sharing problems for feedback from various groups, attending live classes, seminars, webinars, and workshops from any location, attending guest teachers classes from reputable universities, collecting and sharing academic information, and attending live classes, seminars, webinars, and workshops from any location. One respondent added, "I use Facebook to receive educational materials, announcements, study materials, communication with teachers & classmates, linked with teachers, live classes, getting and sharing institutional news/notice/information, group studying, and remote learning".

Another key consideration is that students can use Facebook to communicate with their classmates and teachers. "I can always be connected with classmates and teachers and can see their activities on Facebook," one responder said. Another participant stated "I am able to acquire class-related material on Facebook in a timely manner and using Facebook is engaging and enjoyable." Students also prioritize different educational pages and groups on Facebook for academic purposes. "There are numerous useful education and research related pages and groups on Facebook where students may share their issues and receive professional advice on any academic or non-academic topic," one respondent stated.

Figure 6. Major academic purposes of using Facebook

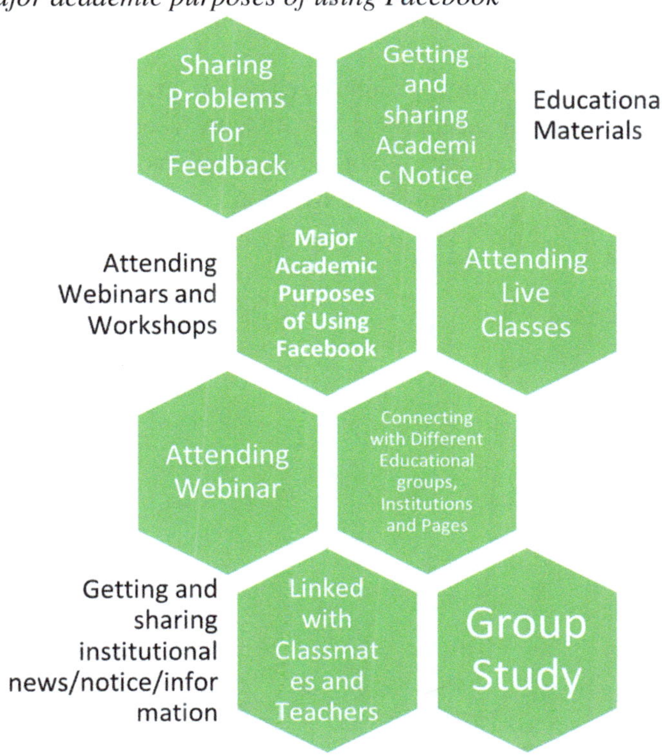

"Students leverage Facebook for educational objectives, including the acquisition of knowledge, monitoring the activities of their friends, and exchanging information," stated another participant. It serves as a special motivator for students to utilize Facebook by allowing them to learn a variety of subjects by connecting with educational groups or sites. Finally, respondents believe that they are utilizing Facebook to improve their academic performance. "We can join any educational groups that serve us in academic goals, and we can be connected to our university sites and groups," one respondent said.

4.5 Challenges do university students confront when using Facebook for educational purposes

Students use Facebook for a range of purposes, as depicted in Figure 7, including those related to their educational objectives. Students, however, face numerous challenges when utilizing Facebook for academic purposes. Many users find themselves easily distracted by the entertaining content on Facebook, which can hinder their ability to use the platform for academic purposes. "As Facebook is also an excellent source of amusement, students might easily become diverted by other topics," one respondent said. Distractions waste time and put mental and physical strain on individuals.

It can lead to wastage of time, addiction, boredom, privacy concerns, and security concerns. Another significant issue that students faced was the authenticity of information and materials. Because all of the information on Facebook is inaccurate and unverified. There is no option for verification.

Figure 7. Major challenges of using Facebook for academic purposes

Survey respondents indicate that even students have a greater inclination towards publishing, exchanging photos and emotions, talking, and watching amusing and explicit movies, memes, news, and memes on Facebook rather than using it for academic reasons. Many students, on the other hand, only use Facebook for recreational purposes. Some students were also unable to utilize Facebook for educational purposes due to financial and technological constraints.

4.6 University students' perception about the effects of Facebook usage on academic performance

According to Figure 8, 89% of students perceive a loss of time awareness while using Facebook, whereas just 11% believe they are effectively managing their workload. Here, 71% agreed that they sometimes or occasionally lose proper sleep owing to Facebook use, whereas 29% indicated that they never lose proper sleep owing to Facebook use. 53% said they never missed an exam or class because of Facebook, while 47% said they have missed an exam or class because of Facebook. In a poll, 51% of students said they never went on Facebook in class, while 49% admitted to doing so. Among students, 49% reported never skipping courses when they are aware in advance that the course materials are accessible online, whereas 51% do skip courses when they are aware in advance that the course materials are available online. Fifty percent of students reported that using Facebook never caused them to receive a poor grade or perform poorly in class, while the other half concurred. They tried to limit their Facebook usage 88% of the time, but just 12% never did.

Figure 8. Perception about the effects of Facebook usage on academic performance

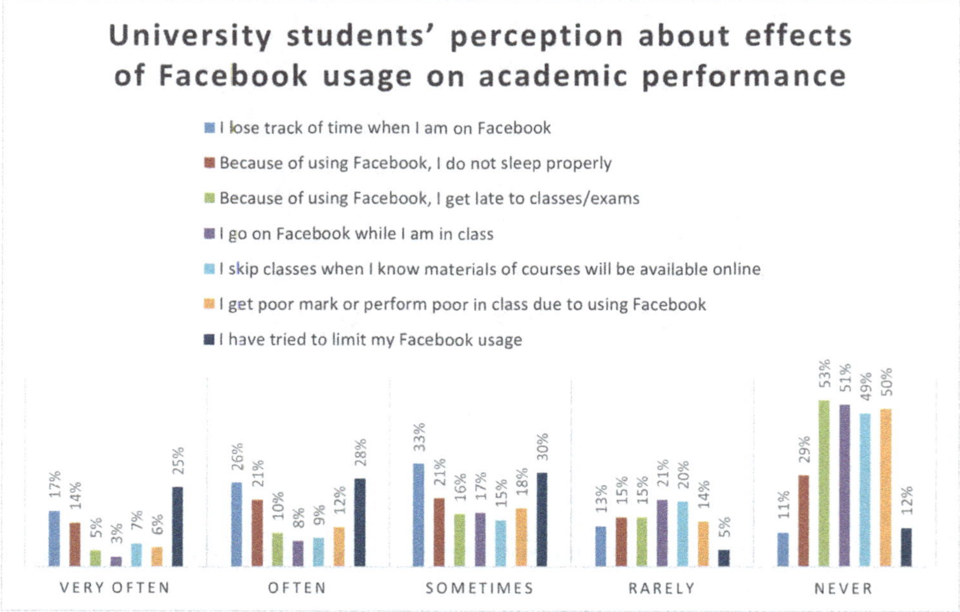

5. DISCUSSION

5.1 University student's perceptions and general usage of Facebook

As per the study's findings, all the respondents' students utilize Facebook. Students use Facebook at home and in public areas such as universities and outings, as well as when they meet up with friends and at social functions. Multiple researches have demonstrated that the student population in higher education, as well as the general population, are significant users of Facebook (Junco, 2012a; Madge et al., 2009; Rhoades et al., 2008). According to Kashif (2013), the most popular mode of contact among UEF students is Facebook, followed by email. The findings also revealed that students generally use cell phones to access Facebook, though some also use laptops, tablets, and desktop computers. However, Selwyn's (2009) study found that students used Facebook to assess their student experiences at universities, share practical and logistical information (such as study schedules, assignment deadlines, or exam dates), and engage in discussions about academic topics covered in class.

Upon careful analysis of all the results, the study concluded that Facebook serves as a pleasant and beneficial means of amusement and relaxation during periods of studying. Moreover, 86% of students say they use Facebook to relax before exams. Median daily usage of Facebook is 73%, with 19% of users engaging with the platform every hour. A significant proportion of students (64%) report dedicating one to two hours to the internet for activities directly connected to their studies, whereas 53% report dedicating one to three hours to the internet for other purposes, such as pleasure. Regrettably, a mere 23% of students assert that they allocate less than one hour each day to internet usage for scholastic reasons. An overwhelming majority of university students use Facebook as a means of communication with their peers, friends, professors, relatives, and family members. Nevertheless, due to the association of social networks with leisure time and reduced stress levels, Facebook can serve not only as a means of relaxation but also as a platform for students and teachers to engage in learning and teaching activities (González et al., 2016).

Regrettably, just 6% of respondents study for academic purposes for five to six hours per day, while 72% claim to study for university reasons for between one and two hours per day and 18% for three to four hours per day. Lampe et al. (2011) found that although most students used Facebook for academic purposes, a subset of them harbored doubts about its educational benefits, indicating a discrepancy between students' real usage and their preconceived notions.

5.2 Perceptions about Facebook usage for educational purpose

The vast majority (99%) of students use Facebook to stay informed about last-minute courses, and classroom or university news, and to interact with their university peers about academic difficulties. Previous research indicates that most students have incorporated social media into their lives for purposes such as communicating with their peers. Facebook, in particular, can facilitate casual interaction during classroom activities and promote collaboration among learners (Toker & Baturay, 2019).

A study conducted in Romania revealed that students exhibited a moderately positive attitude toward utilizing Facebook for educational purposes, particularly in extracurricular activities. This indicates that Facebook may serve as an effective resource for informal learning and community development among students (Coman et al., 2021).

In addition, a majority of individuals also participate in other Facebook groups, communities, or pages that align with their academic interests. Moreover, a significant majority of students, approximately 93%, utilize Facebook as a platform to exchange their university experiences with their predecessors or mentors, as well as to seek guidance on academic matters. Performance expectancy and social influence impact Indian students' behavioral intention to use social networking sites like Facebook for learning, demonstrating general acceptance of these platforms for educational uses (Alvi, 2021).

Facebook live classes and Facebook groups are ideal for studying since they allow students to join free live lectures and webinars taught by the greatest professors and experts. 61% of students have participated in Facebook live classes or sessions and 62% said that Facebook live classes and Facebook groups are excellent for studying from anywhere. Rabbi et al. (2020) also mentioned that with the help of social networking, teaching, and learning may be done anywhere, at any time.

5.3 Challenges of using Facebook for educational purposes

Facebook is a great educational tool that has been ingrained in students' daily lives. Aside from the educational benefits of Facebook, Nguyen (2017) highlighted challenges such as distraction, poor teamwork and communication, information accuracy, and cyberbullying. It was also noted that students used Facebook for educational objectives but faced distractions, harassment, unverified content, false information, time wasting, merging personal and academic life, ads, spam, and cyberbullying.

However, according to the findings, 93% of students report getting distracted by other Facebook content/activities while using Facebook for educational purposes. Facebook's various distractions (advertisements, games, video clips, 18+ content, etc.) may generate work overload for students and academics, who struggle to separate important from useless information. Furthermore, it interferes with their normal growth, leading to sleeplessness, psychological disorders, apprehension, and fluctuations in mood, as well as evasion or lack of awareness of their educational commitments and rejection to enroll in university (Shahid, et al., 2020).

Finally, social media has the potential to diminish educational information asymmetry; however, its effectiveness is contingent upon users' perceptions of the platform's usefulness and trustworthiness. Students are less likely to engage with information shared on Facebook if they do not find it useful or trustworthy (Huang & Chueh, 2023). Facebook is becoming more and more commercialized, which makes some students angry when they see spam or useless posts.

5.4 Impact of Facebook usage on university students' academic performance

The way students act toward Facebook is positive, and they do not regard it as a hindrance to their academic or social lives (*TEFĂNICĂ, 2014*). The research's primary findings revealed that a large percentage of students (90%) feel it has helped students improve their grades and (55%) believe that Facebook usage helps academic success. According to the findings, students generally hold positive impressions regarding Facebook's impact on their academic achievement. They tend to believe that Facebook doesn't significantly affect their ability to succeed academically. Al-Dheleai and Tasir (2017) found that students exhibited positive attitudes towards utilizing Facebook as a means of engaging with their classmates online. Moreover, the data indicate a correlation between students' perceptions of online communication through Facebook and their academic achievement. While various researchers have indeed found a connection between academic achievement and Facebook use, Junco (2015) argues that multitasking can lessen this association. According to Bowers-Campbell (2008), Facebook could improve students' independent learning by promoting communication and collaboration with peers and professors. Students possessing robust peer networks tend to achieve higher academic performance, as these networks offer essential support and motivation (Zhou et al., 2023).

Students use Facebook to bookmark/save useful stuff, interact with teachers and peers, collaborate on group work and assignments, reduce stress, receive information and announcements, and share views and ideas. However, 93% of students bookmark/save study-related content on Facebook. Facebook makes staying in touch with teachers easy, according to 62% of respondents. Facebook makes communicating with professors and classmates easy. Facebook also benefits personal learning, according to 52%. According to the survey, 75% of students believe Facebook is fantastic for university-related information and communication, and 70% think it's great for group work and cooperation. Students in Singapore were content (Wang et al., 2011) with Facebook's fundamental LMS feature despite privacy and technology issues.

Facebook's academic value depends on how it's used. Positive academic outcomes are more likely for students who use Facebook, set academic goals, and balance pleasure and study (Zavala et al., 2023). Researchers have found that students have expressed the most appreciation for Facebook due to its ability to facilitate the sharing of study materials, provide learning resources for references, establish academic groups, and foster interpersonal connections (Manasijević et al., 2016; Hung & Yuen, 2010; Irwin et al., 2012). According to respondents, getting and sharing study materials, improving academic participation, sharing book reviews, crisis communication, receiving university notice, Distributing Materials, communicating with friends and teachers, live classes, and group work are some of Facebook's educational advantages. Facebook facilitates easy access to and exchange of educational resources and information, according to 69% of respondents. Consequently, 54% said Facebook may be a useful supplement to traditional education. Furthermore, Facebook, according to 60% of respondents, encourages and expands academic and professional participation outside of the institution community. Respondents stated that they may interact with Education-related groups, pages, and websites on Facebook and easily gain a lot of information from them, as well as occasionally acquire opportunities for education-related online courses. However, Facebook may be used to assist informal learning, which is defined as learning motivated by daily life or by making connections with other people or tools that meet their interests or needs, according to 60% of respondents. Additionally, Students can participate in live discussions or classes with several world-class lecturers or experts through Facebook at no cost.

Facebook is causing a crisis that is influencing pupils' academic achievement. 73% of students acknowledge that Facebook has a detrimental impact on their academic progress. Whereas 90% of students believe that Facebook prevents them from studying or finishing their schoolwork. Furthermore, the absence of engagement may negatively impact academic performance, as students tend to be less focused on their studies when distracted by social media (Hammill et al., 2023). Even when focused on academic tasks, students are readily sidetracked by the plethora of recreational information that floods Facebook (Cassidy, 2006). Wise et al., (2011) found that Facebook in the classroom was distracting and less likely to boost academic engagement.

There are various reasons why students use Facebook, including educational goals. Students may become easily distracted by other things because Facebook is also a fantastic source of entertainment. It can result in time waste, addiction, boredom, privacy issues, and security concerns. According to the data, 93% of students report being distracted by other Facebook content/activities. 89% of students feel they lose track of time when they are on Facebook. Junco (2012, 2015) discovered a negative link between Facebook use and academic performance, meaning that Students who use Facebook more frequently and for longer periods (for personal usage) perform lower academically. In this study, 71% of those polled claimed to have lost sleep as a result of Facebook use on occasion or regularly.

Facebook addiction causes a slew of issues for students. Students are occasionally late for class or exams because they are on Facebook. They are even using Facebook in class, which is forbidden in Bangladesh. As a result, they are unable to pay their whole attention to the class. 53% of students never skip an exam or class because of Facebook, while 47% have missed an exam or class because of Facebook. In a poll, 51% of students indicated they never go on Facebook in class, while 49% admitted to doing so. Students stated that if they know ahead of time that the course materials are available online, they will skip 51% of the classes. Conversely, however, based on the findings, Moreover, they miss new posts or (urgent) news if they are not regularly available on Facebook which influences their studies also. Meanwhile, in this study, the majority of students (49%) denied being addicted to Facebook.

Using Facebook as an instructional tool that helps students improve their grades while also lowering their grades for access use is a win-win situation. Only 16% of students thought their grades had improved since they began using Facebook. On the other side, 25% of students felt that their grades had not improved since they began using Facebook. Furthermore, 45% thought if they avoided Facebook more, they would do better academically. Finally, 88% of students attempted to minimize their Facebook usage to improve their academic performance. Altaany & Jassim (2013) Moreover, the poll found that a student's grade point average will always perform better the less time they spend on Facebook. Research into the connection between academic success and Facebook use has given a variety of results. Although Facebook's excessive use can have a detrimental effect on academic self-efficacy, its use for self-expression can improve academic self-efficacy and study habits (Valdez & Datu, 2023). Nevertheless, Lambić (2016) and Pasek et al. (2009) asserted that there is no connection between grades and Facebook use. as indicated. There were no differences between Facebook users and non-users' aggregate grade point averages (GPAs), according to Kolek and Saunders (2008). Facebook users had a lower mean GPA and studied for fewer hours a week than those who did not use it (Kirschner & Karpinski, 2010).

5.5 Limitations and Future Research Implications

Since this study focused on students' opinions, more research on the same subject is suggested to better understand teachers' perspectives on employing Facebook as a teaching-learning tool and its impact on university students' academic achievement. Furthermore, it would be interesting to observe if educational level affects students' participation in social media, as well as if there are any discrepancies in social media usage between different educational institutions. During COVID-19, data was collected and universities in Bangladesh stayed closed. This study relies on an online-based questionnaire to acquire primary data from students due to the COVID-19 outbreak. The survey involved a limited number of respondents and was conducted in a short length of time. More research over a longer period and with a larger participant group is recommended. Lastly, this study recommends the implementation of qualitative research or a case study of students to gain a more comprehensive understanding of the correlation between Facebook and academic success.

6. RECOMMENDATIONS

University students use Facebook frequently. Facebook's simplicity and freedom have made it essential to their daily lives. Facebook, a widely used social media site, is also a great teaching-learning tool that students utilize daily. Research on Facebook and academic success has yielded mixed results. It can benefit or harm students depending on how it's used. Based on respondents' facts and key findings, policy recommendations follow.

1. The educational and recreational sections could be divided to mitigate distractions. There is now a distinct area for gaming. Facebook authority should create a distinct educational area. It is also possible by configuring a preference option. This eventually allows students to identify which spectrum they are truly interested in without sending any additional information.
2. Facebook might provide a product like Google Meet, Zoom, or Microsoft Teams for educational purposes. Facebook, on the other hand, may introduce course elements similar to the MOOC platform.
3. Fake news, information, and materials should be removed or banned from Facebook. They might do it by establishing offices in each country to verify data. Facebook, on the other hand, needs to provide all open-source educational materials and authentic educational resources in one place.
4. Parents or guardians should inform their children that other Facebook stuff wastes their time. They should put greater emphasis on educational content on Facebook. Parents, guardians, and teachers must all keep an eye on their children's actions. They must counsel their children frequently.
5. The government should start a program or run commercials for students to raise awareness. Every half-hour, one advertising should remind students that they are wasting their time.
6. Facebook should introduce student accounts with unique features. To enhance student well-being, it is essential for Facebook's administrators to impose time restrictions on social media use. Students must be limited to a maximum of two hours per day on the platform.
7. Students should be mindful of who inspires them, and which groups and pages are beneficial and helpful for learning while connecting with people and groups on Facebook.
8. If the government and other organizations provide students with a low-cost device and internet connection, they should be able to easily join live classes, seminars, and workshops.

7. CONCLUSIONS

Facebook has become part of people's everyday routines, due to its accessibility and user-friendliness. This study thoroughly scrutinized the complex link between Facebook use and university students' academic achievement, focusing on Bangladeshi students and literature. Facebook may be a beneficial tool but also a distraction for schooling, according to the research. On one hand, Facebook serves as an essential platform for communication, collaboration, and provide access to academic resources. It offers educational advantages such as group work, live class participation, and information sharing.

However, excessive Facebook use can cause distractions, time wastage, and impaired focus, all of which may hamper academic success. Nearly 73% of the participants acknowledged that Facebook adversely impacts their academic success due to overindulgence in socializing and irrelevant activities. The results indicate that while a substantial number of students perceive Facebook as a vital educational resource, a notable proportion recognizes its negative consequences, especially when utilized excessively for social interactions. Distractions, harassment, and exposure to stuff that isn't verified make using Facebook for academic reasons even more challenging.

Despite these challenges, the study demonstrates Facebook's potential as a great teaching tool when used responsibly. In order to minimize these detrimental effects, students must use Facebook in a more controlled manner, maintaining a balance between the platform's educational value and the requirement to stay focused on their academics. In addition, educators and policymakers should consider implementing guidelines and raising awareness to assist students in making the most of Facebook's advantages without sacrificing their academic performance. Ultimately, Facebook can continue to be a useful tool in the educational scene if appropriate regulation and purposeful use are implemented.

REFERENCES

Ainin, S., Naqshbandi, M. M., Moghavvemi, S., & Jaafar, N. I. (2015). Facebook usage, socialization and academic performance. *Computers & Education*, *83*, 64–73. DOI: 10.1016/j.compedu.2014.12.018

Al-Dheleai, Y. M., & Tasir, Z. (2017). Using facebook for the purpose of students interaction and its correlation with students academic performance. *The Turkish Online Journal of Educational Technology*, *16*(4), 170–178. https://files.eric.ed.gov/fulltext/EJ1160608.pdf

Al-Hail, M., Zguir, M. F., & Koç, M. (2024). Exploring Digital Learning Opportunities and Challenges in Higher Education Institutes: Stakeholder Analysis on the Use of Social Media for Effective Sustainability of Learning–Teaching–Assessment in a University setting in Qatar. *Sustainability*, *16*(15), 6413. DOI: 10.3390/su16156413

Al-Rahmi, A. M., Shamsuddin, A., Alturki, U., Aldraiweesh, A., Yusof, F. M., Al-Rahmi, W. M., & Aljeraiwi, A. A. (2021). The influence of information system success and technology acceptance model on social media factors in education. *Sustainability*, *13*(14), 7770. DOI: 10.3390/su13147770

Al-rahmi, W. M., Othman, M. S., & Musa, M. A. (2014). Social media through collaborative learning in Malaysian higher education. *Asian Social Science*, *10*(8), 210–221. DOI: 10.5539/ass.v10n8p210

Alsarayreh, M., & Aljaafreh, A. (2023). Factors Influencing Students' Academic Performance in Universities: Mediated by Knowledge Sharing Behavior. *Knowledge Management & E-Learning*, *15*(4), 643–671. DOI: 10.34105/j.kmel.2023.15.036

Altaany, F. H., & Jassim, F. A. (2013). Impact of Facebook usage on Undergraduate students performance in Irbid National University: case study. *arXiv (Cornell University)*. /arxiv.1306.4779DOI: 10.48550

Alvi, I. (2021). College students' reception of social networking tools for learning in India: An extended UTAUT model. *Smart Learning Environments*, *8*(1). Advance online publication. DOI: 10.1186/s40561-021-00164-9 PMID: 40477379

Amjad, A. I., Aslam, S., & Tabassum, U. (2024). Tech-infused classrooms: A comprehensive study on the interplay of mobile learning, ChatGPT and social media in academic attainment. *European Journal of Education*. Advance online publication. DOI: 10.1111/ejed.12625

Bandy, J., & Diakopoulos, N. (2023). Facebook's news feed algorithm and the 2020 US election. *Social Media + Society*, *9*(3). Advance online publication. DOI: 10.1177/20563051231196898

Bicen, H., & Cavus, N. (2011). Social network sites usage habits of undergraduate students: Case study of Facebook. *Procedia: Social and Behavioral Sciences*, *28*, 943–947. DOI: 10.1016/j.sbspro.2011.11.174

Bowers-Campbell, J. (2008). Cyber "Pokes": Motivational antidote for developmental college readers. *Journal of College Reading and Learning*, *39*(1), 74–87. DOI: 10.1080/10790195.2008.10850313

Büyükbaykal, C. I. (2015). Communication Technologies and Education in the information Age. *Procedia: Social and Behavioral Sciences*, *174*, 636–640. DOI: 10.1016/j.sbspro.2015.01.594

Cassidy, J. (2006). *Me Media*. Retrieved from The New Yorker: https://www.newyorker.com/magazine/2006/05/15/me-media

Catanzaro, M. F. (2011). Indirect aggression, bullying and female teen victimization: A literature review. *Pastoral Care in Education*, *29*(2), 83–101. DOI: 10.1080/02643944.2011.573495

Coman, C., Mesesan-Schmitz, L., Tiru, L. G., Grosseck, G., & Bularca, M. C. (2021). Dear student, what should I write on my wall? A case study on academic uses of Facebook and Instagram during the pandemic. *PLoS One*, *16*(9), e0257729. DOI: 10.1371/journal.pone.0257729 PMID: 34555100

Crossette, N., Carr, L. D., & Wilcox, B. R. (2023). Correlations between student connectivity and academic performance: A pandemic follow-up. *Physical Review. Physics Education Research*, *19*(1). Advance online publication. DOI: 10.1103/physrevphyseducres.19.010106

Cui, T., & Wang, J. (2023). Empowering active learning: A social annotation tool for improving student engagement. *British Journal of Educational Technology*, *55*(2), 712–730. DOI: 10.1111/bjet.13403

Dafonte-Gómez, A., García-Crespo, O., & Ramahí-García, D. (2023). Using video for fact-checking on Facebook. Analysis of the trend and reach of Ibero-American production (2016-2021). *El Profesional de la Información*. Advance online publication. DOI: 10.3145/epi.2023.sep.11

De Groot, T., De Haan, M., & Van Dijken, M. (2023). Learning in and about a filtered universe: Young people's awareness and control of algorithms in social media. *Learning, Media and Technology*, *48*(4), 701–713. DOI: 10.1080/17439884.2023.2253730

Duhoki, A. K. (2017). *Students usage of Facebook to enhance learning in higher education, Master's Thesis*. Near East University., https://docs.neu.edu.tr/library/6511073452.pdf

Dule, A., Abdu, Z., Hajure, M., Mohammedhussein, M., Girma, M., Gezimu, W., & Duguma, A. (2023). Facebook addiction and affected academic performance among Ethiopian university students: A cross-sectional study. *PLoS One*, *18*(2), e0280306. DOI: 10.1371/journal.pone.0280306 PMID: 36745630

Dyson, B., Vickers, K., Turtle, J., Cowan, S., & Tassone, A. (2014). Evaluating the use of Facebook to increase student engagement and understanding in lecture-based classes. *Higher Education*, *69*(2), 303–313. DOI: 10.1007/s10734-014-9776-3

Elkhatat, A. M. (2023). Evaluating the authenticity of ChatGPT responses: A study on text-matching capabilities. *International Journal for Educational Integrity*, *19*(1). Advance online publication. DOI: 10.1007/s40979-023-00137-0

Fruehwirth, J. C., Weng, A. X., & Perreira, K. M. (2024). The effect of social media use on mental health of college students during the pandemic. *Health Economics*. Advance online publication. DOI: 10.1002/hec.4871 PMID: 38873817

González, M. R., Gasco, J., & Llopis, J. (2016). Facebook and academic performance: A positive outcome. *The Anthropologist*, *23*(1–2), 59–67. DOI: 10.1080/09720073.2016.11891924

Hamid, S., Waycott, J., Kurnia, S., & Chang, S. (2015). Understanding students' perceptions of the benefits of online social networking use for teaching and learning. *The Internet and Higher Education*, *26*, 1–9. DOI: 10.1016/j.iheduc.2015.02.004

Hammill, J., Nguyen, T., & Henderson, F. (2023). The impact of mindfulness interventions in higher education to enhance engagement. *Journal of Further and Higher Education*, *47*(5), 619–632. DOI: 10.1080/0309877x.2023.2175652

Hasan, H., Lai, C. C., Ibrahim, I. S., Ahmad, S. A., & Meri, A. (2022). The Impact on Usage of Social Media on Academic Performance Among University Students in Sabah – A Conceptual Paper. *International Journal of Law Government and Communication*, *7*(30), 42–50. DOI: 10.35631/ijlgc.730005

He, D. (2024). Navigating academic and everyday life challenges in the US: The role of social media for international graduate students. *Information and Learning Science*. Advance online publication. DOI: 10.1108/ILS-12-2023-0200

Huang, H., & Chueh, H. (2023). Sustained improvement of educational information asymmetry: Intentions to use school social media. *Sustainability*, *15*(3), 2676. DOI: 10.3390/su15032676

Hung, H., & Yuen, S. C. (2010). Educational use of social networking technology in higher education. *Teaching in Higher Education*, *15*(6), 703–714. DOI: 10.1080/13562517.2010.507307

Hurt, N. E., Moss, G. S., Bradley, C. L., Larson, L. R., Lovelace, M., Prevost, L. B., & Camus, M. S. (2012). The 'Facebook'effect: College students' perceptions of online discussions in the age of social networking. *International Journal for the Scholarship of Teaching and Learning*, *6*(2), 10. Advance online publication. DOI: 10.20429/ijsotl.2012.060210

Irwin, C. G., Ball, L. E., Desbrow, B., & Leveritt, M. (2012). Students' perceptions of using Facebook as an interactive learning resource at university. *Australasian Journal of Educational Technology*, *28*(7). Advance online publication. DOI: 10.14742/ajet.798

Javeed, A. (2023). Impact of using social media on the academic performance A case of college going students in Loralai Division. *Siazga Research Journal*, *2*(1). Advance online publication. DOI: 10.58341/srj.v2i1.12

Jiang, Y., Joshi, D. R., & Khanal, J. (2024). From Clicks to Credits: Examining the influence of online engagement and internet addiction on academic performance in Chinese universities. SSRN *Electronic Journal*. DOI: 10.2139/ssrn.4886106

Junco, R. (2012). The relationship between frequency of Facebook use, participation in Facebook activities, and student engagement. *Computers & Education*, *58*(1), 162–171. DOI: 10.1016/j.compedu.2011.08.004

Junco, R. (2012a). Too much face and not enough books: The relationship between multiple indices of Facebook use and academic performance. *Computers in Human Behavior*, *28*(1), 187–198. DOI: 10.1016/j.chb.2011.08.026

Junco, R. (2015). Student class standing, Facebook use, and academic performance. *Journal of Applied Developmental Psychology*, *36*, 18–29. DOI: 10.1016/j.appdev.2014.11.001

Kashif, M. (2013). *Impact of facebook on students' academic performance : analysis through the social capital*. https://erepo.uef.fi/handle/123456789/12939

Kirschner, P. A., & Karpinski, A. C. (2010). Facebook® and academic performance. *Computers in Human Behavior*, *26*(6), 1237–1245. DOI: 10.1016/j.chb.2010.03.024

Klomsri, T., Grebäck, L., & Tedre, M. (2013). Social media in everyday learning: How Facebook supports informal learning among young adults in South Africa. *13th Koli Calling International Conference on Computing Education Research*, (pp. 135-144). Koli, Finland.

Kolek, E. A., & Saunders, D. (2008). Online Disclosure: An Empirical examination of undergraduate Facebook profiles. *NASPA Journal*, *45*(1), 1–25. DOI: 10.2202/1949-6605.1905

Kumi-Yeboah, A., Kim, Y., Yankson, B., Aikins, S., & Dadson, Y. A. (2023). Diverse students' perspectives on privacy and technology integration in higher education. *British Journal of Educational Technology*, *54*(6), 1671–1692. DOI: 10.1111/bjet.13386

Lambić, D. (2016). Correlation between Facebook use for educational purposes and academic performance of students. *Computers in Human Behavior*, *61*, 313–320. DOI: 10.1016/j.chb.2016.03.052

Lampe, C., Wohn, D. Y., Vitak, J., Ellison, N. B., & Wash, R. (2011). Student use of Facebook for organizing collaborative classroom activities. *International Journal of Computer-Supported Collaborative Learning*, *6*(3), 329–347. DOI: 10.1007/s11412-011-9115-y

Lee, N. R. C., & Dioso, N. E. D. (2023). The Effects of Facebook Usage on Academics and Values of the Students. *EPRA International Journal of Environmental Economics Commerce and Educational Management*, 31–44. DOI: 10.36713/epra14012

Liao, C., & Wu, J. (2022). Deploying multimodal learning analytics models to explore the impact of digital distraction and peer learning on student performance. *Computers & Education*, *190*, 104599. DOI: 10.1016/j.compedu.2022.104599

Madge, C., Meek, J., Wellens, J., & Hooley, T. (2009). Facebook, social integration and informal learning at university: 'It is more for socialising and talking to friends about work than for actually doing work.'. *Learning, Media and Technology*, *34*(2), 141–155. DOI: 10.1080/17439880902923606

Manasijević, D., Živković, D., Arsić, S., & Milošević, I. (2016). Exploring students' purposes of usage and educational usage of Facebook. *Computers in Human Behavior*, *60*, 441–450. DOI: 10.1016/j.chb.2016.02.087

Marín, V. I., Carpenter, J. P., Tur, G., & Williamson-Leadley, S. (2022). Social media and data privacy in education: An international comparative study of perceptions among pre-service teachers. *Journal of Computers in Education*, *10*(4), 769–795. DOI: 10.1007/s40692-022-00243-x

Martindale, J., Wiseman, K., Pieper, K., Nascimento, F., Aamodt, W., & Strowd, R. (2024). Social media facilitates lifelong learning for neurologists but is limited by content distrust (P5-7.004). *Neurology*, *102*(17, supplement_1). Advance online publication. DOI: 10.1212/wnl.0000000000206463

Mauludina, Y. S., Hoang, B. L., Wang, T., Jenq, C., Huang, C., & Huang, C. (2024). Medical students' perceptions of integrating social media into a narrative medicine programme for 5th-year clerkship in Taiwan: A descriptive qualitative study. *BMC Medical Education, 24*(1). Advance online publication. DOI: 10.1186/s12909-024-05255-y PMID: 38500075

Mazman, S. G., & Usluel, Y. K. (2010). Modeling educational usage of Facebook. *Computers & Education, 55*(2), 444–453. DOI: 10.1016/j.compedu.2010.02.008

Moghavvemi, S., Sulaiman, A., Aziz, A. A., & Wai, P. S. (2017). *The impact of Facebook usage on academic performance. International Conference on Research and Innovation in Information Systems (ICRIIS)*, IEEE. DOI: 10.1109/icriis.2017.8002518

Mou, Q., Zhuang, J., Wu, Q., Zhong, Y., Dai, Q., Cao, X., Gao, Y., Lu, Q., & Zhao, M. (2024). Social media addiction and academic engagement as serial mediators between social anxiety and academic performance among college students. *BMC Psychology, 12*(1). Advance online publication. DOI: 10.1186/s40359-024-01635-7 PMID: 38582933

Nguyen, T. (2017). Undergraduate students' use of Facebook for educational purposes: Advantages, difficulties, and potential for connected learning, Master's thesis, University of Tampere.

Ning, W., & Inan, F. A. (2023). Impact of social media addiction on college students' academic performance: An interdisciplinary perspective. *Journal of Research on Technology in Education*, •••, 1–16. DOI: 10.1080/15391523.2023.2196456

Pasek, J., More, E., & Romer, D. (2009). Realizing the social internet? Online social networking meets offline civic engagement. *Journal of Information Technology & Politics*, *6*(3–4), 197–215. DOI: 10.1080/19331680902996403

Rabbi, M. F., SmiTa, M. K., & Mohammad, S. (2020). Using social networking sites as medium of instruction at tertiary education during COVID-19 situation in Bangladesh. *International Journal of Educational Research Review*, *5*(3), 258–264. DOI: 10.24331/ijere.741644

Ravichandran, D. (2019). Impact of Social Networking Sites Usage on Students' Performance [IJRISS]. *International Journal of Research and Innovation in Social Science, 3*(1). https://rsisinternational.org/journals/ijriss/Digital-Library/volume-3-issue-1/116-119.pdf

Rhoades, E., Irani, T., Telg, R., & Myers, B. E. (2008). Internet as an informal source: Attitudes, and usage of students enrolled in a college agriculture course. *Journal of Agricultural Education*, *49*(2), 108–117. https://jae-online.org/index.php/jae/article/view/922/767

Rosenberg, J. M., Borchers, C., Stegenga, S. M., Burchfield, M. A., Anderson, D., & Fischer, C. (2022). How educational institutions reveal students' personally identifiable information on Facebook. *Learning, Media and Technology*, *49*(3), 339–355. DOI: 10.1080/17439884.2022.2140672

Rouis, S., Limayem, M., & Salehi-Sangari, E. (2017). Impact of Facebook usage on students' academic achievement: Roles of Self-Regulation and Trust. *Electronic Journal of Research in Educational Psychology*, *9*(25), 961–994. DOI: 10.25115/ejrep.v9i25.1465

Samad, S., Nilashi, M., & Ibrahim, O. (2019). The impact of social networking sites on students' social wellbeing and academic performance. *Education and Information Technologies*, *24*(3), 2081–2094. DOI: 10.1007/s10639-019-09867-6

Selwyn, N. (2009). Faceworking: Exploring students' education-related use of Facebook. *Learning, Media and Technology*, *34*(2), 157–174. DOI: 10.1080/17439880902923622

Shafiq, M., & Parveen, K. (2023). Social media usage: Analyzing its effect on academic performance and engagement of higher education students. *International Journal of Educational Development*, *98*, 102738. DOI: 10.1016/j.ijedudev.2023.102738

Shahid, A., Awan, M. Z., Siddique, W., Nadeem, H. T., & Chaudhary, M. (2020). Negative Impact on Academic Performance, Anxiety and Insomnia Due to Excessive Use of Social Media among University Students of Lahore (Pakistan). *International Journal of Scientific and Engineering Research*, *11*(9).

Shams, M., Shahid, R., & Raza, S. Y. (2022). Social Media and University Students: Trends and Effects Studies. *Pakistan Journal of Social Research*, *4*(04), 763–772. https://pjsr.com.pk/wp-content/uploads/2022/12/81.-Vol.-4-No.-4-December-2022-Shams-Shahid-Raza-Social-Media-and-University-Students-Trends-and-Effects-Studies.pdf

TEFĂNICĂ. S. I. (2014). The Impact of Facebook on University-Students Relationships. *Management Dynamics in the Knowledge Economy*, *2*(3), 492. Retrieved from https://www.managementdynamics.ro/index.php/journal/article/view/72

Tananuraksakul, N. (2015). An Investigation into the Impact of Facebook Group Usage on Students' Affect in Language Learning in a Thai Context. *International Journal on Teaching and Learning in Higher Education*, *27*(2), 235–246. https://files.eric.ed.gov/fulltext/EJ1082882.pdf

Tang, J. K. T., Yau, H., Wong, S., & Wong, S. (2015). The impacts on learning via social media: A study on post-secondary students in Hong Kong. In *Communications in computer and information science* (pp. 195–208). DOI: 10.1007/978-3-662-48978-9_19

Toker, S., & Baturay, M. H. (2019). What foresees college students' tendency to use facebook for diverse educational purposes? *International Journal of Educational Technology in Higher Education*, *16*(1). Advance online publication. DOI: 10.1186/s41239-019-0139-0

Valdez, J. P. M., & Datu, J. a. D. (2023). Does Facebook intensity matter for academic self-efficacy? A path analytic approach. *Research and Practice in Technology Enhanced Learning, 18*, 026. DOI: 10.58459/rptel.2023.18026

Valkenburg, P. M. (2022). Social media use and well-being: What we know and what we need to know. *Current Opinion in Psychology*, *45*, 101294. DOI: 10.1016/j.copsyc.2021.12.006 PMID: 35016087

Valle, A., Rodríguez, S., Cabanch, R.G., Núnez, J.C., & González-Pienda, J.A. and Rosario, & P. (2009). Academic goals: Historical and conceptual perspectives and educational implications. *Electronic Journal of Research in Educational Psychology*, *7*(3), 1073–1106.

Van Huan, D., Tuyet, N. T. B., Dung, T. M., Ha, V. T., & Duc, T. D. (2024). The influence of Facebook intensity on life satisfaction and academic performance of college students during COVID-19 pandemic. *Journal of Affective Disorders Reports*, *16*, 100782. DOI: 10.1016/j.jadr.2024.100782

Vardi, M. Y. (2024). More is different, in social media too. *Communications of the ACM*, *67*(5), 5. DOI: 10.1145/3653683

Wang, Q., Woo, H. L., Quek, C. L., Yang, Y., & Liu, M. (2011). Using the Facebook group as a learning management system: An exploratory study. *British Journal of Educational Technology*, *43*(3), 428–438. DOI: 10.1111/j.1467-8535.2011.01195.x

Willems, J., & Bateman, D. (2011). The potentials and pitfalls of social networking sites such as Facebook in higher education contexts. In G. Williams, P. Statham, N. Brown, & B. Cleland, *Changing Demands, Changing Directions* (pp. 1329-1331). Proceedings ascilite. Retrieved from http://www.ascilite.org.au/conferences/hobart11/procs/Willems-poster.pdf

Wise, L., Skues, J., & Williams, B. (2011). Facebook in higher education promotes social but not academic engagement. In G. Williams, P. Statham, N. Brown, & B. Cleland, *Changing Demands, Changing Directions* (pp. 1332-1342). Proceedings ascilite Hobart 2011. Retrieved from http://www.ascilite.org.au/conferences/hobart11/downloads/papers/Wise-full.pdf

Wohn, D. Y., & LaRose, R. (2014). Effects of loneliness and differential usage of Facebook on college adjustment of first-year students. *Computers & Education*, *76*, 158–167. DOI: 10.1016/j.compedu.2014.03.018

Wolbert, L., & Ünlüsoy, A. (2023). Creating authentic connectedness online through a shared experience of 'not-knowing.'. *Ethics and Education*, *18*(1), 110–122. DOI: 10.1080/17449642.2023.2188725

Yuan, C., He, Y., Lin, R., & Tang, Y. (2021). Graph embedding for scholar recommendation in academic social networks. *Frontiers in Physics*, *9*. Advance online publication. DOI: 10.3389/fphy.2021.768006

Zavala, J., Trenz, R. C., Tzanis, D., Malette, C., & Marin, N. M. (2023). The impact of social media use for news on academic performance in underrepresented undergraduate college students. *Cyberpsychology, Behavior, and Social Networking*, *26*(8), 657–661. DOI: 10.1089/cyber.2022.0303 PMID: 37327047

Zhou, Y., Meng, X., Wang, J., Mo, X., Jiang, S., Dai, C., & Liu, M. (2023). Daily Peer Relationships and Academic Achievement among College Students: A Social Network Analysis Based on Behavioral Big Data. *Sustainability*, *15*(22), 15762. DOI: 10.3390/su152215762

Chapter 10
The Role of Cooperatives in Driving Inclusive Growth and Sustainable Development

V. Venkatakrishnan
https://orcid.org/0009-0008-9800-3096
KIIT School of Rural Management, KIIT University, India

Srilata Patnaik
https://orcid.org/0000-0002-1766-962X
KIIT School of Rural Management, KIIT University, India

Debasish Mohapatra
https://orcid.org/0000-0003-0145-7937
KIIT School of Rural Management, KIIT University, India

Surendra Kumar Jena
https://orcid.org/0009-0003-1456-2709
KIIT School of Rural Management, KIIT University, India

ABSTRACT

India's cooperatives, including Gujarat Cooperative Milk Marketing Federation (GCMMF), Indian Farmers Fertilizer Cooperative Limited (IFFCO), and Krishak Bharati Cooperative Limited (KRIBHCO), have a global reputation for their success and excellence. India's cooperative enterprises, accounting for one-fourth of the world's enterprises, contribute to the economy and promote ethical business practices. A review chapter reveals initial challenges faced by these enterprises, based on secondary data and research. The chapter delves into the fundamental aspects

DOI: 10.4018/979-8-3693-0997-1.ch010

of achieving inclusive growth and sustainable development through various cooperative types. The chapter examines the impact of cooperatives, such as consumer, dairy, fisheries, women's welfare, and sugar cooperatives, on market prices in India, focusing on high-quality products and affordable prices. The chapter discusses recent efforts to support cooperatives and suggests further steps to strengthen them for inclusive growth and sustainable development through their successes.

INTRODUCTION

India has a long history of more than a century old experience of cooperatives. A few of its cooperatives are recognized among the top ten cooperatives in the world due to their continued success. The GCMMF and the IFFCO are some of the India's cooperatives that have been ranked among the top ten cooperatives of the world for the last few years consecutively. The Government of India's Ministry of Cooperation in its National Cooperative Database 2023 has mentioned about close to 8,00,000 cooperatives with 29,12,80,275 members (Attwood & Attwood, 2019). The International Cooperative Alliance (ICA) considered that about 25% of world's cooperative enterprises were in India as on 2023.

The ICA had been highlighting the importance of the cooperatives and the success of the first International Year of Cooperatives in 2012. It was claimed that the first 2012 International Year of Cooperatives had raised the awareness on the cooperatives' roles in promotion of sustainable development and through that inclusive development. It is pertinent to record that the United Nations General Assembly adopted a resolution it is 47th plenary meeting on 3rd November 2023 proclaiming 2025 as an International Year of Cooperatives. It has been extolling all the member States as well as other stakeholders to promote cooperatives and raise awareness on cooperatives' contribution for the achievement of the Sustainable Development Goals (SDGs) and thereby the overall social and economic development. It is claimed that in addition to the ICA, The United Nations and the International Labour Organization (ILO), consider that cooperative types of organizations are the most appropriate ones to address issues of poverty by identifying the economic opportunities for its members. It is also considered by many that the values and principles of cooperatives are strongly interlinked with the SDGs. Dwelling on the roles of cooperatives in achieving the SDGs, Lafont, Saura and Ribeiro-Soriano (2023), are of the view that there are eight different types of cooperatives influencing each of the 17 SDGs (Vishwakarma, 2019).

It is worth noting that the union minister for Cooperation in his address during the National Conference of Scheduled and Multi-State Urban Co-operative Banks and Credit Societies, organized by the Ministry of Cooperation and the National

Federation of Urban Cooperative Banks and Credit Societies Ltd (NAFCUB), in New Delhi on June 23, 2022 has pointed out that there are many issues related to urban cooperative banks. Similarly, there are many different types of cooperatives with their own unique sets of issues, challenges and opportunities (Diwate, 2021; Gupta et al., 2019). If they are addressed earlier, the cooperatives have the potential to improve their contribution to India's economy, their members and also the community in which they are functioning. The present paper is a modest attempt based on the review of the literature in this regard.

Objectives of the chapter

a) To identify the general challenges common to different kinds of cooperatives in India.
b) To delineate specific challenges and prospects of various types of cooperatives such as credit cooperatives, dairy cooperatives, fisheries cooperatives, sugar cooperatives, women cooperatives and consumer cooperatives to achieve the inclusive growth and sustainable development.
c) To suggest various initiatives to address the challenges in order to facilitate the cooperatives to achieve their potential for inclusive growth and sustainable development.

METHODOLOGY

The study is desk-based research to a large extent and also based on the authors' experience of researching and teaching about cooperatives over a period of time. Various reports and research articles have been reviewed and based on their findings this secondary-data based chapter has been prepared. Apart from that the information available in the websites and annual reports of various organizations including Reserve Bank of India (RBI), National Bank for Agricultural and Rural Development (NABARD) and the International Cooperative Alliance (ICA) have been largely utilized(Ghosh, 2021; Singh, 2024).

Sections of the chapter

The chapter has four major sections. The First Section briefly traces the origin, growth and status of various cooperatives in India. The Second Section focuses on the general challenges faced by the cooperatives. The Third Section is devoted to bring out the specific issues and prospects of selected types of cooperatives such as consumer cooperatives, dairy cooperatives, fisheries cooperatives, women cooperatives and sugar cooperatives. The Fourth Section provides suggestions on how to strengthen the cooperatives and ensure that they fulfill their potentials of inclusive growth and sustainable development. Apart from that the limitations of the chapter have also been outlined (Dash et al., 2020; Dohmwirth & Liu, 2020a).

Limitations

The cooperative movement in India is more than 100 years old and has one of the largest memberships among such organizations in the world. Moreover, the level of diversities across the cooperatives within India is also very high. The challenges faced by the cooperatives in India are plenty and the opportunities available to them are also abundant. Hence it is not possible to bring out their range and depth in a short review chapter. Though the authors had the opportunity to closely observe a few types of cooperatives in the distant past, it was not possible for them to undertake a study on these multiple aspects as it needed considerable resources encompassing finance, human and time(Attwood & Attwood, 2019; Ghosh, 2021; Singh, 2024; Vishwakarma, 2019). A few of the many notable challenges that could not be covered in this paper are related to the non-active members of the cooperatives, governance, professionalization and audit. Nonetheless, there is a need to revitalize the cooperatives to ensure they are duly reestablished as contributors to the larger economy and marginalized sections of the society. The authors have to a considerable extent relied upon various reports and publications to bring out the challenges and opportunities identified by various scholars. Most of the issues outlined in this chapter have to be largely credited to the respective reports and authors of various publications.

ORIGIN, GROWTH AND STATUS OF COOPERATIVES IN INDIA

The Indian cooperatives have a recorded history of about 120 years as on 2024. There were also claims as early as 1986 that India's cooperative movement was the largest in the world (Creighton, 1986). Apart from that there were also opinions that it was also the most diverse covering multiple sub-sectors of the economy. Although the initial focus of the cooperatives was on credit, as the first Act was named as the Cooperative Credit Societies Act, 1904 (Ghosh, 2021; Singh, 2024), the cooperatives have grown in many other sub-sectors/domains.

Despite the regional disparities in terms of presence of cooperatives in different parts of India, most of them have the cooperatives in one form or other. Both the Union and the State governments of India have demonstrated strong interest in supporting the cooperatives. They have passed many enabling legislation and also extended their support by forming specialized committees to focus on the functioning of the cooperatives. There could be differences of opinion on the roles of governments with regard to the cooperatives. However, there are numerous examples on how the governments have played active roles in promoting the cooperatives. For instance, various governments have contributed the initial share capital to the fledgling co-operatives and provided preferential treatment to them for establishing the producer cooperatives. The support of the respective governments for the sugar cooperatives in Maharashtra and Gujarat could be notable examples in this regard. It would be extremely difficult to find out any State in India which has not shown interest in promotion of the cooperatives. The Union Government too has been playing a commendable role and displaying strong interest in promoting the cooperatives as could be discerned from the various five-year plan documents.

The National Cooperative Data Base, Ministry of Cooperation, Government of India has rightly lauded the magnificent contributions of the cooperatives to achieve inclusive economic growth. These cooperatives of various sectors covering agriculture, housing, credit and many others domains have been empowering marginalized communities. The Government of India views the cooperative model as a vital component of India's socioeconomic development as it is aligning with the India's strategies for inclusive growth and empowerment.

The renowned Operation Flood resulting in the strengthening of dairy cooperatives numbering 1,41,907 as on 2023 covering 31% of the village *panchayats* and the primary agriculture credit societies (PACS) covering 89% of village *panchayats* (2,41,075) with potential to reduce poverty by promoting sustainable development in agrarian communities are making cooperatives vital part of India's economy. The India's cooperative sugar factories are considered to have more than 50% share in India's sugar export and thereby earning considerable foreign exchange. The cooperatives in the hand loom, textile and weaving sectors numbering around 9200 across the country are important in facilitating the empowerment of women by ensuring direct income leading to their financial independence. Further, the cooperatives that are exclusively focusing on the women's welfare are considered important for the socioeconomic transformation of women. There were 24,264 such cooperatives listed in the 2023 database and they are operating in various sub-sectors like handicrafts, dairy, jewellery making, farming and also Information Technology services (Attwood & Attwood, 2019; Le et al., 2020; Vishwakarma, 2019). These and similar such cooperatives not only provide economic benefits to the marginalized sections of the society but also instrumental in ushering in positive social changes in the society. Despite many ups and downs, the cooperatives in India have started receiving considerable attention in the recent days due to their ability to provide multiple opportunities to the people.

GENERAL CHALLENGES OF COOPERATIVES

Thissub-section focuses on the general challenges faced by many types of co-operatives. The restrictive legal framework on which the cooperatives have been established, the limited resources available to them covering both financial and human resources, multiple control of the cooperatives, for instance, the credit co-operatives controlled by both the State Governments and the RBI, challenges faced due to external forces and events by the cooperatives, for example, demonetization and covid-19 have been outlined in this section(Singh, 2024). The figure 1 depicts the general challenges faced by cooperatives.

Figure 1. General challenges of cooperatives

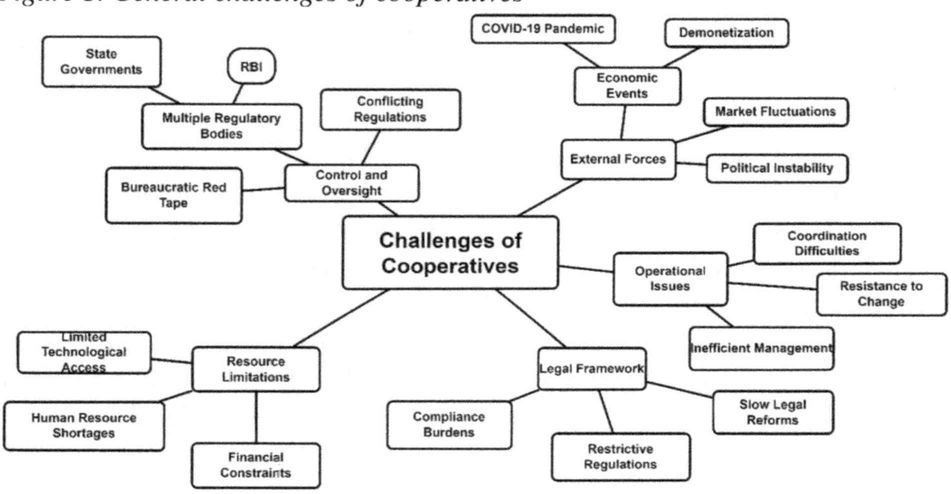

Legal Framework Of Cooperatives

The ICA contends that a enabling legal landscape is crucial for the success of the cooperatives. It further considers that the regulations that ensure a level playing field with other types of enterprises can facilitate the cooperatives. Contrarily, it deems that a lack of specific legal framework or a weak legal framework might hinder the development of cooperatives. Based on the example of Nepal, the ICA reckons that the Nepal's Cooperative Act of 2017 provides an opportunity to improve the cooperative movement's capacity in a competitive, effective and productive manner. It considered that the cooperative legislation of Nepal is cooperative friendly. India's legal framework of cooperatives was similarly analyzed. A report prepared by Paranjothi (2020) on this with inputs from the National Cooperative Union of India (NCUI) was published by the ICA. The following section is based on the information drawn from this report(Gupta et al., 2019).

The India's first Act on Cooperatives was the Cooperative Credit Societies Act, 1904. Later, taking into account the requirements for other types of cooperatives and also for the development of cooperatives, the Cooperative Societies Act II, 1912 was passed. The cooperation became a State subject under the State List of the Constitution once India became a Republic in 1950. Thus, most of the matters relating to the cooperatives were brought under the respective State governments. States like Maharashtra and Gujarat provided a greater emphasis on the cooperatives pursuing their business activities. Contrarily, a few other States were on the other extreme of complete takeover of the cooperatives and running them through special officers employed by them.

The Government of India enacted the Multi-State Cooperative Societies Act (51 of 1984). There were observations by the ICA report that this Act was also comparable to many State Laws in its character due to its obstructive approach. The above 2020 report published by the ICA claimed that even though there have been many changes in this Act subsequently in 2002, the fundamental character remained the same.

There were many other initiatives later on specifically by the Cooperative Initiative Panel (CIP) and many similar organizations. These are considered to have resulted in dual legislation on cooperatives in many States of India. Apart from the existing State Acts on cooperatives, a new Mutually Aided Societies Act was passed in many States since 1995. According to Paranjothi (2020), this development implied that there was a growing demand for autonomy of the cooperatives. The cooperatives registered under the new Act were not receiving the government patronage and also were not subject to much government control. He considered that the parallel existence of the earlier State legislations on the cooperatives indicated the approach of many States to retain control over the cooperatives registered under the pre-existing Acts. The Andhra Pradesh was the first State to pass the Mutually Aided Cooperative Societies Act in 1995. Eight States such as Bihar, Chhattisgarh, Jammu and Kashmir, Jharkhand, Karnataka, Madhya Pradesh, Orissa (Odisha) and Uttaranchal (Uttarakhand) enacted similar legislations to enable, govern and regulate the mutually aided cooperatives (Misra, 2006).

Due to space and many other constraints, the focus of this sub-section has been predominantly on the various Acts of both the States and the Union Governments focusing on the cooperatives. It might be appropriate to record that the Union Government enacted the 97th Constitution Amendment in 2012 conferring the right to form cooperatives. However, in July 2021, a few sections of this 97th Amendments that required provisions by the States were struck down by the Supreme Court of India.

Limited financial and human resources

Many cooperatives suffer due to the limited resources – both financial and human. Finances of the cooperatives were in chronic state of sickness and were prone to recurrent crisis with a very few exceptions. According to him, the public funding accounted for most of the resources of available with the cooperatives for lending. Nevertheless, he further pointed out that there was no mechanism for ensuring prudent and effective fund management by the credit cooperatives (Trivedi et al., 2024).

Some of the credit cooperatives depend upon the share capital/working capital provided by the governments and thereby lose their autonomy. This is the case with the credit cooperatives/ primary agriculture credit societies (PACS) having a weak financial base since they mostly depend on the shares of their members for the capital requirements. A high-power committee established by the RBI observed that there is a probability of a large number of borrowers from cooperatives being under financed as they do not get adequate loan to meet their financial requirements. It observed that some members of the cooperatives might not be getting any loan at all.

Limited or no focus on the non-credit aspects of their members also is a major problem affecting the cooperatives. Many of these cooperatives are single purpose cooperatives. It is pertinent to note that in July 2022, the union minister for Cooperation suggested that cooperative banks in addition to functioning as banks could also focus on other important cooperative activities like irrigation.

The credit cooperatives are saddled with a very high number of non-performing assets (NPAs). A very high dependence of the credit cooperatives on the NABARD, RBI and various governments for refinancing has led to their incapability to fulfill the members' credit requirements on their own. The minimal shares of these credit cooperatives from their members have facilitated even the poorest to join them. Thus, these result in a weak financial base and over dependence on other organizations for fulfilling their members' credit requirements.

Except a very few successful and large credit cooperatives, most of the other cooperatives appear to have very limited qualified human resources for performing various managerial functions. It has also been observed that a few State governments posted some of their staff to the cooperatives. In case of many State level federations of the cooperatives, the key functionaries were deputed from the government.

MULTIPLE CONTROL OF COOPERATIVES

The cooperatives have been facing many other challenges and one of the key challenges was that they were being regulated or controlled by more than one organization. The cooperative banks were being regulated by the rules of the RBI as well as by respective State governments through the Registrar of Cooperative Societies (RCS) (Ziquan et al., 2022). The figure 2 illustrates the challenge of multiple control of cooperatives.

Figure 2. Challenge of multiple control of cooperatives

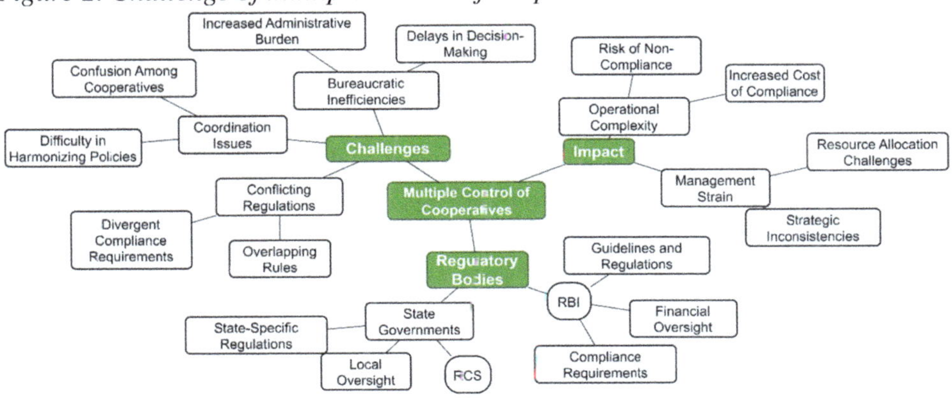

Various functions of the District Central Cooperative Banks (DCCBs) and State Cooperative Banks (StCBs) covering registration/incorporation, audit, regulation and dissolution/liquidation have been regulated by the concerned RCS as they are registered under the State Cooperative Society Acts. The Banking Regulation Act, 1949 has been applied to the banking cooperatives since 1966. The RBI is exercising control over these banking cooperatives for their banking functions covering licensing and supervision. As per the information available in the website of the RBI, the banking functions of the banking cooperatives are regulated through the provisions of Sections 22 and 23, Banking Regulation Act, 1949.

The RBI's report on Trend and Progress of Banking, 2021 mentions that the amendment to the Banking Regulation Act was carried out in 2020 to protect the interests of the depositors and also strengthen the cooperative banks. This was apparently aimed at improving the governance framework and oversight by the RBI, while facilitating better access to the capital. This amendment came into force for the urban cooperative banks (UCBs) with retrospective effect from June 29, 2020 (Zuo et al., 2018). In case of the StCBs and DCCBs, it came into effect from April 1, 2021. It might be pertinent to observe that even the RBI identified in the above report that there are structural impediments that emanate due to the regulatory overlaps. It further pointed out that the cooperative banking sector was facing many other issues such as high level in loan delinquencies and erosion of depositor confidence.

External forces, events and the challenges faced by the cooperatives

Globalization and privatization also posed challenges to the cooperatives. It has been mentioned that the de-licensing of the sugar industry in India from 31 August 1998 also had its impact on the cooperative sugar industry. The demonetization of 2016 also reportedly affected the cooperatives functioning in some parts of India. A few dairy cooperatives were having problems due to it as milk procurement and supply were affected. Some of the dairy cooperatives were unable to access their money because their operations were frozen due to demonetization related issues (Child et al., 2019). Further, due to the uncertainties caused by the Covid-19, the RBI instructed all the banks including the cooperative banks and UCBs in April 2020 to withhold the payment of dividend for the year ending in March 2020. Later, in December 2021, it allowed the cooperative banks to pay the dividend on equity shares. The Covid-19 related challenges were faced by dairy cooperatives and other producers' organizations. Some dairy cooperatives were more resilient than most of the vendor-driven milk markets (Singla, 2020). Many large and leading dairy cooperatives like the GCMMF could ensure seamless procurement and supply of milk and milk products. They also launched many new products even during the Covid-19 induced lockdown.

SPECIFIC ISSUES AND PROSPECTS OF VARIOUS COOPERATIVES

There are various types of cooperatives across the world and in Indian context. Notable among them and consumer cooperatives, financial cooperatives, workers' cooperatives, industrial cooperatives, producer cooperatives and women's welfare cooperatives. The following section is focusing on the specific issues and prospects of a few selected types of cooperatives such as consumer cooperatives, producer cooperatives such as dairy cooperatives and sugar cooperatives, cooperatives with exclusive focus on certain sections of the society fishers and women, financial co-operatives such as credit cooperatives. The specific issues faced by them and their prospects in terms of ensuring inclusive growth and sustainable development in Indian context are deliberated in this section (McKillop et al., 2020). The figure 3 depicts the specific issues and prospects of different cooperatives.

Figure 3. Specific issues and prospects of various cooperatives

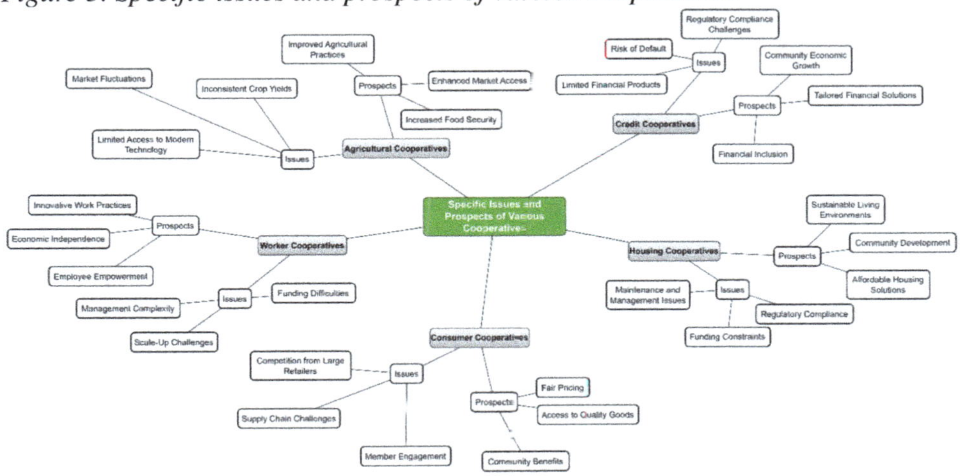

Consumer cooperatives

India's first consumer cooperative was set up in 1904 at Madras (now Chennai) to supply the various necessities of life to its members (Zhang et al., 2020) As on 2023, there were 21, 067 consumer cooperatives with 63,75,920 members. The State of Madhya Pradesh had the highest number of consumer cooperatives (4,959) followed by Chhattisgarh (2,417). The highest number of members of consumer cooperatives were in Madhya Pradesh (12,53,231) and the Maharashtra had 10,61,516 members. There were 20 consumer cooperative federations/unions in 2023.

It was observed by Chaudhary (2007) that entry of major corporate houses into retailing and the potential entry of the many multinational companies presented a challenge to consumer cooperatives like *Mumbai Kamgar Madhyawarti Grahak Sahakari Sanstha Maryadit* (Brand Name: Apna Bazaar). The earlier ICA committee report on the status of consumer cooperatives identified that in case of the India's consumer cooperatives, 16 out of 30 State Federations were either defunct or non-existent. Further, it observed that a large number of wholesale consumer societies and primary/retail societies were either defunct or having huge operational losses. Similar observations have also been made on the primary consumer cooperatives in Delhi numbering around 600 till 1990s. The silver lining with regard to the consumer cooperatives in India is the Warana Bazar Consumer Cooperative Society, Warana Nagar, Kolhapur started in 1976. This is cited as the first rural consumer cooperative society and commended for its several noteworthy aspects such as consistent profit, customer focused approach, fair pricing, high quality products and active member engagement through regular annual meetings (Paliwal, Tripathy and Chatradhi, 2024). It has also been considered as an ethical role model society and it should be an encouragement for others to follow (Naveeenkumar et al., 2024; Ravisankar et al., 2024).

It seems that the cooperatives are also poised to utilize the abundant opportunities provided by the emerging e-commerce in India. Notable efforts in this regard are the launch of google cloud powered e-commerce application for promotion of business in the cooperative sector launched by the Prime Minister of India during the 17th Indian Cooperative Congress in July 2023 and the android phone based mobile application, Coop Bazaar for cooperative products also launched in July 2023 by the Government of Tamil Nadu. These consumer cooperatives are considered to exert a health influence on the market prices of essential commodities, as per the report of the Government of India.

Dairy cooperatives

India became one of the largest milk producers in the world. Its successful dairy cooperatives have been lauded for that (Nath & Arrawatia, 2022). These authors who have studied the Indian dairy cooperatives have arrived at a conclusion that the dairy cooperatives try to maximize their sales and profit. They are also paying attention to the quality of the milk sold by them. Further, they strictly observe the traditional cooperative values particularly the community inclusion. There were criticisms on the government interference on various other types of the cooperatives. The dairy cooperatives contrarily have benefited from the government support particularly due to the protective policies, licensing and financial support from both the Government of India and many State Governments.

It is reported that de-licensing of the dairy sector initially in 1991 due to the liberalization and later concerns about the sustainability of the dairy cooperatives threatened by the entry of private players, led to the Milk and Milk Produce Order (MMPO), 1992. However, a few restrictions of the MMPO were subsequently eliminated with an amendment to the MMPO in 2002. The further opening of the economy and the dairy sector in 2011 resulted in a significant number of private players entering into the dairy sector. It has been pointed out by Katakam (2017) that while the larger dairy cooperatives were modernized and could achieve greater market share by building their own brands, the smaller dairy cooperatives seem to be lagging behind and hence could not do much to their members.

There are a considerable number of studies that eulogize India's dairy cooperatives. However, there are a few others that attempted to bring out their limitations. The study claimed that the share of milk production and marketing by the dairy cooperatives remained modest. It is worth mentioning that this study found out that the incomes gained through the dairy cooperative members were greater for small-scale farmers as the marginal farmers with less than one hectare of land were the greatest beneficiaries of the dairy cooperatives. In case of India's dairy cooperatives, 29.79% out of 16.28 million members were women in 2016-17. A couple of scholars claimed that women in India's dairy sector were empowered due to their membership in cooperatives (Mahida et al., 2018). India's dairy cooperatives have provided gainful employment to women. It is appropriate to claim that dairy cooperatives are instrumental in achieving inclusive growth and sustainable development in the Indian context as they are catering to the small farmers and women who had been deprived of the benefits of the larger development.

The entry of private players in dairy industry leading to increased competition for the procurement of milk and also for milk and milk products' markets, changing food habits and many general issues like lack of resources mainly financial and human resources are the challenges faced by many smaller dairy cooperatives. There are many robust dairy cooperatives in various parts of India and hopefully, they will collectively overcome the various challenges discussed above and ensure the inclusive development.

Fisheries cooperatives

The southern State of Kerala, among the leading marine fishing States of India, had initiated fisheries cooperatives in 1917, even before India's independence in 1947 (Solomon, 2023). Even though, 95 fisheries cooperatives were constituted, their performance was reported to be disappointing. This led to an enquiry committee in 1934 for studying their problems. This committee recommended restructuring of fisher cooperatives as multi-purpose cooperatives. The Kerala government's efforts subsequently resulted in Kerala State Cooperative Federation for Fisheries Development Limited. This federation was linked to 654 village level primary fishers' societies ranged across 10 coastal districts of Kerala (Mahanayak & Panigrahi, 2021).

The South Indian Federation of Fishermen Societies (SIFFS), a top body of primary village-level fisher folk cooperatives was formed in 1980 and achieved notable success. This was reportedly due to the efforts of a group of committed social workers and activists initially. They were later complemented by the professional rural managers. Although it has been hailed as a successful model for fisheries cooperatives, due to the nature of the fish economy, the SIFFS too was considered to have played a partial role in marketing. Moreover, it is also claimed that unlike milk, fish is not a single homogeneous commodity at the time of procurement. It is considered that the SIFFS might not have been rivals or competitors and there may be a very limited overlap between their functions at some points of time. However, it had more access to funds, greater political control and also a longer reach (Kumar, 1988). Nevertheless, it was found out that subsequent events indicated that the government subsidies were mostly accessible for the new members might have opted to join it rather than the SIFFS (Thakur, 2018)

Discussing about the status of the fisheries cooperatives in Tamil Nadu immediately after the tsunami, when the fishing activities came to a standstill, there were questions why they were not an effective vehicle in providing relief or rehabilitation to the fishing community (Kurien, 2005) It was claimed by Kurien that most of the cooperatives were government run-enterprises. It was further asserted by him that the RCS had more powers over the cooperatives than the Registrar of the Companies had over the companies.

The National Cooperative Database (NCD) portal mentions that India had 25,609 primary fishery societies comprising about 46.74 lakhs of fishers as members. There are also exclusive fisher women cooperative societies among them. The newly formed Telangana State had the highest number of fishery cooperative societies (4,985) and it was followed by the Maharashtra State (3,403). The Government of India contends that the cooperatives in the fishery sector considerably improve the livelihoods of the vulnerable fisher groups, their nutritional status and social security. It was claimed that the fishery cooperatives were benefiting around four million people in India (.

There are many cooperatives focusing on reservoir and riverine fisheries. A thought-provoking study on the management of fisheries in Tawa Reservoir in Madhya Pradesh had found out that the community managed cooperative system performed best among the state-management, full privatization, partial privatization, open-access, *Tawa Matsya Sangh* (TMS) and cooperative (collective) management across almost all the factors such as excludability, employment generation and income distribution.

In Dec 2023, the Government of India approved a plan to strengthen the cooperative movement in the country. With regard to the fisheries cooperatives, there are two notable schemes by the Government of India, namely, the *Pradhan Mantri Matsya Sampada Yojana* (PMMSY) and Fisheries and Aquaculture Infrastructure Fund (FIDF). The PMMSY is aimed at overcoming critical gaps in fish production, productivity, quality, technology, infrastructure for post-harvest management, modernizing and strengthening the fish value chain. On the other hand, the FIDF is focusing on creating infrastructure for both inland and marine fisheries sectors. It involves construction of ice plants, transporting fish and cold chain network, cold storage development, brood banks setting up, hatcheries development, fish processing units, fish feed mills and establishing modern fish markets (Mahanayak & Panigrahi, 2021; Solomon, 2023; Thakur, 2018). It is hoped that as and when the fishers' cooperatives get revived, it is expected that they will be contributing to the income and livelihoods of the fishers and reduce inequalities.

Women cooperatives

Compared to many other parts of the world, women's membership in India's cooperatives seems to be very low. When the women membership of the cooperatives itself is very limited, the absence of women in the decision-making leadership positions in cooperatives is not surprising. However, it might be worth mentioning that there are laudable efforts to build cooperatives exclusive for addressing women's welfare(Bharti, 2021).

The dairy cooperatives seem to be an exception and even there are also around only 30 percent of members were reportedly women. The National Dairy Development Board (NDDB) has been focusing on increasing and ensuring women's participation in dairying as members, management committee members, board members and also by forming exclusive women dairy cooperative societies. Women's Dairy Cooperative Leadership Programme (WDCLP), initiated by the NDDB on a pilot basis in 1995, promoting Women Dairy Cooperatives (WDCs) and the National Dairy Plan-I (NDP-I), a central sector implemented from 2012 to 2019 across eighteen major dairying States of India are some of the initiatives that led to women's active participation in dairy cooperatives in India. As per the information obtained from the website of the NDDB, it was observed that more than 45 percent (7.64 lakh) of the total additional members enrolled in the dairy cooperatives under the NDP-I were women. According to the NDDB, the establishment of more than 4,000 all women dairy cooperative societies during the above project period and appointment of Lady Extension Officers enabled women involvement in dairy sector in a large scale(Dohmwirth & Liu, 2020b).

As per the 2023 database of cooperatives published by the Government of India, the number of functional women cooperatives was 10,806. These numbers are too limited compared with the monumental requirements of the women to undertake and participate in various economic activities. The following few paragraphs based on the study of different cooperatives could provide an indication of the many challenges faced by these women focused cooperatives. Similar problems might also be faced by other women welfare cooperatives.

A study of 13 women cooperatives of Kottayam district, Kerala was undertaken. This study found out that these cooperatives were constrained severely due to the method by which the property rights and gender relations are structured. Similarly, Generally, the women cooperatives in India faced multiple constraints from their families as well as their societies(Sahoo et al., 2020a).

According to the International Labour Organization, the Self-Employed Women's Association (SEWA) founded by Elaben Bhatt in 1972, encourages its members to form their own cooperatives. Thus, every member of SEWA is a reported to be member of at least one specific cooperatives of her choice. Further, it is indicated that it is also possible that any SEWA member could be part of more than one cooperative from the fold of SEWA cooperatives. Nevertheless, even this successful and acclaimed SEWA cooperatives movement had faced its own challenges. It is reported that there were a few instances of resistance from the officials in the offices of the RCS. They were stated to have refused to register some of these women cooperatives initially as they were not believing that poor women with very limited literacy could manage their own cooperatives. Some of the reasons such as missing files and interpreting the bye-laws contrary to the interest of the cooperatives were cited as the other challenges. It has been contended that as the SEWA cooperatives were rigorously adopting the ethical principles, some of them could not access the subsidized seeds and fertilizers and they were reportedly allocated to other organizations with clear political affiliations. It is also claimed that a few other SEWA cooperatives lost likely contracts as they refused to pay bribes to the officials who were deciding on awarding of the contracts. Information on this sub-section is liberally drawn mentions many other challenges such as bureaucratization and politicization of cooperative departments, extremely limited financial assets of the cooperatives, and exclusion of cooperatives from the 'new economy'. Similar challenges could be applicable to the non-SEWA cooperatives as well. Further, there were a few specific challenges faced by the SEWA cooperatives. They were (a) procedural restrictions on proposals with the word '*Mahila*' (women) in the nomenclature of the cooperative (b) retaining cooperative membership in a community with high mobility and also (c) the inability of the officials of the RCS to understand the social nature of the activities promoted by the SEWA in its cooperatives (Dash et al., 2020).

The Ministry of Cooperation, claims to have made multiple efforts for betterment, income generation and empowerment of women in India's cooperative sector. Three notable initiatives among them are (a) reservation for women in the Multi State Cooperative Societies' boards (b) reservation to women members in the PACS through adoption of model bye-laws and (c) *Nandini Sahakar* Scheme. Under the *Nandini Sahakar* Scheme, financial assistance scheme for project formulation, capacity building and hand-holding of women cooperatives, the NCDC disbursed Rs.5715 crores to the women cooperatives leading to the benefits for more than 1.56 crores of women cooperative members. The NCDC had provided support for various activities undertaken like processing of food grains and oil seeds, plantation of crops, fisheries, dairy, livestock and poultry farming, storage, spinning mills, handloom and jute and power weaving, *yuva sahakar* and services and many others. A new scheme, *Swayam Shakti Sahakar Yojana* is aimed at providing the financial assistance by the NCDC to the agricultural cooperatives for loans/advances to women self-help groups (SHGs) (Bharti, 2021; Dash et al., 2020; Dohmwirth & Liu, 2020b; Sahoo et al., 2020a).

Sugar Cooperatives

Maharashtra is among the leading States in case of sugar cooperatives. It is reported that the first successful sugar factory in cooperative sector in India at the Pravarangar, Ahmednagar district, Maharashtra state was commissioned in 1954. As per the the National Federation of Cooperative Sugar Factories Limited, the cooperative sector contributed about 35 percent of India's national production of sugar(Sahoo et al., 2020b).

The Annual Report, Department of Food Production and Public Distribution, Government of India for 2021-22, mentioned that there were 506 sugar factories in India as on Feb 2022. Among them, 204 were in the cooperative sector and 292 in the private sector. This status has changed marginally in March 2023 as the number of the installed cooperative sugar factories were 316. The States of Maharashtra (155), Uttar Pradesh (28), Karnataka (26), Gujarat (24), Tamil Nadu and Haryana (16 each) were among the top five states of India in 2023 (Government of India, 2023c). The situation was totally different much earlier on 31 Dec 2004 as there were only 187 factories in private sector, 316 in cooperative sector and 62 in public sector as indicated by Annual Report of the same department (Abnave Vikas, n.d.).

Gujarat is presenting an interesting policy of promoting only cooperatives in the sugar sector. It is the second most important state in case of sugar cooperative in India. As on June 2024, there were 22 sugar cooperatives in Gujarat as per the information available from the website of the Gujarat Federation of cooperative sugar factories limited. However, in 2022-23, only 13 factories were in operation in Gujarat. A study identified that south Gujarat's sugar cooperatives had been successful engines of large-scale agricultural and capitalist production. Nevertheless, they reportedly failed as agents of equity. In an analysis of sugar cooperatives in Maharashtra, Through the sugar cooperatives, the rich persons who controlled them had been enriching themselves at the cost of many other stakeholders such as the consumers, labourers and the poor peasants (Banerjee & Banerjee, 2021).

The Union Government and the concerned State Governments have been taking strong efforts to rejuvenate the sugar cooperatives in India. The Union Government has resolved to find solutions to the decade old income tax issues faced by the sugar cooperatives. The Central Board of Direct Taxation (CBDT) in its circular No.14 dated 27 July 2023 with a view to enable the relevant cooperative sugar mills has issued a Standard Operating Procedure (SOP). It was expected that a relief to the extent of Rs. 10,000 crores might be available to the cooperative sugar mills by treating the payments to the sugarcane farmers as expenditure. It has been mentioned in the above circular that in a few States of India, the sugar cooperative factories have been paying the sugarcane farmers a final amount, referred to as the Final Cane Price (FCP). This was over and above the Statutory Minimum Price (SMP) mandated by Union Government based on Sugarcane Control Order, 1996 (Banerjee & Banerjee, 2021; Nomani et al., 2022).

Further, the Union Government has decided to treat the cooperative sugar mills at par with the private companies with regard to the ethanol procurement under the Ethanol Blending Programme (EBP) of the Ministry of Petroleum. It is reported that co-generation power plants from sugarcane bagasse are also being set up. The Goods and Services Tax (GST) on molasses has been reduced by the Union Government to five percent from 28% to enable the cooperative sugar mills earn more profits for their members through selling the molasses to distilleries with higher margins. All these steps are expected to enlarge the business of the sugar cooperative mills and resultant increase in their profits.

PROSPECTS OF THE COOPERATIVES FOR INCLUSIVE GROWTH AND SUSTAINABLE DEVELOPMENT

There are a few scholars who considered that the traditional cooperatives had a poor performance. They expressed the need to provide freedom to the cooperatives to operate as business entities. It is believed that the cooperatives have not failed by they have been failed by other entities (Schoneveld, 2020). The cooperatives in India and elsewhere have to be lauded and credited not only for their survival for such a long time in adverse conditions but also for their appreciable contribution to their members and the larger society. It has to be noted that the cooperatives had faced continuous onslaught from the external as well as the internal forces inimical to the interest of cooperatives. The figure 4 depicts the potential of cooperatives for inclusive growth and sustainable development.

Figure 4. Prospects of the cooperatives for inclusive growth and sustainable development

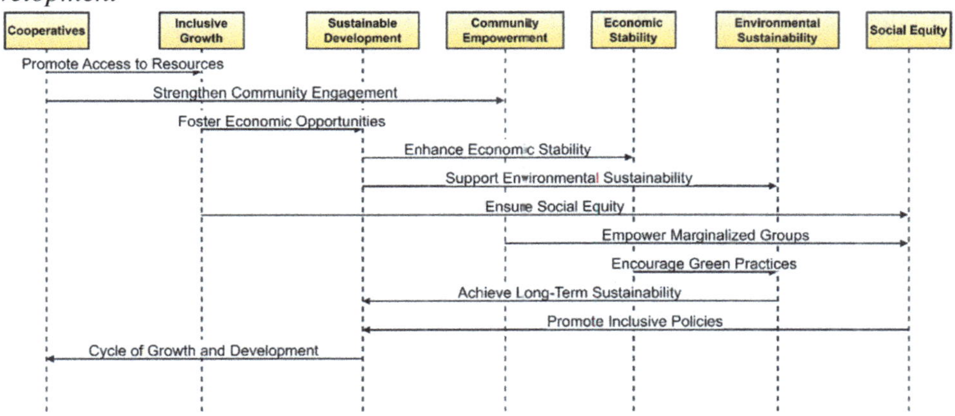

The debates on the Constitutional Amendments related to the cooperatives, formation of an exclusive Ministry of Cooperation at the union government level in 2021 and celebration of the 100th International Day of Cooperatives on 2 July 2022 have all brought the cooperatives into limelight again. The apex level organizations on cooperatives at the national level such as the NCUI, National Centre for Cooperative Education (NCCE), National Cooperative Development Corporation (NCDC) and various academic institutions are organizing consultations, offering courses and conducting policy-oriented conferences across India. This renewed interest in cooperatives have to be sustained to ensure that the cooperatives overcome some of the challenges they have been facing. They have to be enabled to perform fulfilling their members' needs and expectations.

It is worth noting that the cooperatives have got the wherewithal and capacity to sustain the external onslaughts by forming alliances among themselves. For instance, in 2013, six cooperative sugar factories in Gujarat had joined together to form a consortium and acquired a sick sugar cooperative for ensuring that large corporates would not be able to enter the space. Further, two other sugar cooperatives in Gujarat have jointly been taking efforts to revive another cooperative in Bharuch district in Gujarat (SINGH et al., 2022). It may be worth recording that despite the grim challenges faced by the cooperatives intermittently, they continue to retain the zeal to serve the society and thus continue to remain relevant in the Indian context. It is laudable that they are facilitating considerable sections of poor and marginalized although at a lower scale than their capabilities. The sugar, dairy and fisheries cooperatives can be classified as producer cooperatives as defined. These authors have identified that the producers' cooperatives were found to have links with various SDGs such as No Poverty (SDG1), Zero Hunger (SDG2), Responsible Consumption and Production (SDG12) and Life on Land (SDG15). These cooperatives by their potential relationship with the above SDGs are uniquely positioned to achieve sustainable and inclusive development.

The Government of India had been taking substantial efforts to strengthen the cooperatives. With regard to the PACS, plans are afoot to make them multi-purpose cooperatives so that they will be more empowered and economically viable. As these PACS are covering around 89% of the villages panchayats in India, once they are strengthened, they would be in a position to enable the small and marginal farmers to access financial and other related services. This is likely to result in inclusive development focusing on these marginalized sections of the farming community. In addition to those existing PACS, 2,00,000 new multipurpose PACS /dairy / fisheries cooperatives were being planned in 2023 with a view to ensure that the remaining panchayats/villages will also have them in the next five years. The proposal to converge various schemes of the Government of India at the level of PACS, as and when implemented, would ensure that the PACS would be in a stronger footing to deliver multiple services to the small and marginal farmers and also the other excluded sections of the society. The proposed world's largest decentralized grain storage programme, to ensure food security under the aegis of the PACS, was approved by the Union Government's cabinet in May 2023. It is aimed at having various types of agricultural infrastructure such as godowns, custom hiring centres, fair price shops and processing units at the PACS level. Apart from that, the PACS are expected to deliver more than 300 e-services and become common service centres (CSCs). As on Oct 2023, it was reported that 14,000 PACS have started providing services like the CSCs (Gutberlet, 2021; Sahoo et al., 2020c). Moreover, there are strong efforts by the Union Government for providing the opportunities to the PACS for the LPG distribution, assigning priority to them for petrol/diesel pump dealerships and approving them for selling cheaper generic medicines for the common people. Provision of micro automatic teller machines (ATMs) to the PACS by making them the business correspondents of the District Central Cooperative Banks (DCCBs) and pilot projects in distribution of *Kisan* credit cards (farmer credit cards) to the account holders of the cooperative societies are aimed at the financial inclusion. If the PACS could make use of the above-mentioned opportunities and deliver the services to the small, marginal farmers and the other poorer sections of the society effectively, it will result in inclusive development.

We concur with the following views expressed that cooperative form of organization is a panacea for development. They are of the view that whoever comes forward to invigorate the cooperative ideology and take a lead in that direction should be welcomed wholeheartedly(Imaz & Eizagirre, 2020; Schoneveld, 2020; SINGH et al., 2022). The initiatives could be from the Union government or State governments or corporates or any individual leader. It is believed that the cooperatives have nothing to lose but everything to gain. Their earnest hope is that scholars, practitioners and policy makers committed to the cooperatives will earnestly strive to ensure the cooperatives their rightful place.

CONCLUSION

The cooperative movement in India, more than 100 years old, has been facing multiple issues and challenges. Some of the general challenges faced by them were a restrictive legal framework, limited financial and human resources and multiple control of the cooperatives specifically, the credit cooperatives by the concerned RCS and the RBI. Apart from that there were also challenges related to the external events that proved to be hurdles in the progress of cooperatives such as demonetization and covid-19. There were also some specific challenges faced by a few types of cooperatives. The credit/finance cooperatives were having limited financial resources, faced dual control by the concerned RCS and the RBI and had been saddled with a very high NPAs. The dairy cooperatives seem to be relatively more successful, albeit in a few States of India. The opening up of the dairy sector to the private players and also other movements like vegan and plant based products have become major challenges to the dairy cooperatives. The women welfare focused cooperatives though successful in many cases are inadequate to take care of the interests of the women in major parts of the country. Fishers cooperatives seem to be less effective and defunct in some cases. Sugar cooperatives have lost their pre-eminent position in the recent past and there are also criticisms that they are favourable to large farmers and neglect other stakeholders.

Notwithstanding the above, it is expected that the renewed interest in the cooperatives both nationally and globally will lead to strengthening of the cooperatives. As cooperatives are owned by their members and not by a handful of individuals, their success is likely to percolate to its members and the larger society. The credit cooperatives, as and when they are able to convert themselves as multipurpose cooperatives and start delivering multiple services to their members such as small and marginal farmers, they will be contributing to the inclusive growth and reduce inequalities. There is a need to free them from restrictive controls by the RCS to ensure that they achieve their potential in this regard. Similarly, the women cooperatives in various parts of the country need stronger support from both the concerned State governments and the Union Government. It is essential that the *Nandini Sahakar* benefits women cooperatives in all States of India than focusing on only a couple of States like Andhra Pradesh and Telangana. Among the producer cooperatives, the dairy cooperatives seem to have contributed for women empowerment and reduced inequalities by facilitating the small holder farmers. The second International Year of Cooperatives, 2025 is likely to bring the cooperative forms of organizations to the centre stage again resulting in the inclusive growth and sustainable development.

ABBREVIATIONS

ATM: Automated Teller Machine
CB: Cooperative Bank
CBDT: Central Board of Direct Taxes
CIP: Cooperative Insurance Program
CSC: Customer Service Center
DCCB: District Central Cooperative Bank
EBP: Employee Benefit Plan
FCP: Financial Credit Program
FIDF: Fisheries and Aquaculture Infrastructure Development Fund
GCMMF: Gujarat Cooperative Milk Marketing Federation
GST: Goods and Services Tax
ICA: International Cooperative Alliance
IFFCO: Indian Farmers Fertilizer Cooperative Limited
II: Insurance Institute
ILO: International Labour Organization
LPG: Liquefied Petroleum Gas
MMPO: Multi-State Cooperative Societies Act, 2002
NABARD: National Bank for Agriculture and Rural Development
NAFCUB: National Federation of Urban Cooperative Banks and Credit Societies
NCCE: National Council for Cooperative Education
NCD: National Cooperative Dairy Federation
NCDC: National Cooperative Development Corporation
NCUI: National Cooperative Union of India
NDDB: National Dairy Development Board
NDP: National Development Program
NPA: Non-Performing Asset
PACS: Primary Agricultural Credit Societies
PMMSY: Pradhan Mantri Matsya Sampada Yojana
RBI: Reserve Bank of India
RCS: Registrar of Cooperative Societies
SDG: Sustainable Development Goals
SEWA: Self-Employed Women's Association
SHG: Self-Help Group
SIFFS: South Indian Federation of Fishermen Societies

SINGH: Specific Information Not Given
SMP: Strategic Management Plan
SOP: Standard Operating Procedure
TMS: Technical Management Services
UCB: Urban Cooperative Bank
WDC: Women's Development Corporation
WDCLP: Women Development Cooperative Loan Program

REFERENCES

Abnave Vikas, B. (n.d.). *Sugar Co-operatives in Maharashtra: Challenges Ahead.*

Attwood, D. W., & Attwood, D. (2019). *Raising cane: The political economy of sugar in western India*. Routledge.

Banerjee, A. N., & Banerjee, R. (2021). Farming: Cooperatives in India: Problems and Prospects. *Supremo Amicus*, *24*, 481.

Bharti, N. (2021). Role of cooperatives in economic empowerment of women: A review of Indian experiences. *World Journal of Entrepreneurship, Management and Sustainable Development*, *17*(4), 617–631.

Child, J., Faulkner, D., Tallman, S., & Hsieh, L. (2019). *Cooperative strategy: Managing alliances and networks.* Oxford University Press.

Dash, B. M., Prashad, L., Singh, K. K., & Dash, M. (2020). Women and poverty in india: Poverty alleviation and empowerment through cooperatives. *Social Work & Society*, *18*(2).

Diwate, A. (2021). Growth of private medical colleges in Maharashtra and its implications for universal healthcare. *Universalising Healthcare in India: From Care to Coverage*, 83–102.

Dohmwirth, C., & Liu, Z. (2020). Does cooperative membership matter for women's empowerment? Evidence from South Indian dairy producers. *Journal of Development Effectiveness*, *12*(2), 133–150.

Ghosh, J. (2021). *Informal women workers in the Global South: Policies and practices for the formalisation of women's employment in developing economies*. routledge.

Gupta, R., & Gupta, A. (2019). *Cooperative Business System of Dairy Sector in India: Role of State*. Caste and Gender.

Gutberlet, J. (2021). Grassroots waste picker organizations addressing the UN sustainable development goals. *World Development*, *138*, 105195.

Imaz, O., & Eizagirre, A. (2020). Responsible innovation for sustainable development goals in business: An agenda for cooperative firms. *Sustainability*, *12*(17), 6948.

Le, N. K., Garg, M., Izurieta, R., Garg, S. M., Papadimos, T. J., Arquilla, B., Miller, A. C., Khan, A. M., Worlton, T., & Firstenberg, M. S. (2020). International health security: A summative assessment by ACAIM consensus group. In *Contemporary Developments and Perspectives in International Health Security-Volume 1*. InteChOpen.

Mahanayak, B., & Panigrahi, A. K. (2021). Sustainable management of the aquatic ecosystem and the fishermen cooperative societies in India: A brief review. *Uttar Pradesh Journal of Zoology*, *42*(16), 28–35.

Mahida, D., Sendhil, R., Sirohi, S., Chandel, B., Ponnusamy, K., & Sankhala, G. (2018). Potential impact of dairy cooperatives on sustainable milk production: Evidence from Gujarat, India. *Indian Journal of Economics and Development*, *14*(1a), 402–409.

McKillop, D., French, D., Quinn, B., Sobiech, A. L., & Wilson, J. O. (2020). Co-operative financial institutions: A review of the literature. *International Review of Financial Analysis*, *71*, 101520. PMID: 38620621

Nath, S., & Arrawatia, R. (2022). Trade-offs or synergies? Hybridity and sustainable performance of dairy cooperatives in India. *World Development*, *154*, 105862.

Naveeenkumar, N., Rallapalli, S., Sasikala, K., Priya, P. V., Husain, J., & Boopathi, S. (2024). Enhancing Consumer Behavior and Experience Through AI-Driven Insights Optimization. In *AI Impacts in Digital Consumer Behavior* (pp. 1–35). IGI Global.

Nomani, A., Khan, M., Shajar, S. N., Afzal, M. A., & Salman, M. (2022). Financial crisis of Indian sugar industry: Case study of Uttar Pradesh. *Journal of Statistics and Management Systems*, *25*(5), 1303–1317.

Ravisankar, A., Shanthi, A., Lavanya, S., Ramaratnam, M., Krishnamoorthy, V., & Boopathi, S. (2024). Harnessing 6G for Consumer-Centric Business Strategies Across Electronic Industries. In *AI Impacts in Digital Consumer Behavior* (pp. 241–270). IGI Global.

Sahoo, A. K., Meher, S. K., Panda, T. C., Sahu, S., Begum, R., & Barik, N. (2020). Critical review on cooperative societies in agricultural development in India. *Current Journal of Applied Science and Technology*, *39*(22), 114–121.

Schoneveld, G. C. (2020). Sustainable business models for inclusive growth: Towards a conceptual foundation of inclusive business. *Journal of Cleaner Production*, *277*, 124062.

SINGH, S., GAUTAM, R. S., AGARWAL, B., PUSHP, A., BARGE, P., & RASTOGI, S. (2022). Impacts of financial inclusion on sustainable development in India. *The Journal of Asian Finance, Economics and Business*, *9*(10), 235–242.

Singh, U. K. (2024). Implementation Of Sustainable Development Goals In India: Progress And Challenges. *Regional Dimensions of Human Development in India and South Africa: Through Sustainable Development Goals*, 39–91.

Solomon, P. (2023). Can cooperatives be a tool for poverty reduction? Social capital perspectives of fisher's cooperatives in India. *Marine Policy*, *147*, 105373.

Thakur, A. (2018). Assessment of status of the fishery cooperatives, SHGs and fishermen groups in Baster district of Chhattisgarh: A review. *Journal of Pharmacognosy and Phytochemistry*, *7*(3), 1748–1754.

Trivedi, P., Ravisankar, A., Kumar, G. P., Krishnamoorthy, V., Shukla, S., & Boopathi, S. (2024). Finance and Technology-Integrated Digital Economy: Circular Age of a Sustainable Digital Revolution. In *Navigating the Circular Age of a Sustainable Digital Revolution* (pp. 91–120). IGI Global. DOI: 10.4018/979-8-3693-2827-9.ch004

Vishwakarma, M. M. (2019). E-commerce: Emerging trend for business management education. *Challenges and Opportunities in Social Sciences, Humanities and Business Management, 114*.

Zhang, S., Sun, Z., Ma, W., & Valentinov, V. (2020). The effect of cooperative membership on agricultural technology adoption in Sichuan, China. *China Economic Review*, *62*, 101334.

Ziquan, Y., Zhang, Y., Jiang, B., Jun, F., & Ying, J. (2022). A review on fault-tolerant cooperative control of multiple unmanned aerial vehicles. *Chinese Journal of Aeronautics*, *35*(1), 1–18.

Zuo, Z., Han, Q.-L., Ning, B., Ge, X., & Zhang, X.-M. (2018). An overview of recent advances in fixed-time cooperative control of multiagent systems. *IEEE Transactions on Industrial Informatics*, *14*(6), 2322–2334.

Chapter 11
Pioneering Pathways:
Future Directions and Innovations in Fostering Well-Being and Genuine Connections in the Digital Era

Gregory Harrison
The Citadel, USA

Emily Duplantis
https://orcid.org/0009-0003-1374-7488
Dorchester School District Two, USA

ABSTRACT

As digital technology rapidly evolves, education has shifted from face-to-face interactions to more virtual experiences, especially following the COVID-19 pandemic. This shift has emphasized the need to examine the impact of technology on students' mental well-being, personal growth, and authentic relationships. The integration of artificial intelligence (AI) and virtual reality (AR) in education offers new possibilities for personalized learning and fostering stronger connections between students and teachers. However, as technology transforms the educational landscape, there is a growing concern that it may impair meaningful human interactions, which are crucial for academic performance and emotional health. This chapter explores how AI and other emerging technologies can be thoughtfully integrated to support both learning outcomes and student well-being, ensuring that technology enhances, rather than diminishes, the importance of human connections in education.

DOI: 10.4018/979-8-3693-0997-1.ch011

THE EVOLVING DIGITAL LANDSCAPE

Having lived through the past several decades and witnessing the rapid explosion of technology serves as a profound reminder of how quickly our world is changing. As a young child, I vividly recall the arrival of the first computer in my house. I remember looking at this large, unfamiliar piece of equipment and wondering what purpose it could possibly serve. Over time, I observed the progression of technology becoming smaller and more powerful, culminating in devices that fit into our pockets and provide access to more information than the Library of Congress. This rapid progression of innovation and technology has not only transformed my life but has also had a profound impact on education at all levels. The changes brought about by technological advancements are evident in our schools, classrooms, and universities. The impact extends beyond the simple transfer of knowledge from teacher to student; it permeates down to the granular level of human relationships and interactions. Without a doubt, innovation and technology have fundamentally altered how we communicate, meet, and collaborate with one another.

As this shift has moved us from face-to-face interactions to more virtual experiences, especially for our students, we must pause to consider the implications on mental well-being, authentic relationships, and personal growth. The convenience and accessibility of technology brings many benefits, but they also pose just as many challenges (Doan, 2020). We must carefully examine how this digital transformation affects the social and emotional development of the next generations of learners. While technology opens new avenues for learning and connection, it is crucial to ensure that it does not come at the expense of meaningful human interactions and the overall well-being of our students.

The emerging "digital age" has witnessed a transformation in digital technology and its impact on how we educate our students in the 21st Century (Cardona et al., 2023). We have seen a shift to online and blended learning platforms where students can access information online or by a hybrid method of in-person and online. An increasing trend across the globe has seen the integration of artificial intelligence (AI) and virtual reality (VR) into the classrooms. For the first time in human history our students are engaging with machine learning to enhance their learning opportunities and growth potential. What will the next decade look like as our learners engage more with these technology tools and how will technology reshape our educational practices. Understanding these trends is crucial for preparing educators to effectively integrate technology into their teaching practices and for equipping students with the skills they need to thrive in an increasingly digital world. This chapter seeks to provide valuable insights and practical guidance for navigating the complex interplay between digital technology and education, ensuring that we harness the full potential of these tools to enhance learning outcomes and foster a more innovative and inclusive educational environment.

EMERGING TECHNOLOGIES AND THEIR IMPACT ON WELL-BEING

Technology and its innovations have become deeply interwoven into our working and home lifestyles, influencing every aspect of our daily existence. However, the integration of technology into our personal lives and its application within K-12 education are two fundamentally different discussions, each with unique challenges and opportunities. While technology in personal life often focuses on convenience and entertainment, its role in education is increasingly becoming crucial for enhancing student well-being and learning outcomes. This potential has remained largely untapped, especially in relation to student mental health and well-being, a concern that has gained prominence in educational discussions (Panesi et al., 2020).

Over the past decade, the mental health and well-being of students have become central to the focus of educators worldwide (Doan, 2020). The onset of the COVID-19 pandemic exacerbated this focus, as the global crisis highlighted and, in many cases, intensified the mental health challenges faced by students. The pandemic's impact on education, coupled with the social isolation and emotional stress experienced by students, necessitated a shift in educators' priorities towards supporting the whole student. This includes not only the student's academic and school-related well-being but also their self-related well-being, encompassing emotional, psychological, and social dimensions.

In the post-pandemic educational landscape, educators have increasingly recognized the importance of fostering a comprehensive approach to student development (Cardona et al., 2023). This approach aims to help students achieve their personal and social goals by placing renewed emphasis on their cognitive, psychological, and social well-being. The integration of emerging technologies into the educational framework has been critical. These technologies offer innovative tools and platforms that can enhance traditional teaching methods, provide personalized learning experiences, and support the mental and emotional health of students.

Emerging technologies, such as virtual reality, artificial intelligence, and hybrid learning opportunities, have introduced new possibilities for educators to engage with students in more meaningful and supportive ways. Virtual reality, for example, can create immersive environments that promote relaxation and mindfulness, while AI-driven platforms can offer personalized feedback and mental health resources tailored to individual student needs (Doan, 2020). Additionally, mental health applications provide accessible support and coping strategies for students, contributing to a more resilient and emotionally healthy student body.

Virtual Reality

Virtual reality (VR) first entered our world around 50 years ago, and like all technology has evolved over the decades into a much more sophisticated form. The first VR would have seen head-mounted displays, head tracking, and computer-generated images (Slater & Sanchez-Vives, 2016). Given the fact that VR has been around for many decades, to some it is still a foreign technology advancement, so what exactly is VR and what is its potential impact on the well-being of our students? Slater and Sanchez-Vives (2016) describe VR as, "Virtual reality is 'reality' that is virtual. This means that in principle, anything that can happen in 'reality' can be programed to happen virtually" (pg. 16). However, VR doesn't stop there, as we can reach outside the boundaries of reality. Our consciousness relies on the data gathered by our senses that surround us daily including taste, touch, smell, sound, and vision. Understanding the way our consciousness works allows us to dive deeper into VR in what is called immersive virtual reality, where the use is to totally immersed "present" in a virtual reality. Slater and Sanchez-Vives state, "This fundamental aspect of VR to deliver experience that gives rise to illusory sense of place and an illusory sense of reality is what distinguishes it fundamentally from all other types of media" (2016). Virtual reality has the potential to be a powerful tool for providing an authentic experience for the user. Educators can embrace this powerful tool to provide authentic learning simulations to actively engage students. In doing so, teachers can motivate students by boosting self-confidence and self-efficacy.

Virtual reality offers numerous educational benefits, such as increased motivation, gamification of learning, enhanced enjoyment, and personalized learning experiences. These benefits are particularly valuable for students who are unmotivated, disengaged, or unable to attend school to benefit from social interactions. Among the various advantages of VR in education, enhancing student motivation stands out as a primary outcome. Simply interacting with technology, including VR, can significantly boost student motivation, as noted by Kavanagh et al. (2017). This increase in motivation is closely linked to improved learning outcomes and is also associated with a more positive emotional state for students.

The gamification of learning through VR can transform the educational experience, making it more engaging and enjoyable for students. By integrating elements of gaming into the learning process, VR can capture students' attention and interest, encouraging them to participate actively in their education. This gamified approach not only enhances the enjoyment of learning but also fosters a sense of achievement and accomplishment, which is crucial for students' emotional well-being. When students find joy in the learning process, they are more likely to succeed academically and develop a positive attitude towards education (Kavanagh et al., 2017). Besides making learning and introduction of new concepts fun, VR can also have a positive impact on a student's anxiety level associated with learning. As Doan (20202) stated, "After experiencing virtual situations, the anxiety level decreased significantly, students can also propose solutions for themselves such as actively exploring the environment, seeking support from teachers or friends" (pg. 20).

Moreover, the personalized learning (PL) opportunities provided by VR can cater to the unique needs and preferences of each student. PL has become a catchy trend in the educational sector stemming from technological advancements. There is much debate still over what PL truly is, but most educators will agree that it involves personalization of the learning process. The organization for Economic Co-operation and Development (OECD) defines PL as holistic, person-centered approach that moves away from the traditional one-size-fits- all approach to education (Gerasimova & Schevlyagin, 2021). Advances in educational technology have enabled scaling of personalized learning to personalize the learning experience of students. VR has great potential to facilitate personalized learning experiences that target to meet the individual needs of students (Kavanagh et al., 2017). This customization allows students to learn at their own pace and explore topics that interest them, leading to a more fulfilling and effective educational experience. Table 1 highlights sample PL tools available to educators and students.

Table 1. AI-Powered Personalized Learning Tools in K-12 Education

Tool	Description
DreamBox	A personalized learning software that uses AI to provide individualized math learning pathways.
Edmentum Exact Path	An AI-driven platform offering customized learning paths across all core content areas.
Carnegie Learning	Offers AI-based tutoring services in ELA, math, and other subjects to support personalized learning.
ALEKS	An adaptive AI learning program that delivers tailored learning activities for student needs.

By addressing individual learning styles and preferences, VR can help students overcome learning barriers and achieve their full potential. Kavanagh et al. (2017) state, "Educational virtual reality software potentially allows students to explore and learn at their own pace. This is appealing to both students and educators attempting to teach students of different abilities" (pg. 5). In recent years, personalized learning through virtual reality (VR) has gained significant attention in the field of special education, especially as a means of helping students cope with social and emotional challenges. The focus on students' social and emotional well-being has intensified in the aftermath of the COVID-19 pandemic, and VR-based personalized learning offers a promising avenue for addressing these needs.

VR software designed for personalized learning allows students to engage with lessons that adapt dynamically to their academic levels and individual needs. This tailored approach not only fosters a sense of success but also helps students develop perseverance and grit. According to Gerasimova and Schevlyagin (2021), "Studies have shown that students' perceived ability to achieve results through effort serves as a predictor of their perseverance." (pg. 6). Thus, a student's level of grit and perseverance can be directly influenced by their learning environment. Implementing personalized learning technologies in VR settings could significantly enhance students' social-emotional skills by providing a supportive and adaptive learning environment.

Another critical factor in enhancing students' social and emotional well-being is addressing the challenge of overcrowded classrooms. In such environments, it is often difficult for teachers to provide individualized instruction, which can lead to frustration, academic failure, and a lack of motivation among students. VR technology can mitigate this issue by enabling teachers to create personalized lessons that engage and motivate each student, irrespective of the class size. This personalized approach has shown great promise in helping students achieve success and cope effectively within the classroom.

The marked increase in enjoyment of learning facilitated by VR has powerful implications for the overall mental state of students. As students experience success in the classroom, they are more likely to develop a positive self-image and a stronger sense of self-efficacy. This, in turn, contributes to their overall well-being and prepares them for future academic and personal challenges. Studies highlight that VR interventions promoted a significant reduction in stress and increased positive outcomes for overall well-being (Xu et al., 2024). VR can serve as an affordable tool to help students cope with stress. By fostering a supportive and engaging learning environment, VR can play a crucial role in promoting student motivation, enjoyment, and emotional well-being, ultimately leading to a more positive and successful educational journey. Table 2 highlights some sample AI tools available to educators and students that support student wellness.

Table 2. Virtual Reality Tools Supporting Student Wellness

Tool	Description
TRIPP	A VR tool offering guided meditation and mindfulness activities to reduce stress by immersing users in calming visuals and sounds.
Relax VR	Similar to TRIPP, it provides guided meditation sessions in peaceful virtual settings such as beaches, rainforests, and other natural environments.
Limbix VR	A therapeutic VR tool used under clinical supervision to treat anxiety, PTSD, and phobias through controlled exposure therapy.
Nature Treks VR	Offers immersive explorations of natural environments like oceans, forests, and mountains, aimed at reducing stress and enhancing relaxation.
FitXR	Engages students in physical fitness through immersive workouts including dance, aerobics, and HIIT, promoting physical health and wellness.
Engage VR	A multi-institution VR platform that hosts virtual wellness rooms for guided relaxation activities and peer connection in a safe digital space.

These VR tools and platforms offer innovative ways to address various individual needs of student well-being, from mental and emotional health to social skills and physical fitness. By integrating VR into educational settings, schools can provide a holistic approach to student well-being that supports both their academic and personal growth.

Artificial Intelligence

Advancements in Artificial Intelligence (AI) have become a transformative agent in the past five years in the educational ecosystem. Educator concerns have been well documented in the research surrounding AI and student mental health. Growing concerns over screentime, social media, and AI engagement has become a center of focus as AI and social media have become indispensable in the educational and personal lives of students (Shahzad et al., 2024). The specific impact of AI, particularly in the transformative era of Generative AI, on both academic and emotional well-being remains under-explored. Additionally, the role of smart learning within the context of AI and user experiences is under-researched.

The integration of AI into the educational ecosystem is much more than mere academic in nature. AI technological advancements around natural language processing and sentiment analysis can identify signs of stress, anxiety and depression. (Empowering mental well-being: The intersection of AI and Student Mental Health - U-M Ross Business+Tech, 2023). By providing emotional support, stress management, and personalized interventions AI can have a positive impact in the mental health space. The powerful information gleaned from AI can be of great value to educators when used to provide personalized interventions, resources, and support. Stress management, time management and recommended counselor interventions could all be outcomes of this AI generated data on students. Shahzad et al. (2024) highlight, “AI technologies serve as robust tools for effective time management, task prioritization, and as repositories of supplemental educational resources” (pg. 4). Table 3 Highlights some sample AI tools available to educators and students to support student mental health and emotional wellness.

Table 3. AI Tools Supporting Student Mental Health and Emotional Wellness

Tool	Description
ChatGPT	An AI tool that offers both academic and emotional support, including relaxation exercises, meditation techniques, coping strategies, and communication tips for student wellness.
Wysa	A mental health app driven by AI and supported by live human coaching. It tracks mood and offers therapeutic interventions for emotional regulation.
Breathhh	A Chrome extension that monitors students' online activity to identify mental health concerns and suggest timely interventions.
WoeBot	An AI chatbot integrated with social media messengers that delivers mental health guidance based on user conversations.
MyUBot	An AI-driven chatbot providing direct feedback and mental wellness advice to students through interactive conversation.
Headspace	An AI-powered mindfulness app offering guided meditations focused on reducing stress and anxiety.
Calmn	A mindfulness app with guided meditations, sleep aids, and relaxation tips aimed at improving overall well-being.
Peekapak	An SEL platform that leverages AI to generate personalized activities for developing students' social and emotional skills.

These AI tools provide innovative solutions to enhance various aspects of student well-being, including mental and emotional health and social-emotional learning. By integrating AI into educational settings, schools can offer a personalized, supportive, and engaging learning environment to meet the individual needs of all students.

Hybrid Learning Environments

Social isolation from peers in asynchronous learning environments show a significant correlation to a student's mental health and well-being (Gandhi et al., 2023). Advancements in technology have vastly improved online course delivery methods allowing teachers to reach students in ways they have never been able to in and out of the classroom. The hybrid model of learning is an educational model where some students attend class in-person, while other students join the class virtually. El-Gayar and Dennis (2005) state, “Hybrid learning environment (HLE) is a classroom- and computer-based environment that is an open system, allowing synchronous and asynchronous interactions and encounters with other participants” (pg. 5). By providing both formats in a hybrid learning format, students still enjoy healthy relationships and social interaction with their peers and teacher.

One example of technology extending the classroom to meet the needs of students is called the hybrid inclusive classroom model. This model provides homebound students with the opportunities to participate and take part in daily classroom activities from a remote location (Panesi et al., 2020). This inclusive classroom approach has marked great improvements in student well-being as students are no longer isolated from their peers or classroom teacher. As Panesi et al. (2020) state, "Hybrid inclusive classrooms unfold within dynamic hybrid spaces formed when participants use their (mobile or fixed) devices to connect online at any time, thereby integrating remote (and/or virtual) spaces and situations within the actuality of a visual/perceptual location/situation". The hybrid inclusive classroom model is critically important as it allows students to remotely maintain social relationships with their classmates, and this is an important aspect of development of the mind and overall well-being of the whole student. One study found that students in the virtual classroom setting where students had the benefit from flexibility and availability of hybrid learning environments had reduced anxiety and feeling of isolation by being afforded the live classroom experience virtually (El-Gayar & Dennis, 2005). This approach strengthens the mind's development, and the underlying importance of a healthy student-teacher relationship is also strengthened.

Another hybrid model is the Enriched Virtual Learning Model. The enriched virtual model combines online learning with occasional in-person sessions. The main method of instruction in this model is online but requires students attend in person on specific days (Kayalar, 2021). By allowing students flexibility to work online, but still require in-person days for group activities and SEL check-in's this model has seen great success with student outcomes holistically. This model offers a great balance of flexibility of online learning and the benefits of the traditional face-to-face learning environment. It has been suggested at all levels of education to improve student academic success, increase participation in the lesson, and increase social interactions with students (Kayalar, 2021).

The Flex Model is another hybrid model that offers both online and in person learning opportunities. The flex model can be defined as a course where online learning is the course's backbone, students have an individualized schedule of activities, and the teacher is onsite to provide additional support as needed (Maxwell, 2018). Students complete online modules at their pace of learning, but attend on campus for tutoring, group projects, and SEL activities. This model offers many potential positive benefits including flexible learning that allows students to take ownership in their work all while having the support of their teachers and fellow peers in the classroom.

The last major hybrid model is the Personalized Learning Model (PLM). In this model instruction is based on the students individual learning path, needs, interest, and educational goals. When looking at the PLM, it's more than the use of technology in instruction. It involves a combination of learning modalities focused on student outcomes (Fisher, 2020). PLM provides learning pathways, adaptive AI learning, and teacher support. By allowing students to take responsibility for their own learning, this model ensures they are provided with the essential resources to excel academically and maintain their mental health.

By leveraging these technological advancements, educators can better address the diverse needs of their students, fostering a more inclusive and supportive educational environment. As technology continues to evolve, it presents an opportunity for educators to innovate and enhance their approaches to student well-being, ultimately leading to improved educational outcomes and a more positive learning experience for all students. In this way, emerging technologies have not only made the job of supporting student well-being easier but have also opened new avenues for addressing the complex and multifaceted challenges that students face today.

Figure 1. Flowchart depicting personalized learning pathways through AI integration in K-12 settings

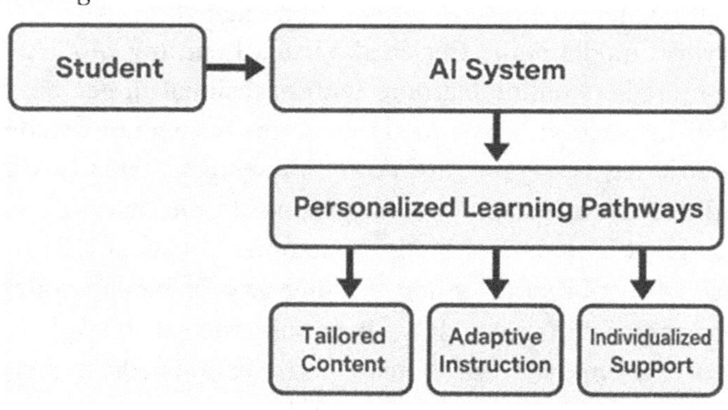

INNOVATIONS IN BUILDING AUTHENTIC RELATIONSHIPS

We are currently living in a time when technology is changing quicker than teenagers change friends, so it is no wonder that Artificial Intelligence (AI) is transforming the way we approach relationships. Younger generations, especially those ages 18-40 are not only interested in AI relationships, but they are open to having AI companions (Nosta, 2024). With over forty percent of Gen Z being open to AI companions, the future for AI and authentic relationships is showing great promise. Not only does this advancement in AI hold great potential for relationships, but AI-driven personalization can facilitate more meaningful and impactful interactions between educators and students. This AI technology advancement could potentially change the student-teacher relationship forever aiding to increased academic performance, because the research shows that the more connected a student is the better they perform.

In the education world, the relationship between teacher and student is constantly evolving which leads to challenges with connectiveness, but it also leaves the door open for innovation in the space. Guilherme (2019) states, "the level of connectedness between teacher and students, and between students has either decreased or become impaired by the increasing technologization of education. Running parallel to this and perhaps exacerbating the problem is the so-called process of 'learnification', which understands that teachers are mere facilitators of the learning process, rather than someone with an expertise who has something to teach others" (p.47). As highlighted, this evolution of the relationship and role of the teacher in the educational process has opened the door for AI Personalization to facilitate stronger more meaningful connections between student and teacher. By delivering customized feedback, recommendations, and resources, these technologies can help educators better understand and address the unique needs of each student, fostering stronger relationships and improving academic outcomes. Additionally, AI can enhance communication between students, parents, and educational institutions, promoting a more collaborative and supportive learning environment.

AI in Education

With the recent surge in AI technology and release of updated versions of ChatGPT, a generative AI software, technology now has the potential to generate human-like responses on various subjects and topics. Many have questioned if AI potentially the power to replace the classroom teacher entirely, and it seems like that could be a real possibility as more than five million jobs could be replaced by AI in the future (Chan & Tsi, 2023). AI in education goes as far back as the 1950's, but over the last few decades AI has evolved from the once tutoring technology to so much more. AI educational technology ranges from personalized tutoring to virtual assistants (Zhang & Yu, 2021). Goksel and Bozkurt (2019) identified three primary themes in AI space that have captivated researchers: adaptive learning, expert systems and ITS, and the future role of AI in educational processes. Other technological innovations that have enhanced student-teacher relationships are the Learning Management Systems (LMS) and virtual office hours.

Learning Management Systems

Learning management systems have changed how we view traditional classrooms. The traditional concept of learning taking place in a single physical location is a thing of the past. Gone are the days where students had to pile into a classroom and sit in front of a live teacher to consume content, and most learners today are becoming less and less attracted to the stand-and-deliver approach to education (Turnbull, D. et al., 2020). Advancements in educational software have paved the way for systems that can facilitate courses remotely. These learning management systems facilitate personalized feedback and foster deeper student-teacher relationships. Table 4 highlights are some examples of Learning Management Systems currently available to educational institutions.

Table 4. Comparison of Learning Management Systems in K-12 and Higher Education

LMS Platform	Primary Audience	Key Features	Unique Characteristics
Canvas	K-12 and Higher Education	Customizable rubrics, modules, schedules, quizzes, advanced analytics	Offers deep insights into student progress; intuitive interface; widely adopted in both K-12 and higher ed
Schoology	Primarily K-12	Course management tools, communication features	Branded as a "learning hub"; integrates with PowerSchool for seamless data and course management
Blackboard Learn	Higher Education (expanding to K-12)	Course customization, analytics, intuitive design, rubrics, modules, schedules, quizzes	Traditionally higher ed-focused; expanding into K-12; offers full customization
Google Classroom	K-12 and Higher Education	Course materials, assignments, surveys, integrated communication and collaboration tools	Strong integration with Google Suite (Drive, Gmail); emphasizes ease of use and collaboration

Learning Management has taken remote learning to a whole new level and completely changed how we see the traditional classroom. With a variety of software platforms to choose from, educators have choices as to which platform meets the needs of their students and organization. This innovative technological advancement has enhanced the evolving relationship between student and teacher in a remote classroom setting. LMS systems positively impact students by providing well-designed units that include high-quality resources, individualized feedback, and effective communication.

Virtual Office Hours

With current advancements in technology, a new trend is starting to pop up throughout schools around the country called virtual office hours. Virtual office hours can be best described as computer-generated office hours in lieu of in-person office hours in the traditional sense. Cox and Williams (2011), state, “Virtual office hours often refer to set times when an instructor is available to learners for one-on-one or small-group consultations” (p.136). Typical class structures along with the normal office hours teachers have could limit student-teacher interaction due to the formal structure. Many students aren't comfortable approaching their teacher in the classroom or other formal traditional setting leading to a missed opportunity to connect with their teacher (Li & Pitts, 2009). Advancements in online platforms and the internet have provided teachers with an innovative way to connect with students. Research has been clear that an increase in informal contact between a student and teacher is associated with a student's personal, social, and intellectual growth (Li & Pitts, 2009). Teachers that have embraced this innovative technology are reaching students synchronously from any location.

Reaching student through a synchronous method involves video conferencing via Zoom, TEAMS, or other online video conferencing software. Teachers also have access to other forms of asynchronous communication to use like email, chat, IM, and discussion post online. Regardless of the format, this form of virtual communication improves the connection between student and teacher regardless of time or location. Virtual office hours can help students accomplish many goals by providing a space for students who may have missed in-person office hours or don’t feel comfortable asking questions in front of their peers (Cox & Williams, 2011). Regardless of what type of virtual office a teacher chooses to use evidence suggest that these methods of reaching students not only helps academically but can build collaboration and community in a classroom helping students communicate with the instructor and their peers (Cox & Williams, 2011). Teachers should encourage students to participate in virtual office hours early in the course to help ignite that sense of community early. Teachers as good practice should also engage the families of students in office hours to further build and develop a sense of community in the learning process. By taking office hours a step further and offering virtual office hours teachers can tap into unrealized potential of students and develop stronger relationships with their students. The result is students not feeling disconnected or isolated but feeling connected and engaged.

Peer-to-Peer Relationship Building through Technology Innovation

Innovation in technology has not only opened new avenues for building relationships between teachers and students but has also positively impacted peer-to-peer relationships. Educators recognize that students who collaborate and engage with their peers not only deepen their understanding of the content but also gain social benefits from these interactions. Advancements in technology have paved the way in helping students connect through collaborative learning platforms like Padlet, Kahoot, video-conferencing breakout rooms, and innovative peer mentoring programs.

Padlet is a free multimedia program that engages students in real-time interactions with both their teachers and classmates. Because Padlet is free to educators and simple to use, teachers have embraced this technology over the past several years. Padlet is useful to improve collaboration instantly among students, but it also allows teachers and students to place all content in this one online platform. Padlet also works on many devices making it more mobile and assessable to students and teachers alike (Beltrán-Martín, 2019). As a multimedia platform, Padlet provides and digital platform where students can gather resources like class resources, class diary, frequently asked questions, brainstorming wall, and online collaboration space. Padlet allows students to engage and reflect on their learning from any device anytime. In addition, Padlet promotes online collaboration that increases a student's social skills like communication, teamwork, time management, and negotiation skills (Beltrán-Martín, 2019).

Kahoot is a game-based student interaction platform that turns the traditional classroom into a competitive gaming process. Kahoot aims to enhance the learning environment by encouraging curricular interaction between students and teachers (Zhang & Yu, 2021). Research in the gamification of learning and academic performance is heavily debated over, but one thing is clear, gamification tools like Kahoot clearly increase learner motivation, engagement, and enjoyment of learning (Zhang & Yu, 2021). Social interaction between students and teachers is a focus of Kahoot enhancing interaction and collaboration in the classroom. While creating a fun engaging learning platform, Kahoot can also promote a positive classroom community and reduce student anxiety levels (Zhang & Yu, 2021). Kahoot has been a successful tool in transforming the learning environment and increased student collaboration and interaction through the gamification of learning. Research also highlights that students views on the use of breakout rooms to be exciting, innovative, motivating, and fosters class participation.

Video-conferencing breakout rooms came to a dynamic start with the onset of the Covid-19 pandemic as students shifted to online learning. Educations immediately saw the challenges associated with virtual learning as many students struggled both academically and socially as learners faced new challenges from their computers at home. Isolation, lack of engagement, and decreasing morale were just a few of those challenges students and teachers had to overcome. Zoom, Microsoft TEAMS, and Google Classroom are all internet-based video-conferencing software designed to allow students and teachers to interact and collaborate virtually (Healey-Benson et al., 2024). Video-conferencing software have been a gamechanger and innovative in the virtual education space showing great promise for small-group collaboration and engagement among students, but the impact grows well beyond academics as the impact on relationships, presences, and student identity have been noted in research (Healey-Benson et al., 2024). Research also highlights that student views on the use of breakout rooms to be exciting, innovative, motivating, and fosters class participation (Bamidele, 2021). Breakout rooms allow teachers to put students into small-group collaborative learning teams that allow students to develop stronger peer interactions and have become a central part for collaborative learning in a virtual classroom.

Innovation in online peer mentoring, peer support, or peer coaching have also gained in popularity as educators continue to look for ways to support students in a virtual classroom setting. Peer mentoring is also key in developing healthy relationships for learners.

Global Classroom Connections

Innovations in technology have created new opportunities to engage with students from around the world through virtual exchanges and global classrooms. Advancements in technology allow teachers the opportunity to take students on virtual field trips, engage in intercultural exchanges, and global collaboration by connecting students online (Patterson et al., 2012). These innovative technology platforms have created an international shift if educational programs allowing students to build relationships with peers from different cultural backgrounds. As with all innovation there are challenges to facilitate authentic collaboration in a global classroom (Lock, 2015). If structured correctly, this global collaboration and relationship building classroom can produce some amazing benefits for students on both sides of the screen. In addition to teaching students to think more globally on key issues, global classrooms allow students to sharpen their critical thinking skills, embrace diversity, and build global relationships (Patterson et al., 2012). These connections with peers across the world allow students to share ideas, learn about other cultures, and foster relationships in ways the traditional classroom can't. Through introductions, icebreakers, collaborative teambuilding activities, students experience different cultures, experiences, and perceptions from around the world (Patterson et al., 2012). Global classrooms and the interpersonal exchanges that happen help to breakdown cultural barriers and help students to understand the commonalities in the cultures and the people that make up those cultures (Patterson et al., 2012). Thanks to advancements in technology, we now have the tools necessary to make these global connections and help students build authentic relationships across country borders all over the internet without leaving their classrooms in their home country.

ENHANCING PERSONAL AND PROFESSIONAL GROWTH WITH TECHNOLOGY

The unprecedented disruption in education brought about by the COVID-19 pandemic presented challenges that were beyond anyone's prior experience. Teachers, who had long relied on traditional, face-to-face methods, were suddenly thrust into a new, digital learning environment that many were not prepared for. As a result, there was a rapid and massive shift in educational practices, as educators had to adapt to online platforms, digital tools, and remote teaching methodologies (Kit Ng, 2023). Fast forward four years, and the educational landscape looks markedly different. The digital transformation that began during the pandemic has not only persisted but has also deepened its roots in the education system. This section aims to provide a thorough understanding of how these digital innovations are revolutionizing the realms of professional development and mentorship in education.

In March 2020, the global educational community faced an unprecedented challenge (Kit Ng, 2023). Educators worldwide were compelled to transition from their conventional pedagogical approaches to the relatively uncharted waters of distance learning. This transition was not merely about ensuring that students continued to learn despite the physical separation but also involved finding ways to support educators as they navigated this new terrain. School systems encountered the urgent need to develop digitally proficient teaching communities capable of addressing the needs of 21st-century learners (Anis, 2024).

The shift to online education exposed significant gaps in how professional development had been delivered historically. For decades, traditional methods of professional development included workshops, seminars, peer mentoring, and face-to-face conferences. These methods were deeply embedded in the educational system but came under scrutiny for their effectiveness, particularly as the demands of modern education evolved. The pandemic forced a reevaluation of these methods, leading to a broader and more nuanced understanding of how professional development could be delivered in a way that was both effective and adaptable to the needs of today's educators (Haleem et al., 2022).

The forced transition to remote learning provided an unexpected opportunity for educational leaders to reassess and innovate professional development supports.

This period of upheaval catalyzed a pedagogical shift that integrated technology with traditional pedagogy and content knowledge. Educators quickly recognized that digital professional development approaches offered several advantages, including greater flexibility and individualization. Online courses, webinars, virtual peer coaching, and digital learning communities emerged as viable and often preferable alternatives to traditional professional development methods (Canaran, 2023).

The benefits of these new digital approaches are manifold. Online courses and webinars allow educators to access training and resources from anywhere, overcoming the geographical limitations of in-person events. Virtual peer coaching offers a platform for educators to collaborate and reflect on their practices without the constraints of time and location. Digital learning communities provide ongoing support and networking opportunities, facilitating continuous professional growth beyond the confines of traditional models. These innovations enhance professional development accessibility and contribute to a more personalized and responsive learning experience for educators.

Mentoring and Coaching Innovations

Mentoring and coaching have always been integral components of professional development. Traditional peer mentoring and coaching approaches have been well-documented, with substantial research indicating their positive impact on improving retention rates for early-career educators. However, the effectiveness of digital mentoring and coaching in the evolving educational landscape necessitates further exploration. Current research emphasizes that, now more than ever, teachers need continuous professional development support to stay current with the rapid advancements in digital education tools and methodologies (Haleem et al., 2022).

Traditional mentoring and coaching methods have been criticized for their hierarchical nature, wherein a "master teacher" often leads an early-career educator. This hierarchical model, while effective in some contexts, has been challenged by the demands of the digital era. The rise of online, flexible peer coaching presents a compelling alternative. This approach is characterized by a collaborative, non-hierarchical model, where educators work together to reflect on and address professional challenges. Online peer coaching typically involves at least two educators who engage in reflective discussions on topics previously covered by traditional mentoring methods (Canaran, 2023).

One of the key advantages of online peer coaching is its ability to foster a collaborative environment that transcends traditional power dynamics. Educators who participate in online peer coaching often report improved teaching practices, enhanced reflection on their teaching, and better overall well-being (Canaran, 2023). This positive feedback suggests that the non-hierarchical nature of online peer coaching, combined with the ability to connect with peers who share similar personal and professional experiences, contributes to its effectiveness. The digital tools that facilitate this model also enable a level of personalization that was previously unattainable in traditional settings.

Participants in online peer coaching often find that the less formal and more collaborative nature of these interactions reduces intimidation and promotes open dialogue. The ability to connect with peers who have similar experiences or challenges fosters a sense of community and shared purpose (Kit Ng, 2023). Additionally, digital tools provide the flexibility to engage in peer coaching on demand, allowing educators to balance their professional development with their personal responsibilities. This flexibility is particularly valuable in the context of the ongoing demands of modern education.

While the landscape of coaching and mentoring has undeniably shifted in the digital era, these approaches remain effective in enhancing educators' confidence in both pedagogical and technical domains (Klimova et al., 2023). Several digital mentoring and coaching programs exemplify this shift and have demonstrated success in integrating technology with professional development. Notable programs include:

Table 5. Digital Mentoring and Professional Development Programs for Educators

Program	Description
Google Certified Educator	Provides training and certification in using Google tools for teaching. Offers multiple levels to meet diverse educator needs and skill levels.
Apple Distinguished Educator	Recognizes innovative educators using Apple technology to inspire creativity and supports collaboration within a global professional network.
Microsoft Educator Community	A comprehensive platform offering training, resources, and certifications to help educators integrate Microsoft tools into their instruction.
Digital Learning Consortia	Collaborative groups that unite educators, researchers, and developers to advance innovative strategies in digital teaching and learning.

These programs have proven successful because they incorporate key aspects of flexible online peer mentoring. They offer customizable learning paths, promote collaboration among educators with shared interests, and leverage technology to integrate new tools with traditional teaching methods (Klimova et al., 2023). Moreover, school systems have adopted intra-district supports like Microsoft Teams and Google Meet, which facilitate peer mentoring and coaching without geographical constraints.

Professional Development Shift

The evolution of professional development in the digital age highlights the importance of adaptability and continuous learning. As technology continues to advance, it is essential for educators to embrace new tools and methodologies to enhance their teaching practices and meet the evolving needs of their students. The integration of digital tools into professional development not only provides more accessible and personalized learning opportunities but also fosters a more connected and collaborative educational community (Larsen et al., 2023).

In conclusion, the digital transformation of education, accelerated by the COVID-19 pandemic, has fundamentally changed the landscape of professional development and mentorship (Kit Ng, 2023). While traditional methods have been reevaluated and adapted, the rise of digital approaches has provided new opportunities for growth and collaboration. As we continue to navigate this evolving landscape, it is crucial to embrace these innovations and leverage technology to support educators in their ongoing professional development. Education's future will be shaped by the continued integration of digital tools and methodologies, fostering a more dynamic and responsive learning environment for educators and students.

FUTURE CHALLENGES AND ETHICAL CONSIDERATIONS

The incorporation of technology into the classroom has always been a dynamic process, with educators striving to stay updated on evolving tools and methodologies. In the contemporary education system, artificial intelligence (AI) emerges as a potential game-changer, poised to transform the way educators teach, and students learn (Yue et al., 2024). AI can automate mundane tasks, offer personalized learning experiences, and open the door to innovative teaching methods. However, just like any technological advancement, AI in education brings both opportunities and challenges. The debate over whether the benefits of adaptive learning, automated task delegation, and other AI-powered solutions outweigh the challenges is ongoing (Larsen et al., 2023). Among the key concerns are issues of academic integrity, reliability, bias, and the dissemination of false information. Educators are caught between the promise of AI and the ethical dilemmas it presents, leading to questions about how best to integrate these tools into educational practices (Rasul et al., 2023; Saaida, 2023).

Academic Integrity in the Era of AI

A major concern for educators is the impact AI could have on academic integrity. The rapid advancements in generative AI tools, such as language models and automated essay generators, have created a situation where it is difficult to determine whether a student's work is truly their own (Yue et al., 2024). This issue is compounded by the fact that many educational institutions do not yet have formal policies in place regarding AI use. Even in cases where AI policies exist, there remains a significant level of distrust among educators. Teachers often feel uncertain about how to manage student submissions that may have been partially or wholly produced by AI.

AI detection tools, which have been developed to address this concern, only offer probabilistic evaluations, meaning that they cannot definitively state whether content was generated by AI (Larsen et al., 2023). This leaves educators in a gray area, unsure whether to penalize students for potential dishonesty or to trust the AI-detection software's results (Memarian & Doleck, 2023). Moreover, this situation can create a negative atmosphere in classrooms, where the traditional trust between teachers and students is eroded by the fear that assignments may not be authentic. This uncertainty presents a significant hurdle to embracing AI in education.

Staff Readiness and Training

Another critical factor influencing the successful integration of AI in education is staff readiness. According to a recent study by Saaida (2023), only 28% of teachers reported having received any form of training on incorporating AI resources into their instruction. This lack of preparedness is problematic because the effective use of AI in the classroom requires more than just knowledge of the tools—it requires an understanding of how to integrate these technologies into pedagogical practices meaningfully. Furthermore, even fewer educators have been trained to use AI detection software, which adds to the frustration around managing student submissions and maintaining academic integrity (Yue et al., 2024).

In the K-12 sector, many teachers report that they have higher priorities in their classrooms and do not have the time or bandwidth to learn yet another instructional resource (Lee & Kwon, 2024). Without a clear directive from school districts regarding AI usage, teachers may continue to view AI tools as unnecessary or even detrimental to their work, particularly when there are no administrative consequences for students who misuse AI. If districts fail to provide guidance and support for AI integration, educators may be reluctant to adopt these tools fully, which will limit the potential benefits that AI could bring to the classroom.

Faculty Adoption and Concerns

Faculty acceptance of AI is crucial for its successful adoption (Yue et al., 2024). However, concerns about job displacement, academic integrity, and the pedagogical implications of AI use can deter educators from embracing these tools. One of the most significant potential benefits of AI in education is its ability to automate grading and administrative tasks. For many teachers, this would free up valuable time, allowing them to focus more on individualized instruction and higher-order thinking skills (Saaida, 2023). However, there is a growing concern that AI tools may replace essential human elements of teaching, such as building personal connections with students and understanding their unique needs.

AI tools excel at tasks like automating repetitive tasks, but they are less adept at fostering the kind of human connection that is critical for student success. If AI begins to take over too many aspects of day-to-day classroom management, it could diminish the relational elements of teaching that are so important for student motivation and engagement (Larsen et al., 2023). This tension between automation and the human touch in education is a critical issue that needs to be addressed before AI can be fully embraced.

Financial and Logistical Challenges

Implementing AI in schools also presents financial and logistical challenges. Many school districts lack the funds to purchase and maintain the technology necessary to support an AI-driven learning environment (Nguyen et al., 2023). The costs associated with hardware, software, and ongoing maintenance can be prohibitive, particularly in underfunded schools. Furthermore, technology departments within school districts are working tirelessly to protect their systems from cyber threats. In this landscape, AI tools—which often require access to external applications or networks—can introduce additional vulnerabilities. As a result, many districts are opting to lock down their networks, which limits teachers' ability to use AI resources effectively in the classroom (Memarian & Doleck, 2023).

The integration of AI tools into pre-existing educational systems is also complex. Schools may lack the infrastructure needed to support AI, and there may be compatibility issues between new AI platforms and older technologies still in use. Addressing these challenges will require significant investment, careful planning, and collaboration between educational institutions, technology providers, and policymakers (Larsen et al., 2023).

Equity, Access, and Bias in AI Algorithms

One of the most significant concerns related to AI in education is the potential for algorithms to exacerbate existing biases and inequalities. AI systems are trained on data, and if that data reflects societal biases, the resulting algorithms can reinforce those biases (Nguyen et al., 2023). This is especially concerning in education, where equity and access are already pressing issues. Minority students, who often face barriers to digital equity and access, could be further disadvantaged by AI tools that do not account for their unique needs (Nguyen et al., 2023).

Ensuring fairness, transparency, and accountability in AI algorithms is essential for mitigating these risks. However, many AI systems operate as "black boxes," meaning that the decision-making processes within the algorithm are opaque (Larsen et al., 2023). This lack of transparency makes it difficult to identify and address biases, leaving educators and students vulnerable to the negative consequences of biased AI systems. Furthermore, issues of data privacy and security add another layer of complexity to the use of AI in education. The collection of student data by AI tools raises concerns about consent, data breaches, and the potential misuse of personal information.

Cybersecurity Concerns

As educational institutions increasingly rely on digital tools, including AI, cybersecurity has become a growing concern (Cardona et al., 2023). Schools are now prime targets for cyberattacks, which can disrupt learning, compromise sensitive information, and lead to costly recovery efforts. With AI tools requiring access to cloud-based services and external applications, the risk of cyber threats increases (Lee & Kwon, 2024). Keeping students safe in an AI-driven educational environment will require robust cybersecurity measures, which may be beyond the capacity of many school districts to implement.

In conclusion, while AI holds tremendous potential to revolutionize education, the challenges associated with its adoption must not be overlooked (Canaran, 2023). Educators must navigate concerns about academic integrity, staff readiness, equity, and cybersecurity as they consider how best to integrate AI into their teaching practices. Ultimately, the success of AI in education will depend on careful planning, thoughtful policy development, and a commitment to ensuring that these powerful tools are used ethically and equitably.

Figure 2. Conceptual model of how emerging digital tools (VR and AI) support student mental health, motivation, and engagement

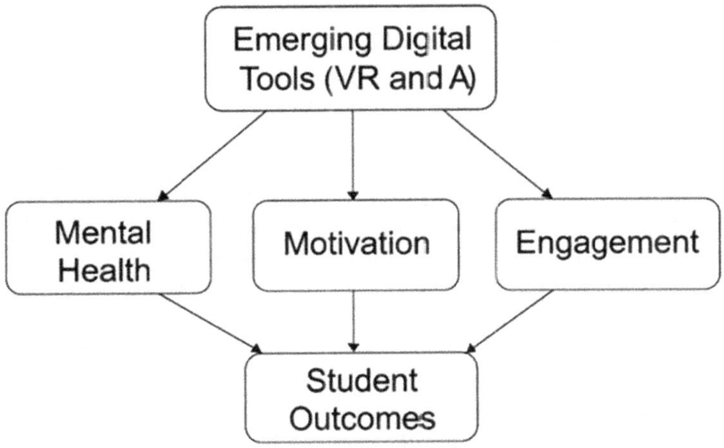

CONCLUSION

As we continue to watch the evolution of technology, it is important to reflect on the shift from face-to-face interactions to more virtual experiences, especially for our students, and to fully understand the implications for their mental well-being, authentic relationships, and personal growth. While the convenience and accessibility of technology offer numerous benefits, they also present significant challenges that must be addressed with care. As we continue to integrate digital tools into education, we must continue to examine how this transformation affects the social and emotional development of our learners. Although technology provides new opportunities for learning and connection, it is essential to ensure that these advancements do not negatively impact meaningful human interactions and the overall well-being of our students.

The rapid evolution of technology, particularly artificial intelligence, presents both challenges and opportunities in education. AI-driven tools like virtual reality and machine learning have the potential to enhance personalized learning, offer mental health resources, and foster stronger student-teacher connections. In an era where AI can even transform relationships, especially among younger generations, educators must thoughtfully leverage these innovations to promote student engagement and success. Research shows that the more connected a student feels, the better they perform academically, and AI can play a vital role in strengthening these relationships by providing customized feedback, recommendations, and support. As technology continues to shape education, we must be mindful of balancing innovation with authentic relationships. The challenge lies in ensuring that AI and other emerging technologies enhance, rather than impair, the connections that are crucial for student success and well-being. By thoughtfully integrating these tools, we can create a more supportive, collaborative, and emotionally healthy learning environment, equipping students with the skills they need to thrive in the digital world.

The transformation brought about by the digital age has fundamentally reshaped the educational landscape, marking a significant shift in how we teach, learn, and lead. Online and blended learning platforms, once considered supplemental, have become essential components of instructional design in both K–12 and higher education settings. This chapter has explored how emerging technologies—including artificial intelligence (AI), virtual reality (VR), and machine learning—are not only enhancing academic instruction but also redefining student engagement, personalization, and access.

Key to this transformation is the role of educational leaders in navigating this rapidly evolving terrain. The effective integration of digital tools is not a matter of simply adopting the latest technology, but rather requires strategic vision, ethical considerations, and a deep understanding of pedagogy. As demonstrated throughout the chapter, tools such as learning management systems (LMS), adaptive learning platforms, and immersive simulations can elevate student learning when implemented with purpose and supported by sound instructional practices.

Moreover, the chapter has highlighted the importance of fostering digital equity and inclusion. The digital divide remains a pressing challenge; thus, educational leaders must advocate for equitable access to devices, internet connectivity, and high-quality digital content. Additionally, professional development must be prioritized to ensure that educators are not only technologically proficient but also pedagogically empowered to use these tools to support diverse learners.

As we look to the future, the convergence of AI, data analytics, and immersive technologies presents both promise and responsibility. These tools have the potential to support student motivation, resilience, and well-being, but only when their use is grounded in intentional design and a commitment to human-centered learning. Educational leaders must remain vigilant stewards of these innovations, ensuring that technology serves as a bridge rather than a barrier, strengthening authentic relationships, promoting critical thinking, and supporting the holistic development of every student.

In summary, the digital age offers unprecedented opportunities to transform education, but it requires thoughtful leadership to translate technological potential into meaningful impact. By embracing a forward-thinking and inclusive approach, we can build responsive, engaging, and equitable learning environments that prepare students not only to thrive in a digital world; but to lead within it.

REFERENCES

Anis, M. (2024, January-February). Teacher professional development in the digital age: Addressing the evolving needs post-COVID. *International Journal for Multidisciplinary Research*, *6*(1), 1–14. DOI: 10.36948/ijfmr.2024.v06i01.12386

Bamidele, A. (2021, July). Student-centered interactions within an ESL classroom using online breakout room. In *Proceedings of the AUBH E-Learning Conference*.

Beltrán-Martín, I. (2019). Using Padlet for collaborative learning. *5th International Conference on Higher Education Advances (HEAd'19)*, 1–8. DOI: 10.4995/head19.2019.9188

Canaran, O. (2023). Teacher educators' professional development through online peer-coaching. International *Journal of Curriculum and Instruction, 15(*2), 892-911. https://ijci.globets.org/index.php/IJCI/article/view/1240/623

Cardona, M. A., Rodriguez, R. J., & Ishmael, K. (2023). Artificial intelligence and the future of teaching and learning. Office of Educational Technology. https://tech.ed.gov/ai-future-of-teaching-and-learning/

Chan, C. K. Y., & Tsi, L. H. (2023). The AI revolution in education: Will AI replace or assist teachers in higher education? /arXiv.2305.01185DOI: 10.48550

Cox, T. C., & Williams, A. (2011). Virtual office hours. The professor's guide to taming technology: Leveraging digital media. *Web*, *2*, 135–150.

Doan, V. A. (2020). Primary students' school anxiety: An initiative study on virtual reality therapy. *VNU Journal of Science: Education Research*, *36*(4). Advance online publication. DOI: 10.25073/2588-1159/vnuer.4399

El-Gayar, O., & Dennis, T. (2005). Effectiveness of hybrid learning environments. *Issues in Information Systems*, *6*(1), 176–182. DOI: 10.48009/1_iis_2005_176-182

Empowering mental well-being: The intersection of AI and Student Mental Health - U-M Ross Business+Tech. U. (2023, September 10).

Fisher, J. F. (2020, March 26). *Defining personalized learning and blended learning: Is there a difference?* Education Next. https://www.educationnext.org/defining-personalized-learning-blended-learning-difference/

Gandhi, M., Egner, C., Coyle, M. C., Mehta, B. H., McAuley, J. W., & Cline, K. M. (2023). Impact of asynchronous virtual learning on student well-being and success. *Currents in Pharmacy Teaching & Learning*, *15*(3), 266–273. DOI: 10.1016/j.cptl.2023.03.006 PMID: 37055317

Gerasimova, I., & Schevlyagin, M. (2021). How personalized learning platforms could improve social-emotional skills. In *INTED2021 Proceedings* (pp. 10033-10040). IATED.

Goksel, N., & Bozkurt, A. (2019). Artificial intelligence in education: Current insights and future perspectives. In Sisman-Ugur, S., & Kurubacak, G. (Eds.), *Handbook of Research on Learning in the Age of Transhumanism* (pp. 224–236). IGI Global.

Guilherme, A. (2019). AI and education: The importance of teacher and student relations. *AI & Society*, *34*, 47–54. DOI: 10.1007/s00146-017-0693-8

Haleem, A., Javaid, M., Qadri, M. A., & Suman, R. (2022). Understanding the role of digital technologies in education: A review. *Sustainable Operations and Computers*, *3*, 275–285. DOI: 10.1016/j.susoc.2022.05.004

Healey-Benson, F., Johnson, M. R., Adams, C., & Turville, J. (2024). What is it like for a learner to participate in a Zoom breakout room session? In *Phenomenology in Action for Researching Networked Learning* (pp. 125–152). Springer Nature Switzerland., DOI: 10.1007/978-3-031-62780-4_7

Kavanagh, S., Luxton-Reilly, A., Wuensche, B., & Plimmer, B. (2017). A systematic review of virtual reality in education. *Themes in Science and Technology Education*, *10*(2), 85–119. Retrieved August 11, 2024, from https://www.learntechlib.org/p/182115/

Kayalar, F. (2021). Importance of enriched virtual learning model in hybrid teaching application. *Proceedings of IAC in Budapest*, 23-27.

Kit Ng, D. T., Leung, J. K. L., Su, J., Wui Ng, R. C., & Wah Chu, S. K. (2023). Teachers' AI digital competencies and twenty-first century skills in the post-pandemic world. *Educational Technology Research and Development*, *71*, 137–161. DOI: 10.1007/s11423-023-10203-6 PMID: 36844361

Klimova, B., Pikhart, M., & Kacetl, J. (2023). Ethical issues of the use of AI-driven mobile apps for education. *Public Health*, *10*. Advance online publication. DOI: 10.3389/fpubh.2022.1118116 PMID: 36711343

Larsen, E., Jensen-Clayton, C., Curtis, E., Loughland, T., & Nguyen, H. T. M. (2023, February). *Re-imaging teacher mentor for the future*. Professional Development in Education, https://www.tandfonline.com/doi/full/10.1080/19415257.2023.2178480

Li, L., & Pitts, J. P. (2009). Does it really matter? Using virtual office hours to enhance student-faculty interaction. *Journal of Information Systems Education*, *20*(2), 175.

Lock, J. V. (2015). Designing learning to engage students in the global classroom. *Technology, Pedagogy and Education*, *24*(2), 137–153.

Maxwell, C. (2018, October 9). *A deeper look at the flex model*. Blended Learning Universe. https://www.blendedlearning.org/a-deeper-look-at-the-flex-model/

Memarian, B., & Doleck, T. (2023). Fairness, accountability, transparency, and ethics (FATE) in artificial intelligence (AI) and higher education: A systemic review. *Computers and Education: Artificial Intelligence*, *5*(100152), 1–12. DOI: 10.1016/j.caeai.2023.100152

Nguyen, A., Ngo, H. N., Hong, Y., Dang, B., & Thi Nguyen, B. P. (2023). Ethical principles for artificial intelligence in education. *Education and Information Technologies*, *28*, 4221–4241. DOI: 10.1007/s10639-022-11316-w PMID: 36254344

Nosta, J. (2024). *How artificial intelligence is reshaping relationships*. Psychology Today. https://www.psychologytoday.com/us/blog/the-digital-self/202406/how-artificial-intelligence-is-reshaping-relationships

Panesi, S., Bocconi, S., & Ferlino, L. (2020). Promoting students' well-being and inclusion in schools through digital technologies: Perceptions of students, teachers, and school leaders in Italy expressed through SELFIE piloting activities. *Frontiers in Psychology*, *11*, 1563. DOI: 10.3389/fpsyg.2020.01563 PMID: 32848988

Patterson, L. M., Carrillo, P. B., & Salinas, R. S. (2012). Lessons From a Global Learning Virtual Classroom. *Journal of Studies in International Education*, *16*(2), 182–197. DOI: 10.1177/1028315311398665

Rasul, T., Nair, S., Kalendra, D., Robin, M., de Oliveira Santini, F., Ladeira, W. J., Sun, M., Day, I., Rather, R. A., & Heathcote, L. (2023). The role of ChatGPT in higher education: Benefits, challenges, and future research directions. *Journal of Applied Learning & Teaching*, *6*(1), 1–16. https://journals.sfu.ca/jalt/index.php/jalt/index

Saaida, M. B. (2023). AI-driven transformations in higher education: Opportunities and challenges. *International Journal of Educational Research and Studies*, *5*(1), 29–36. DOI: 10.5281/zenodo.8164414

Shahzad, M. F., Xu, S., Lim, W. M., Yang, X., & Khan, Q. R. (2024). Artificial intelligence and social media on academic performance and mental well-being: Student perceptions of positive impact in the age of smart learning. *Heliyon*, *10*(8). Advance online publication. DOI: 10.1016/j.heliyon.2024.e29523 PMID: 38665566

Slater, M., & Sanchez-Vives, M. V. (2016). Enhancing our lives with immersive virtual reality. *Frontiers in Robotics and AI*, *3*, 74. DOI: 10.3389/frobt.2016.00074

Turnbull, D., Chugh, R., & Luck, J. (2020). Learning management systems, an overview. *Encyclopedia of education and information technologies*, 1052-1058. DOI: 10.1007/978-3-030-10576-1_248

Xu, J., Khanotia, A., Juni, S., Ku, J., Sami, H., Lin, V., Walterson, R., Payne, E., Jo, H., & Rahimpoor-Marnani, P. (2024). Effectiveness of virtual reality-based well-being interventions for stress reduction in young adults: Systematic Review. *JMIR Mental Health*, *11*, e52186. DOI: 10.2196/52186 PMID: 38551625

Yue, M., Jong, M. S. Y., & Kit, Nj. D. T. (2024). Understanding K-12 teachers' technological pedagogical content knowledge readiness and attitudes toward artificial intelligence education. *Education and Information Technologies*. Advance online publication. DOI: 10.1007/s10639-024-12621-2

Zhang, Q., & Yu, Z. (2021). A literature review on the influence of Kahoot! On learning outcomes, interaction, and collaboration. *Education and Information Technologies*, *26*(4), 4507–4535. DOI: 10.1007/s10639-021-10459-6

Compilation of References

Abhari, K., Klase, M., Koobchehr, F., Olivares, F., Pesavento, M., Sosa, L., & Vaghefi, I. (2021). Toward a theory of digital mindfulness: a case of Smartphone-Based self-monitoring. In *Lecture notes in computer science* (pp. 549–561). https://doi.org/DOI: 10.1007/978-3-030-77750-0_35

Abnave Vikas, B. (n.d.). *Sugar Co-operatives in Maharashtra: Challenges Ahead.*

Ainin, S., Naqshbandi, M. M., Moghavvemi, S., & Jaafar, N. I. (2015). Facebook usage, socialization and academic performance. *Computers & Education*, *83*, 64–73. DOI: 10.1016/j.compedu.2014.12.018

Al-Dheleai, Y. M., & Tasir, Z. (2017). Using facebook for the purpose of students interaction and its correlation with students academic performance. *The Turkish Online Journal of Educational Technology*, *16*(4), 170–178. https://files.eric.ed.gov/fulltext/EJ1160608.pdf

Alexander, R. D. (1974). The evolution of social behavior. *Annual Review of Ecology, Evolution, and Systematics*, *5*, 325–383.

Al-Hail, M., Zguir, M. F., & Koç, M. (2024). Exploring Digital Learning Opportunities and Challenges in Higher Education Institutes: Stakeholder Analysis on the Use of Social Media for Effective Sustainability of Learning–Teaching–Assessment in a University setting in Qatar. *Sustainability*, *16*(15), 6413. DOI: 10.3390/su16156413

Allen, K., Kern, M. L., Rozek, C. R., McInerney, D. M., & Slavich, G. M. (2021). Belonging: A review of conceptual issues, an integrative framework, and directions for future research. *Australian Journal of Psychology*, *73*(1), 87–102. DOI: 10.1080/00049530.2021.1883409

Aloni, N. (2002). Enhancing humanity. *The philosophical foundations of humanistic education. Bos*. https://link.springer.com/book/10.1007/978-1-4020-6168-4

Al-Rahmi, A. M., Shamsuddin, A., Alturki, U., Aldraiweesh, A., Yusof, F. M., Al-Rahmi, W. M., & Aljeraiwi, A. A. (2021). The influence of information system success and technology acceptance model on social media factors in education. *Sustainability*, *13*(14), 7770. DOI: 10.3390/su13147770

Al-rahmi, W. M., Othman, M. S., & Musa, M. A. (2014). Social media through collaborative learning in Malaysian higher education. *Asian Social Science*, *10*(8), 210–221. DOI: 10.5539/ass.v10n8p210

Alsarayreh, M., & Aljaafreh, A. (2023). Factors Influencing Students' Academic Performance in Universities: Mediated by Knowledge Sharing Behavior. *Knowledge Management & E-Learning*, *15*(4), 643–671. DOI: 10.34105/j.kmel.2023.15.036

Altaany, F. H., & Jassim, F. A. (2013). Impact of Facebook usage on Undergraduate students performance in Irbid National University: case study. *arXiv (Cornell University)*. /arxiv.1306.4779DOI: 10.48550

Alvi, I. (2021). College students' reception of social networking tools for learning in India: An extended UTAUT model. *Smart Learning Environments*, *8*(1). Advance online publication. DOI: 10.1186/s40561-021-00164-9 PMID: 40477379

Amjad, A. I., Aslam, S., & Tabassum, U. (2024). Tech-infused classrooms: A comprehensive study on the interplay of mobile learning, ChatGPT and social media in academic attainment. *European Journal of Education*. Advance online publication. DOI: 10.1111/ejed.12625

Anggraeni, A. (2020). Blended humor and mind mapping in improving 21st century skills. *Jurnal Ilmu Pendidikan*, *25*(1), 1. DOI: 10.17977/um048v25i1p1-5

Anis, M. (2024, January-February). Teacher professional development in the digital age: Addressing the evolving needs post-COVID. *International Journal for Multidisciplinary Research*, *6*(1), 1–14. DOI: 10.36948/ijfmr.2024.v06i01.12386

Apple, M. W. (2004). *Ideology and curriculum*. Routledge.

Ardelt, M., & Kingsbury, J. (2024). Wisdom, Virtues, and Well-Being: An Empirical test of Aristotle's Theory of Flourishing. *Topoi*. Advance online publication. DOI: 10.1007/s11245-023-10002-x

Arthur, W. B. (2009). *The nature of technology: What it is and how it evolves*. Free Press.

Attwood, D. W., & Attwood, D. (2019). *Raising cane: The political economy of sugar in western India*. Routledge.

Audrin, C., & Audrin, B. (2022). Key factors in digital literacy in learning and education: A systematic literature review using text mining. *Education and Information Technologies*, *27*(6), 7395–7419. DOI: 10.1007/s10639-021-10832-5

Audrin, C., & Audrin, B. (2023). More than just emotional intelligence online: Introducing "digital emotional intelligence.". *Frontiers in Psychology*, *14*. Advance online publication. DOI: 10.3389/fpsyg.2023.1154355 PMID: 37205063

Aznia, N., Utina, R., & Hamidun, M. (2022). Using jigsaw learning model to improve collaboration and communication skills of high school students on environmental change. *Jurnal Pendidikan Mipa*, *23*(4), 1610–1619. DOI: 10.23960/jpmipa/v23i4.pp1610-1619

Baker, J. O., Perry, S. L., & Whitehead, A. L. (2020, September). Crusading for moral authority: Christian nationalism and opposition to science. In *Sociological Forum* (Vol. 35, No. 3, pp. 587-607). DOI: 10.1111/socf.12619

Bamidele, A. (2021, July). Student-centered interactions within an ESL classroom using online breakout room. In *Proceedings of the AUBH E-Learning Conference*.

Bandura, A. (1971). *Social learning theory*. General Learning Press.

Bandy, J., & Diakopoulos, N. (2023). Facebook's news feed algorithm and the 2020 US election. *Social Media + Society*, *9*(3). Advance online publication. DOI: 10.1177/20563051231196898

Banerjee, A. N., & Banerjee, R. (2021). Farming: Cooperatives in India: Problems and Prospects. *Supremo Amicus*, *24*, 481.

Basilotta-Gómez-Pablos, V., Matarranz, M., Casado-Aranda, L., & Otto, A. (2022). Teachers' digital competencies in higher education: A systematic literature review. *International Journal of Educational Technology in Higher Education*, *19*(1). Advance online publication. DOI: 10.1186/s41239-021-00312-8

Bateson, G. (2002). *Mind and nature: A necessary unity*. Hampton Press.

Bavinck, H. (2013). Essays on Religion, Science, and Society. Bolt, John (Ed). Baker Academic. Chapters 9 and 10. Original work published in 1921.

Bawuro, F., Danjuma, I., & Wajiga, H. (2018). Factors influencing innovative behaviour of teachers in secondary schools in the north east of nigeria. *Path of Science*, *4*(3), 1007–1017. DOI: 10.22178/pos.32-9

Beltrán-Martín, I. (2019). Using Padlet for collaborative learning. *5th International Conference on Higher Education Advances (HEAd'19)*, 1–8. DOI: 10.4995/head19.2019.9188

Benavot, A., Hoppers, C. A. O., Lockhart, A. S., & Hinzen, H. (2022). Reimagining adult education and lifelong learning for all: Historical and critical perspectives. *International Review of Education*, *68*(2), 165–194. DOI: 10.1007/s11159-022-09955-9 PMID: 35668894

Bharti, N. (2021). Role of cooperatives in economic empowerment of women: A review of Indian experiences. *World Journal of Entrepreneurship, Management and Sustainable Development*, *17*(4), 617–631.

Bhattacharya, S., Murthy, V., & Bhattacharya, S. (2022). The social and ethical issues of online learning during the pandemic and beyond. *Asian Journal of Business Ethics*, *11*(1), 275–293. DOI: 10.1007/s13520-022-00148-z

Bicen, H., & Cavus, N. (2011). Social network sites usage habits of undergraduate students: Case study of Facebook. *Procedia: Social and Behavioral Sciences*, *28*, 943–947. DOI: 10.1016/j.sbspro.2011.11.174

Bishop, S. (2017). Understanding legitimacy: political theory and neo-Calvinist social thought, Philip D. Shadd. *Journal for Christian Scholarship= Tydskrif vir Christelike Wetenskap, 53*(1-2), 331-333. https://hdl.handle.net/10520/EJC-86a05b35a

Bishop, S. (2024). Everything Matters: Gordon Spykman-A Neo-Calvinist Theologian. *Pro Rege, 52*(3), 1-15. https://digitalcollections.dordt.edu/pro_rege/vol52/iss3/1

Bizerril, M. X. A., Arrais, A. A. M., & Silva, N. P. M. (2022). The culture of care and sense of belonging as drivers of sustainability in higher education. *Revista Tempos e Espaços em Educação*, *15*(34), 1–13. DOI: 10.20952/revtee.v15i34.18037

Boersma, H. (2017). Blessing and Glory: Abraham Kuyper on the Beatific Vision. *Calvin Theological Journal, 52*(2), 205-241. https://www.hansboersma.org/articles-1/blessing-and-glory-kuyper-beatific-vision

Bolt, J. (2004). From Princeton to Wheaton: The Course of Neo-Calvinism in North America. In *Vicissitudes of Reformed Theology in the Twentieth Century* (pp. 163-184). Brill. DOI: 10.1163/9789004389168_010

Boulos, M. N. K., Maramba, I., & Wheeler, S. (2006). Wikis, blogs and podcasts: A new generation of Web-based tools for virtual collaborative clinical practice and education. *BMC Medical Education*, *6*(1). Advance online publication. DOI: 10.1186/1472-6920-6-41 PMID: 16911779

Bowers-Campbell, J. (2008). Cyber "Pokes": Motivational antidote for developmental college readers. *Journal of College Reading and Learning*, *39*(1), 74–87. DOI: 10.1080/10790195.2008.10850313

Boyatzis, R. (2012). Neuroscience and the link between inspirational leadership and resonant relationships. *Ivey Business Journal, 76*(1), 26–28.

Braxton, J. M., Milem, J. F., & Sullivan, A. S. (2004). The influence of active learning on the college student departure process: Toward a revision of Tinto's theory. *The Journal of Higher Education, 71*(5), 569–590.

Brika, S. K. M., Chergui, K., Algamdi, A., Musa, A. A., & Zouaghi, R. (2022). E-Learning Research Trends in Higher Education in light of COVID-19: A Bibliometric analysis. *Frontiers in Psychology, 12*. Advance online publication. DOI: 10.3389/fpsyg.2021.762819

Brock, C. C., & Sutanto, N. G. (2023). *Neo-Calvinism: A theological introduction*. Lexham Academic. https://books.google.co.uk/books?hl=en&lr=&id=eLANEQAAQBAJ&oi=fnd&pg=PT5&dq=neocalvinism+sutanto&ots=Nqo55L3tK3&sig=qAVuLdxUbgowE_XI8y5-Dp_hIzM&redir_esc=y#v=onepage&q=neocalvinism%20sutanto&f=false

Brodsky, J. E., Brooks, P. J., Scimeca, D., Todorova, R., Galati, P., Batson, M., Grosso, R., Matthews, M., Miller, V. B., & Caulfield, M. P. (2021). Improving college students' fact-checking strategies through lateral reading instruction in a general education civics course. *Cognitive Research: Principles and Implications, 6*(1). Advance online publication. DOI: 10.1186/s41235-021-00291-4

Brookfield, S. D., & Preskill, S. (2005). *Discussion as a way of teaching: Tools and techniques for democratic classrooms*. Jossey-Bass.

Brooks, W. S., Deweese, J. E., & Wilson, A. B. (2024). Faith and facts: Exploring the intersection of religion and science among anatomy educators. *Anatomical Sciences Education*. Advance online publication. DOI: 10.1002/ase.2400 PMID: 38409570

Büchi, M. (2021). Digital well-being theory and research. *New Media & Society, 146144482110568*. Advance online publication. DOI: 10.1177/14614448211056851

Burgis, L., & Miller, J. (2023). *Unrepeatable: Cultivating the unique calling of every person*. Emmaus Road.

Burns, M., & Seligman, M. E. P. (1991). *Explanatory style, helplessness, and depression. Handbook of Social and Clinical Psychology*. Pergamon Press.

Burr, C., Taddeo, M., & Floridi, L. (2020). The Ethics of Digital Well-Being: A Thematic Review. *Science and Engineering Ethics, 26*(4), 2313–2343. DOI: 10.1007/s11948-020-00175-8 PMID: 31933119

Butin, D. W. (2010). *Service learning in theory and practice: The future of community engagement in higher education*. Palgrave Macmillan.

Butler, J., & Kern, M. (2016). The PERMA-Profiler: A brief multidimensional measure of flourishing. *International Journal of Wellbeing*, *6*, 1–48. DOI: 10.5502/IJW.V6I3.526

Büyükbaykal, C. I. (2015). Communication Technologies and Education in the information Age. *Procedia: Social and Behavioral Sciences*, *174*, 636–640. DOI: 10.1016/j.sbspro.2015.01.594

Canaran, O. (2023). Teacher educators' professional development through online peer-coaching. International *Journal of Curriculum and Instruction, 15(*2), 892-911. https://ijci.globets.org/index.php/IJCI/article/view/1240/623

Cannon, M. (2018). Digital media in education. In *Springer eBooks*. https://doi.org/DOI: 10.1007/978-3-319-78304-8

Cao, S., & Li, H. (2023). A scoping review of Digital Well-Being in Early Childhood: Definitions, Measurements, contributors, and Interventions. *International Journal of Environmental Research and Public Health*, *20*(4), 3510. DOI: 10.3390/ijerph20043510 PMID: 36834204

Capra, F. (1996). *The web of life: A new scientific understanding of living systems*. Anchor Books.

Capra, F. (2007). Sustainable living, ecological literacy, and breath of life. *Canadian Journal of Environmental Education*, *12*, 9–18.

Capra, F., & Luisi, P. L. (2016). *The systems view of life: A unifying vision*. Cambridge University Press.

Cardona, M. A., Rodriguez, R. J., & Ishmael, K. (2023). Artificial intelligence and the future of teaching and learning. Office of Educational Technology. https://tech.ed.gov/ai-future-of-teaching-and-learning/

Carrigan, M., & Jordan, K. (2021). Platforms and Institutions in the Post-Pandemic University: A Case Study of Social Media and the Impact Agenda. *Postdigital Science and Education*, *4*(2), 354–372. DOI: 10.1007/s42438-021-00269-x

Case, L., Harris, K., & Mamlin, N. (2001, Winter). A methodological analysis of research on locus of control and learning disabilities: Rethinking a common assumption. *The Journal of Special Education*, •••, 11–15.

Cassidy, J. (2006). *Me Media*. Retrieved from The New Yorker: https://www.newyorker.com/magazine/2006/05/15/me-media

Catanzaro, M. F. (2011). Indirect aggression, bullying and female teen victimization: A literature review. *Pastoral Care in Education, 29*(2), 83–101. DOI: 10.1080/02643944.2011.573495

Caudill, D. S. (2019). The Dutch Effect: Kuyper and Neo-Calvinism in Professor Cochran's Scholarship. *Pepp. L. Rev., 47*, 419. https://heinonline.org/HOL/LandingPage?handle=hein.journals/pepplr47&div=23&id=&page=

Cervantes, J. M., Craik, L., Kreil, D., Wiest, D., & Wong, E. (2001, Spring). Intrinsic motivation among regular, special, and alternative education high school students. *Adolescence, 5*(4).

Cham, S., Algashami, A., Aldhayan, M., McAlaney, J., Phalp, K., Almourad, M. B., & Ali, R. (2019). Digital Addiction: Negative life experiences and Potential for Technology-Assisted Solutions. In *Advances in intelligent systems and computing* (pp. 921–931). https://doi.org/DOI: 10.1007/978-3-030-16184-2_87

Chang, M. L. Y., & Lee, I. O. (2024). Functional connectivity changes in the brain of adolescents with internet addiction: A systematic literature review of imaging studies. *PLOS Mental Health*. Advance online publication. DOI: 10.1371/journal.pmen.0000022

Cheng, L. J., Fang, G., Zhang, X., Lv, Y., & Liu, L. (2022). Impact of social media use on critical thinking ability of university students. *Library Hi Tech*. Advance online publication. DOI: 10.1108/lht-11-2021-0393

Chen, P., Chavez, O., Ong, D. C., & Gunderson, B. (2017). Strategic resource use for learning: A self-administered intervention that guides self-reflection on effective resource use enhances academic performance. *Psychological Science, 28*(6), 774–785. DOI: 10.1177/0956797617696456 PMID: 28447894

Cherkowski, S. (2018). Positive teacher leadership: Building mindsets and capacities to grow wellbeing. *International Journal of Teacher Leadership, 9*(1), 63–78. https://eric.ed.gov/?id=EJ1182707

Child, J., Faulkner, D., Tallman, S., & Hsieh, L. (2019). *Cooperative strategy: Managing alliances and networks*. Oxford University Press.

Choi, J. (2018). Chapter twelve science and faith: from conflict to integration. *Christian Mind in the Emerging World: Faith Integration in Asian Contexts and Global Perspectives*, pp. 268-285.

Choi, Y. J. J. (2016). *Research on the Christian Philosophy of Education in the Netherlands: a historical approach*. Faith and Learning. DOI: 10.30806/fs.21.2.201606.231

Cilliers, E. J. (2021). Reflecting on social learning tools to enhance the Teaching-Learning Experience of Generation Z learners. *Frontiers in Education*, *5*. Advance online publication. DOI: 10.3389/feduc.2020.606533

Çimer, A., Çimer, S. O., & Vekli, G. S. (2013). How does reflection help teachers to become effective teachers. *International Journal of Educational Research*, *1*(4), 133–149. https://www.researchgate.net/publication/337992327_How_does_Reflection_Help_Teachers_to_Become_Effective_Teachers

Clausing, C. (2016). Bavinck on the Christian Life: Following Jesus in Faithful Service. *European Journal of Theology*, *25*(2). https://bavinckinstitute.org/.well-known/sgcaptcha/?r=%2F2015%2F09%2Fannouncing-bavinck-on-the-christian-life-following-jesus-in-faithful-service-by-john-bolt%2F&y=ipr:194.61.41.35:1723894769.632

Collier, P. J. (2017). Why peer mentoring is an effective approach for promoting college student success. *Metropolitan Universities*, *28*(3), 9–19. DOI: 10.18060/21539

Colliver, J. A. (2000). Effectiveness of problem-based learning curricula. *Academic Medicine*, *75*(3), 259–266. DOI: 10.1097/00001888-200003000-00017

Coman, C., Mesesan-Schmitz, L., Tiru, L. G., Grosseck, G., & Bularca, M. C. (2021). Dear student, what should I write on my wall? A case study on academic uses of Facebook and Instagram during the pandemic. *PLoS One*, *16*(9), e0257729. DOI: 10.1371/journal.pone.0257729 PMID: 34555100

Cox, T. C., & Williams, A. (2011). Virtual office hours. The professor's guide to taming technology: Leveraging digital media. *Web*, *2*, 135–150.

Cremin, T., Burnard, P., & Craft, A. (2006). Pedagogy and possibility thinking in the early years. *Thinking Skills and Creativity*, *1*(2), 108–119. DOI: 10.1016/j.tsc.2006.07.001

Crossette, N., Carr, L. D., & Wilcox, B. R. (2023). Correlations between student connectivity and academic performance: A pandemic follow-up. *Physical Review. Physics Education Research*, *19*(1). Advance online publication. DOI: 10.1103/physrevphyseducres.19.010106

Cui, T., & Wang, J. (2023). Empowering active learning: A social annotation tool for improving student engagement. *British Journal of Educational Technology*, *55*(2), 712–730. DOI: 10.1111/bjet.13403

Dafonte-Gómez, A., García-Crespo, O., & Ramahí-García, D. (2023). Using video for fact-checking on Facebook. Analysis of the trend and reach of Ibero-American production (2016-2021). *El Profesional de la Información*. Advance online publication. DOI: 10.3145/epi.2023.sep.11

Damasio, A. (2018). *The strange order of things: Life, feeling, and the making of culture*. Pantheon Books.

Dash, B. M., Prashad, L., Singh, K. K., & Dash, M. (2020). Women and poverty in india: Poverty alleviation and empowerment through cooperatives. *Social Work & Society*, *18*(2).

Davis, B. & Sumara, D. (2006). *Complexity and education.* Routledge: Taylor & Francis Group.

De Groot, T., De Haan, M., & Van Dijken, M. (2023). Learning in and about a filtered universe: Young people's awareness and control of algorithms in social media. *Learning, Media and Technology*, *48*(4), 701–713. DOI: 10.1080/17439884.2023.2253730

De Jong, M. (2015). *The Heart of the Academy: Herman Bavinck in Debate with Modernity on the Academy, Theology, and the Church. The Kuyper Center Review* (Vol. 5). Church and Academy.

de Ruyter, D., & Wolbert, L. (2020). Human flourishing as an aim of education. In *Oxford research encyclopedia of education*. DOI: 10.1093/acrefore/9780190264093.013.1418

Della Longa, L., Valori, I., & Farroni, T. (2022). Interpersonal affective touch in a virtual world: Feeling the social presence of others to overcome loneliness. *Frontiers in Psychology*, *12*. Advance online publication. DOI: 10.3389/fpsyg.2021.795283 PMID: 35087455

Dey, A. K. (2024). The CARE model: Reimagining education through an emancipatory framework that disrupts coloniality in school systems. *Canadian Journal for New Scholars in Education*, *15*(1). https://journalhosting.ucalgary.ca/index.php/cjnse/article/view/78965

Diwate, A. (2021). Growth of private medical colleges in Maharashtra and its implications for universal healthcare. *Universalising Healthcare in India: From Care to Coverage*, 83–102.

Doan, V. A. (2020). Primary students' school anxiety: An initiative study on virtual reality therapy. *VNU Journal of Science: Education Research*, *36*(4). Advance online publication. DOI: 10.25073/2588-1159/vnuer.4399

Dohmwirth, C., & Liu, Z. (2020). Does cooperative membership matter for women's empowerment? Evidence from South Indian dairy producers. *Journal of Development Effectiveness*, *12*(2), 133–150.

Du Toit-Brits, C. (2022). Exploring the importance of a sense of belonging for a sense of ownership in learning. *South African Journal of Higher Education*, *36*(5). DOI: 10.20853/36-5-4345

Duhoki, A. K. (2017). *Students usage of Facebook to enhance learning in higher education, Master's Thesis*. Near East University., https://docs.neu.edu.tr/library/6511073452.pdf

Dulany, A., Rook, R., Reister, M., & Utz, B. (2022, September). Forming the Student Experience from Start to Finish: Education Day: Enabling potential students to see themselves at our Institution of higher education. *Best Practices in Christian Higher Education Conference*, Abilene, Texas.

Dule, A., Abdu, Z., Hajure, M., Mohammedhussein, M., Girma, M., Gezimu, W., & Duguma, A. (2023). Facebook addiction and affected academic performance among Ethiopian university students: A cross-sectional study. *PLoS One*, *18*(2), e0280306. DOI: 10.1371/journal.pone.0280306 PMID: 36745630

Du, M. (2023). Research and effectiveness analysis of innovative teaching models of physical education in colleges and universities under convergent network architecture. *Applied Mathematics and Nonlinear Sciences*, *9*(1). Advance online publication. DOI: 10.2478/amns.2023.2.01099

Dung, Q. (2024). Outdoor teaching aims to enhance the positive learning attitude of 6th-grade students in biology at tuyen quang school for excellence. *International Journal of Multidisciplinary Research and Growth Evaluation*, *5*(1), 644–648. DOI: 10.54660/.ijmrge.2024.5.1.644-648

Duran, M. (2022). Legal and ethical issues in educational technology. In *Springer eBooks* (pp. 89–122). https://doi.org/DOI: 10.1007/978-3-031-18111-5_6

Dykstra, G. (1982). *Basic concepts for art curricula development in neo-calvinistic education* (Doctoral dissertation, University of British Columbia). http://hdl.handle.net/2429/23288

Dyson, B., Vickers, K., Turtle, J., Cowan, S., & Tassone, A. (2014). Evaluating the use of Facebook to increase student engagement and understanding in lecture-based classes. *Higher Education*, *69*(2), 303–313. DOI: 10.1007/s10734-014-9776-3

Ebil, S., Salleh, S. M., & Shahrill, M. (2020). Using E-portfolio for self-reflection to promote learning: A case of TVET students. *Education and Information Technologies, 25*(6), 5797–5814. DOI: 10.1007/s10639-020-10248-7

Eckert, J. (2022). *Just teaching: Feedback, engagement, and well-being for each student.* Corwin Press. https://uk.sagepub.com/en-gb/eur/just-teaching/book282609

Ehrenfeld, J. R. (2019). Flourishing: Designing a brave new world. *The Journal of Design, Economics, and Innovation, 5*(2), 105–116.

Ehrenfeld, J. R. (2020). *The right way to flourish: Reconnecting to the real world.* Routledge Press.

Ehrenfeld, J. R., & Hoffman, A. J. (2013). *Flourishing: A frank conversation about sustainability.* Stanford University Press.

Ekkekakis, P. (2012). Affect, mood, and emotion. In Tenenbaum, G., Eklund, R. C., & Kamata, A. (Eds.), *Measurement in sport and exercise psychology* (pp. 321–332). Human Kinetics., DOI: 10.5040/9781492596332.ch-028

Elbahri, M., Soliman, A., Yliniemi, K., Abdelaziz, R., Homaeigohar, S., & Zarie, E. (2018). Innovative education and active teaching with the leidenfrost nanochemistry. *Journal of Chemical Education, 95*(11), 1966–1974. DOI: 10.1021/acs.jchemed.7b00973

Elenany, Y. (2023). A proposed framework for the classification of game-based learning in construction management. *European Conference on Games Based Learning*, 17(1), 799-806. DOI: 10.34190/ecgbl.17.1.1712

El-Gayar, O., & Dennis, T. (2005). Effectiveness of hybrid learning environments. *Issues in Information Systems, 6*(1), 176–182. DOI: 10.48009/1_iis_2005_176-182

Elkhatat, A. M. (2023). Evaluating the authenticity of ChatGPT responses: A study on text-matching capabilities. *International Journal for Educational Integrity, 19*(1). Advance online publication. DOI: 10.1007/s40979-023-00137-0

Empowering mental well-being: The intersection of AI and Student Mental Health - U-M Ross Business+Tech. U. (2023, September 10).

Erdem, C., Oruç, E., Atar, C., & Bağcı, H. (2022). The mediating effect of digital literacy in the relationship between media literacy and digital citizenship. *Education and Information Technologies, 28*(5), 4875–4891. DOI: 10.1007/s10639-022-11354-4

Erdemir, N., & Yeşilçınar, S. (2021). Reflective practices in micro teaching from the perspective of preservice teachers: Teacher feedback, peer feedback and self-reflection. *Reflective Practice, 22*(6), 766–781. DOI: 10.1080/14623943.2021.1968818

Eurboonyanun, C., Petrusa, E., Eurboonyanun, K., McKinley, S. K., Phanphruk, W., Gee, D. W., & Phitayakorn, R. (2023). Relationship of high self-directed learning readiness and growth mindset among general surgery resident. *Global Surgical Education : Journal of the Association for Surgical Education*, *2*(1). Advance online publication. DOI: 10.1007/s44186-023-00115-7

Falloon, G. (2020). From digital literacy to digital competence: The teacher digital competency (TDC) framework. *Educational Technology Research and Development*, *68*(5), 2449–2472. DOI: 10.1007/s11423-020-09767-4

Ferrer, J., Ringer, A., Saville, K., Parris, M. A., & Kashi, K. (2020). Students' motivation and engagement in higher education: The importance of attitude to online learning. *Higher Education*, *83*(2), 317–338. DOI: 10.1007/s10734-020-00657-5

Firth, J., Torous, J., Stubbs, B., Firth, J. A., Steiner, G. Z., Smith, L., Alvarez-Jimenez, M., Gleeson, J., Vancampfort, D., Armitage, C. J., & Sarris, J. (2019). The "online brain": How the Internet may be changing our cognition. *World Psychiatry; Official Journal of the World Psychiatric Association (WPA)*, *18*(2), 119–129. DOI: 10.1002/wps.20617 PMID: 31059635

Fisher, J. F. (2020, March 26). *Defining personalized learning and blended learning: Is there a difference?* Education Next. https://www.educationnext.org/defining-personalized-learning-blended-learning-difference/

Fisher, J. W. (2011). The four domains model: Connecting Spirituality, Health and Well-Being. *Religions*, *2*(1), 17–28. DOI: 10.3390/rel2010017

Flanigan, A. E., Brady, A. C., Dai, Y., & Ray, E. (2023). Managing Student Digital Distraction in the College Classroom: A Self-Determination Theory Perspective. *Educational Psychology Review*, *35*(2). Advance online publication. DOI: 10.1007/s10648-023-09780-y

Forbes, R. (2021). Descriptions of learning and teaching innovations; using project-based learning to support clinical education. *Australian Journal of Clinical Education*, *9*(1). Advance online publication. DOI: 10.53300/001c.25453

Forrester, J. (2009). Thinking creatively; thinking critically. *Asian Social Science*, *4*(5). Advance online publication. DOI: 10.5539/ass.v4n5p100

Freire, P. (1970). *Pedagogy of the oppressed*. Seabury Press.

Fruehwirth, J. C., Weng, A. X., & Perreira, K. M. (2024). The effect of social media use on mental health of college students during the pandemic. *Health Economics*. Advance online publication. DOI: 10.1002/hec.4871 PMID: 38873817

Gandhi, M., Egner, C., Coyle, M. C., Mehta, B. H., McAuley, J. W., & Cline, K. M. (2023). Impact of asynchronous virtual learning on student well-being and success. *Currents in Pharmacy Teaching & Learning*, *15*(3), 266–273. DOI: 10.1016/j.cptl.2023.03.006 PMID: 37055317

Gao, Z. (2012). An arduous but hopeful journey: Implementing project-based learning in a middle school of china. *Frontiers of Education in China*, *7*(4), 608–634. DOI: 10.1007/bf03396956

Gerasimova, I., & Schevlyagin, M. (2021). How personalized learning platforms could improve social-emotional skills. In *INTED2021 Proceedings* (pp. 10033-10040). IATED.

Ghosh, J. (2021). *Informal women workers in the Global South: Policies and practices for the formalisation of women's employment in developing economies*. routledge.

Giroux, H. A. (1988). *Teachers as intellectuals: Toward a critical pedagogy of learning*. Bergin & Garvey.

Goksel, N., & Bozkurt, A. (2019). Artificial intelligence in education: Current insights and future perspectives. In Sisman-Ugur, S., & Kurubacak, G. (Eds.), *Handbook of Research on Learning in the Age of Transhumanism* (pp. 224–236). IGI Global.

Goldman, B. (2021, October 29). Addictive potential of social media, explained. *Stanford Medicine*. https://scopeblog.stanford.edu/2021/10/29/addictive-potential-of-social-media-explained/

Goleman, D. (1995). *Emotional intelligence*. Bantam Books.

González, M. R., Gasco, J., & Llopis, J. (2016). Facebook and academic performance: A positive outcome. *The Anthropologist*, *23*(1–2), 59–67. DOI: 10.1080/09720073.2016.11891924

Gordon, R. M. (2004). *The GRAM: Learned helplessness and school failure*. Retrieved July 8, 2004 from http://www.ldaca.org/gram/gordon.htm

Gouseti, A., Ilomäki, L., & Lakkala, M. (2024). Re-thinking critical digital literacies in the context of compulsory education. In *Springer eBooks* (pp. 261–281). https://doi.org/DOI: 10.1007/978-3-031-30438-5_15

Graham, C. (2012). Developing creativity across cultures. Text, 16(Special 16). DOI: 10.52086/001c.31193

Grant, D. (2024). How recognized addiction models and our relationships with digital media intersect. In Rich, G. J., Kumar, V. K., & Farley, F. H. (Eds.), *Handbook of media psychology* (pp. 233–245). Springer., DOI: 10.1007/978-3-031-56537-3_12

Greenhow, C., Graham, C. R., & Koehler, M. J. (2022). Foundations of online learning: Challenges and opportunities. *Educational Psychologist, 57*(3), 131–147. DOI: 10.1080/00461520.2022.20903644

Guilherme, A. (2019). AI and education: The importance of teacher and student relations. *AI & Society, 34*, 47–54. DOI: 10.1007/s00146-017-0693-8

Gumede, J. T. (2020). Living Educational Theory Development of a Black African (Zulu) Male Educator. *Educational Journal of Living Theories, 13*(1). https://ejolts.net/node/354

Guo, H. (2023). An innovative approach to teaching physical education integrating modern network technology. *Applied Mathematics and Nonlinear Sciences, 9*(1). Advance online publication. DOI: 10.2478/amns.2023.2.00433

Gupta, R., & Gupta, A. (2019). *Cooperative Business System of Dairy Sector in India: Role of State*. Caste and Gender.

Gusti, D. & Ratnawulan, A. (2021). Validity of student worksheetswith the theme of energy in daily life by problem based learning of integrated in 21st century learning. *International Journal of Advanced Research, 9*(02), 403–407. DOI: 10.21474/ijar01/12459

Gutberlet, J. (2021). Grassroots waste picker organizations addressing the UN sustainable development goals. *World Development, 138*, 105195.

Hachem, H., & Westberg, J. (2022). On older learners' naïveté: An examination of the emancipatory function of critical older adult education. *International Journal of Lifelong Education, 42*(1), 101–116. DOI: 10.1080/02601370.2022.2152117

Haleem, A., Javaid, M., Qadri, M. A., & Suman, R. (2022). Understanding the role of digital technologies in education: A review. *Sustainable Operations and Computers, 3*, 275–285. DOI: 10.1016/j.susoc.2022.05.004

Hällström, J. (2020). Embodying the past, designing the future: Technological determinism reconsidered in technology education. *International Journal of Technology and Design Education, 32*(1), 17–31. DOI: 10.1007/s10798-020-09600-2

Hamid, S., Waycott, J., Kurnia, S., & Chang, S. (2015). Understanding students' perceptions of the benefits of online social networking use for teaching and learning. *The Internet and Higher Education, 26*, 1–9. DOI: 10.1016/j.iheduc.2015.02.004

Hammill, J., Nguyen, T., & Henderson, F. (2023). The impact of mindfulness interventions in higher education to enhance engagement. *Journal of Further and Higher Education, 47*(5), 619–632. DOI: 10.1080/0309877x.2023.2175652

Hanipah, H., Jiea, P., Rosly, R., & Omar, S. (2019). Integrated 21st century science, technology, engineering, mathematics (stem) education through robotics project-based learning. *Humanities & Social Sciences Reviews*, *7*(2), 204–211. DOI: 10.18510/hssr.2019.7222

Han, S.-J., Nagduar, S., & Yu, H.-J. (2023). Digital addiction and related factors among college students. *Health Care*, *11*(22), 2943. DOI: 10.3390/healthcare11222943 PMID: 37998435

Harinck, G. (2014). 'We must no longer restrict our horizon to one country': Neo-Calvinism and Internationalism in the Interbellum Era. In *European Encounters* (pp. 225–245). Brill., DOI: 10.1163/9789401210775_014

Hartogsohn, I., & Vudka, A. (2022). Technology and addiction: What drugs can teach us about digital media. *Transcultural Psychiatry*, *60*(4), 651–661. DOI: 10.1177/13634615221105116 PMID: 35799499

Hasan, H., Lai, C. C., Ibrahim, I. S., Ahmad, S. A., & Meri, A. (2022). The Impact on Usage of Social Media on Academic Performance Among University Students in Sabah – A Conceptual Paper. *International Journal of Law Government and Communication*, *7*(30), 42–50. DOI: 10.35631/ijlgc.730005

Hayes, S. (2019). *A liberated mind: How to pivot toward what matters*. Avery.

Healey-Benson, F., Johnson, M. R., Adams, C., & Turville, J. (2024). What is it like for a learner to participate in a Zoom breakout room session? In *Phenomenology in Action for Researching Networked Learning* (pp. 125–152). Springer Nature Switzerland., DOI: 10.1007/978-3-031-62780-4_7

He, D. (2024). Navigating academic and everyday life challenges in the US: The role of social media for international graduate students. *Information and Learning Science*. Advance online publication. DOI: 10.1108/ILS-12-2023-0200

Herodotou, C., Sharples, M., Gaved, M., Kukulska-Hulme, A., Rienties, B., Scanlon, E., & Whitelock, D. (2019). Innovative Pedagogies of the Future: An Evidence-Based Selection. *Frontiers in Education*, *4*. Advance online publication. DOI: 10.3389/feduc.2019.00113

Hmelo-Silver, C. E. (2004). Problem-based learning: What and how do students learn? *Educational Psychology Review*, *16*(3), 235–266. DOI: 10.1023/b:edpr.0000034022.16470.f3

Holdahl, E. (2023). The Earth as an Altar: Understanding Humanity's Place and Duty in Creation through Neo-Calvinism. *Pro Rege, 51*(4), 26-31. https://digitalcollections.dordt.edu/pro_rege/vol51/iss4/4?utm_source=digitalcollections.dordt.edu%2Fpro_rege%2Fvol51%2Fiss4%2F4&utm_medium=PDF&utm_campaign=PDFCoverPages

Horton, M. (2011). *The Christian faith: A systematic theology for pilgrims on the way*. Zondervan Academic.

Huang, H., & Chueh, H. (2023). Sustained improvement of educational information asymmetry: Intentions to use school social media. *Sustainability, 15*(3), 2676. DOI: 10.3390/su15032676

Hübner, J. A. (2021). Anti-reductionist christian philosophy in the twentieth century: Owen Barfield and Neo-Calvinists. *Pro Rege., 49*(3), 25-40. https://vl.lcc.lt/object/elaba:105963484/

Hung, H., & Yuen, S. C. (2010). Educational use of social networking technology in higher education. *Teaching in Higher Education, 15*(6), 703–714. DOI: 10.1080/13562517.2010.507307

Huong, N. (2022). Innovating teaching methods at the university level: Necessity and problems issues for higher education. *Global Academic Journal of Humanities and Social Sciences, 4*(6), 207–212. DOI: 10.36348/gajhss.2022.v04i06.002

Huppert, F. A., & So, T. T. C. (2013). Flourishing across Europe: Application of a new conceptual framework for defining well-being. *Social Indicators Research, 110*(3), 837–861. DOI: 10.1007/s11205-011-9966-7

Hurt, N. E., Moss, G. S., Bradley, C. L., Larson, L. R., Lovelace, M., Prevost, L. B., & Camus, M. S. (2012). The 'Facebook'effect: College students' perceptions of online discussions in the age of social networking. *International Journal for the Scholarship of Teaching and Learning, 6*(2), 10. Advance online publication. DOI: 10.20429/ijsotl.2012.060210

Hutchison, K., Paatsch, L., & Cloonan, A. (2020). Reshaping home–school connections in the digital age: Challenges for teachers and parents. *E-Learning and Digital Media, 17*(2), 167–182. DOI: 10.1177/2042753019899527

Imaz, O., & Eizagirre, A. (2020). Responsible innovation for sustainable development goals in business: An agenda for cooperative firms. *Sustainability, 12*(17), 6948.

Immordino-Yang, M. H., & Damasio, A. (2011). We feel, therefore we learn: The relevance of affective and social neuroscience of education. *LEARNing Landscapes, 5*(1), 115–131. DOI: 10.1111/j.1751-228X.2007.00004

Immordino-Yang, M. H., & Damasio, A. (2016). We feel, therefore we learn: The relevance of affective and social neuroscience to education. In Immordino-Yang, M. H. (Ed.), *Emotions, Learning, & the Brain: Exploring the Educational Implications of Affective Neuroscience* (pp. 26–42). W.W. Norton & Company.

Irwin, C. G., Ball, L. E., Desbrow, B., & Leveritt, M. (2012). Students' perceptions of using Facebook as an interactive learning resource at university. *Australasian Journal of Educational Technology*, *28*(7). Advance online publication. DOI: 10.14742/ajet.798

Islas, O., & Bernal, J. (2016). Media Ecology: A complex and systemic meta discipline. *Philosophies*, *1*(3), 190–198. DOI: 10.3390/philosophies1030190

Jahankhani, H., Jamal, A., Brown, G., Sainidis, E., Fong, R., & Butt, U. (2023). AI, Blockchain and Self-Sovereign Identity in Higher Education. In *Advanced sciences and technologies for security applications*. https://doi.org/DOI: 10.1007/978-3-031-33627-0

Jahn, D., & Kenner, A. (2017). Critical Thinking in Higher Education: How to foster it using Digital Media. In *Springer eBooks* (pp. 81–109). https://doi.org/DOI: 10.1007/978-3-658-19925-8_7

Jalinus, N., Nabawi, R., & Mardin, A. (2017). The seven steps of project based learning model to enhance productive competences of vocational students.. DOI: 10.2991/ictvt-17.2017.43

Janicke-Bowles, S. H., Buckley, T. M., Rey, R. T., Wozniak, T., Meier, A., & Lomanowska, A. M. (2023). Digital Flourishing: Conceptualizing and assessing positive perceptions of mediated social interactions. *Journal of Happiness Studies*, *24*(3), 1013–1035. DOI: 10.1007/s10902-023-00619-5

Javeed, A. (2023). Impact of using social media on the academic performance A case of college going students in Loralai Division. *Siazga Research Journal*, *2*(1). Advance online publication. DOI: 10.58341/srj.v2i1.12

Jiang, Y., Joshi, D. R., & Khanal, J. (2024). From Clicks to Credits: Examining the influence of online engagement and internet addiction on academic performance in Chinese universities. SSRN *Electronic Journal*. DOI: 10.2139/ssrn.4886106

Jiang, Y., Liu, H., Yao, Y., Li, Q., & Li, Y. (2023). The Positive Effects of Growth Mindset on Students' Intention toward Self-Regulated Learning during the COVID-19 Pandemic: A PLS-SEM Approach. *Sustainability*, *15*(3), 2180. DOI: 10.3390/su15032180

Jong, M. D. (2019). *The Church is the Means, the World is the End: The Development of Klaas Schilder's Thought on the Relationship between the Church and the World* (Doctoral dissertation). https://theoluniv.ub.rug.nl/337/

Joustra, J. R., & Joustra, R. J. (Eds.). (2022). *Calvinism for a secular age: a twenty-first-century reading of Abraham Kuyper's Stone lectures*. InterVarsity Press. https://books.google.co.uk/books?hl=en&lr=&id=T1I2EAAAQBAJ&oi=fnd&pg=PT5&dq=calvinism+is+life+system+kuyper&ots=3kljDaY1Tj&sig=9xjCPBqcuBUF-yUYxSc5iA_Lxm8&redir_esc=y#v=onepage&q=calvinism%20is%20life%20system%20kuyper&f=false

Junco, R. (2012). The relationship between frequency of Facebook use, participation in Facebook activities, and student engagement. *Computers & Education*, *58*(1), 162–171. DOI: 10.1016/j.compedu.2011.08.004

Junco, R. (2012a). Too much face and not enough books: The relationship between multiple indices of Facebook use and academic performance. *Computers in Human Behavior*, *28*(1), 187–198. DOI: 10.1016/j.chb.2011.08.026

Junco, R. (2015). Student class standing, Facebook use, and academic performance. *Journal of Applied Developmental Psychology*, *36*, 18–29. DOI: 10.1016/j.appdev.2014.11.001

Kahraman, A. D. (2015). Relationship of modernism, postmodernism and reflections of it on education. *Procedia: Social and Behavioral Sciences*, *174*, 3991–3996. DOI: 10.1016/j.sbspro.2015.01.1146

Kandasamy, V., Hirai, A. H., Ghandour, R. M., & Kogan, M. D. (2018). Parental perception of flourishing in school-aged children: 2011–2012 National Survey of Children's Health. *Journal of Developmental and Behavioral Pediatrics*, *39*(6), 497–507. DOI: 10.1097/dbp.0000000000000559 PMID: 29521665

Kantar, N., & Bynum, T. W. (2021). Global ethics for the digital age – flourishing ethics. *Journal of Information. Communication and Ethics in Society*, *19*(3), 329–344. DOI: 10.1108/jices-01-2021-0016

Kaplan, D. (2019). Creativity in education: Teaching for creativity development. *Psychology (Irvine, Calif.)*, *10*(02), 140–147. DOI: 10.4236/psych.2019.102012

Karakose, T., Tülübaş, T., & Papadakis, S. (2022). Revealing the Intellectual Structure and evolution of Digital Addiction Research: An Integrated bibliometric and science mapping approach. *International Journal of Environmental Research and Public Health*, *19*(22), 14883. DOI: 10.3390/ijerph192214883 PMID: 36429603

Kashif, M. (2013). *Impact of facebook on students' academic performance : analysis through the social capital*. https://erepo.uef.fi/handle/123456789/12939

Kavanagh, S., Luxton-Reilly, A., Wuensche, B., & Plimmer, B. (2017). A systematic review of virtual reality in education. *Themes in Science and Technology Education*, *10*(2), 85–119. Retrieved August 11, 2024, from https://www.learntechlib.org/p/182115/

Kawai, T. (2021). A theoretical framework on reflection in service learning: Deepening Reflection through Identity Development. *Frontiers in education*, p. *5*. https://doi.org/DOI: 10.3389/feduc.2020.604997

Kayalar, F. (2021). Importance of enriched virtual learning model in hybrid teaching application. *Proceedings of IAC in Budapest*, 23-27.

Keinänen, M., & Kairisto-Mertanen, L. (2019). Researching learning environments and students' innovation competences. *Education + Training*, *61*(1), 17–30. DOI: 10.1108/et-03-2018-0064

Kemmery, M., Appenzeller, M., & Gardiner-Walsh, S. (2014, January). Creating new collaboration…One car ride at a time! *North Carolina Council for Exceptional Children*, Pinehurst, NC.

Khairnar, C. (2015). Advance pedagogy: Innovative methods of teaching and learning. *International Journal of Information and Education Technology (IJIET)*, *5*(11), 869–872. DOI: 10.7763/ijiet.2015.v5.629

Kilgour, P., Reynaud, D., Northcote, M. T., & Shields, M. (2015). Role-playing as a tool to facilitate learning, self-reflection and social awareness in teacher education. *International Journal of Innovative Interdisciplinary Research*, *2*(4), 8–20. https://www.academia.edu/81758080/Role_Playing_as_a_Tool_to_Facilitate_Learning_Self_Reflection_and_Social_Awareness_in_Teacher_Education

Kincheloe, J. L. (2008). *Critical pedagogy primer*. Peter Lang.

Kirschner, P. A., & Karpinski, A. C. (2010). Facebook® and academic performance. *Computers in Human Behavior*, *26*(6), 1237–1245. DOI: 10.1016/j.chb.2010.03.024

Kit Ng, D. T., Leung, J. K. L., Su, J., Wui Ng, R. C., & Wah Chu, S. K. (2023). Teachers' AI digital competencies and twenty-first century skills in the post-pandemic world. *Educational Technology Research and Development*, *71*, 137–161. DOI: 10.1007/s11423-023-10203-6 PMID: 36844361

Klimova, B., Pikhart, M., & Kacetl, J. (2023). Ethical issues of the use of AI-driven mobile apps for education. *Public Health, 10*. Advance online publication. DOI: 10.3389/fpubh.2022.1118116 PMID: 36711343

Klomsri, T., Grebäck, L., & Tedre, M. (2013). Social media in everyday learning: How Facebook supports informal learning among young adults in South Africa. *13th Koli Calling International Conference on Computing Education Research*, (pp. 135-144). Koli, Finland.

Kokotsaki, D., Menzies, V., & Wiggins, A. (2016). Project-based learning: A review of the literature. *Improving Schools, 19*(3), 267–277. DOI: 10.1177/1365480216659733

Kolek, E. A., & Saunders, D. (2008). Online Disclosure: An Empirical examination of undergraduate Facebook profiles. *NASPA Journal, 45*(1), 1–25. DOI: 10.2202/1949-6605.1905

Kristjánsson, K. (2016). Flourishing as the aim of education: Towards an extended, 'enchanted' Aristotelian account. *Oxford Review of Education, 42*(6), 707–720. DOI: 10.1080/03054985.2016.1226791

Kumar, M., Ingale, V. S., Kaur, A., & Bhatia, K. (2023). Consequences of brain health in the digital era. In Battineni, G., Mittal, M., & Chintalapudi, N. (Eds.), *Computational methods in psychiatry* (pp. 123–145). Springer., DOI: 10.1007/978-981-99-6637-0_6

Kumi-Yeboah, A., Kim, Y., Yankson, B., Aikins, S., & Dadson, Y. A. (2023). Diverse students' perspectives on privacy and technology integration in higher education. *British Journal of Educational Technology, 54*(6), 1671–1692. DOI: 10.1111/bjet.13386

Kümmel, E., Moskaliuk, J., Cress, U., & Kimmerle, J. (2020). Digital Learning Environments in Higher Education: A Literature Review of the Role of Individual vs Social Settings for Measuring Learning Outcomes. *Education Sciences, 10*(3), 78. DOI: 10.3390/educsci10030078

Kuyper, A. (2008). *Lectures on calvinism*. Hendrickson Publishers. Originally published in 1931. https://books.google.co.uk/books?hl=en&lr=&id=-OMa70AxqvAC&oi=fnd&pg=PR7&dq=calvinism+is+life+system+kuyper&ots=0STFPosxaS&sig=CyBGYxMaPioQam_XePep4qPX8Fs&redir_esc=y#v=onepage&q=calvinism%20is%20life%20system%20kuyper&f=false

Ladson-Billings, G. (2021). Three decades of culturally relevant, responsive, & sustaining pedagogy: What lies ahead? *The Educational Forum, 85*(4), 351–354. DOI: 10.1080/00131725.2021.1957632

Lambić, D. (2016). Correlation between Facebook use for educational purposes and academic performance of students. *Computers in Human Behavior*, *61*, 313–320. DOI: 10.1016/j.chb.2016.03.052

Lampe, C., Wohn, D. Y., Vitak, J., Ellison, N. B., & Wash, R. (2011). Student use of Facebook for organizing collaborative classroom activities. *International Journal of Computer-Supported Collaborative Learning*, *6*(3), 329–347. DOI: 10.1007/s11412-011-9115-y

Lange, E. (2009). Fostering a learning sanctuary for transformation in sustainability education. In Mezirow, J., & Taylor, E. W. (Eds.), *Transformative learning in practice: Insights from community, workplace, and higher education* (pp. 193–204). Jossey-Bass, John Wiley & Sons, Inc.

Lang, P. (1998). Towards an understanding of affective education in a European context. In P.

Larsen, E., Jensen-Clayton, C., Curtis, E., Loughland, T., & Nguyen, H. T. M. (2023, February). *Re-imaging teacher mentor for the future*. Professional Development in Education, https://www.tandfonline.com/doi/full/10.1080/19415257.2023.2178480

Lee, N. R. C., & Dioso, N. E. D. (2023). The Effects of Facebook Usage on Academics and Values of the Students. *EPRA International Journal of Environmental Economics Commerce and Educational Management*, 31–44. DOI: 10.36713/epra14012

Lee, L., Cheung, S. T., & Kwok, L. F. (2020). Learning analytics: Current trends and innovative practices. *Journal of Computers in Education*, *7*(1), 1–6. DOI: 10.1007/s40692-020-00155-8

Le, N. K., Garg, M., Izurieta, R., Garg, S. M., Papadimos, T. J., Arquilla, B., Miller, A. C., Khan, A. M., Worlton, T., & Firstenberg, M. S. (2020). International health security: A summative assessment by ACAIM consensus group. In *Contemporary Developments and Perspectives in International Health Security-Volume 1*. IntechOpen.

Li, K. C., & Wong, B. (2020). Social media in Higher Education: A Review of Their uses, benefits and Limitations. In *Communications in computer and information science*. https://doi.org/DOI: 10.1007/978-981-33-4594-2_21

Li, L., Ting-ting, Z., Liu, B., Wu, L., & Huang, H. (2021). Observation and thinking of innovative courses in colleges and universities.. DOI: 10.2991/assehr.k.210121.071

Liao, C., & Wu, J. (2022). Deploying multimodal learning analytics models to explore the impact of digital distraction and peer learning on student performance. *Computers & Education*, *190*, 104599. DOI: 10.1016/j.compedu.2022.104599

Li, L., & Pitts, J. P. (2009). Does it really matter? Using virtual office hours to enhance student-faculty interaction. *Journal of Information Systems Education*, *20*(2), 175.

Lim, Z. Y., Yap, J. H., Lai, J. W., Mokhtar, I. A., Yeo, D. J., & Cheong, K. H. (2024). Advancing Lifelong Learning in the Digital Age: A narrative review of Singapore's SkillsFuture programme. *Social Sciences*, *13*(2), 73. DOI: 10.3390/socsci13020073

Lin, Y. (2011). Fostering creativity through education – a conceptual framework of creative pedagogy. *Creative Education*, *02*(03), 149–155. DOI: 10.4236/ce.2011.23021

Liu, K. (2015). Critical reflection as a framework for transformative learning in teacher education. *Educational Review*, *67*(2), 135–157. DOI: 10.1080/00131911.2013.839546

Liu, Z. (2023). The influence of ai chatgpt on improving teachers' creative thinking. *International Journal of Learning Teaching and Educational Research*, *22*(12), 124–139. DOI: 10.26803/ijlter.22.12.7

Lock, J. V. (2015). Designing learning to engage students in the global classroom. *Technology, Pedagogy and Education*, *24*(2), 137–153.

London, M. (2011). *Lifelong Learning: Introduction*. The Oxford Handbook of Lifelong Learning., DOI: 10.1093/oxfordhb/9780195390483.013.0013

Loureiro, P., & Gomes, M. J. (2023). Online Peer Assessment for Learning: Findings from Higher Education Students. *Education Sciences*, *13*(3), 253. DOI: 10.3390/educsci13030253

Low, R. (2014). 'Fulfilling Their God-given Talents': Neo-Calvinist 'Parent-controlled' Schooling and Neo-liberal Education Policy. *Crucible, 6*(1). chrome-extension://efaidnbmnnnibpcajpcglclefindmkaj/https://www.crucibleonline.net/wp-content/uploads/2016/08/Low-Fulfilling-their-God-given-talents-Crucible-6-1-November-2014.pdf

Madge, C., Meek, J., Wellens, J., & Hooley, T. (2009). Facebook, social integration and informal learning at university: 'It is more for socialising and talking to friends about work than for actually doing work.'. *Learning, Media and Technology*, *34*(2), 141–155. DOI: 10.1080/17439880902923606

Mahanayak, B., & Panigrahi, A. K. (2021). Sustainable management of the aquatic ecosystem and the fishermen cooperative societies in India: A brief review. *Uttar Pradesh Journal of Zoology*, *42*(16), 28–35.

Mahida, D., Sendhil, R., Sirohi, S., Chandel, B., Ponnusamy, K., & Sankhala, G. (2018). Potential impact of dairy cooperatives on sustainable milk production: Evidence from Gujarat, India. *Indian Journal of Economics and Development*, *14*(1a), 402–409.

Mamuaja, M. (2023). The role of m-learning in project-based learning models in elementary schools. *IJITE*, *2*(3), 118–132. DOI: 10.62711/ijite.v2i3.131

Manasijević, D., Živković, D., Arsić, S., & Milošević, I. (2016). Exploring students' purposes of usage and educational usage of Facebook. *Computers in Human Behavior*, *60*, 441–450. DOI: 10.1016/j.chb.2016.02.087

Marciano, L., & Viswanath, K. (2023). Social media use and adolescents' well-being: A note on flourishing. *Frontiers in Psychology*, *14*. Advance online publication. DOI: 10.3389/fpsyg.2023.1092109 PMID: 37089739

Marín, V. I., Carpenter, J. P., Tur, G., & Williamson-Leadley, S. (2022). Social media and data privacy in education: An international comparative study of perceptions among pre-service teachers. *Journal of Computers in Education*. Advance online publication. DOI: 10.1007/s40692-022-00243-x

Martindale, J., Wiseman, K., Pieper, K., Nascimento, F., Aamodt, W., & Strowd, R. (2024). Social media facilitates lifelong learning for neurologists but is limited by content distrust (P5-7.004). *Neurology*, *102*(17, supplement_1). Advance online publication. DOI: 10.1212/wnl.0000000000206463

Mason, M. (2008). Complexity theory and the philosophy of education. In Mason, M. (Ed.), *Complexity Theory and the Philosophy of Education* (pp. 1–15). Wiley-Blackwell. DOI: 10.1002/9781444307351.ch1

Maturana, H. R., & Varela, F. J. (1980). *Autopoiesis and cognition: The realization of the living*. D. Reidel Publishing Company. DOI: 10.1007/978-94-009-8947-4

Mauludina, Y. S., Hoang, B. L., Wang, T., Jenq, C., Huang, C., & Huang, C. (2024). Medical students' perceptions of integrating social media into a narrative medicine programme for 5th-year clerkship in Taiwan: A descriptive qualitative study. *BMC Medical Education*, *24*(1). Advance online publication. DOI: 10.1186/s12909-024-05255-y PMID: 38500075

Mauriz, B. P., Anaya, P. B., & Bargiela, I. M. (2020). A Systematic Review on E-learning Environments for Promoting Critical Thinking in Higher Education. In *Springer eBooks* (pp. 345–362). https://doi.org/DOI: 10.1007/978-3-030-36119-8_15

Maxwell, C. (2018, October 9). *A deeper look at the flex model*. Blended Learning Universe. https://www.blendedlearning.org/a-deeper-look-at-the-flex-model/

Mayer, C. (2017). The holistic wellness model. In *Springer eBooks* (pp. 95–117). https://doi.org/DOI: 10.1007/978-3-319-59638-9_4

Mazman, S. G., & Usluel, Y. K. (2010). Modeling educational usage of Facebook. *Computers & Education, 55*(2), 444–453. DOI: 10.1016/j.compedu.2010.02.008

McKillop, D., French, D., Quinn, B., Sobiech, A. L., & Wilson, J. O. (2020). Co-operative financial institutions: A review of the literature. *International Review of Financial Analysis, 71*, 101520. PMID: 38620621

McLaren, P. (2003). *Life in schools: An introduction to critical pedagogy in the foundations of education*. Allyn & Bacon.

Meadows, D. (2008). *Thinking in systems: A primer*. Chelsea Green Publishing.

Mehedintu, A., & Soava, G. (2022). A structural framework for assessing the digital resilience of enterprises in the context of the technological revolution 4.0. *Electronics (Basel), 11*(15), 2439. DOI: 10.3390/electronics11152439

Melo, V. (2019). Emancipatory education and youth engagement in Brazil: A study bridging the theory and practice of education for social transformation. *Education Sciences, 9*(23), 1–14. https://files.eric.ed.gov/fulltext/EJ1211912.pdf

Memarian, B., & Doleck, T. (2023). Fairness, accountability, transparency, and ethics (FATE) in artificial intelligence (AI) and higher education: A systemic review. *Computers and Education: Artificial Intelligence, 5*(100152), 1–12. DOI: 10.1016/j.caeai.2023.100152

Mezirow, J. (1991). *Transformative dimensions of adult learning*. Jossey-Bass.

Miranda, P., Isaías, P., & Pífano, S. (2018). Digital literacy in higher education. In *Lecture Notes in Computer Science* (pp. 71–87). https://doi.org/DOI: 10.1007/978-3-319-91152-6_6

Mirbabaie, M., Stieglitz, S., & Marx, J. (2022). Digital Detox. *Business & Information Systems Engineering, 64*(2), 239–246. DOI: 10.1007/s12599-022-00747-x

Mirbahaeddin, E., & Chreim, S. (2024). Transcending technology boundaries and maintaining sense of community in virtual mental health peer support: A qualitative study with service providers and users. *BMC Health Services Research, 24*(1). Advance online publication. DOI: 10.1186/s12913-024-10943-y PMID: 38658968

Mitsea, E., Drigas, A., & Skianis, C. (2023). Digitally Assisted Mindfulness in Training Self-Regulation Skills for Sustainable Mental Health: A Systematic review. *Behavioral Sciences (Basel, Switzerland), 13*(12), 1008. DOI: 10.3390/bs13121008 PMID: 38131865

Moghavvemi, S., Sulaiman, A., Aziz, A. A., & Wai, P. S. (2017). *The impact of Facebook usage on academic performance. International Conference on Research and Innovation in Information Systems (ICRIIS)*, IEEE. DOI: 10.1109/icriis.2017.8002518

Montag, C., Sindermann, C., Becker, B., & Panksepp, J. (2016). An Affective Neuroscience Framework for the molecular study of Internet Addiction. *Frontiers in Psychology*, *7*. Advance online publication. DOI: 10.3389/fpsyg.2016.01906 PMID: 28018255

Montgomery, B. L. (2018). Building and sustaining diverse functioning networks using social media and digital platforms to improve diversity and inclusivity. *Frontiers in Digital Humanities*, *5*. Advance online publication. DOI: 10.3389/fdigh.2018.00022

Motz, R., Porta, M., & Reategui, E. (2023). Building resilient educational Systems: the power of digital technologies. In *Lecture notes in educational technology* (pp. 370–383). https://doi.org/DOI: 10.1007/978-981-99-7353-8_28

Mou, Q., Zhuang, J., Wu, Q., Zhong, Y., Dai, Q., Cao, X., Gao, Y., Lu, Q., & Zhao, M. (2024). Social media addiction and academic engagement as serial mediators between social anxiety and academic performance among college students. *BMC Psychology*, *12*(1). Advance online publication. DOI: 10.1186/s40359-024-01635-7 PMID: 38582933

Murphy Odo, D. (2022). An action research investigation of the impact of using online feedback videos to promote self-reflection on the microteaching of preservice EFL teachers. *Systemic Practice and Action Research*, *35*(3), 327–343. DOI: 10.1007/s11213-021-09575-8 PMID: 34248347

Murray, J. (2018). Early childhood pedagogies: Spaces for young children to flourish. In *Early Childhood Pedagogies* (pp. 1–18). Routledge., https://www.taylorfrancis.com/chapters/edit/10.4324/9781315473536-1/early-childhood-pedagogies-spaces-young-children-flourish-jane-murray

Nath, S., & Arrawatia, R. (2022). Trade-offs or synergies? Hybridity and sustainable performance of dairy cooperatives in India. *World Development*, *154*, 105862.

Naude, L., van den Bergh, T. J., & Kruger, I. S. (2014). "Learning to like learning": An appreciative inquiry into emotions in education. *Social Psychology of Education*, (17), 211–228. DOI: 10.1007/s11218-014-9247-9

Naveeenkumar, N., Rallapalli, S., Sasikala, K., Priya, P. V., Husain, J., & Boopathi, S. (2024). Enhancing Consumer Behavior and Experience Through AI-Driven Insights Optimization. In *AI Impacts in Digital Consumer Behavior* (pp. 1–35). IGI Global.

Nguyen, T. (2017). Undergraduate students' use of Facebook for educational purposes: Advantages, difficulties, and potential for connected learning, Master's thesis, University of Tampere.

Nguyen, A., Ngo, H. N., Hong, Y., Dang, B., & Thi Nguyen, B. P. (2023). Ethical principles for artificial intelligence in education. *Education and Information Technologies*, *28*, 4221–4241. DOI: 10.1007/s10639-022-11316-w PMID: 36254344

Nichols, M. (2023, April 14). Cultivating virtue in education: Insights from Socrates and Aristotle. https://www.linkedin.com/pulse/cultivating-virtue-education-insights-from- socrates-mark-nichols

Nīmante, D., Kalniņa, D., & Baranova, S. (2022). Towards an Inclusive Digital Learning Environment in Higher Education: Opportunities and Limitations Gleaned from Working Students' Remote Learning Experiences During COVID-19. In *Springer eBooks* (pp. 213–226). https://doi.org/DOI: 10.1007/978-3-031-14775-3_14

Ning, W., & Inan, F. A. (2023). Impact of social media addiction on college students' academic performance: An interdisciplinary perspective. *Journal of Research on Technology in Education*, •••, 1–16. DOI: 10.1080/15391523.2023.2196456

Nkomo, L. M., Daniel, B. K., & Butson, R. (2021). *Synthesis of student engagement with digital technologies: a systematic literature review*. PubMed., DOI: 10.1186/s41239-021-00270-1

Noble, T., & McGrath, H. (2015). PROSPER: A New Framework for Positive Education. *Psychology of Well-Being*, *5*, 2. DOI: 10.1186/s13612-015-0030-2

Nomani, A., Khan, M., Shajar, S. N., Afzal, M. A., & Salman, M. (2022). Financial crisis of Indian sugar industry: Case study of Uttar Pradesh. *Journal of Statistics and Management Systems*, *25*(5), 1303–1317.

Nosta, J. (2024). *How artificial intelligence is reshaping relationships*. Psychology Today. https://www.psychologytoday.com/us/blog/the-digital-self/202406/how-artificial-intelligence-is-reshaping-relationships

Novozhenina, A., & López Pinzón, M. M. (2018). Impact of a professional development program on EFL teachers' performance. *How, 25*(2), 113-128. DOI: 10.19183/how.25.2.406

O'Brien, C. (2010). Sustainability, happiness and education. *Journal of Sustainability Education*, *1*(1), 1–18.

O'Brien, C. (2012). Sustainable happiness and education: Educating teachers and students in the 21st Century. In Bartels, K. A., & Parker, K. A. (Eds.), *Teaching Sustainability / Teaching Sustainably* (pp. 41–52). Routledge. DOI: 10.4324/9781003447429-5

O'Brien, C. (2013). Happiness and sustainability together at last! Sustainable happiness. *Canadian Journal of Education*, *36*(4), 228–256.

Oliver, M. (2011). Technological determinism in educational technology research: Some alternative ways of thinking about the relationship between learning and technology. *Journal of Computer Assisted Learning*, *27*(5), 373–384. DOI: 10.1111/j.1365-2729.2011.00406.x

Ong, A. (2018). Neo-Calvinism and Ethnic Churches in Multiethnic Contexts. *Journal of Reformed Theology*, *12*(3), 296–320. https://brill.com/view/journals/jrt/12/3/article-p296_6.xml

Ott, C. R. (2017). *Assessing awareness, perception of importance, and intention to practice new skills in team emotional intelligence with Ohio State University Extension teams* [Master's thesis, Ohio State University]. OhioLINK Electronic Theses and Dissertations Center. https://rave.ohiolink.edu/etdc/view?acc_num=osu15119902457882

Otto, S., Bertel, L. B., Lyngdorf, N. E. R., Markman, A. O., Andersen, T. F., & Ryberg, T. (2023). Emerging Digital Practices Supporting Student-Centered Learning Environments in Higher Education: A Review of Literature and Lessons Learned from the Covid-19 Pandemic. *Education and Information Technologies*. Advance online publication. DOI: 10.1007/s10639-023-11789-3

Panesi, S., Bocconi, S., & Ferlino, L. (2020). Promoting students' well-being and inclusion in schools through digital technologies: Perceptions of students, teachers, and school leaders in Italy expressed through SELFIE piloting activities. *Frontiers in Psychology*, *11*, 1563. DOI: 10.3389/fpsyg.2020.01563 PMID: 32848988

Pappas, S. (2021). Fighting fake news in the classroom. https://www.apa.org. https://www.apa.org/monitor/2022/01/career-fake-news

París, G., & Hay, P. (2019). 5x5x5=creativity: Art as a transformative practice. *International Journal of Art & Design Education*, *39*(1), 69–84. DOI: 10.1111/jade.12229

Park, J. (2024). An examination of why smartphone use gradually leads to addiction. In *Communications in computer and information science* (pp. 394–398). https://doi.org/DOI: 10.1007/978-3-031-61963-2_40

Pasek, J., More, E., & Romer, D. (2009). Realizing the social internet? Online social networking meets offline civic engagement. *Journal of Information Technology & Politics*, *6*(3–4), 197–215. DOI: 10.1080/19331680902996403

Patterson, L. M., Carrillo, P. B., & Salinas, R. S. (2012). Lessons From a Global Learning Virtual Classroom. *Journal of Studies in International Education*, *16*(2), 182–197. DOI: 10.1177/1028315311398665

Payne, C., Plaus, V., Reister, M., Miller, J., Frezza, S., Jauregui, J., & Pilsner, J. (2023). Toward a comprehensive approach to personal vocation. *Christian Higher Education*, *22*, 3–4. DOI: 10.1080/15363759.2023.2223163

Pedrosa-de-Jesus, H., Guerra, C., & Watts, M. (2016). University teachers' self-reflection on their academic growth. *Professional Development in Education*, *43*(3), 454–473. DOI: 10.1080/19415257.2016.1194877

Pérez-Juárez, M. A., González-Ortega, D., & Aguiar-Pérez, J. M. (2023). Digital Distractions from the Point of View of Higher Education Students. *Sustainability*, *15*(7), 6044. DOI: 10.3390/su15076044

Peterson, J. B., Doidge, N., & Van Sciver, E. (2019). *12 rules for life: an antidote to chaos* [London]. Penguin Books.

Postholm, M. B. (2008). Teachers developing practice: Reflection as key activity. *Teaching and Teacher Education*, *24*(7), 1717–1728. DOI: 10.1016/j.tate.2008.02.024

Potenza, M. N. (2013). How central is dopamine to pathological gambling or gambling disorder? *Frontiers in Behavioral Neuroscience*, *7*. Advance online publication. DOI: 10.3389/fnbeh.2013.00206 PMID: 24391562

Prayogi, S. (2024). Inquiry vs. inquiry-creative: Emphasizing critical thinking skills of prospective stem teachers in the context of stem learning in indonesia. *Education Sciences*, *14*(6), 593. DOI: 10.3390/educsci14060593

Pumptow, M., & Brahm, T. (2020). Students' Digital Media Self-Efficacy and Its Importance for Higher Education Institutions: Development and Validation of a survey instrument. *Technology, Knowledge, and Learning*, *26*(3), 555–575. DOI: 10.1007/s10758-020-09463-5

Qi, C., & Yang, N. (2024). Digital resilience and technological stress in adolescents: A mixed-methods study of factors and interventions. *Education and Information Technologies*. Advance online publication. DOI: 10.1007/s10639-024-12595-1

Rabbi, M. F., SmiTa, M. K., & Mohammad, S. (2020). Using social networking sites as medium of instruction at tertiary education during COVID-19 situation in Bangladesh. *International Journal of Educational Research Review*, *5*(3), 258–264. DOI: 10.24331/ijere.741644

Rasul, T., Nair, S., Kalendra, D., Robin, M., de Oliveira Santini, F., Ladeira, W. J., Sun, M., Day, I., Rather, R. A., & Heathcote, L. (2023). The role of ChatGPT in higher education: Benefits, challenges, and future research directions. *Journal of Applied Learning & Teaching*, *6*(1), 1–16. https://journals.sfu.ca/jalt/index.php/jalt/index

Ravichandran, D. (2019). Impact of Social Networking Sites Usage on Students' Performance [IJRISS]. *International Journal of Research and Innovation in Social Science*, *3*(1). https://rsisinternational.org/journals/ijriss/Digital-Library/volume-3-issue-1/116-119.pdf

Ravisankar, A., Shanthi, A., Lavanya, S., Ramaratnam, M., Krishnamoorthy, V., & Boopathi, S. (2024). Harnessing 6G for Consumer-Centric Business Strategies Across Electronic Industries. In *AI Impacts in Digital Consumer Behavior* (pp. 241–270). IGI Global.

Reisner, P. (2019). Modernity and the Early Modern: Fifty Years of Reformation Scholarship. *The Sixteenth Century Journal*, *50*(1), 29–36. DOI: 10.1086/SCJ5001004

Reister, M. (2023). Teachable Moments: What can we learn from peer mentors and teacher workshops? *Teaching and Teacher Education*, *135*. Advance online publication. DOI: 10.1016/j.tate.2023.104330

Reister, M., & Rook, R. (2021). Perceptions of preparedness for online teaching due to the COVID-19 pandemic as a graduate of an education program at a university in the Midwest. *Journal of Digital Learning in Teacher Education*. Advance online publication. DOI: 10.1080/21532974.2021.1908920

Rhoades, E., Irani, T., Telg, R., & Myers, B. E. (2008). Internet as an informal source: Attitudes, and usage of students enrolled in a college agriculture course. *Journal of Agricultural Education*, *49*(2), 108–117. https://jae-online.org/index.php/jae/article/view/922/767

Rikowski, G., & McLaren, P. (2002). Postmodernism in educational theory. *Marxism against postmodernism in educational theory*, 3-13. https://www.researchgate.net/publication/344154923_Postmodernism_in_Educational_Theory_Education_and_the_Politics_of_Human_Resistance

Riva, G., Baños, R. M., Botella, C., Wiederhold, B. K., & Gaggioli, A. (2012). Positive technology: Using interactive technologies to promote positive functioning. *Cyberpsychology, Behavior, and Social Networking*, *15*(2), 69–77. DOI: 10.1089/cyber.2011.0139

Robinson, S., & Moraes-Robinson, M. (2017). *Customer experiences with soul: A new era in design*. Holonomics Publishing.

Roche, S. (2018). The contribution of lifelong learning to development – personal and communal. *International Review of Education*, *64*(1), 1–7. DOI: 10.1007/s11159-018-9706-1

Rosenberg, J. M., Borchers, C., Stegenga, S. M., Burchfield, M. A., Anderson, D., & Fischer, C. (2022). How educational institutions reveal students' personally identifiable information on Facebook. *Learning, Media and Technology*, *49*(3), 339–355. DOI: 10.1080/17439884.2022.2140672

Roth, D. (2021). Neo-Calvinism for the Nations: Reviewing Part 2 & 3 of Reformed Public Theology. https://digitalcollections.dordt.edu/faculty_work/1356/

Rötzel, P. (2018). Information overload in the information age: A literature review from business administration, business psychology, and related disciplines with a bibliometric approach and framework development. *Business Research*, *12*(2), 479–522. DOI: 10.1007/s40685-018-0069-z

Rouis, S., Limayem, M., & Salehi-Sangari, E. (2017). Impact of Facebook usage on students' academic achievement: Roles of Self-Regulation and Trust. *Electronic Journal of Research in Educational Psychology*, *9*(25), 961–994. DOI: 10.25115/ejrep.v9i25.1465

Ruggeri, K., Garcia-Garzon, E., Maguire, Á., Matz, S., & Huppert, F. A. (2020). Well-being is more than happiness and life satisfaction: A multidimensional analysis of 21 countries. *Health and Quality of Life Outcomes*, *18*(1). Advance online publication. DOI: 10.1186/s12955-020-01423-y PMID: 32560725

Rusk, R. D., & Waters, L. (2015). A psycho-social system approach to well-being: Empirically deriving the five domains of positive functioning. *The Journal of Positive Psychology*, *10*(2), 141–152. DOI: 10.1080/17439760.2014.920409

Saaida, M. B. (2023). AI-driven transformations in higher education: Opportunities and challenges. *International Journal of Educational Research and Studies*, *5*(1), 29–36. DOI: 10.5281/zenodo.8164414

Sadoughi, M., Hejazi, S. Y., & Lou, N. M. (2022). How do growth mindsets contribute to academic engagement in L2 classes? The mediating and moderating roles of the L2 motivational self-system. *Social Psychology of Education*, *26*(1), 241–261. DOI: 10.1007/s11218-022-09744-0

Safaei, N., & Shahrokhi, M. (2019). Relationship between teacher self-disclosure and teaching style: Perception of EFL teachers. *Cogent Education*, *6*(1), 1678231. DOI: 10.1080/2331186x.2019.1678231

Sahoo, A. K., Meher, S. K., Panda, T. C., Sahu, S., Begum, R., & Barik, N. (2020). Critical review on cooperative societies in agricultural development in India. *Current Journal of Applied Science and Technology*, *39*(22), 114–121.

Salkeld, B. (2023). *Educating for eternity: A teacher's companion for making every class Catholic*. Our Sunday Visitor.

Samad, S., Nilashi, M., & Ibrahim, O. (2019). The impact of social networking sites on students' social wellbeing and academic performance. *Education and Information Technologies*, *24*(3), 2081–2094. DOI: 10.1007/s10639-019-09867-6

Schäfer, S. K., Von Boros, L., Schaubruch, L. M., Kunzler, A. M., Lindner, S., Koehler, F., Werner, T., Zappalà, F., Helmreich, I., Wessa, M., Lieb, K., & Tüscher, O. (2024). Digital interventions to promote psychological resilience: A systematic review and meta-analysis. *NPJ Digital Medicine*, *7*(1). Advance online publication. DOI: 10.1038/s41746-024-01017-8 PMID: 38332030

Schoneveld, G. C. (2020). Sustainable business models for inclusive growth: Towards a conceptual foundation of inclusive business. *Journal of Cleaner Production*, *277*, 124062.

Schroeder, R. (2002). Social interaction in virtual environments: key issues, common themes, and a framework for research. In *Springer eBooks* (pp. 1–18). https://doi.org/DOI: 10.1007/978-1-4471-0277-9_1

Schutz, P. A., Hong, J., Cross, D. I., & Osbon, J. N. (2006). Reflections on investigating emotion in educational activity settings. *Educational Psychology Review*, *18*, 343–360. DOI: 10.1007/s10648-006-9030-3

Scott, D. A., Valley, B., & Simecka, B. A. (2016). Mental health concerns in the digital age. *International Journal of Mental Health and Addiction*, *15*(3), 604–613. DOI: 10.1007/s11469-016-9684-0

Seligman, M. E. P. (2011). *Flourish: A visionary new understanding of happiness and well-being*. Atria Books.

Selwyn, N. (2009). Faceworking: Exploring students' education-related use of Facebook. *Learning, Media and Technology*, *34*(2), 157–174. DOI: 10.1080/17439880902923622

Sensoy, Ö., & Diangelo, R. J. (2014). Respect differences? Challenging the common guidelines in social justice education. *Democracy & Education*, *22*, 1.

Shafiq, M., & Parveen, K. (2023). Social media usage: Analyzing its effect on academic performance and engagement of higher education students. *International Journal of Educational Development*, *98*, 102738. DOI: 10.1016/j.ijedudev.2023.102738

Shahid, A., Awan, M. Z., Siddique, W., Nadeem, H. T., & Chaudhary, M. (2020). Negative Impact on Academic Performance, Anxiety and Insomnia Due to Excessive Use of Social Media among University Students of Lahore (Pakistan). *International Journal of Scientific and Engineering Research*, *11*(9).

Shahzad, M. F., Xu, S., Lim, W. M., Yang, X., & Khan, Q. R. (2024). Artificial intelligence and social media on academic performance and mental well-being: Student perceptions of positive impact in the age of smart learning. *Heliyon*, *10*(8). Advance online publication. DOI: 10.1016/j.heliyon.2024.e29523 PMID: 38665566

Shams, M., Shahid, R., & Raza, S. Y. (2022). Social Media and University Students: Trends and Effects Studies. *Pakistan Journal of Social Research*, *4*(04), 763–772. https://pjsr.com.pk/wp-content/uploads/2022/12/81.-Vol.-4-No.-4-December-2022-Shams-Shahid-Raza-Social-Media-and-University-Students-Trends-and-Effects-Studies.pdf

Simonsmeier, B. A., Peiffer, H., Flaig, M., & Schneider, M. (2020). Peer feedback improves students' academic Self-Concept in higher education. *Research in Higher Education*, *61*(6), 706–724. DOI: 10.1007/s11162-020-09591-y

SINGH, S., GAUTAM, R. S., AGARWAL, B., PUSHP, A., BARGE, P., & RASTOGI, S. (2022). Impacts of financial inclusion on sustainable development in India. *The Journal of Asian Finance, Economics and Business*, *9*(10), 235–242.

Singh, U. K. (2024). Implementation Of Sustainable Development Goals In India: Progress And Challenges. *Regional Dimensions of Human Development in India and South Africa: Through Sustainable Development Goals*, 39–91.

Skaff, J. (2015). Common Grace and the Ends of Creation in Abraham Kuyper and Herman Bavinck. *Journal of Reformed Theology*, *9*(1), 3–18. DOI: 10.1163/15697312-00901003

Slater, M., & Sanchez-Vives, M. V. (2016). Enhancing our lives with immersive virtual reality. *Frontiers in Robotics and AI*, *3*, 74. DOI: 10.3389/frobt.2016.00074

Slepcevic-Zach, P., & Stock, M. (2018). ePortfolio as a tool for reflection and self-reflection. *Reflective Practice*, *19*(3), 291–307. DOI: 10.1080/14623943.2018.1437399

Small, G. W., Lee, J., Kaufman, A., Jalil, J., Siddarth, P., Gaddipati, H., Moody, T. D., & Bookheimer, S. Y. (2020). Brain health consequences of digital technology use. *Dialogues in Clinical Neuroscience*, *22*(2), 179–187. DOI: 10.31887/dcns.2020.22.2/gsmall PMID: 32699518

Solomon, P. (2023). Can cooperatives be a tool for poverty reduction? Social capital perspectives of fisher's cooperatives in India. *Marine Policy*, *147*, 105373.

Spendlove, Z., & Best, R. (2018). Innovation in assessment: Building student confidence in preparation for unfamiliar assessment methods. *British Journal of Midwifery*, *26*(3), 180–184. DOI: 10.12968/bjom.2018.26.3.180

TEFĂNICĂ. S. I. (2014). The Impact of Facebook on University-Students Relationships. *Management Dynamics in the Knowledge Economy, 2*(3), 492. Retrieved from https://www.managementdynamics.ro/index.php/journal/article/view/72

Sternberg, R. J. (1997). The concept of intelligence and its role in lifelong learning and success. *The American Psychologist*, *52*(10), 1030–1037. DOI: 10.1037/0003-066x.52.10.1030 PMID: 9329294

Sturm, J. C. (2006). Education between indoctrination and emancipation. *Religious Education (Chicago, Ill.)*, *88*(1), 40–51. DOI: 10.1080/0034408930880104

Sturm, J., & Groenendijk, L. (1998). Gender Education and the Transformation of Calvinism in the Netherlands, 1870-1970. *Journal of Beliefs & Values*, *19*(1), 83–96. DOI: 10.1080/1361767980190107

Subramanian, D., & Kelly, P. (2018). Effects of introducing innovative teaching methods in engineering classes: A case study on classes in an indian university. *Computer Applications in Engineering Education*, *27*(1), 183–193. DOI: 10.1002/cae.22067

Summerville, J., & Johnson, C. S. (2006). Rural creativity: A Study of District Mandated Online Professional Development. *Journal of Technology and Teacher Education*, *14*(2), 347–361.

Sutanto, N. G. (2015). Neo-Calvinism and the French Revolution. James Eglinton and George Harinck (Eds). DOI: 10.1093/jts/flv082

Sutanto, N. G. (2018). Organic knowing: the theological epistemology of Herman Bavinck. https://era.ed.ac.uk/handle/1842/31241

Tanana, S. (2022). Innovative format of organization teaching of foreign languages in the professional preparation of future teachers-philologists. *European Humanities Studies State and Society*, (2), 138–150. DOI: 10.38014/ehs-ss.2022.2.08

Tananuraksakul, N. (2015). An Investigation into the Impact of Facebook Group Usage on Students' Affect in Language Learning in a Thai Context. *International Journal on Teaching and Learning in Higher Education*, *27*(2), 235–246. https://files.eric.ed.gov/fulltext/EJ1082882.pdf

Tang, J. K. T., Yau, H., Wong, S., & Wong, S. (2015). The impacts on learning via social media: A study on post-secondary students in Hong Kong. In *Communications in computer and information science* (pp. 195–208). DOI: 10.1007/978-3-662-48978-9_19

Taylor, D. M. (1999). Education in the neo-Calvinist Reformed Christian tradition, the meaning of a religious worldview and philosophy for the practice of education. https://mspace.lib.umanitoba.ca/handle/1993/2327

Taylor, S. E. (2007). Social support. In Friedman, H. S., & Silver, R. C. (Eds.), *Foundations of health psychology* (pp. 145–171). Oxford University Press.

Tereshchenko, S. Y. (2023). Neurobiological risk factors for problematic social media use as a specific form of Internet addiction: A narrative review. *World Journal of Psychiatry*, *13*(5), 160–173. DOI: 10.5498/wjp.v13.i5.160 PMID: 37303928

Thakur, A. (2018). Assessment of status of the fishery cooperatives, SHGs and fishermen groups in Baster district of Chhattisgarh: A review. *Journal of Pharmacognosy and Phytochemistry*, *7*(3), 1748–1754.

Thwe, W. P., & Kálmán, A. (2023). Lifelong Learning in the Educational Setting: A Systematic Literature Review. *The Asia-Pacific Education Researcher*. Advance online publication. DOI: 10.1007/s40299-023-00738-w

Tila, D. (2023). Open pedagogy, renewable assignments, and course content creation in economics. *Creative Education*, *14*(12), 2394–2404. DOI: 10.4236/ce.2023.1412153

Timotheou, S., Miliou, O., Dimitriadis, Y., Sobrino, S. V., Giannoutsou, N., Cachia, R., Martínez-Monés, A., & Ioannou, A. (2022). Impacts of digital technologies on education and factors influencing schools' digital capacity and transformation: A literature review. *Education and Information Technologies*, *28*(6), 6695–6726. DOI: 10.1007/s10639-022-11431-8

Tinto, V. (1993). *Leaving college: Rethinking the causes and cures of student attrition* (2nd ed.). University of Chicago Press.

Tinto, V. (1997). Classrooms as communities: Exploring the educational character of student persistence. *The Journal of Higher Education*, *68*(6), 599–623.

Toker, S., & Baturay, M. H. (2019). What foresees college students' tendency to use facebook for diverse educational purposes? *International Journal of Educational Technology in Higher Education*, *16*(1). Advance online publication. DOI: 10.1186/s41239-019-0139-0

Tran-Duong, Q. H. (2022). The effect of media literacy on effective learning outcomes in online learning. *Education and Information Technologies*, *28*(3), 3605–3624. DOI: 10.1007/s10639-022-11313-z

Trivedi, P., Ravisankar, A., Kumar, G. P., Krishnamoorthy, V., Shukla, S., & Boopathi, S. (2024). Finance and Technology-Integrated Digital Economy: Circular Age of a Sustainable Digital Revolution. In *Navigating the Circular Age of a Sustainable Digital Revolution* (pp. 91–120). IGI Global. DOI: 10.4018/979-8-3693-2827-9.ch004

Tseng, S. K. (2022). Emerging Neo-Calvinistic Barth Interpretation in Sinophone Scholarship: Its Significance for Sino-Christian Theology. *Journal of Chinese Theology, 1*(aop), 1-23. https://brill.com/view/journals/jct/10/1/article-p97_5.xml

Turnbull, D., Chugh, R., & Luck, J. (2020). Learning management systems, an overview. *Encyclopedia of education and information technologies*, 1052-1058. DOI: 10.1007/978-3-030-10576-1_248

Ulrich, D. (1998) *A New Mandate for Human Resources*. Harvard Business Review. https://hbr.org/1998/01/a-new-mandate-for-human-resources

Ursavaş, Ö. F. (2022). Unified Theory of Acceptance and Use of Technology Model (UTAUT). In *Springer eBooks* (pp. 111–133). https://doi.org/DOI: 10.1007/978-3-031-10846-4_6

Vacca, R. T., Vacca, J. A. L., & Mraz, M. (2014). *Content area reading: Literacy and learning across the curriculum* (11th ed.). Pearson.

Valdez, J. P. M., & Datu, J. a. D. (2023). Does Facebook intensity matter for academic self-efficacy? A path analytic approach. *Research and Practice in Technology Enhanced Learning, 18*, 026. DOI: 10.58459/rptel.2023.18026

Valkenburg, P. M. (2022). Social media use and well-being: What we know and need to know. *Current Opinion in Psychology*, *45*, 101294. DOI: 10.1016/j.copsyc.2021.12.006 PMID: 35016087

Valle, A., Rodríguez, S., Cabanch, R.G., Núnez, J.C., & González-Pienda, J.A. and Rosario, & P. (2009). Academic goals: Historical and conceptual perspectives and educational implications. *Electronic Journal of Research in Educational Psychology*, *7*(3), 1073–1106.

Van der Kooi, C. (2021). The Relevance of Neo-Calvinism for Church and Theology. *European Journal of Theology*, *30*(2). Advance online publication. DOI: 10.5117/EJT2021.2.004.KOOI

Van der Kroef, J. M. (2009). Abraham Kuyper and the rise of neo-Calvinism in the Netherlands. *Church History, 17*(4), 316-334. Originally published in 1948. DOI: 10.2307/3160320

Van Huan, D., Tuyet, N. T. B., Dung, T. M., Ha, V. T., & Duc, T. D. (2024). The influence of Facebook intensity on life satisfaction and academic performance of college students during COVID-19 pandemic. *Journal of Affective Disorders Reports*, *16*, 100782. DOI: 10.1016/j.jadr.2024.100782

Van Zyl, L. E., & Stander, M. W. (2019). Flourishing Interventions 2.0: A Practical Guide to Student Development. In Van Zyl, L., & Rothmann, S.Sr., (Eds.), *Positive Psychological Intervention Design and Protocols for Multi-Cultural Contexts*. Springer., DOI: 10.1007/978-3-030-20020-6_20

VanderVliet, C. F. (2020). Negotiating a Gendered Neo-Calvinist Pillar: Immigrant Loss, Transformation, and Lifelong Learning. http://hdl.handle.net/10464/14613 accessed July 11, 2024.

VanderWeele, T. J. (2017). On the promotion of human flourishing. *Proceedings of the National Academy of Sciences of the United States of America*, *114*(31), 8148–8156. DOI: 10.1073/pnas.1702996114 PMID: 28705870

Vanderwoerd, J. R. (2015). All things new: Neo-Calvinist groundings for social work. *Social Work & Christianity*, *42*(2), 121. Retrieved August 15, 2024, from https://www.researchgate.net/publication/301553141_All_Things_New_Neo-Calvinist_Groundings_for_Social_Work

Vanhoozer, K.J. (2003). Scripture and Tradition in Modernity: From Reformation to Enlightenment. *The Cambridge Companion to Postmodern Theology*, 149.

Vanides, J. (2007). Online professional development that works. *Learning and Leading with Technology*, *34*(8), 10–14.

Vardi, M. Y. (2024). More is different, in social media too. *Communications of the ACM*, *67*(5), 5. DOI: 10.1145/3653683

Vargas-Nieto, J., Zambrano, D., Montcrio, I., & Sanabria, L. M. (2024). Efficacy of Digital Mindfulness-Based Interventions for Repetitive Negative Thinking: A Systematic review and Bibliometric analysis. *Mindfulness, 15*(3), 523–538. DOI: 10.1007/s12671-024-02321-w

Vass, V. (2024). The coherence between innovative teaching methods and formative assessment in higher education. *International Journal of Advanced Corporate Learning (Ijac), 17*(3), 108–116. DOI: 10.3991/ijac.v17i3.45657

Vaughan, M. (2019). Learning who I am: The exploration of my guiding values through a Living Theory methodology. *Educational Journal of Living Theories,* vol. 12 issue 1, pp. 62-80. https://ejolts.net/node/336

Vedechkina, M., & Borgonovi, F. (2021). A review of evidence on digital technology's role in shaping children's attention and cognitive control. *Frontiers in Psychology, 12*. Advance online publication. DOI: 10.3389/fpsyg.2021.611155

Villamil, A., & Heshmati, S. (2023). Engaging in the good with technology: A framework for examining positive technology use. *Frontiers in Psychology, 14*, 1175740–1175740. DOI: 10.3389/fpsyg.2023.1175740

Vimbelo, S. (2023). Current pedagogical practices employed by technical vocational education and training college's mathematics lecturers. *South African Journal of Higher Education, 37*(4). Advance online publication. DOI: 10.20853/37-4-5292

Vishwakarma, M. M. (2019). E-commerce: Emerging trend for business management education. *Challenges and Opportunities in Social Sciences, Humanities and Business Management, 114*.

Volk, T., & Bloom, J. W. (2007). The use of metapatterns for research into complex systems of teaching, learning, and schooling, Part II: Applications. *Complicity: An International Journal of Complexity and Education, 4*(1), 45–68. http://ejournals.library.ualberta.ca/index.php/complicity/issue/archive

Vrieling-Teunter, E., Henderikx, M., Nadolski, R., & Kreijns, K. (2022). Facilitating peer interaction Regulation in online settings: The role of social presence, social space and sociability. *Frontiers in Psychology, 13*. Advance online publication. DOI: 10.3389/fpsyg.2022.793798

Wahl, K. (2020). Defying gravity: An affective photovoice lens on transformative sustainability learning. (Publication No. 28156446). [Doctoral Dissertation, UW-Stevens Point, WI]. ProQuest Dissertations & Theses Global.

Wang, G., Simkute, D., & Griskova-Bulanova, I. (2023). Neurobiological Link between Stress and Gaming: A Scoping Review. *Journal of Clinical Medicine*, *12*(9), 3113. DOI: 10.3390/jcm12093113 PMID: 37176554

Wang, Q., Woo, H. L., Quek, C. L., Yang, Y., & Liu, M. (2011). Using the Facebook group as a learning management system: An exploratory study. *British Journal of Educational Technology*, *43*(3), 428–438. DOI: 10.1111/j.1467-8535.2011.01195.x

Wanyama, T., & Singh, I. (2015). Laboratory based project for experiential learning in plc systems integration and plc systems data access. *Proceedings of the Canadian Engineering Education Association (Ceea)*. DOI: 10.24908/pceea.v0i0.5866

Wehmeyer, M. L., Little, T. D., & Sergeant, J. (2009). Self-determination. In Lopez, S. J., & Snyder, C. R. (Eds.), *Oxford handbook of positive psychology* (2nd ed., pp. 357–366). Oxford University Press.

Weller, M.J. (2011). The digital scholar: How technology is changing academic practice.

Whitehead, J. (2008) Using a living theory methodology in improving practice and generating educational knowledge in living theories. Educational Journal of Living Theories. Vol 1. Issue 1. pp. 103-126. https://ejolts.net/node/80

Whitehead, J., & Huxtable, M. (2024). *Living Educational Theory Research as an epistemology for practice: the role of values in practitioners' professional development*. Taylor & Francis. DOI: 10.4324/9781003429074

Widhalm, B. (2011). Nature as guide for vibrant learning – a living systems framework for academic learning experience design toward a thriving sustainable world. (Publication No. 3489705) [Doctoral Dissertation, California Institute of Integral Studies, CA]. ProQuest Dissertations & Theses Global.

Widhalm, B. (2013). Teaching living systems awareness as a change agent skill for a vibrant sustainable world. In *Proceedings of the 56th Annual Meeting of the ISSS-2012, San Jose, CA, USA*. https://journals.isss.org/index.php/proceedings56th/article/view/1852

Widiastuti, I. (2023). Implementing problem-based learning to develop students' critical and creative thinking skills. [Jurnal Pendidikan Indonesia]. *Jpi*, *12*(4), 658–667. DOI: 10.23887/jpiundiksha.v12i4.63588

Willems, J., & Bateman, D. (2011). The potentials and pitfalls of social networking sites such as Facebook in higher education contexts. In G. Williams, P. Statham, N. Brown, & B. Cleland, *Changing Demands, Changing Directions* (pp. 1329-1331). Proceedings ascilite. Retrieved from http://www.ascilite.org.au/conferences/hobart11/procs/Willems-poster.pdf

Willson, C. B. (2016). *Poetics of everyday work: A neo-Calvinist approach to vocational discipleship in local churches*. Fuller Theological Seminary, Center for Advanced Theological Study. https://www.proquest.com/openview/0f653db331773c65a8004754940f4129/1?pq-origsite=gscholar&cbl=18750

Wise, L., Skues, J., & Williams, B. (2011). Facebook in higher education promotes social but not academic engagement. In G. Williams, P. Statham, N. Brown, & B. Cleland, *Changing Demands, Changing Directions* (pp. 1332-1342). Proceedings ascilite Hobart 2011. Retrieved from http://www.ascilite.org.au/conferences/hobart11/downloads/papers/Wise-full.pdf

Wohn, D. Y., & LaRose, R. (2014). Effects of loneliness and differential usage of Facebook on college adjustment of first-year students. *Computers & Education*, *76*, 158–167. DOI: 10.1016/j.compedu.2014.03.018

Wolbert, L., & Ünlüsoy, A. (2023). Creating authentic connectedness online through a shared experience of 'not-knowing.'. *Ethics and Education*, *18*(1), 110–122. DOI: 10.1080/17449642.2023.2188725

Xu, R., Li, J., & Zou, Y. (2017). Research on the innovation of teaching method and the cultivation of innovative undertaking talents in colleges.. DOI: 10.2991/icemc-17.2017.176

Xu, J., Khanotia, A., Juni, S., Ku, J., Sami, H., Lin, V., Walterson, R., Payne, E., Jo, H., & Rahimpoor-Marnani, P. (2024). Effectiveness of virtual reality-based well-being interventions for stress reduction in young adults: Systematic Review. *JMIR Mental Health*, *11*, e52186. DOI: 10.2196/52186 PMID: 38551625

Yang, D. (2017). Instructional strategies and course design for teaching statistics online: Perspectives from online students. *International Journal of STEM Education*, *4*(1). Advance online publication. DOI: 10.1186/s40594-017-0096-x

Yuan, C., He, Y., Lin, R., & Tang, Y. (2021). Graph embedding for scholar recommendation in academic social networks. *Frontiers in Physics*, *9*. Advance online publication. DOI: 10.3389/fphy.2021.768006

Yue, M., Jong, M. S. Y., & Kit, Nj. D. T. (2024). Understanding K-12 teachers' technological pedagogical content knowledge readiness and attitudes toward artificial intelligence education. *Education and Information Technologies*. Advance online publication. DOI: 10.1007/s10639-024-12621-2

Zahid, M., & Khanam, A. (2019). Effect of reflective teaching practices on the performance of prospective teachers. *Turkish Online Journal of Educational Technology-TOJET, 18*(1), 32-43. https://eric.ed.gov/?id=EJ1201647

Zalat, M. M., Hamed, M., & Bolbol, S. A. (2021). The experiences, challenges, and acceptance of e-learning as a tool for teaching during the COVID-19 pandemic among university medical staff. *PLoS One*, *16*(3), e0248758. DOI: 10.1371/journal.pone.0248758

Zarate, D., Stavropoulos, V., Ball, M., De Sena Collier, G., & Jacobson, N. C. (2022). Exploring the digital footprint of depression: A PRISMA systematic literature review of the empirical evidence. *BMC Psychiatry*, *22*(1). Advance online publication. DOI: 10.1186/s12888-022-04013-y PMID: 35733121

Zavala, J., Trenz, R. C., Tzanis, D., Malette, C., & Marin, N. M. (2023). The impact of social media use for news on academic performance in underrepresented undergraduate college students. *Cyberpsychology, Behavior, and Social Networking*, *26*(8), 657–661. DOI: 10.1089/cyber.2022.0303 PMID: 37327047

Zhang, Q., & Yu, Z. (2021). A literature review on the influence of Kahoot! On learning outcomes, interaction, and collaboration. *Education and Information Technologies*, *26*(4), 4507–4535. DOI: 10.1007/s10639-021-10459-6

Zhang, S., Sun, Z., Ma, W., & Valentinov, V. (2020). The effect of cooperative membership on agricultural technology adoption in Sichuan, China. *China Economic Review*, *62*, 101334.

Zhou, S., Lin, L., Shu, Y., & Xiong, N. (2020). The construction and practice of computer network course driven by innovative thinking. Matec Web of Conferences, 309, 05017. DOI: 10.1051/matecconf/202030905017

Zhou, Y., Meng, X., Wang, J., Mo, X., Jiang, S., Dai, C., & Liu, M. (2023). Daily Peer Relationships and Academic Achievement among College Students: A Social Network Analysis Based on Behavioral Big Data. *Sustainability*, *15*(22), 15762. DOI: 10.3390/su152215762

Ziquan, Y., Zhang, Y., Jiang, B., Jun, F., & Ying, J. (2022). A review on fault-tolerant cooperative control of multiple unmanned aerial vehicles. *Chinese Journal of Aeronautics*, *35*(1), 1–18.

Zulkifli, H., Tamuri, A. H., & Azman, N. A. (2022). Understanding creative teaching in twenty-first century learning among Islamic education teachers during the COVID-19 pandemic. *Frontiers in Psychology, 13*. Advance online publication. DOI: 10.3389/fpsyg.2022.920859

Zuo, Z., Han, Q.-L., Ning, B., Ge, X., & Zhang, X.-M. (2018). An overview of recent advances in fixed-time cooperative control of multiagent systems. *IEEE Transactions on Industrial Informatics, 14*(6), 2322–2334.

About the Contributors

Raymond Aaron Younis was educated at the University of Oxford and the University of Sydney. He has held professorial positions at three universities in Sydney, Australia. He is the recipient of several teaching and learning awards and commendations for excellence, and has published over one hundred papers in philosophy, ethics, media and cultural studies, in books, journals and refereed online collections. He is also an experienced wine consultant (in Oxford and Sydney).

***

Sabbir Ahmed is currently pursuing the Master of Science in educational technology and Engineering (EdTE) at the University of Frontier Technology, Bangladesh. His role as a Research Assistant in a University Grant Commission (UGC) funded project showcased his dedication and expertise. He is familiar with educational topics like instructional design and technology-enhanced learning (TEL), as well as various programming languages, including C, Python, TensorFlow, PyTorch, MATLAB, and Java. His research interests include educational technology, learning design, deep learning, deep reinforcement learning, human activity recognition, medical imaging, federated learning, and natural language processing. His commitment to academic excellence, as evidenced by his inclusion in the prestigious Deans List, is truly mentionable.

Liz Allgood is a Senior Instructional Designer in the Center for Excellence in Teaching and Learning at Franciscan University of Steubenville. With a deep commitment to the advancement of education through thoughtful design and innovation, Liz has played a pivotal role in supporting faculty development and enhancing student learning experiences across diverse disciplines. She earned her Master of Education degree from Kent State University in May 2014, where she focused on educational technology. Since joining Franciscan University in

August 2016, Liz has contributed significantly to the university's mission by integrating pedagogical best practices with cutting-edge learning tools, fostering academic excellence rooted in the Catholic intellectual tradition. Passionate about learner-centered design, Liz brings both strategic vision and practical insight to the evolving landscape of higher education. Her work continues to influence teaching methodologies and course development at Franciscan and beyond.

Md. Ashrafuzzaman is an Assistant Professor in the Department of Educational Technology and Engineering (EdTE) at the University of Frontier Technology, Bangladesh. Previously, he worked as a Research Coordinator in the EIA-DU-OU (UK) Research Collaboration Programme at the Institute of Education and Research (IER), University of Dhaka (DU). He has completed his BEd (Hons), MEd, and MPhil from IER, DU. He has fourteen years of experience in teaching and educational research, focusing on teachers' training programs, underprivileged children's education, English language education, classroom practice, teaching methods and techniques, assessment and feedback practice, ICT in education, online, blended and hybrid learning, and educational technology.

Ajay Chandel is working as an Associate Professor at Mittal School of Business, Lovely Professional University, Punjab. He has 14 years of teaching and research experience. He has published papers in SCOPUS, WOS, and UGC listed Journals in areas like Social Media Marketing, E-Commerce, and Consumer Behaviour. He has published cases on SMEs and Social Entrepreneurship in The Case Centre, UK. He also reviews The Case Journal, Emerald Group Publishing, and International Journal of Business and Globalisation, Inderscience. He has authored and developed MOOCs on Tourism and Hospitality Marketing under Epg-Pathshala- A gateway to all postgraduate courses (a UGC-MHRD project under its National Mission on Education Through ICT (NME-ICT).

Emily Duplantis is the Assistant Director of CTE for the Dorchester District Two Schools and an adjunct professor at the University of Phoenix. Recent publications include Secondary Teachers' Perceptions on How Administrators Affect the Induction Process for New Teachers: An Explanatory Case Study. Dr. Duplantis is a 22-year veteran educator. Serving in roles such as a middle and high school CTE teacher, assistant principal, Work-Based Learning Coordinator, and Executive Vice President of Professional Development.

Pam Epler, Ph.D., has a master's degree in special education and a doctorate degree in curriculum and instruction. Her doctoral research focused on the Response to Intervention (RTI) service delivery model in the secondary educational environment. She has taught and been an administrator in both the public and private sectors, from the elementary through collegiate levels. She currently teaches graduate-level courses and serves as a doctoral chairperson for Grand Canyon University and teaches pre-service undergraduate students about special education at Youngstown State University. Her research interests include RTI strategies, special education teachers' roles in RTI, special education service delivery models, and pre-service teachers' perceptions of special education students, personalized learning and teaching math to at-risk students.

Greg Harrison is an Assistant Professor of Educational Leadership in the Zucker Family School of Education at The Citadel Military College in Charleston, S.C. Recent publications include the following: Secondary Teachers' Perceptions on How Administrators Affect the Induction Process for New Teachers: An Explanatory Case Study and Developing a Virtual Learning Option for Students. Prior to working with the Citadel, Dr. Harrison has over 23 years in k-12 education to include high school classroom teacher, assistant principal, principal, and Executive Director at the district office.

Jeremiah Paul G. Manuel is an educator with over twenty years of experience dedicated to advancing literacy development among children across diverse educational contexts worldwide. He is currently a Doctor of Philosophy (PhD) candidate in Reading Education at the Philippine Normal University. He previously served as an instructor in Pedagogy and English at the College of Education of Pamantasan ng Lungsod ng Muntinlupa. At present, he is an associate researcher at the National Research Council of the Philippines, with research interests spanning Christian education, early and adult literacy, technology-integrated instruction, brain-based learning, educational management, and Physical Education. Jeremiah is currently based in Jakarta, Indonesia, where he teaches at Sekolah Pelita Harapan Kemang Village, continuing to support and enrich students' learning through his expertise and commitment to quality education.

Megan Reister enjoys conducting research, writing, and teaching as a Special Education and Early Childhood Professor in the Education Department at Franciscan University of Steubenville. Her primary areas of research, when not spending time with her husband, young daughter, and two pups, include self-advocacy and identity in students with and without disabilities, itinerant teaching, and fostering collaboration among parents, general education, and special education teachers in addition to mentoring pre-service teachers.

Belinda Rudinger's background is interdisciplinary, including a BA in Literature, an MEd in Special Education specializing in Behavior Analysis, and an EdD in Educational Sustainability. Her experience includes serving as a special educator, an educational consultant, and an assistant professor. Approaching special education through an educational sustainability lens informs her instructional practices, her relationships with both students and colleagues, and her research in braille and assistive technology.

Ranjit Singha is a Doctorate Research Fellow at Christ (Deemed to be University) and holds the prestigious American Psychological Association (APA) membership. With a strong background in Research and Development, he has significantly contributed to various fields such as Mindfulness, Addiction Psychology, Women Empowerment, UN Sustainable Development Goals, and Data Science. With over 15 years of experience in Administration, Teaching, and Research, both in Industry and Higher Education Institutions (HEI), Mr Ranjit has established himself as a seasoned professional. Mr Ranjit is dedicatedly involved in research and teaching endeavours, primarily focusing on mindfulness and compassion-based interventions. His work in these areas aims to promote well-being and foster positive change in individuals and communities.

Surjit Singha is an academician with a broad spectrum of interests, including UN Sustainable Development Goals, Organizational Climate, Workforce Diversity, Organizational Culture, HRM, Marketing, Finance, IB, Global Business, Business, AI, K12 & Higher Education, Gender and Cultural Studies. Currently a faculty member at Kristu Jayanti University, Dr. Surjit also serves as an Editor, reviewer, and author for prominent global publications and journals, including being on the Editorial review board of Information Resources Management Journal and contributor to various publications. With over 15 years of experience in Administration, Teaching, and Research, Dr. Surjit is dedicated to imparting knowledge and guiding students in their research pursuits. As a research mentor, Dr. Surjit has nurtured young minds and fostered academic growth. Dr. Surjit has an impressive track record of over 150+ publications (SCOPUS Indexed 122), including articles, book chapters, and textbooks, holds two US Copyrights, and has successfully completed and published two fully funded minor research projects from Kristu Jayanti College. PhD, M.Phil, MBA (Distinction) from Christ University, M.Com, BBM from KJC (Bangalore University), PGDHE (Higher Education) from IGNOU (Central University), UGC-NET Commerce, Examiner for IB.

Kim Wahl is a Sustainability Teaching Faculty member for the Nelson Institute for Environmental Studies and Office of Sustainability at the University of WI-Madison, Kim Wahl teaches classes focused on sustainability and systems thinking. Her research is transdisciplinary and builds upon a transformative sustainability framework.

Mohit Yadav is an Associate Professor in the area of Human Resource Management at Jindal Global Business School (JGBS). He has a rich blend of work experience from both Academics as well as Industry. Prof. Mohit holds a Ph.D. from Department of Management Studies, Indian Institute of Technology Roorkee (IIT Roorkee) and has completed Master of Human Resource and Organizational Development (MHROD) from prestigious Delhi School of Economics, University of Delhi. He also holds a B.Com (Hons.) degree from University of Delhi and UGC-JRF scholarship. He has published various research papers and book chapters with reputed publishers like Springer, Sage, Emerald, Elsevier, Inderscience etc. and presented research papers in national and International conferences both in India and abroad. He has many best paper awards on his credit too. He is reviewer of various international journals like Computers in Human Behavior, Policing etc. His areas of interest are Organizational Behavior, HRM, Recruitment and Selection, Organizational Citizenship Behavior, Quality of work life and role.

Index

H

I

K

L

M

N

P

R

S

T

U

V

W

www.ingramcontent.com/pod-product-compliance
Lightning Source LLC
LaVergne TN
LVHW060005031026
849161LV00025B/1449